MASS TERMS:
SOME PHILOSOPHICAL PROBLEMS

SYNTHESE LANGUAGE LIBRARY

TEXTS AND STUDIES IN
LINGUISTICS AND PHILOSOPHY

VOLUME 6

MASS TERMS:
SOME PHILOSOPHICAL
PROBLEMS

Edited by

FRANCIS JEFFRY PELLETIER
University of Alberta, Edmonton

D. REIDEL PUBLISHING COMPANY

DORDRECHT : HOLLAND / BOSTON : U.S.A.
LONDON : ENGLAND

Library of Congress Cataloging in Publication Data

Main entry under title:

Mass terms: some philosophical problems.

    (Synthese language library; v. 6)
    "A bibliography of recent work on mass terms",
by F. J. Pelletier: p.
    Includes indexes.
    1.   Grammar, Comparative and general – Mass nouns – Addresses,
essays, lectures.   2.   Languages – Philosophy – Addresses, essays,
lectures.   3. Grammar, Comparative and general – Quantifiers –
Addresses, essays, lectures.   I.   Pelletier, Francis Jeffry, 1944–
II. Series. P271.M3   415   78–23806
ISBN 90–277–0931–9

Published by D. Reidel Publishing Company,
P.O. Box 17, Dordrecht, Holland

Sold and distributed in the U.S.A., Canada, and Mexico
by D. Reidel Publishing Company, Inc.
Lincoln Building, 160 Old Derby Street, Hingham,
Mass. 02043, U.S.A.

Printed in The Netherlands

TABLE OF CONTENTS

EDITORIAL INTRODUCTION

1. MASS TERMS, COUNT TERMS, AND SORTAL TERMS

Central examples of mass terms are easy to come by. 'Water', 'smoke', 'gold', etc., differ in their syntactic, semantic, and pragmatic properties from count terms such as 'man', 'star', 'wastebasket', etc. Syntactically, it seems, mass terms do, but singular count terms do not, admit the quantifier phrases 'much', 'an amount of', 'a little', etc. The typical indefinite article for them is 'some' (unstressed)[1], and this article cannot be used with singular count terms. Count terms, but not mass terms, use the quantifiers 'each', 'every', 'some', 'few', 'many'; and they use 'a(n)' as the indefinite article. They can, unlike the mass terms, take numerals as prefixes. Mass terms seem not to have a plural. Semantically, philosophers have characterized count terms as denoting (classes of?) individual objects, whereas what mass terms denote are cumulative and dissective. (That is, a mass term is supposed to be true of any sum of things (stuff) it is true of, and true of any part of anything of which it is true). Pragmatically, it seems that speakers use count terms when they wish to refer to individual objects, or when they wish to reidentify a particular already introduced into discourse. Given a "space appropriate" to a count term C, it makes sense to ask how many C's there are in that space. Mass terms, on the other hand, are used more frequently when we wish to state what a particular is constituted of. Given a "space appropriate" to a mass term M, it makes sense to ask how much M there is in that space.

The syntactic distinction has been in the linguistic literature for many years. The semantico-pragmatic distinction was introduced into philosophy in the 1950's; it was sometimes called the 'count/mass' distinction, but even more often called the 'sortal/mass' distinction. In this philosophic literature (especially in Geach, Strawson, Anscombe) the role of sortal terms was claimed to be central to our conception of the world.

One difficulty with the philosophic literature has been a lack of agreement as to what is a sortal term and what is a mass term. For,

F. J. Pelletier (ed.), Mass Terms, vii–xii. All Rights Reserved.
Copyright © 1979 by D. Reidel Publishing Company, Dordrecht, Holland.

differing conceptions about what "our conception of the world" is, lead to different words being sortal. For example, does symbiosis show that 'animal' is not sortal? Does it follow from the fact that some tables are made of smaller tables, that 'table' is not a sortal? Can any word which denotes artifacts be sortal? Can complex noun phrases be sortal? Can parts of speech other than noun phrases be sortal? What is the status of "measures on mass nouns" – e.g., 'gallon of gasoline'? Finally, why are words like 'thing', 'object', etc., decreed non-sortal, given that they are syntactically count?

Questions such as these are dealt with in my 'Non-Singular Reference: Some Preliminaries.' In this article I try to give an account of how the philosophically interesting distinction "sortal/non-sortal" can be generated from the syntactical distinction "count/mass", which latter distinction is claimed to be philosophically uninteresting. The account depends upon being able to decide, for any specific use (or alternatively, any specific sense), whether it is a count or mass use (or sense). R. X. Ware's article 'Some Bits and Pieces' deals also with these issues, but his "skeptical" conclusion is that there is no way to decide for many uses. Helen Cartwright's 'Some Remarks about Mass Nouns and Plurality' tries to establish the philosophical interest of the count/mass distinction, and show that the "skeptical" remarks to the contrary made in both my and Ware's articles can be circumvented by a notion of "structural ambiguity". (See her remarks at the beginning of Section 4).

2. QUESTIONS OF ONTOLOGY

Drawing the count/mass or sortal/non-sortal distinction(s) and deciding what these types of terms are supposed to do is but preliminary to the philosophical purposes that this (these) distinction(s) is (are) supposed to have. One area of philosophical application is in the realm of metaphysics: mass terms apparently denote *stuff* and count terms apparently denote *things*. Many writers have taken the position that our conceptual scheme presupposes an ontology of things, and therefore that sortal terms set the paradigm for predication.[2] But since things are made up of or are constituted by or are defined in terms of stuff, it would seem that the proper statement of an ontology should include a discussion of the denotation of these kinds of terms and a discussion of how the constitution-relation operates. Most of the rest of the articles in this book have explicit claims to make on these matters.[3]

Richard Sharvy tries to establish that there is a parallel between Quine's "indeterminacy of reference" of count terms and certain properties of mass reference. I argue in response that it is not proved that Sharvy's mass-indeterminacy is any different from the count-indeterminacy. Eddy Zemach's well-known article. 'Four Ontologies', lays out a "type ontology" according to which "types" are fully real particulars bounded neither in space nor time. Zemach thinks the ontology is most plausible when talking about masses, but that there are sufficient similarities between masses and other types ("count types") to make it acceptable for describing ordinary discourse in the count as well as the mass case. This type ontology has been criticized by John Bacon in 'Do Generic Descriptions Denote?', *Mind* (1973) and 'The Untenability of Genera', *Logique et Analyse* (1974), and Zemach answers these criticisms in his 'On the Adequacy of a Type Ontology'. One might compare the type ontology offered by Zemach for the mass case with the analyses given by Parsons and Bealer in this issue. (More about them below).

Henry Laycock's article 'Theories of Matter' is a defense of the view that the basic ontological category is that of matter, and that correspondingly, mass predication is more basic than any sort of count predication. This article is a refinement or advance on his earlier 'Some Questions of Ontology', *Phil. Rev.* (1972) and his 'Chemistry and Individuation' (read to the Canadian Philosophical Association 1973). In these articles Laycock also took to task Helen Cartwright's doctrine that occurrences of a mass term M are to be understood by the phrase 'quantity of M' (see her 'Heraclitus and the Bath Water', *Phil. Rev.* (1965) and 'Quantities' *Phil. Rev.* (1970)).[4] K. C. Cook's article 'On the Usefulness of Quantities' is designed to explicate the Cartwright doctrine and defend it from these kinds of criticisms.

3. THE LOGICAL FORM OF SENTENCES WITH MASS TERMS

One way a certain kind of philosopher explains his ontological doctrines is by showing how to cast ordinary language sentences into a formalized language. The earliest account along these lines is probably Quine's – in *Word and Object*, pp. 90–124. However, such an account did not seem to satisfy the people who later discussed the problem.[5] The earliest of the criticisms based on the logic of the matter was Terry Parsons' 'An

Analysis of Mass Terms and Amount Terms', which is reprinted here. The article has evoked criticisms from many sides (e.g., in the articles cited in Note 5), and Parsons responds to them in his 'Afterthoughts on Mass Terms'. An article with a position similar to Parsons' is Montague's (as Montague himself observes). The article is printed here with the title originally given it by Montague (and under which it was circulated in mimeographed form). It unfortunately was not included in the collection of his works on language, *Formal Philosophy*, edited by Richmond Thomason (Yale U.P. 1974); it was also inadvertently omitted from the "complete bibliography" at the end of the anthology. The title is by analogy with his 'The Proper Treatment of Quantifiers in English' – the work he obliquely refers to in his opening remarks.

In her 'Amounts and Measures of Amount', Helen Cartwright investigates some ramifications of her earlier work on quantities (*op. cit.*); in particular, she is here interested in the formal properties of measurements of quantities. Besides the continuation of her work on quantities that this article presents, it also brings out rather clearly how Parsons's (*op. cit.*) work on "applied amount phrases" can be adapted to fit her intuitions about quantities.

Tyler Burge, in his 'Mass Terms, Count Nouns, and Change', contrasts two approaches to the logical representation of sentences containing the phrases 'is M' and 'is the same M as' (where 'M' stands for some mass term). One approach – the Constitution-Approach – alters the analysis of 'is M' from the traditional '$M(x)$'. The other approach – the Relational Approach – alters the analysis of 'is the same M as' from the traditional '$M(x)$ & $x = y$'. Burge brings out difficulties in the Relational Approach, and therefore opts for the Constitution-Approach. Richard Grandy's 'Stuff and Things' is an attempt to defend the Relational Approach.[6] The approach, as given by Grandy, distinguishes between first- and second-level predicates, where mass predicates are first-level and sortal predicates are second-level. Things will be relations between quantities of stuff and moments of time. Brian Chellas, in his commentary on Grandy's paper, brings out some further difficulties with the Relational Approach. Gabbay and Moravcsik's paper 'Sameness and Individuation' presents a theory which is "somewhere between the Constitution- and Relational-Approaches", to use Burge's characterization. In this article, they bring out some different uses of the phrase 'is the same as' and give a formal semantics which will characterize how it is to be accounted for in its various occurrences – both those which are intuitively cases of 'is made of' and those which are intuitively cases of 'is a temporal stage of'.

One way of formalizing our semantic intuitions about mass terms is to invoke mereology.[7] This method is appealing, because mereology mirrors the semantics of mass terms by presupposing that the denotations of the terms satisfy the cumulativity and divisiveness conditions (characterized above in Section 1). The method has been applied, in various ways and with varying degrees of success, by Moravcsik ('Mass Terms in English' in Hintikka *et. al.*, *op. cit.*), Sharvy ('Mixtures' read to the Pacific Division of the American Philosophical Association in 1976), and H. Cartwright *opera cit.*, especially 'Amounts and Measures of Amount'. In this volume, H. C. Bunt gives a detailed presentation of his "ensemble theory", which is an adaptation of mereology. The use of mereology has been criticized before[8], and one might profitably try to see whether Bunt's presentation can overcome these objections.

In this final article of this volume, George Bealer investigates an analysis of the logical form of sentences involving mass terms according to which 'is' is an unambiguous term, but where different sentences using 'is' get different "readings" depending upon the sort of term in the predicate. Thus, 'this ring is gold', 'Socrates is the teacher of Plato', 'Socrates is pale', 'Socrates is a man', 'man is an animal', etc., all have the same logical form, but the "reading" or "understanding" of them is conditioned by the sort of term in the predicate – *viz.*, whether it be the name of a quality, a species, a particular, a stuff, etc. Such an approach obviously depends heavily upon being able to distinguish what kind of term is in the predicate. Bealer distinguishes "extensional entities" such as species, stuffs, and particulars, from "intensional entities" such as propositions, qualities, and relations; and he introduces a relation called 'comprehension'. Within this framework, he tries to answer the logico-linguistic puzzles which have exercised our other writers.

The volume closes with a reasonably thorough bibliography of the work done recently on mass terms.

F. J. PELLETIER

NOTES

¹ This 'some' is to be distinguished from the (stressed) quantifier 'some'. Contrast their pronounciation in the sentences *Some boy was hit by a car yesterday* (stressed quantifier) and *I would like some water* (unstressed indefinite article). Phonetically, they are represented [sʌm] and [sm̩] respectively. In many of the articles on mass terms, the quantifier is written 'some' and the article 'sm'. The distinction was first made popular in the philosophical literature by Helen Cartwright, 'Heraclitus and the Bath Water', *Phil. Rev.* **74** (1965), 466–485.

² See various works of P. T. Geach, such as *Reference and Generality* (Cornell 1962) and *Logic Matters* (Blackwell's 1975). See also the discussion in Strawson's *Individuals* (Methuen 1959), and in W. V. Quine, *Word and Object* (MIT Press 1960) – especially pp. 91–100, where he talks of mass predication as 'pre-individuative', 'immature', and 'archaic'. A particularly good source of information on the doctrine can be found in David Wiggins's *Identity and Spatio-Temporal Continuity* (Blackwell's 1967), wherein an attempt to relate the "primacy of sortal predication" to Aristotle's doctrine of substance is made.

³ The three previous articles also make some remarks on these topics, although such remarks are not central to these articles.

⁴ The Cartwright doctrine is also discussed and criticized in my 'On Some Proposals for the Semantics of Mass Terms', *Journ. Phil. Logic* **3** (1973), 87–108.

⁵ For example, Donald Davidson, 'Truth and Meaning', *Synthese* **17** (1967), 304–323 (see Note 9), F. J. Pelletier, *Some Problems of Non-Singular Reference* (Ph.D. Dissertation, UCLA 1971) and 'On Some Proposals for the Semantics of Mass Terms' *loc. cit.*, J. M. E. Moravcsik, 'Mass Terms in English' in Hintikka, Moravcsik, and Suppes (eds.) *Approaches to Natural Language* (Reidel 1973), Tyler Burge, *Truth and Some Referential Devices* (Ph.D. Dissertation, Princeton 1971) and 'Truth and Mass Terms' *Journ. Phil.* **69** (1972), 263–282, in addition to Parsons' article cited in the text.

⁶ It is therefore a repudiation of his earlier approach in 'Response to Moravcsik' in Hintikka *et al.*, *op. cit.*, wherein he defended a view that made a mass term *M* be a predicate true of all the bits, lumps, puddles, etc., of *M*.

⁷ The term is from Lesniewski; see Nelson Goodman & H. S. Leonard, 'The Calculus of Individuals and its Uses', *Journ. Symb. Logic* **5** (1940), 45–55, or Nelson Goodman, *The Structure of Appearance* (3rd Edition, Reidel 1977) for general statements of mereology.

⁸ E.g., by Terry Parsons, 'An Analysis of Mass Terms and Amount Terms', Pelletier, 'On Some Proposals for the Semantics of Mass Terms', R. E. Grandy, 'Response to Moravcsik'.

ACKNOWLEDGEMENTS

The majority of these papers were first published in *Synthese* Vol. 31, Nos. 3/4; and I thank the authors for permitting their republication in the present volume. F. J. Pelletier, 'Non-Singular Reference: Some Preliminaries' originally appeared in *Philosophia* Vol. 5, No. 4 (1975) and is reprinted here with permission of the Editor of *Philosophia*. Eddy Zemach, 'Four Ontologies' originally appeared in *Journal of Philosophy* Vol. 67, No. 8 (1970) and is reprinted here with permission of the author and the Editor of the *Journal of Philosophy*. Terence Parsons, 'An Analysis of Mass Terms and Amount Terms' originally appeared in *Foundations of Language* Vol. 6, No. 3 (1970) and is reprinted here with permission of the author.

Richard Montague, 'The Proper Treatment of Mass Terms in English' was originally published under the title 'Response to Moravcsik' in K. J. J. Hintikka, J. M. E. Moravcsik, and P. Suppes (eds.), *Approaches to Natural Language* (Reidel Publishing Co., 1973) and is reprinted here with the permission of Reidel Publishing Co. H. M. Cartwright, 'Amounts and Measures of Amount' originally appeared in *Noûs* Vol. 9 (1975) and is reprinted here with the permissions of the author and the Editor of *Noûs* Dov Gabbay and J. M. E. Moravcsik, 'Sameness and Individuation' was originally published in the *Journal of Philosophy* Vol. 70, No. 16 (1973) and is reprinted with the permission of the authors and the Editor of *Journal of Philosophy*.

Richard Sharvy, 'The Indeterminancy of Mass Predication', F. J. Pelletier, 'Sharvy on Mass Predication', and H. C. Bunt, 'Ensembles and the Formal Semantic Properties of Mass Terms' are all original to this volume.

F. J. P.

FRANCIS JEFFRY PELLETIER

NON-SINGULAR REFERENCE:
SOME PRELIMINARIES[1]

One of the goals of a certain brand of philosopher has been to give an
account of language and linguistic phenomena by means of showing how
sentences are to be translated into a "logically perspicuous notation" (or
an "ideal language" – to use passé terminology). The usual reason given
by such philosophers for this activity is that such a notational system
will somehow illustrate the "logical form" of these sentences. There are
many candidates for this notational system: (almost) ordinary first-
order predicate logic (see Quine [1960]), higher-order predicate logic
(see Parsons [1968, 1970]), intensional logic (see Montague [1969,
1970a, 1970b, 1971]), and transformational grammar (see Harman
[1971]), to mention some of the more popular ones. I do not propose to
discuss the general question of the correctness of this approach to the
philosophy of language, nor do I wish to adjudicate among the notational systems mentioned here. Rather, I want to focus on one problem
which must be faced by all such systems – a problem that must be
discussed *before* one decides upon a notational system and tries to
demonstrate that it in fact can account for all linguistic phenomena.
The general problem is to determine what we shall allow as linguistic
data; in this paper I shall restrict my attention to this general problem
as it appears when we try to account for certain words with non-singular
reference, in particular, the words that are classified by the count/mass
and sortal/non-sortal distinctions.

Nouns are normally divided into two classes: proper and common.
Proper nouns themselves fall into two classes: those in one very rarely
occur with a determiner, and those in the other usually with 'the' (*Connecticut* is a state, *The Connecticut* is a river).[2] In the case of common
nouns, there is general recognition that there are two quite distinct
classes – at least "quite distinct" for the paradigms. The syntactical
behavior of words like 'water', 'mud', and 'oatmeal' is quite different
from the behavior of words like 'man', 'statue', and 'eye'. [I shall call
the former 'mass' and the latter 'count', in keeping with accepted usage].
For elementary purposes, textbooks (e.g. Gleason [1965]) often give
criteria like the following: Count nouns are so-called because they can

1

F. J. Pelletier (ed.), *Mass Terms*, 1–14. *All Rights Reserved.*
Copyright © 1975 *by Philosophia.*

occur with numerals and can be used as either singular or plural. They admit of 'a' and 'every' with the singular, and 'few' with the plural. Mass nouns do not exhibit the singular-plural distinctions; when used as subjects, they take singular verbs. The determiners used with mass nouns, however, are more like those used with plural count nouns than those used with singulars. This may be brought out by a tabulation of grammatically comparable constructions (from Gleason [1965], p. 135):

the man is	the men are	the water is
a man	men	water
this man	these men	this water
—	few men	little water
every man	all men	all water
one man	two men	—
some man	some men	some water (*some* stressed)
—	some men	some water (*some* unstressed)

Unfortunately, this simple and elegant explanation of the syntactical difference between count and mass nouns will not suffice. First, it is claimed that count nouns, but not mass nouns, admit of numerals (and along with this is some related claim for pluralization). This at least needs some kind of qualification, for consider the (supposed) mass noun 'oatmeal': given an appropriate setting (such as a customer in a diner to his waitress), it is clear that such questions as 'How many oatmeals are in your kitchen?' have as a perfectly clear answer 'Three oatmeals', thus violating the two related criteria of mass nouns accepting neither pluralization nor numeral prefixes. Of course one might always retort "You've either changed the sense of 'oatmeal' or you have deleted from the surface structure some such phrase as 'kinds of' or 'bowls of', etc." True, I suppose I have, but such a claim makes clear that either (1) surface structure is not what the criteria are talking about or (2) we need to distinguish not between mass and count *nouns* but between mass and count *senses* of nouns. More about this will appear below, but for now it is well to cast a wary eye on such simplistic claims as we started with.

The next criterion is pluralization: that mass nouns do not exhibit it. Even ignoring such difficulties as noted above, there are mass nouns that *without change of sense* admit of apparent (syntactical) pluralization: e.g., 'beans' and 'potatoes' ('Pass the (mashed) potatoes', etc.). That is, it is the syntactically plural form that is used in the mass sense. Another rather straightforward attempt might be: mass nouns but not count nouns admit of the prefixes 'much' and 'amount of'. But as we shall see below, these expressions *can* be used with apparent count nouns.

There still remains more to the story of the count/mass distinction, but let's leave off for now and turn to a distinction given to us by traditional wisdom: sortal vs. non-sortal terms. Frege ([1884], p. 66) explains for us:

The concept "letters in the word 'three' " isolates the 't' from the 'h', the 'h' from the 'r', and so on. The concept "syllables in the word 'three' " picks out the word as a whole, and as indivisible in the sense that no part of it falls any longer under the same concept. Not all concepts possess this quality. We can, for example, divide up something falling under the concept "red" into parts in a variety of ways, without the parts ceasing to fall under the concept "red". To a concept of this kind no finite number will belong. The proposition asserting that units are isolated and indivisible can, accordingly, be formulated as follows:
Only a concept which isolates what falls under it in a definite manner, and which does not permit any arbitrary division of it into parts, can be a unit relative to a finite number.

The distinction is supposed to divide predicates that "provide a criterion for counting" from predicates that do not provide such a criterion. In a space appropriate to the sortal 'S', we can count how many S's there are in that space; but in a space appropriate to a non-sortal 'M' we cannot straightforwardly ask how many M's there are. Thus we can ask how many men are in a room, but not how many waters (without changing the sense of 'water'). Non-sortal terms are *collective* – if 'M' is a non-sortal term, then 'M' is true of any sum of things of which 'M' is true – and *divisive* – 'M' is true of any part of a thing of which 'M' is true (down to a certain lower limit, the setting of which is generally an empirical matter).

This distinction is only clear in its broadest outline, and not much at all in the details, in spite of the fact that so much of the recent philosophical literature presupposes it. Nonetheless, we are in a position to compare, generally, the grammatical distinction, i.e., the count/mass distinction, with the philosophical one, i.e., the sortal/non-sortal distinction. That there are two distinctions here is, I think, insufficiently recognized; Wallace [1964] p. 70 runs the two together, Gleason [1965] pp. 135–137 tries to show that count nouns do what we admit only sortals do, Quine [1960] uses the criteria for sortals and calls them count, and Moravcsik [1970], while recognizing the two ways to make these distinctions, uses the sortal/non-sortal distinction and thinks that he has adequately characterized the count/mass distinction.

It strikes me that there are five important differences between the two distinctions. First, the grammatical distinction applies only to nouns whereas the philosophical distinction is usually asserted to apply to all monadic predicates. For example, the grammatical distinction does not treat 'red' or 'spherical' at all, but the philosophical distinction is sometimes held to classify 'red' as a non-sortal and 'spherical' as a sortal. Second, the grammatical distinction applies only to simple nouns, whereas the philosophical distinction applies to complex terms. E.g., it makes 'white man' a sortal and 'dirty water' a non-sortal. Third, certain count nouns are classified as non-sortals, e.g., 'thing', 'object', 'entity'. Fourth, the grammatical distinction will make abstract nouns such as 'speed' and 'knowledge' mass nouns, and make 'plot' and 'virtue' (in one sense) count. The philosophical distinction is vague at this point; some philosophers do, but others do not, want the distinction to apply to such terms at all. And fifth, measures on mass nouns (e.g., 'lump of coal', 'gallon of gasoline') raise special problems. Some of these are divisive (e.g., 'lump of coal' or 'amount of dirt') and would probably be classified as non-sortal (although Wallace [1964] calls 'lump of coal' sortal and 'amount of dirt' non-sortal). But others are more problematic: for instance, 'blade of grass' is not obviously divisive or collective. There are certain affinities between these "measured mass nouns" and "counted count nouns" (e.g., 'busload of teams of basketball players'), but I shall not pursue them here.[3] In fact, I shall completely ignore these occurrences of mass terms in what follows. In any case, all of these "measured mass nouns", even 'amount of dirt', if treated at all, would be classified as count by the grammatical distinction.

The difference between the distinctions is a matter of focus. The grammatical distinction is supposed to describe the syntax of our language – it tries, *without theory*, to show us how to tell the one kind of word from the other. It is supposed to be a *starting point for* a theory – that is, it is supposed merely to *describe* some phenomenon that any general account (i.e., theory) of language must face up to. For this reason, in order to succeed, the distinction must not appeal to any theory, but only to surface structure and other pre-theoretic information. (In fact, the distinction cannot appeal to the theory in which it is being used without being circular.)[4] We've seen above that for the criteria given to work, we must (1) have recourse to structures other than surface structure, or (2) be able to distinguish senses of words before we apply the criteria. Now, (1) is clearly theory-laden, and so this preliminary distinction can have no recourse to such structures; but (2) seems different – one would like to think that the ability to distinguish different senses of the same word is pre-theoretic. We should, therefore, be able to use at least some of the criteria given to make the desired mass/count distinction (e.g., we should be able to give as a criterion: When X is used in a mass sense, phrases like 'an amount of X' and 'much X' are not anomalous; when X is used in a count sense, phrases like 'an X' and 'four X's' are not anomalous; but the reverse is not true).

But is (1) so clearly theory-laden? The fact that speakers can discriminate between senses of sentences might be taken as evidence supporting a deep structure analysis.[5] One consideration which can be brought out as a reason for rejecting this support for (1) is: speakers can indeed tell that sentences are ambiguous, but sometimes they can also pinpoint *where* the ambiguity comes from. In the case given here, they will point to the word 'oatmeal'. It is no good to say that the informants might not be able to say what the ambiguity is or to what it is due in any theoretically interesting way. Such claims find their home in the analysis of sentences like 'Two soldiers shot two students'; in such sentences informants may well be unable to give an accounting of the ambiguity. But at least they will be able to discern that it is *not* due to any lexical ambiguity. Conversely, when they *can* attribute the ambiguity to a lexical item, as in the present case, that cuts in favor of (2), and against (1).

I think that reflection on the example of above, 'How many oatmeals are in your kitchen?' provides convincing evidence that every word which would normally be called a mass noun can be given a perfectly clear count sense. This sense might be the same as that of 'kind of oatmeal', or 'bowl of oatmeal', etc., or it may be different. There are many nouns which have mass/count senses related in other ways. 'I like chicken*s*' versus 'I like chicken', 'Pass the five potatoes' versus 'Pass the (mashed) potatoes' show the distinction occurring between a naturally-constituted object (i.e., structured according to biological, geological, or cultural norms,[6] etc.) and the matter of which it is made.

Can all words that one is tempted to call count nouns be given a mass sense? A "thought experiment" like the following might be described in order to persuade one that it is possible to do so. Let's agree that a mass or count sense of a word exists if one can describe a circumstance or set of circumstances in which that word with the requisite sense can (or would) be normally employed. Consider a machine, the "universal grinder".[7] This machine is rather like a meat grinder in that one introduces something into one end, the grinder chops and grinds it up into a homogeneous mass and spews it onto the floor from its other end. The difference between the universal grinder and a meat grinder is that the universal grinder's machinery allows it to chop up any object no matter how large, no matter how small, no matter how soft, no matter how hard. Now if we put into one end of a meat grinder a steak, and ask what is on the floor at the other end, the answer is 'There is steak all over the floor' (wherein 'steak' has a mass sense). It may be true that we have a special term for the mass sense of 'steak', such as 'ground sirloin', but in general this will not be the case. And in any case, it is only relevant to note that the sense of 'steak' in the answer given above is mass, and the answer is normal. The reader has doubtless guessed by now the purpose of our universal grinder: Take an object corresponding to any (apparent) count noun he wishes (e.g., 'man'), put the object in one end of the grinder and ask what is on the floor (answer: 'There is man all over the floor'), Perhaps there are other answers to this question, such as 'There are pieces of a man all over the floor', but this is irrelevant to the test. All that needs be the case is for *one* of the possible normal answers to use the mass sense of our "normal" count noun, and this has been supplied. It is apparent that this test can be employed at will, always giving us a mass sense of count nouns having physical objects as their extension.

There is still some question about nouns which do not have physical objects in their extension – ungrindable tings like unicorns (ungrindable because there are none of them to grind): are they the only *true* count nouns? The answer is no: it is not necessary that the object actually be grindable, but only that a normal sentence use the word in a mass sense. The sentence 'If there were any unicorns and if we were to put one into the grinder, there would be unicorn all over the floor' uses 'unicorn' in the required sense. A harder example is 'number', but perhaps one would be satisfied with the sentence 'If numbers were physical objects, and if we were to put one into the grinder, there would be number all over the floor'.[8] At any rate, there can be made a *prima facie* case that nothing is immune from the grinder treatment. So there is at least a *prima facie* reason to believe that every noun must have (perhaps hidden) both a count and a mass sense. Reasoning similar to this is used by Gleason [1965], pp. 136–37:

Are there limitations to this shifting [between count and mass senses]? At first there seems to be. . . . But it is soon found that many of the ones with both uses are very much more frequent in one than in the other. The less frequent use occurs only in rather unusual circumstances. *Water* as a mass noun is common and widespread; as a count noun is nearly restricted to waiters. Even if the restaurant usage had not been observed, the pattern would remain and this use might arise at any time. Perhaps some of the other words would also show both uses if sufficiently unusual situations were conceived. This seems to be the case. For example, *book* and *shelf* are both fairly typical count nouns. With the present vogue for speaking – animal stories, we can imagine one featuring a mother termite concerned over her child: *Johnny is very choosey about his food. He will eat book, but he won't touch shelf.* This is far-fetched, of course. But it does suggest that every noun, given the right context, can occur in either type of usage, count or mass.

There are two kinds of objections one can make to this. First, we might object to this use of the counterfactual: if the counterfactual's antecedent is contradictory, can we always be assured of grammaticality? In cases like 'If 4 were the smallest even prime number, then 2 would not be' we have clearly true (and hence grammatical) sentences. But with sentences like 'If all of mathematics were entirely different than it is, then 4 would be the smallest even prime number' we are quite at a loss. Does the 'If numbers were physical objects. . .' belong to the first or the second class? Furthermore, what about such words as 'individual' or 'thing'? It seems that if an individual or a thing is put into the grinder, then (in the absence of any other information about *what* the individual or thing is) the *only* natural answer is that there is *stuff* all over the floor. Such problems restrict the *extent* of Gleason's claim. We might also try to deny the applicability of the grinder in particular and "thought experiments" in general by calling into question the underlying assumption that a sense of a word exists if one can describe circumstances wherein that sense would normally be employed. The matter is cannot easily be put aside by simply saying, "We are not interested in how language *might* be if the world were different; we are interested in the structure of English *now*." Or in Grandy's language (see fn. 1), if the world were different, and water, sand, etc., came in large, relatively stable and permanent chunks, we would no doubt speak of sands, waters, etc. "If the world were different, our syntax (as well as our beliefs and semantics) would probably change as well. This should not be a surprising discovery. . ." But this is not exactly what is at issue here. If one looks at the discussion of a few pages ago, he will notice a series of sentences in which the phrase 'universal grinder' occurs. Also there will be various occurrences of 'man' that one *has* to understand in a mass sense. Furthermore, all of it is written in present-day English – thus this phenomenon arises *within* language, and is not simply a peculiarity of the relation *between* language and the world. But this is giving too much. We would not say that 'Ugga Bugga bo' is grammatical English, even though it makes sense when considered as part of the series of sentences: "When I say 'Ugga Bugga bo' I mean that grass is green. Ugga Bugga bo". Perhaps the reason this is an unacceptagle example is that, intuitively speaking, we would call this a code, and furthermore because sentences of this sort are not uniformly generated. But this is not all, and I do not know the rest. At any rate, every obvious criterion I can think of either rules out suppositions from being English or else admits the "grinder" as generating present-day English uses or ordinary count terms in a mass sense.

In contrast to this descriptive purpose stands the purpose of the philosophical distinction, which is not intended to give a *syntactical* characterization but rather something we might want to call a *semantical* one. The criteria usually proffered (as by Frege above) tell us that we should look to the *reference* of the term in question: if it "provides a criterion for counting" or if it is not divisive or if it is not collective then it is sortal: otherwise it is non-sortal. (The results obtained above should be kept in mind. Namely, it seems that many predicates – almost all nouns – have both a sortal and non-sortal sense.)

Using the *semantic* criteria to judge whether a word (or word sense) is *mass* or *count* will lead to impossible difficulties. Any criterion which concerns itself with the nature of the reference of a word will find no interesting differences between 'thing' and 'water'. To hold (as Quine [1960] and Moravcsik [1970] do) that such criteria are sufficient to make this distinction, will be to hold that a syntactical theory cannot make use of the distinction (even if it were allowed that semantics can be settled before developing the related syntax). For any *syntactical* theory will group 'thing' with 'man' and its like, and it will separate this group from the group containing 'water' and its like. The reason for this grouping is, of course, that 'thing' admits the same prefixes, figures in the same kinds of transforms, etc., as does 'man' – and these are radically different from the ones 'water', etc., admit of. So a syntactical theory could not use the Quine/Moravcsik distinction because it does *not* group in this way, and the point of making the distinction at all will be lost (except of course for its *philosophical* interest, but this is then the sortal/non-sortal distinction and ought to be called such. The *philosophical* distinction would be of little interest for anyone constructing a *syntactical* theory). Both Quine and Moravcsik would find it difficult to give an account of a sentence containing 'thing'. According to the semantic criteria given by Quine, 'thing' is mass, so a sentence containing 'things' (plural) must be either ill-formed or else elliptical for a more complex sentence. (As e.g., when we use a sentence containing 'waters' – as 'There are two waters in this room', this is elliptical for something like 'kinds of water' or 'bodies of water' – as in 'There are two kinds of [or 'bodies of', etc.] water in this room'). One should note that the apparent count use gets replaced by an individuator term (measure?) plus mass use of the term. But clearly the sentence 'There are two things in this room' is not ill-formed, so it must be elliptical for 'There are two kinds of thing in this room' (where 'thing' has its "true" mass sense). However, the first sentence can be true when the second is false, as when we have two distinct things falling under all the same kinds (as perhaps if there are two men in the room, or two atoms in the room, or whatever one's metaphysical biases dictate). The problem is that 'thing' is a count noun, and any syntactical account must recognize this fact. Giving *semantic* criteria along the lines that Moravcsik and Quine have suggested will never make 'thing' come out count.

Part of the problem here seems to be that we want to cling to the grammatical distinction because it stands some chance of being clearly made (bearing in mind the above discussion about *words* vs. *senses* of words). But on the other hand it does not make quite the distinction one wants for philosophical purposes. Thus the goal should be now to show how to "generate" the sortal/non-sortal distinction from the mass/count distinction; i.e., to show how to overcome the five differences noted above. (From now on I will use 'term' or 'noun', etc., but in keeping with the discussion, I mean senses of the terms or nouns.) We can get rid of the first and fifth differences by merely expanding the grammatical distinction to include complex terms and from this strike out measures on mass terms (like 'lump of coal', 'gallon of water') – the latter for separate treatment. The second dispute, that the philosophical distinction treats even non-substantival phrases (like adjectives), I think should be resolved in favor of the grammatical distinction – i.e., the philosophical distinction should *not* attempt to classify these terms as *either* sortal or non-sortal. To understand why, we should look at the accounts given by those who think that, for example, adjectives should be so classified. In the Frege quote there is a certain problem surrounding his statement "we can divide something falling under the concept 'red' in a variety of ways. . ." *What* is it that we are dividing up? Surely it is not *the red*, for consider the red book on my desk, and contrast it with the coffee which is also on my desk. To show that 'coffee' is a non-sortal term, the *coffee on my desk* must be divided to see if each of these *parts of my original coffee* are coffee (they are). However, the *red* on my desk is divided by dividing the red book. These *parts of my book* must be examined to determine if they are red (they are, if I started out with an entirely red book). The point is that we are to divide up the X, and see if the parts are still X – we are *not* supposed to divide up Y and see if those parts are still X. There *is* a sense in which we can divide up *the red*, but this is a sortal sense of a noun ("How many reds are there on the desk?" "Three: scarlet, crimson, and brick"). And even if we ignore this problem, we *still* cannot give a clear sense to sortal or non-sortal senses of adjectives. Words such as 'heavy' and 'light' would seem to be examples of non-sortal terms, since they do not "divide their reference into discrete objects". But also they do not seem to pass the divisibility test (not all parts of things that are heavy are themselves heavy) nor the collectivity test (not all sums of things that are light are themselves light).[9] I think this should justify us giving up the idea that adjectives and other non-substantival terms can have sortal or non-sortal senses.

The fourth point of dispute, terms with non-physical objects in their extension, seems to me to be best settled by not having the philosophical distinction applied to them at all – i.e., strike them from the (revised) grammatical distinction which we have when we are generating the sortal/non-sortal distinction. The reason for this is that such terms have no "appropriate space" within which to judge whether it is or is not possible to count how many there are. Consider the most likely candidates for being sortal: words for geometrical figures (in the *abstract* sense) like 'triangle', 'square', etc. It is clear that the main sense of these sorts of words are *count*, since they admit numerical prefixes, can be used with 'a' and 'every', etc. However, one of the purposes of the 'sortal' designation is, as Frege notes, to be able to apply a number to it in a *definite* manner, and not to permit any arbitrary division of it into parts. Yet, since an abstract geometrical figure needs no physical bounds, it follows that there are an indefinite number of triangles within each triangle.[10] And this violates the intent of the sortal designation. Yet it is also not right to call them *non-sortal*, for it is not true that there is a space appropriate to 'triangle' such that one *cannot* count how many there are in that space (as there was a space appropriate to 'water' but one could not count how many there were in that space).

Only the third difference, non-sortal count terms, remains to be settled. Some examples of these are 'thing', 'white thing', and 'physical object'. According to traditional wisdom, some phrases containing these are sortal, some not. Predicates like 'thing that is wise' or 'physical object that is thinking of Vienna' are sortal, since only a *person* could be wise or think of Vienna (and 'person' is a sortal predicate). On the other hand the simple phrases 'physical object', 'white thing', etc., are taken to be non-sortal since they pick out no definite thing or things – do not provide a criterion for counting, are divisive, etc. – to which a property can be applied. Many people (e.g., Geach [1962], p. 148) brand sentences with such phrases as 'meaningless', because they do not refer to a particular thing or group of things. But surely the "meaningless phrases" can, in the following sentences, be interpreted in at least one way that makes sense (and they might even be true): 'Every physical object is extended', 'All white objects are white'. The problem is to understand just what the interpretation shall be.

I suggest the following: In the sentences where 'thing' (or a phrase containing 'thing') is being used as a proxy for some other term (as in 'thing that is wise') if 'thing' is replaced by what it is going proxy for, reflection will show that the replacement will always be by a sortal. ('Thing that is wet' cannot be replaced by 'water', rather, 'stuff that is wet' is what 'water' can replace.) In the remaining (non-proxy) cases we should take the sentence in the question to be a quantification over (normal) sortals. E.g., 'All white things are white' is to be construed as 'For all sortals S, and any x, if x is a white S, then x is white', and so on. This explains both why 'thing' is a count noun (since it either "stands for" or indicates quantification over sortals) and also why it is not itself a sortal noun.[11] Thus in any proposed "logically perspicuous notation" there should be no word 'thing' or phrase 'physical object' since they should all be replaced by a sortal or by a quantifier phrase of some sort.

A similar phenomenon appears to happen on the mass noun side also. Sentences like 'Water is wet', 'Mercury is dry', etc., are perfectly normal (from both the grammatical and philosophical point of view) and yet 'All stuff is fluid in nature' seems to pass only the tests for grammaticality, but not those for straightforward intelligibility, since no definite stuff has been picked out for us to say something about or predicate anything of. Words like 'stuff' seem to have the two uses corresponding to those we distinguished for words like 'thing' – first, as a proxy for a normal mass noun, and second, as an indication of quantification over (normal) stuffs. The above sentence, for example, is to be construed as 'For any (normal) stuff M, M is fluid in nature'. For simplicity let's agree to call normal sortal predicates "sortals", normal mass nouns "mass nouns", 'thing' and its relatives "secondary sortals" and "super sortals" corresponding to whether it "goes proxy" for a sortal or it is construed as quantification over sortals, and 'stuff' and its relatives "secondary mass nouns" and "super mass nouns" for the corresponding two cases for mass nouns. Again, no "logically perspicuous notation" should contain any of these sorts of words, but rather will have replaced them by a normal mass noun or by some kind of quantification.

Thus for monadic noun phrases that are not measures on mass nouns at least, we have a pretty clear grasp of what is a sortal according to traditional wisdom. They are what I call sortal and secondary sortals. Non-Sortals according to traditional wisdom are what I call supersortals, together with all our mass nouns (normal, secondary, and super). So we see that the philosophic distinction can, in a way, be "generated" from the grammatical one. For instance, to get the sortals from the counts, all that we have to do is to (a) include all noun phrases, (b) delete abstract noun phrases and measures on mass nouns, (c) distinguish "proxy" and "super" count nouns from the rest, and (d) reconstrue these two kinds of count nouns correctly (find the right word it goes "proxy" for, or find the proper quantifier phrase).

I think I have sufficiently shown that it is not easy to make these two distinctions. What I have not here demonstrated is that these distinctions must be accounted for in any philosophically adequate theory of language. Perhaps it is easy enough to see that the mass/count distinction should be preserved in a canonical notation, since it looms so large and on the surface of English grammar.[12] As for the sortal/non-sortal distinction: if one takes any of a number of closely related views prevalent in recent philosophical literature, one will believe that sortal terms are "the glasses through which we view the world", or the solution to the "paradox of confirmation", or how we "identify" and "reidentify" objects, or how we "pick out domains of discourse", or how we learn to think and talk, etc., etc. Any proponent of such a position who also views the construction of a "logically perspicuous notation" as an aid in understanding our ordinary language, must insist on the inclusion of this distinction in the artificial language if it is to be of any help in achieving his goal.

University of Alberta

NOTES

[1] The penultimate version of this paper was read at the Pacific APA meeting, April 1972. I want to thank the meeting's chairman, J. M. E. Moravcsik, and my commentator, Richard Grandy, for their comments. I have not addressed myself to all the points raised by Grandy, but only a few of the more important ones. Various still earlier versions of this paper were read by David Lewis, Barbara Hall Partee, and John Perry. The paper is considerably better as a result.

[2] Contra Quine [1960] p. 90.

[3] The interested reader will find at least a wealth of examples bearing on this similarity in Celce and Schwarcz [1969].

[4] Already, of course, we have *some* theory invoked with the notion of "surface structure". It seems to me, though, that it would be difficult to find a clear boundry between theoretic and non-theoretic; rather, descriptions of phenomena form a continuum from one to the other. But we can at least judge that "deep structure" invokes *more* theory than "surface structure", and for that reason the latter is preferable as a description of the data upon which our theory is to be built.

[5] This objection was raised by Grandy (see note 1).

[6] An example of each: 'blade of grass', 'vein of gold', 'ream of paper'. Of course, in the examples given, the noun in question is clearly count without the help of an explicit "constitutional" term like 'blade of', 'vein of' or 'ream of'. So to speak, the noun in its count sense has "built into it" the "constitutional" feature of being a single chicken or single potato.

[7] The "universal grinder" was suggested to me by a joke made by David Lewis in 1968.

[8] This application of the "grinder" is also due to David Lewis.

[9] This last criticism is from Moravcsik [1970], although he does not seem to believe its conclusion.

[10] This point was brought to my attention by David Lewis in 1970.

[11] This treatment is different from that given in Wallace [1964] pp. 77–78, where he gives the "proxy" treatment essentially as I have done, and instead of considering the other cases higher level quantification he calls it "use as a philosophical substantive" which is "conceptual or theoretical in what it affirms" and is "not confirmed by its instances". All this seems to me to be false.

[12] Although it should be noted that some people, e.g., Quine [1960], seem to think that the mass category is "archaic". Moravcsik's [1970] rejoinder to this is that it is only through mass concepts that quantative measurements, and thus scientific advancement, is possible.

WORKS CITED

[1969] Celce, M. and Schwarcz, R. M., *Counting, Collecting, Measuring and Quantifying In English* (Santa Monica, Cal.: System Development Corporation document SP-3378).

[1884] Frege, Gottlob, *Die Grundlagen der Arithmetik*. Translated by J. L. Austin as *The Foundations of Arithmetic* (Oxford: Basil Blackwell, 1950). References are to the translation.

[1962] Geach, Peter T., *Reference and Generality* (Ithaca, N.Y.: Cornell University Press).

[1965] Gleason, H. A. *Linguistics and English Grammar* (Toronto, Canada: Holt Reinhard Winston of Canada).

[1971] Harmon, Gilbert, 'Deep Structure as Logical Form', *Synthese* **21**, 275–297.

[1973] Hintikka, K. J. J., Moravcsik, J. M. E. and Suppes, P. (eds)., *Approaches to Natural Language* (Dordrecht, Reidel).

[1969] Montague, Richard, 'On the Nature of Certain Philosophical Entities', *The Monist* **53**, 159–194.

[1970a] Montague, Richard, 'English as a Formal Language', *Linguaggi Nella Societa e Nella Tecnica* (Milan, Italy).

[1970b] Montague, Richard, 'The Proper Treatment of Quantifiers in English' in Hintikka, Moravcsik and Suppes (eds.) [1973], pp. 177–188.

[1971] Montague, Richard, 'Universal Grammar', *Theoria* **36**, 378–398.

[1970] Moravcsik, J. M. E. 'The Problem of the Semantics of Mass Terms in English' in Hintikka, Moravcsik and Suppes (eds.) [1973].

[1968] Parsons, Terence, 'A Semantics for English' (unpublished paper).

[1970] Parsons, Terence, 'An Analysis of Mass Terms and Amount Terms', *Found. Lang.* (which is a part of Parsons [1968]); reprinted in this volume, pp. 137–166.

[1960] Quine, W. V., *Word and Object* (Cambridge, Mass.: M. I. T. Press).

[1964] Wallace, John, 'Philosophical Grammar' (unpublished Ph.D. dissertation, Stanford).

SOME BITS AND PIECES

These are some bits and pieces on the distinction between count nouns and mass nouns in an attempt to investigate the semantic and/or ontological significance of that distinction.[1] Count nouns are nouns like 'label', 'fable' and 'table', and mass nouns are nouns like 'milk' and 'honey' and 'silk' and 'money'. My question is whether count nouns correspond to counting things and mass nouns to amassing stuff and also whether there is a corresponding ontological difference in what we talk about.

The distinction between count nouns and mass nouns is notoriously difficult to make and a variety of criteria have been used, so part of what I argue is that the distinction that I make is appropriate to the reality of our language and the world. I maintain that the distinction between count nouns and mass nouns is determined by the quantifiers and determiners that are appropriate to the nouns.[2] Count nouns are distinguished by their taking the indefinite article, 'many', 'few', 'one', and other number words. I shall call these enumeratives. Mass nouns are distinguished by the appropriateness of what I shall call amassives, words like 'much', 'little', and 'less'. (There are differing views about the appropriateness of the definite article, a subject that I take up later.) What I am claiming is that in a particular occurrence a noun is count if enumeratives are appropriate to it, and it is mass if amassives are appropriate to it, giving us a sufficient condition for the distinction between count nouns and mass nouns.

It is necessary to speak of the *appropriateness* of quantifiers and determiners to nouns, since nouns in their various occurrences do not always appear with the distinguishing quantifiers or determiners. When we read 'Her iron is hot', we do not know on the face of it whether her iron is some stuff or something used for pressing (or golfing or whatever). But there are ways of knowing what the meaning of a word is in its particular occurrence, and from knowing the meaning we can know, for example, the appropriate predications even though they are not found in that occurrence. In a similar way, I am maintaining that we can know the appropriate quantifiers and determiners for a noun occurrence. There is a

15

F. J. Pelletier (ed.), Mass Terms, 15–29. All Rights Reserved.
Copyright © 1975 by D. Reidel Publishing Company, Dordrecht, Holland.

determinate grammar of an occurrence of 'He's at the bank' just as there is a determinate meaning. Just as we can know that the utterer is talking about a financial institution we can also know that the utterer is talking about something of which there can be many (and is thus using a count noun). Thus the proverbial 'chicken' has a grammar that accompanies it corresponding to the distinction between the stuff and the animal.

The plural has also been taken as a way of distinguishing count nouns from mass nouns, but this can have the danger of clouding the issue. For one thing, it is not always clear whether a word is in the singular or plural. We can easily become confused by words like 'news', 'woods', and 'politics'. ('His politics *are* atrocious, but then politics *is* not his bag.') I take it that the correct grammatical distinction is that a word is plural if plural verbs and plural anaphoric pronouns are appropriate to it and it is singular if the appropriate verbs and pronouns are singular. But being able to isolate the grammatical plural does not assure us of making the distinction between mass and count. The costs of doing something may be prohibitive and the blues are debilitating, but neither the costs nor the blues are many or much. Perhaps a plural occurrence is a criterion for a word *not* being mass. Some people think this; but I do not find it clearly wrong to ask how much beans (or vitamins) are in the cassoulet and how much politics are involved. So I prefer to stick with the criteria of enumeratives and amassives, although recognizing that plurality provides a rough indicator. This means that some nouns like 'blues' and 'wares' will be neither count nor mass, and although people will differ, this may also be true of 'groceries' and 'contents'.

The lack of both count and mass is also found with most nouns with the suffix '-hood' (some exceptions are 'falsehood' and 'brotherhood') and some nouns with the suffix '-ness' or '-ity', as in 'nearness', 'appropriateness', and 'chastity'.[3] (Although more nouns formed with '-ness' seem to be mass than count there are 'kindness' and 'thickness'. I see no interesting generalizations here.) Thus the distinction between count nouns and mass nouns using enumeratives and amassives is not exhaustive; nor need it be. One might also argue that the count noun/mass noun distinction does not apply to proper names, depending on what one says about 'There have been many John Does but only one Bertrand Russell'. I will avoid this issue here. I will also avoid developing a theory about generics and types. To say that there are two jades, jadeite and nephrite, looks for all the world like using 'jade' as a count noun, but most of what I will have to say will have little if anything to do with talking about kinds of stuff (or kinds of things).

One final consideration is whether the distinction is a unitary distinction, remembering that it uses a variety of determiners and quantifiers. We cannot use number words in talking about tidings, clothes, and groceries, although I think we can talk about many of them. Furthermore, we cannot have one of them or use the indefinite article with the respective noun. If this were to make our distinction unsatisfactory, we could restrict our criterion to the appropriateness of 'many' and 'much'; but there are very few words that show this lack of unity, and in any case I think my remarks will be independent of any decision on this matter. So I will continue with the convenience of using the variety of enumeratives and amassives to distinguish count nouns and mass nouns.

Something now needs to be said about the exclusiveness of the distinction and the reason for my putting the distinction in terms of noun occurrences. The problem arises when we realize that some tokens of homophonic nouns (with or without the same meaning) are count nouns while others are mass nouns. Consider, for example, 'paper', 'glass', and 'iron'. A paper like the *New York Times* uses too much paper; many glasses do not have any glass in them; and I don't know how much iron most flatirons have in them. Granted these words have differences in meaning and must be distinguished just as we distinguish 'wood' ('the wood in our woodpile') and 'woods' ('the woods that we hide in'). But this is the very reason that we have to look at noun occurrences, that is in order not to beg the question about whether the same noun can be both a count noun and a mass noun. So at this point I will remain neutral on the question of meaning and the number of words by talking about homophones, expression types with the same phonology.

Now it is important to remember just how many homophones are commonly used both as mass nouns and count nouns. Just for a start, we should notice that we can ask how many masses there are in a room and how much mass each has. We can also speak of how many counts we made of how much count a bridge hand has. There can also be too much or too many body(ies) or material(s). Even if there is a difference, we can have a number of pains and an amount of pain as well as a number of times (spaces) and an amount of time (space). Such variation is also common when we get away from the concrete. We speak of needing much more theory or needing many more theories, of finding more truth or finding more truths, of not having much hope or having many hopes. There can also be much or many justification(s), consideration(s), and similarity(ies). We can say either that there are many more similarities than differences between them or that there is much more similarity than difference between them.

Our kitchens and cafes are also good places to find this variation. What causes trouble is that in some of our lowlier cafes people have been known to order three waters, four ice creams, and two coffees, while in the adjoining bar they ask for three beers and a scotch. We know that these things come in glasses, dishes, cups, and bottles, so it is tempting to say that these are not instances of the homophones having count occurrences at all but of there being instead the proper deletions of the appropriate nouns that do have count occurrences. We want dishes of ice cream or orders of ice cream, but I will return to this question of deletion shortly. For the moment I am trying to exhibit what is on the surface, and it has been my experience that even the classiest restaurants will take an order for two coffees. And this is not meant to deprecate the language in the lowliest cafes. We have to be able to understand the communications of the people there too.

I have given some cases of homophones that typically and frequently have mass occurrences which also appear to have count occurrences, but our language goes the other way as well. Back in the kitchen, there are the well known cases of not getting much lamb (from a lamb) and of using too much apple (from many apples). Also I ask for a dozen chicken eggs but for a plateful of scrambled eggs. I tell them how many chicken eggs but how much scrambled eggs. But moreover, it is not unheard of to ask how many scrambled eggs someone wants. Sometimes, not to prejudice the issue I say that I want a lot of eggs or more eggs, both expressions being neutral between count and mass occurrences. We do similar things with potatoes, although in this case we sometimes ask for more potato, particularly when they are mashed.

I do not think it is too farfetched to imagine a universal grinder (as does Pelletier[4]) that can grind up anything and everything such that whatever spills out is an amount of what goes in. If you put a few large trees in, what you will get out is a large amount of tree. This will be true even if it is also sawdust. Pelletier's claim is that since everything can go in, everything can also come out as stuff, and the appropriate homophones have mass as well as count occurrences. He also claims that it is enough that it only works for physical objects. The universal grinder does help us realize how our language can be used (and is used in describing these examples) with mass occurrences. But it is not just grinding and mashing that does the job.

We don't grind sculptures to get sculpture nor kleenexes to get kleenex. Homophones with count occurrences can take on mass occurrences very easily in a variety of ways. You may be impressed by the number of glasses in my cupboard, or it may be the amount of glass that impresses you. In the same context either a mass occurrence or a count occurrence can be appropriate. Similarly, it may be that the National Gallery of England has many more Rembrandts than the National Gallery of the United States, but those who are interested in expanse and expense may find out that the latter has much more Rembrandt than the former. This might incline us to talk about how much David is in the Louvre and how many Vermeers are in the Mauritshuis. Here are just a few other cases to show the variety and extent of mass occurrences. We speak of how much family someone has. Hunters ask if there is much elk in the province. We can also ask how much city we go through before we get to the country. Nor do I think it is absurd to say that there is much more car than garage.

So there are a number of cases where homophones that normally have count occurrences also have mass occurrences and vice versa. This is coupled with the fact that there are many homophones for which count occurrences and mass occurrences are equally common. A few examples to add to the list are 'hamburger', 'candy', 'ballet', 'meaning', and 'hope'. I do want to make it clear, however, that I do not think that *all* homophones with count occurrences have mass occurrences and vice versa. Words for orifices seem to have count but not mass occurrences, for example: 'opening', 'hole', and 'mouth'. We would also be hard pressed to find mass occurrences for 'peculiarity', 'trick', 'act', and 'occurrence'. On the other hand the following seem to be homophones with mass occurrences but no count occurrences: 'fun', 'moisture', 'gratitude', 'carelessness', and 'audacity'.[5] Depending on one's imagination and tolerance, many more data or much more data could be suggested, but I want now to turn to a discussion of the examples that we have.

Consider again the language of the cafe where people order waters, milks, and coffees. As I said above, it is tempting to say that these orders are to be understood as having deletions of appropriate count nouns, like 'glass' and 'cup', with a movement of the pluralization. There is very little known about deletion, and it should be treated with suspicion in general. One principle, however, that is universally accepted is that what is deleted should be readily recoverable – we should be able to say what has been deleted from the sentence. Our linguistic intuitions and the corresponding linguistic theories do tell us the difference in deletions in 'John promised to go' and 'John told Harry to go'. We know that in one case we can expect John to go and in the other case we can expect Harry to go. In the case of ordering milks and coffees, there is no obvious recoverability. There is certainly no way of telling that deep down there was 'cup', 'mug', 'order', or 'bit' deleted, and certainly no general deletion can be found for all of these expressions. I see no way that a deletion theory could deal with my ordering a dinner. Much worse would be the attempt to explain the various uses of 'irons' and 'glasses'. Moreover, even if 'an iron' did mean 'a golf iron' there would be no reason to postulate a deletion any more than when 'a bank' means 'a river bank'.

Another problem with attempting a deletion theory is that it does not give us any understanding of homophones for which count occurrences are prior or primary, as appears to be the case, for example, with 'lamb' and 'steak'. Anything that would make any sense at all would be far too complicated to allow for recoverability. Even if we were to have a deletion theory that could go from count to mass as well as from mass to count, we would have to know which way it went with words like 'consideration' and 'difference'. There are numerous cases of homophones with both count and mass occurrences that are well established. It is not clear what the historical relation is between the count and mass occurrences of 'hamburger' and 'candy'. When we see the variation in 'faculty' as when we wonder whether his faculties are intact and how much faculty he has for the project or when we talk about the faculty that teaches in a faculty of medicine, it then becomes clear that deletion theories should be laid to rest.

What seems more likely is that there are words with a double life – sometimes occurring as count nouns and sometimes occurring as mass nouns.[6] This vitiates the need for deletions. Quine suggests that one of the two kinds of occurrences will be the shadow of the other, but this need not be the case as it appears with 'hamburger'. Nouns cannot be divided into those that are count and those that are mass with a saving grammatical theory for irregularities. Most nouns can have a role as either a mass noun or a count noun. 'Cup' and 'saucer' are usually count nouns, and 'sugar' and 'spice' are usually mass nouns. They all have their double lives, but one is more dominant than the other. Some nouns like 'iron', 'candy', 'faculty', and 'experience' are equally at home in either role. A word can be well established in both count and mass occurrences without any deletions being necessary.

Before turning to a further discussion of the significance and difference between the two roles, there are three other linguistic contexts that are worth considering. We speak of someone being at home but at the house. Some people speak of others being in the hospital but in prison. Others speak of people being in a cast but in hospital. The question obviously arises about whether 'home', 'prison', and 'hospital' are mass nouns or count nouns in these occurrences. The same question arises about nouns when they occur as noun modifiers as in 'snow man' and 'tape recorder'. I think we can ask how much snow there is in a snow man, but it is not to the point to ask how many tapes or how much tape a tape recorder is for. Certainly nose drops do not quantify or enumerate nose(s). It might also be to the point to ask how much or how many when told that she is dressed in silk(s), but this is clearly inappropriate with respect to hospitals and jails. These constructions seem to give us the nearest thing to mentioning features rather than referring to stuff or things.

On the other hand we have constructions that give us what look more like mass occurrences, often of nouns that we expect usually to have count occurrences. We can pass a stretch of road or use a length of rope, and in this case 'road' and 'rope' are being used as mass nouns. We also speak of a head of hair with many strands of hair, and in neither case is it appropriate to ask how many hairs there are. In a rather common construction we ask for a piece of newspaper, of bone, and of other things that are usually enumerated. *Larousse Gastronomique* gives directions for making essence of onion and shallot and of tomato.[7] We all know the taste of banana and there is Dr Fowler's extract of wild strawberry to cure us of diarrhea. These constructions seem to depend upon what constitutes these things, i.e. the stuff of which they are made, and we can ask how much of the stuff there is. Our interest, as in the game, is whether they are made of animal, vegetable, or mineral. In this context there are *some* noun modifiers, as in 'log cabin', 'brick building', and 'stone wall', that have mass occurrences giving us the stuff of the thing.

Turning now to why it is that words sometimes have count occurrences and sometimes mass occurrences, we are immediately faced with the problem of a tremendous amount of variation that appears unnecessary and inexplicable. I have already pointed out the variation of non-concrete terms like 'truth', 'hope', and 'justification'. If counting and measuring have anything to do with count nouns and mass nouns, it is certainly not here. Exactly the same thing(s) will provide as much justification or as many justifications as we need. We also find other variations of occurrences for basically the same part of the world. There is a count/mass difference between 'fruit' and 'vegetable', but they apply to things that for all accounts and purposes seem to be alike. Nor can I see anything that would explain the count/mass difference between 'footwear' and 'shoe', 'clothing' and 'clothes', 'shit' and 'turd', or 'fuzz' and 'cop'.[8] These are normally mass nouns and count nouns for basically the same thing. It is also difficult to understand why 'knowledge' is a mass noun while 'belief' is normally a count noun when our theories tell us that they are about such similar material. It is equally curious that 'success' is often a mass term while 'failure' is rarely, if ever, a mass term. And the only difference that I can see between 'coal' and 'furniture' on the one hand and 'coals' and 'furnishings' on the other is that what is referred to by the mass nouns is more easily counted.

Moreover it is surprising that 'art' and 'architecture' are mass terms when it is pieces of the stuff that are created and sold. Bread and, particularly, toast are also taken by the piece, but they are referred to by mass nouns. Similarly, in trying to understand why some nouns are mass nouns and others are count nouns, 'furniture' is a difficult case. Although we usually count the pieces in a set, we still talk about how much or how little furniture someone has. Counting is much easier when we are dealing with furniture, but we put up with the mass noun. It would seem more sensible to use a count noun as do the Germans and French. When they talk about many pieces of furniture, the Germans talk about *die vielen Möbel*. (Although it is interesting to note that when they talk about three pieces of furniture, they refer to *die drei Möbelstücke*.) It is also peculiar that we talk about how much whiskey and how much gin and orange we drink but how many martinis and how many orange blossoms we drink.

Faced with evidence like this and examples like these, I become sceptical of finding a general distinction between count and mass occurrences with respect to individualizing or anything else. I have no reason to think that the Germans treat or regard their furniture in any way different from the English, Canadians, Australians, and Americans. And I want the same thing whether I call it gin and orange or an orange blossom. From these examples, it appears that the distinction between count and mass occurrences does not tell us about nor depend upon any distinctions in the world at least in these cases. Looking back at a great many other cases, we can see that we cannot get directly at the structure of our world through our language. This is as one would expect and want, however. Our language ossifies according to established linguistic conventions so that grammatical distinctions are not sensitive to scientific progress and change. We would certainly not want our language to restrict scientific progress or even popular understanding of that progress. I have no doubt that science will tell us what the real distinctions are between particular things and stuff and what the nature of the world is. I agree with Laycock that scientists will have to be able to refer to stuff and things, and moreover the language is flexible enough to provide the appropriate means.[9] I also expect the difference in counting and measuring in science to be reflected in the scientific use of count nouns and mass nouns. The scientist needs to quantify appropriately in the best scientific theory.

Such care about the way we are quantifying is often not needed in our ordinary dealings in the world. We follow the linguistic conventions of our language and form our communicative intentions without necessarily having corresponding commitments about counting or measuring. We know that saying how much toast we want usually involves some counting, while asking for beans usually involves measuring. What I am claiming is that the mass/count distinction is often not reflected in the meaning of an utterance; the relation between the language and the world is not so simple. Before developing this further, I turn to the role of the definite article in the count/mass distinction.

Some have said that the definite article is appropriate only to count nouns and not to mass nouns.[10] This would give a certain unity to the articles (definite and indefinite), and it could perhaps explain some matters about reference. On the other hand, it would appear to give all nouns a count occurrence. For any stuff on the table we can speak of *the* stuff on the table, whether it be sugar, water, dust, or whatever. And we can always speak of *the* stuff here or there. So a question arises about how we are to understand a request to pass the sugar. There is a definite reference in this case to some particular sugar – that sugar which is contextually indicated – and this is why it makes sense to ask what sugar I want. (I may not have noticed, for example, that there is a bowl of cubed sugar as well as a jar of loose sugar.) Furthermore, if someone replaces that sugar with some other sugar, then I don't still have the sugar (I had before) although I still have sugar. So asking for sugar is different from asking for the sugar. The difference is between asking for some (any old) sugar and asking for some particular (bit of) sugar. There is a similar difference between saying that wheat is in great demand in the Sahara and saying that the wheat (in the Sahara) is in great demand. In the first case, there is no presupposition at all that there is wheat, but in the second case there is a presupposition that there is the wheat one is referring to. Similarly, one normally doesn't ask for sugar unless there is sugar around, but asking for *the* sugar presupposes that there is some particular sugar. There is perhaps a problem that sugar bowls are constantly replenished, but then so are the toothpicks we ask for and refer to in asking for them.

Laycock claims that there cannot be any reference to particulars in the examples I have given above because there are no criteria of distinctness incorporated.[11] It seems to me that I do refer to something distinct and discrete (unlike the cases where I refer to the stuff), but this might be considered quibbling, for Laycock does accept that we have criteria of identity when we talk about, e.g., the water in a glass.[12] It can be distinguished from the water that is not in the glass, but the problem is that even though 'the water' refers to a quantity of water (in Helen Cartwright's sense)[13] we cannot go from the definite 'the water' to the indefinite 'a water'. We might say that there is something *distinctive* about the water (e.g. on the table). We have no established criteria for treating it as an individual (object) with convenient individuation and reidentification.

I would be happy to call the water on the table a particular, but terminology is difficult and unstable in this area. What needs to be clear is that by referring to this water and that water we have not thereby referred to countables. We cannot say how many waters we have referred to. We can always say how many bits (or quantities in Cartwright's sense) of water we have referred to, because that is as easy as picking out a bit of time here and a bit of time there for a project. We usually do not have reason to pick out adjoining bits of stuff, but I see nothing unintelligible about it. So although we pick out something to refer to, we do not necessarily pick out an individual object, something that can be counted in ways that have been established by linguistic convention. On the other hand we are not referring to stuff as we do with the normal mass occurrences of nouns. ('Iron is an element'. Not: 'The iron is an element'.) So picking out these particulars (as I have called them) is different from picking out stuff as well as from picking out individuals. There may be reason not to call such occurrences either count occurrences or mass occurrences.

In using the definite article, context allows us to pick out and refer to particular bits of stuff. I have pointed out that the coffee, e.g. in the pot, is not necessarily a coffee, but I have also pointed out above that we can speak of a coffee (and many coffees) using a count occurrence of the noun. Usually coffee does not stick together so well in neat little bits. But after a few stops at the local coffee house, we begin to get it in standard quantities, and the coffee is neatly massed together. This happens in many other cases as well. At first our cheese comes in little bits and pieces with little cohesion or regularity. The stilton is scooped out in scoops of the stuff. Then we begin to notice that it all comes from the same containers, and we begin to speak of a stilton or of many stiltons. It depends upon whether the stuff travels in the same regular packages. When the material is packaged together, we frequently begin to use count nouns.[14]

The conventions of packaging constitute one factor in determining criteria for individualizing that get established in our linguistic conventions. The influence of packaging is strong but by no means decisive. We still talk about how much soup is in a can and how much milk is in a carton. Also it is not the packages that hamburgers come in but the way they stick together as they get commercialized that seems to be important. But there are many other factors coming from our interests and practices that account for the establisment of linguistic conventions, without any broad generalizations available. Branding irons, golf irons, and laundry irons are only a few of the kinds of things that are made predominantly of iron, and it has just happened that linguistic conventions have not been established to call most of the other kinds of things irons. And of course there are things like nickels and tins that have little, if any, of the stuff. We also get 'apple' from 'apples' and 'lamb' from 'lambs', because the words have become established in that use because of linguistic conventions.

We can have such a large variety of nouns that have both mass and count occurrences because everything can be individuated, divided into parts, and everything can be measured, en masse. Linguistic conventions can establish the appropriateness of count and mass occurrences, depending on our interests and practices. And as I have said before, this is not always a matter of cutting, mashing, or grinding. We don't do anything to the world when we ask how much space there is at each space at the table or at what times the film begins and how much time it takes. Much of this goes on independent of what science says the world is like.

What the scientist says is not all that there is to be said, and for a variety of good reasons. We do not have to know the best scientific theory to put in our orders at the restaurant, and the scientific theory does not have to make reference to glasses although we do require that it refer to the stuff glass. Furthermore, we can get on with the way we talk about justification(s) and difficulty(ies) without even expecting these to form part of the ontology in a scientific theory. It is important that the subject of science(s) can always be individualized, i.e., divided into parts, or measured, en masse. This does not mean that we have machinery to break it up, but rather that we always have the conceptual capabilities of regarding the parts of the world in at least two different ways.[15] Science is of course important in determining how we regard our world, but its importance can be overemphasized.

The point of all this is that we have numerous ways of individualizing the world, which means that we also have numerous ways of gathering stuff together. The stuff in a jar can vary from sand to marbles and from scotch to martinis. When we talk about a candy or about a glass it is usually because we are individualizing in the way established by convention. We can also talk about the candy or the glass when we want to refer to a definite individual.

It will not always be the case that we will use a count noun when we are individualizing and a mass noun when we are not. Linguistic conventions get established without necessarily being reflected in communication intentions. As I mentioned above, we can use a count noun for beans without individualizing and a mass noun for toast while individualizing. When we use 'consideration' and 'difference' as count nouns or as mass nouns there is no reason to believe that we are either counting or measuring. In some contexts it is not appropriate to ask whether we are talking about it as stuff or as things. We can talk about it without talking about it as either. The neutral terms 'a lot of' and 'more of' are used when we don't want to indicate either a count occurrence or mass occurrence.

Moreover, even when we are using nouns for which individualizing or amassing is normally appropriate there is sometimes an indefiniteness in the meaning and the grammar of the noun occurrence. This can be seen most clearly if we notice that the definite article can be either the definite article corresponding to the indefinite article or the article which indicates the picking out of particulars which are not individuals. When I speak of the candy, I can be speaking either of the definite candy (one of the many candies) or of the particular bit of candy (but not a candy). Often it is not obvious from what we hear or see on the surface which group of quantifiers, enumeratives or amassives, are appropriate to a noun occurrence. This can be a communication loss, but frequently it is not important which quantifiers are appropriate. We can respond to a request for the candy without knowing whether the speaker is individualizing or amassing. In these cases, the communication intentions of the speaker are all we have to determine the appropriateness of quantifiers.

My final point is that sometimes we do not even have the communication intentions that would determine appropriateness. Sometimes not even the speakers themselves will make the distinction. When I ask what the justification was for something, I can be totally devoid of intentions that involve individualizing or amassing, and there is no need to answer either in terms of a justification or in terms of justification. Where there is an absence of communication intention like this I will speak of there being a communicative gap. If one Beethoven sonata was played and I say that I liked the Beethoven I don't have to be either using a count noun or a mass noun, or individualizing or amassing. That is something that may not be determined by my communication intentions, thus leaving a communicative gap. There can be a communicative gap with respect to mass and count occurrences when I say that I like smelt. I don't have to determine whether it is the stuff or the things. Such a communicative gap will be acceptable.

Not all communicative gaps will be acceptable, however. It is highly unlikely that I can speak of the iron without establishing whether or not I am individualizing or even how I am individualizing. I cannot speak of wanting the iron without the principles of individualizing being established. That would be as bad as saying that one wanted to go to the bank without it being established that it was the river bank or the financial bank. This might even provide a criterion for individualizing words, by saying that there is a difference of words if the communicative gap is unacceptable. In the case of 'iron' we would have to speak of different words, while in the case of 'justification' we could speak of just one word. At this point, however, it seems unimportant how we individualize words as long as we can establish the grammar and the meaning of the occurrences of homophones. I might add that when I speak of the meaning it is not clear to me whether or not or how I am individualizing meaning.

I have claimed that there are two sources of indefiniteness with respect to count and mass occurrences of nouns. One concerns the communicative gap where the count/mass distinction is sometimes left out of the communicative situation, and the other concerns a difference between the grammatical distinction and semantic accounts. Even where the count/mass distinction is included in the communicative situation individualizing and amassing does not always follow according to count and mass occurrences. Here we have the source(s) of my scepticism about there always being a sharp line between our individualizing and our amassing. I wish I could say many more things at this point, but I have said about as much as I can.

University of Calgary

NOTES

[1] It would be too cumbersome to mention all of my sources at the appropriate point in the text, but I am happy to acknowledge here the very important help of Jude Carlson, Helen Cartwright, Henry Laycock, Brian Loar, Jeffry Pelletier, and Haj Ross. I have also had the benefit of comments on very different ancestors of this paper read at the University of Wisconsin, Brandeis University, and a meeting of the Western Canadian Philosophical Association in Edmonton. Some of my examples also come from the seminal work of Otto Jespersen in *The Philosophy of Grammar* (New York, Norton Library; 1965 (first published 1924)), pp. 198–201.

[2] I speak of nouns here, but the distinction can easily be extended to noun phrases.

[3] Notice that these nouns occur in the singular without determiners or quantifiers but are not therefore considered mass nouns, although this can still be taken as a rough indicator of a mass noun occurrence, as in 'There is milk in the refrigerator'.

[4] See F. J. Pelletier, 'Non-Singular Reference: Some Preliminaries', in this volume, pp. 1–14.

[5] Much of this comes from Haj Ross, following, I think, the work of Bob Fiengo.

[6] Such a view is suggested by W. V. Quine, *Word and Object*, esp. pp. 90–95.

[7] On the other hand, *Larousse Gastronomique* also gives recipes for essence of mushrooms and of truffles.

[8] There is some slight semantic difference in some of these pairs, for example boots are footwear but not shoes, but such semantic difference does not seem to account for the mass/count distintion. For a note on the distinction between 'shit' and 'turd', see Quang Phuc Dong, 'Three Lexicographic Notes on Individuation', *Quarterly Regress Report*, No. 38 (South Hanoi Institute of Technology, no date).

[9] I am largely in agreement with the main points in Henry Laycock's 'Some Questions of Ontology', *Philosophical Review* 81 (1972), 3–42.

[10] Cf. Quine, *Word and Object*, p. 91.

[11] See Henry Laycock's 'Some Questions of Ontology', esp. pp. 30–34 and his 'Chemistry and Individuation', a paper read to the Canadian Philosophical Association, 6 June, 1973.

[12] See Laycock, 'Chemistry and Individuation', p. 7. This seems to be a refinement of the things he said in 'Some Questions of Ontology'.

[13] See Helen Cartwright, 'Quantities', *Philosophical Review* 79 (1970), 25–42.

[14] See Laycock, 'Some Questions of Ontology', p. 18 for another statement of this view.

[15] Cf. Eddy Zemach, 'Four Ontologies', *Journal of Philosophy* 67 (1970), 231–247, for an interesting discussion of this kind of view.

HELEN M. CARTWRIGHT

SOME REMARKS ABOUT MASS NOUNS
AND PLURALITY

There is a distinction, well marked in English, between words and phrases with the grammatical features of a count noun, a noun regularly used with 'many' and 'few' in the plural and 'an' in the singular, and words and phrases with the grammar of a mass noun, a word which, among other things, lacks these features along with the contrast between plural and singular. 'Ring', 'gold ring', 'metal', 'rope', 'rope from which he hung' are examples of the former; examples of the latter are 'water', 'metal', 'rusty metal', 'rope all over the floor'.

Both count nouns and mass nouns *are* nouns; they occur with demonstratives and with 'the' and 'the same'. 'This water', 'the water in the pot' and 'the same water' look very much like 'this ring', 'the ring on my finger' and 'the same ring'; and the analogy invites the suggestion that the grammatical distinction reflects a systematic semantic difference, in particular, an ontological difference. Rings are *individuals*, full-fledged objects or *substances*; words like 'water' are names of stuff or *matter*. But if the ontological difference in question is Aristotle's, the bricks of which a house is made, the letters in a word and the orange which was my breakfast may fairly be classified as matter; and since 'brick', 'letter' and 'orange' are count nouns, *this* difference, so one might argue, is no more neatly reflected in grammar than the difference between plants and animals or men and machines.

And those sceptical of the existence of anything here of philosophical interest can only draw comfort, as it seems to me, from at least one way in which Jespersen introduces the distinction. By contrast with 'countables' or 'thing words',

There are a great many words which do not call up the idea of some definite thing with a certain shape or precise limits. I call these 'mass-words'; they may be either material, in which case they denote some substance in itself independent of form, such as *silver, quicksilver, water, butter, gas, air*, etc., or else immaterial, such as *leisure, music, traffic, success, tact, commonsense*, and ... *satisfaction, admiration, refinement*, from verbs, or ... *restlessness, justice, safety, constancy*, from adjectives.[1]

31

F. J. Pelletier (ed.), Mass Terms, 31–46. All Rights Reserved.

Plainly a classification based on no more than the grammatical features mentioned above far outruns the examples that first come to mind. And the added hints here quoted – especially the opening remark – are of little help in trying to grasp the general contrast he is after.

1.   There is an important contrast to be made nonetheless, I think. Quine follows Jespersen only in part in his use of 'mass term'[2], a label which covers what Strawson has called 'material names',[3] and there is here perhaps the basis for a more conservative classification. Strawson's distinction between 'material names' and 'substance names'[4] does not coincide with Quine's distinction between 'mass terms' and 'general terms'; but where their usage overlaps, so in some important ways do their views.

Substance names (count nouns), according to Strawson, "provide a principle for distinguishing, enumerating and reidentifying particulars of a sort" (II, 202). According to Quine, general terms, by contrast with mass terms, "possess built-in modes, however arbitrary, of dividing their reference" (91). Whereas 'this river' and 'the same river' are connected logically as well as grammatically with 'a river' and 'another river', there are no such connections in the case of 'this water' or 'the same water'. In order to grasp the purported references of such phrases "some special individuating standard is understood from the circumstances"[5] – perhaps, as Strawson suggests, some standard of a sort provided by adjuncts like 'puddle' or 'pool' or 'glassful'. What Strawson calls 'feature-placing' statements, e.g., 'There is gold here' or 'Snow is falling, – a class of sentences which correspond to what Quine calls 'occasion sentences' – "do not bring particulars into our discourse", they do not involve "expressions referring definitely or indefinitely to individual instances" (I, 244).

Such words in fact belong to an "archaic category" (95) associated with "one of the earliest things children do with language" (II, 206). In adult English, material names are missing an ingredient typically present in the case of substance names, which ingredient enables a speaker to pick out and identify, hence refer to or mention something. Mass terms, on Quine's account, fall outside a scheme of classification intended to illuminate the nature of reference and the ontological issues associated with it. Philosophical parsing, for Quine at any rate, begins with singular terms and predication, and in sentences parsed accordingly, a mass term borrows from its context and takes on another function.

2. Now I have argued elsewhere [6] that mass nouns like 'water' and 'gold' contribute no less to the adult business of reference than count nouns do, and I mean to pursue the point again. But I shall here be concerned first to defend what seems to me to be right in this brief sketch. And while any very complete defense would call for further elaboration of the views of Quine and Strawson – doubtless also some general discussion of various other ways in which linguistic phenomena are currently described, these remarks are intended primarily to ward off sceptics by simply calling attention to some misconceptions as to just where – in the context of anyone's theory – the difference marked by grammar is to be located; and I shall have very little to say beyond this.

I mean to argue first that, contrary to what I have so far suggested, what is in question is not at bottom a difference between two classes of words or classes of words and phrases, or their occurrences, or their senses. There is another alternative; and in connection with this alternative I shall consider some examples, familiar in contemporary discussion couched in terms of the general framework of Quine's program of "regimenting" English in the notation of quantification theory. In the end I mean to suggest that for rather obvious reasons these examples are unfortunate. But by dwelling on their defeats, I hope to shed some light on another source of misunderstanding and a more fruitful way of looking at the matter.

3. I began with a rough description of a syntactic distinction – a grammatical distinction between classes of nominal forms. If there is more to be said then this, then at the very least some account is needed for the fact that hosts of words and phrases cut across the distinction, however stringently it is drawn. Jespersen's cases include:

a little more cheese	two big cheeses
It is hard as iron.	a hot iron (flat iron)
Cork is lighter than water.	I want three corks for these bottles.
a parcel in brown paper	state papers
little talent	few talents
much experience	many experiences

And cases like Quine's

Put some apple in the salad.
Mary had a little lamb.

serve to show that not only words and phrases but their occurrences need not be exclusively mass or count.

We can agree that all these cases involve a difference in sense of one kind or another; and that some involve 'lexical' ambiguity – i.e., very roughly, word ambiguity of a sort one would expect to find recorded in a dictionary. 'Iron' and 'cork' in the contexts given are of this nature; 'lamb' functions like 'calf' on the one hand and 'veal' on the other. And one may, for one reason or another, be inclined to pass on this and other cases as well; that is, to locate a shift in the sense of some word or words, whose ambiguity then serves to account for a corresponding shift in grammar. But if this way of looking at the difference seems to work in some cases it does not, I think, work in general.

It is not obvious, in the first place, that Quine's 'apple' is ambiguous at all. The ambiguity of the *sentence* is clear enough, given some latitude about 'some'. It involves a shift familiar in the language of cookery and elsewhere. But it is worth noticing that 'Put *an* apple in the salad' would do as well in the most likely circumstances, since a recipe would probably call for an apple – peeled, cored and diced (not sliced or mashed). A comparable switch would probably *not* do, had we begun with 'Put some chicken in the salad' – unless it were a very large salad. And the point is that the shift in grammar, assuming that it involves a shift in sense, reflects something about what we do with apples, not – or not at all obviously – a shift in the sense of the count noun 'apple'.

And for the same sorts of reasons it seems to me implausible to say in the other direction that there is a shift in the sense of the mass noun 'beer' if one says 'He had a couple of beers' – or, for that matter, that Jespersen's 'cheese' and 'paper' are ambiguous. 'Two big cheeses' is not at all like 'two large beers', but this seems to be an accident of the manufacture and consumption of cheese and beer. Unhappily I have recently heard 'two milks' and 'three oatmeals' passed off by philosophers as English; and, e.g., in the idiom of short order restaurants perhaps they do pass. Perhaps also in such a setting one might order one small cheese or two apple pies without risk of confusion. But we do standardly use 'piece' here, and although I have no desire to defend the claim that there must be some sort of ellipsis or 'deletion' in every such case, short orders *are* short. A grilled cheese and a hot pastrami are sandwiches – the ellipsis is easy, as it is with 'one scrambled without' and 'a large orange' if one knows the idiom at all.

It is not as obvious with 'one ham on rye' or 'two over easy', nor is it with 'a beer'. (Notice, e.g., that with no apparent shift in sense, it may or may not be superfluous to ask someone who wants a beer whether or not he'd like a glass.) But surely this is not enough to establish that 'beer' is ambiguous.

Given sufficient imagination one might find occasion to say 'Put some table in the salad' and 'I'll have two large potting soils'. If, in every such case, a shift in sense is to be laid to the sense of a word – count noun or mass noun – a sceptic might well argue that the choice of one form or the other depends on nothing of systematic interest, but on a variety of factors, psychological and practical, perhaps on nothing at all.[7]

Again, there are shifts in sense – not to be confused with the short order sort just discussed – that are, if anything, too systematic for lexical treatment. The shift from 'some scrap metal' to 'a heavy metal' is just comparable to that from 'They are drinking wine' to 'They are drinking a (French) wine'; and hosts of mass nouns shift in this systematic and familiar way – *a* metal or wine or liquid or gas is, roughly speaking, a *kind* or *sort* of metal or wine or some other stuff. For whatever reason, 'water' and 'gold' are not, I think, regularly used in this way, and again I am not supposing one who says 'Gold is a metal' has deleted or elided 'kind of'. The point has to do with reference, and I shall have more to say of kinds below. For the moment it is worth noting only that one would no more expect a dictionary to account for it wherever it occurs than one would expect a separate entry for the use of 'bird' in 'Audubon's *Birds of America*'. A bird, here, is, again roughly speaking, a kind of bird; the shift in question occurs with both mass nouns and count nouns.

Finally, the differences recorded above involving 'talent' and 'experience' are not like those so far considered nor, in any obvious way, like one another. But again it will not do, I think, to assume the ambiguity in question is lexical; at any rate if one knows the use of either word in its capacity as mass noun or count noun, he knows as much as any dictionary is likely to tell him about its use in the other capacity. And similar considerations apply to such hard cases as 'noise', 'thought', and 'pain'. Doubtless a dictionary should record illustrative uses along with the fact that both forms regularly occur, if they do. But if it is assumed that a shift in syntax is to be explained in terms of the senses of these words or their occurrences, it is once again open to a sceptic to argue that there is nothing here of systematic interest.[8]

4. What I want to suggest – vague as it is – is plain enough, I think, nonetheless. The crucial difference in all these cases is not lexical but 'structural'; the *relevant* ambiguity is not to be gleaned from the sense of such words as 'apple', 'beer', 'metal', or 'experience' but from the grammatical structure of those contexts in which they occur. Moreover, what is needed is a *twofold* comparison between the features of mass nouns and those of *singular* count nouns, on the one hand, and the features of mass nouns and those of *plural* forms, on the other. For if it is plausible to say that there is no interesting lexical difference between the singular count noun 'apple' and its occurrence as a mass noun, the suggestion is, if anything, even more plausible with respect to the plural 'apples'.[9] And it is perhaps worth mentioning in this connection some of the rather mixed bag of apparently plural forms Jespersen lists among mass words as a lexical class: 'dregs', 'proceeds', 'belongings', 'sweepings', 'measles', 'rickets', 'blues', 'creeps' – to which we may add 'nosedrops', 'contents', and, I suppose, 'data', and 'groceries'.

In a recent controversy between linguists, it has been said that, contrary to the general claim that selectional restrictions reflect semantic differences, 'footwear' and 'articles of wearing apparel for the feet' are "identical in meaning".[10] Since the former is mass and the latter is count, the claim is again that the distinction makes no semantic difference. But surely there are grounds for suspicion in the fact that if the purported paraphrase comes close to meaning the same as 'footwear', 'articles of *footwear*' comes much closer, and in the fact that the paraphrase is plausible only with the count noun 'article' in the plural. There is no *lexical* difference between 'article' and 'articles'; they are the same word, in one straightforward sense of the word 'word'. But 'footwear' does *not* mean the same as 'article of wearing apparel for the feet', and what the case shows at most is that the *structural* contrast between some mass nouns and some *plural* nominals is not as sharp as the contrast between some mass nouns and some singular count noun constructions.

I have argued elsewhere that mass nouns contribute no less to the adult business of reference than count nouns do – i.e., count nouns in the *plural*. And what seems right in views like these of Quine and Strawson depends at least in part on attending only to the difference between mass nouns and count nouns *in the singular*. Trivially, 'an apples' and 'another rivers' are no better than 'a gold' and 'another gold'. If 'the same water' requires some special understanding as to what is being individuated, so, one might say, does 'the same apples'. Again what is needed is a twofold structural comparison; in particular we need to explore the grammatical analogy between mass nouns and plural forms. We can agree with Quine that "the dichotomy between singular terms and general terms, inconveniently similar in nomenclature to the grammatical one between singular and plural, is less superficial" (90). But to leave it at that is to miss the *non*-superficiality of the analogy between the singular *form* of singular mass nouns and that of plural count nouns.

Quine's program calls for only two categories of nominal forms – singular and general – in the philosophical parsing of English sentences.[11] Contrary to Quine's treatment, the suggestion I am making requires, in the first place, that some status be granted the features of mass nouns, and in the second, that the grammar of plural forms be described in parallel fashion.

5. Consider now

(1)   Water is a fluid.
        Water is fluid (colorless).
        Water flows.
        Lamb is scarce (plentiful, disappearing).
        Petroleum is various in origin.
        Fuel is a necessity.

(2)   Lions are a carnivore.
        Lions are carnivores.
        Lions like red meat.
        Lions are scarce (numerous, disappearing, widespread).
        Apples are various in origin.
        Shoes are a necessity.

Most of these examples are Quine's, and according to his well known view the unmodified mass nouns in (1) are singular terms designating objects which are or may be 'scattered'; 'Water' there "differs none from such singular terms as 'mama' and 'Agnes', unless the scattered stuff it names be denied the status of a single sprawling object" (98). The fact that 'water' is not elsewhere interchangeable with 'Agnes' preserving grammar is irrelevant, since, according to Quine, elsewhere mass terms are general terms and 'Agnes' is not. And to object that proper names are normally reserved for continuous objects with shapes and sizes would be to beg the question at issue; at any rate independent reasons are needed for with-holding the status of proper names from 'Schlitz', 'Pepsi Cola', 'Oxidel', 'Tijuana Gold', etc.

Further, Quine has on his side, as it seems to me, the fact that the result of prefixing 'all' to any of the sentences in (1) results at best in a question-able paraphrase. One who would base an argument on the purported paraphrase 'All water is fluid' must account somehow for the existence of slush and ice; for on one quite straightforward reading, the supposed paraphrase is false and the original true. It has been argued[12] that Quine's treatment of mass nouns unduly complicates such simple inferences as that from 'Snow is white' and 'The stuff in the yard is snow' to 'The stuff in the yard is white', since 'snow' in the second premise is, according to Quine, a general term. After regimentation we have something like:

W (snow), S (the stuff in the yard); therefore
W (the stuff in the yard),

and it is not clear what non-logical principles are to be invoked to save the argument. But it is worth pointing out that its validity is in any case open to question. Though it is true that snow is white, it may be that the stuff in the yard, though snow, is dirty snow – i.e., not white. This scarcely ends the matter, but if the second premise has been properly parsed, the infer-ence only goes through if what is meant in the first premise is *all* snow.

Now it seems to me that the sentences in (2) can be described in analo-gous fashion and for the same sorts of reasons. Quine says of sentences like 'Lions are numerous' that the plural "... does the work of an abstract singular term designating the extension of the general term (i.e., the class of all the things of which the general term is true)..." (134). So presumably the unmodified plurals in the last three sentences in (2) and in the first *are* singular terms.

The trouble is that, according to Quine, the plural form 'lions' in 'Lions like red meat' "... does the work merely of the singular with 'every' " (134). So the second and third cases in (2) are to be paraphrased by sentences beginning 'Every lion...', hence by sentences beginning '*All* lions...'. And, as with the corresponding cases in (1), the paraphrases are surely open to question. One can agree that lions are carnivores and

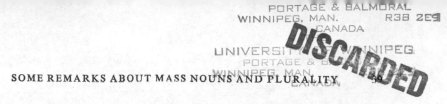
suppose nonetheless that there are lions who, through some fluke of body chemistry, are vegatarians, lacking even the disposition to eat meat given the chance.

Moreover, if according to Quine we are permitted the paraphrase with 'all' in the plural case, we should similarly read 'Snow is white' as 'All snow is white' after all, and Quine would reject my defense of his claim about the unmodified mass nouns in (1).[13] But then an obvious counter to his claim is to say that unmodified mass nouns in subject position as well elsewhere may be general terms; that, in particular, the inference mentioned above turns up after regimentation with 'snow' as a general term throughout: I.e., as

$$(x)\,(\text{if } Sx \text{ then } Wx);\ S\,(\text{the stuff in the yard});\ \text{therefore}$$
$$W\,(\text{the stuff in the yard}),$$

and in general to assimilate description of the sentences in (1) to Quine's account of the function of the plural in (2) rather than vice versa.[14]

Such a view is in keeping with the suggestion that the subjects of (1) and (2) function in parallel fashion. But it is open to objection on other grounds;[15] and I am not sure that I am really at odds with Quine about the parsing of (2). My claim is only that if any of the unmodified plurals of (2) is a singular term, then at *some* level of precision all of them may be so described. We can put alongside the complaint about assuming a double function for 'snow', the undue complication of the inference from 'Lions are carnivores' and 'Carnivores are scarce' to 'Lions are scarce', if in the first premise 'lions' means 'every lion'; and I can see no reason why Quine should disagree.

6. At some level of precision Quine would, I think, agree to parse (2) in such a way that 'lions' throughout is a singular term. There is a harder question as to what he takes 'lions' – as a singular term – to designate. Lions are a species, a large feline animal, native to Africa, frequently found in zoos. 'Lions' as a singular term designates the species *Panthera Leo*, and in general it seems that where it makes sense to suppose an unmodified plural form is a singular term, what is designated is a species or genus or type – roughly speaking, a *kind* of thing.

But if this is right, there is good reason to say that nowhere in (2) does 'lions' designate a class whose members are all the things of which the general term 'lion' is true. It is customary to distinguish attributes from classes – humility from the class of humble persons – as Quine does, by recourse to identity conditions: Classes are identical just in case their members are identical; and the analogue of this principle fails for attributes. It is necessary but not sufficient for the identity of attributes that those things which have them be identical; so we are to conclude that attributes are not classes. And similarly one might argue that it is not a sufficient condition for the identity of kinds that things of these kinds be identical; that distinct kinds, like distinct committees, may have a common membership. But if my claims about the non-equivalence of 'lions' and 'all lions' are sound, the suggestion is rather that such a condition is not necessary. The assumption that men and rational animals are the same species – i.e., in no sense distinct kinds – is compatible with the fact that not all men are rational animals, and the identity of the species does not require that all those things of which the pair of general terms is true be identical. And if the class of lions is to be distinguished from the attribute of lionhood, the species, Panthera Leo is to be distinguished from both. We can suppose 'lions' in 'Lions are numerous' does the work of an abstract singular term; but it does not designate a class of lions.

There is a difference between a kind of thing and a class; with very few resources for saying what it is, I think there is a corresponding difference between an object which may be scattered and a kind of stuff. And here, I suppose, I am siding with Strawson against Quine at a point where their views diverge. My claim rests again on the non-superfluity of 'all' with (1) as with (2). We may add to (1) 'Water is liquid H_2O'. And water and liquid H_2O *are* the same (kind of) stuff. But if 'water' here designates a concrete object – the world's water – it seems we ought to be able to infer from this that *all* water – all of that object which is water – is liquid H_2O. And it is just not obvious that the inference is valid.[16]

And notice there is yet a third possibility for the regimentation of the argument discussed above, whose major premise is 'Snow is white':

W (snow); the stuff in the yard = snow, therefore
W (the stuff in the yard).

If we suppose 'the stuff in the yard' designates the kind of stuff we call 'snow', then that kind of stuff, dirty or not, is white; and, so understood, the argument is valid.

7. Now it may be that all that sound metaphysics can salvage of such Aristotelian talk of kinds is rough paraphrase in terms of classes and scattered objects. In part I mean only to adopt the sort of attitude about kinds that Quine takes up with respect to attributes (119–20). It is important to be as clear as possible about differences among the candidates for one's ontology before making any decisions as to which of them is to be eschewed and talk about it assimilated in some fashion to a more manageable idiom.

But sound metaphysics aside there is an important difference between (1) and (2) on the one hand and

(3)   This water is frozen.
           The wine in the cupboard is fast disappearing.

and

(4)   The lions in the cage like red meat.
           These apples are various in origin.

on the other. In (3) and (4), where grammar permits its occurrence, 'all' really *is* superfluous; and here it seems altogether natural to speak of sets and particular scattered objects. Moreover, if 'The lions in the cage eat red meat' when regimented as,

$$(y) \, (\text{if } y \in \{x \mid x \text{ is a lion in the cage}\} \text{ then } y \text{ eats red meat})$$

it is obviously equivalent to 'Every lion in the cage eats red meat'. Quine's view, so I am suggesting, involves assimilating the semantics of (1) and (2) to that of (3) and (4). But especially in light of his differences with Strawson, it seems important to give them separate treatment.

Indeed it is at least tempting to say that the unmodified mass nouns and plurals of (1) and (2) are not to be salvaged as full-fledged singular terms at all, that these sentences share some of the characteristics of Strawson's feature-placing statements and "do not introduce particulars into our discourse" but only 'general features', and that their unmodified subjects function in the way Quine describes the use of mass nouns as a lexical class. They do not divide their reference, not because of their function as singular terms, but because they do not in (1) and (2) "go along with singular terms... in purporting to name a unique object each" (p. 91). Their use is as in Quine's 'Ernest is hunting lions', "if what is meant is not that he is intent on a certain lion or lions but just that in his unfocussed way he is out for lions" (p. 134). This reading of the sentence need not be laid to the opacity of the verb 'hunt';[17] consider

> Ernest breeds lions.
> John grows house plants.

with which we may compare

> Ernest produces furniture.
> John grows corn.

This sort of use is one which is self-consciously vague and non-commital, available for deception as well as honest communication. On the label of a certain product for pets there appears the claim "Used in cat shows across the land". There are weasel words; here, we might say, is a weasel construction.

And given this suggestion, there *is* something primitive or archaic about the unmodified mass nouns in (1); for unless the function of the subjects of the sentences in (1) is assimilated to that of the subjects of the sentences in (3), there is no obvious connection between such constructions and the sophisticated apparatus of quantification theory. For the moment I mean only to emphasize that what is involved is not merely a feature of mass nouns but of plural forms as well. And whatever shift occurs in the function of 'water' from (1) to (3) – evidence on Quine's view of the 'protean' character of mass terms – is shared by 'lions' in going from (2) to (4). But I would prefer to regard the pre-singular term use of both forms as degenerate rather than archaic; for one obvious comment to make about the examples in (1) and (2) is that they are just unfortunate. And one reason I have discussed them at such length is that in recent discussion sentences like those of (1) have been regarded as basic to any illuminating account of the function of mass nouns.

My claims about the non-superfluity of 'all' may seem picayune; but if they do, this is perhaps just because '*All* snow is white', '*All* lions are carnivores' are what are of interest to one sympathetic to Quine's general program. Quantification theory gets a purchase only in the presence of those particles which are reflected somehow in its notation. And in this connection notice that for 'an apple' there are the modified forms 'some water' and 'some lions'. The following are not pairwise equivalent.

(5)   John sold some butter and Bill bought it.
         John sold some eggs and Bill bought them.
(6)   John sold butter and Bill bought it.
         John sold eggs and Bill bought them.

(5) but not (6) requires a reading according to which Bill bought the same butter and eggs John sold. (6) may well be compatible with their having respectively bought and sold not the same butter and eggs but, one is tempted to say again, the same *kinds* of things. (6) may be classed with (1) and (2).

'Some' like 'an' is often logically superfluous, but those cases in which it is 'understood' – since unlike 'an' grammar does not require it[18] – need to be distinguished from those in which it is not. Consider

(7)   My ring is gold,

another example some take to be basic to any account of the function of mass nouns. (7) invites a rendering of the copula as 'is made of' or 'is composed of'. Rival views, of which Quine's is one, would leave the copula alone and read 'gold' as a general term dividing its reference among bits and pieces of gold as well as gold rings. (7) seems to me unfortunate for other reasons; but surely the view one chooses to adopt depends heavily on whether or not (7) is equivalent to

My ring is some gold.

8.   I have suggested that views like those of Quine and Strawson are in need of supplementation by some account of the significance of the grammatical analogy between mass nouns and plural forms. I should like to say further that within the general framework of a program like Quine's, consideration of unmodified forms is no more promising than the attempt to base a general lexical contrast on the syntax of mass nouns and count nouns. We need to *begin* with cases as complex as (3), (4) and (5). And notice that it is only here that we can speak of the *same* butter or water and the *same* eggs or lions. For

This lion is the same lion as that

we have

(8)　　　These lions are the same lions as those
　　　　　This water is the same water as that

but not

(9)　　　?Lions are the same lions as...
　　　　　?Water is the same water as....

And there is here also, I think, some hope of organizing Jespersen's very general classification. At any rate it is worth thinking about the oddities of

(10)　　?John's leisure (success, music, tact, satisfaction, safety) is the same leisure (success, ...) as...

and the fact that 'experience', 'talent', 'thought', and 'pain' in such contexts can only be count nouns.

In light of what has been said about the language of cooking, the short order idiom, and words like 'metal' and 'wine', sentences like (8) are often ambiguous. But if the ambiguity is no worse than that which constructions containing 'metal' share with those containing 'bird', and sentence like (3) and (4) are parsed in Quine's way; then my suggestion can be put in straigthforwardly ontological terms. We need to ask what, if anything, distinguishes a full-fledged object from whatever can be said to be some so-and-so – water, gold, butter, etc. Since, on Quine's account, 'water', and 'wine' in (3) are simply general terms, an appropriate answer, I take it, is nothing at all but possibly scatter. A prior question, so I claim, is what, if anything, distinguishes what can be said to be some water, gold, etc. from a class of so-and-so's – lions or men. For here Quine finds a sharp distinction, and grammar suggests the opposite.

Tufts University

NOTES

[1] Jespersen, O., *The Philosophy of Grammar* (1924), pp. 198f.
[2] Quine, W. V., *Word and Object* (1960). Page numbers without further qualification refer to this volume.
[3] Strawson, P. F., 'Particular and General', *Proceedings of the Aristotelian Society* **59** (1953–54). Page numbers with (I) refer to this article.

4 *Ibid.*, In *Individuals* (1959) Strawson casts the distinction in terms of 'feature universals' and 'sortal universals'; for present purposes I have not attempted to explicitly accommodate the shift. Page numbers with (II) refer to this later work.

5 Quine, W. V., review of P. T. Geach, *Reference and Generality*, *Philosophical Review* 73 (1964), p. 102.

6 Cartwright, H. M., 'Heraclitus and the Bath Water', *Philosophical Review* 74 (1965). Cartwright, H. M., 'Quantities', *Philosophical Review* 79 (1970).

7 F. J. Pelletier argues (in 'Non-Singular Reference: Some Preliminaries', a paper presented at the 1971 meetings of the American Philosophical Association, Pacific Divisision) that every count noun has a 'mass sense' from the possibility of a 'universal grinder': "... one introduces something into one end, the grinder chops and grinds it up into a homogeneous mass and spews it onto the floor from its other end.... Take an object corresponding to any (apparent) count noun he wishes (e.g., 'man'), put the object in one end of the grinder and ask what is on the floor (answer: 'There is man all over the floor')".

If we assume 'man' really has shifted in sense in Pelletier's 'answer', the explanation for the shift (the grinder) is no more illuminating than Jespersen's remarks about material mass words (and surely does not extend beyond these). Are we to suppose that men are made up of or constituted by man? Are they man on the hoof? Neither suggestion is very promising. But in any case, as R. E. Grandy points out in his comments on this paper, the possibility of giving a word a sense (and I am not convinced that the grinder story succeeds even in this) is not enough to establish that it has that sense.

8 See Robert X. Ware, 'Some Bits and Pieces' this volume, pp. 15–29, for sceptical arguments with respect to all of the lexical classes touched upon above.

9 Compare the oft-cited '(mashed) potatoes', '(stewed) tomatoes', '(scrambled) eggs', etc.

10 J. J. Katz, 'Interpretive Semantics vs. Generative Semantics', *Foundations of Language* 6 (1970), 238.

11 This is an overstatement. Quine's threefold lexical classification is 'retrospective', and in sentences 'lamb' has three functions: as a singular term (discussed below), as a general term (a count noun, plural or singular) and as a mass noun used as a general term (99).

12 R. E. Grandy, 'Reply to Moravcsik' in Hintikka *et al.*, *Approaches to Natural Language*, D. Reidel Publ. Co., Dordrecht, 1973, p. 295. Tyler Burge, 'Truth and Mass Terms', *Journal of Philosophy* 69 (May 18, 1972).

13 Or perhaps not; but see, e.g., p. 139 of *Word and Object*.

14 Grandy defends this view in the paper cited in footnote 11; and Burge (p. 277) analyzes the argument in question this way.

15 Ignoring 'Snow is white' for the moment, it seems outrageous to regard 'water' in 'Water is widespread' as designating 'the class of objects which are water', as Grandy does. (I shall not pursue the matter here, but see 'Quantities', section 9 for an attack on a more conservative claim.) At the same time, I am in sympathy with Grandy's scepticism with respect to views like that of Burge which invoke the apparatus of the calculus of individuals (Henry Leonard and Nelson Goodman, 'The Calculus of Individuals and Ite Uses', *Journal of Symbolic Logic* 5, No. 2 (1940) or Leśniewski's mereology (A. Tarski, 'Foundations of the Geometry of Solids', *Logic, Semantics, Metamathematics*, J. H. Woodger, trans. 1956) in order to specify what *is* designated in such cases. There is, I think, a 'natural' mereology for a given set of quantities of, e.g., water in the sense of 'quantity of ——', as I have elsewhere tried to explain. But this claim is intended to be open to debate – i.e., it depends on an independent specification of any such set.

[16] V. C. Chappell gives some arguments in support of Strawson on this point in 'Stuff and Things', *Proceedings of the Aristotelian Society* 71 (1970–71), pp. 67–68. T. Parsons in 'An Analysis of Mass Terms and Amount Terms', *Foundations of Language* 5 (1970) argues in the other direction that "even if all and only furniture were composed of wood, it would not follow that wood = furniture, since parts of chairs might be wood without being furniture". We are to suppose that under the circumstances described, we have a single Goodman-individual though not, Parsons argues, a single object designated by 'wood' and 'furniture'. But the argument seems to be invalid. If as singular terms 'wood' and 'furniture' designate the same Goodman-individual, then their parts are identical in some sense of 'part' appropriate to the calcules of individuals. But all that follows from 'Some parts of chairs are wood and not furniture' is that, in Quine's terms, the *general* term 'furniture' is not true of every part of the object designated by the *singular term* 'furniture', as he notices (99), and some such parts are wood. Parsons needs a principle according to which something is a part of F only if it is F; and any such principle appears to beg the question against Quine. I find the appropriate uses of 'part' especially obscure in application to (the world's) wood, furniture, water. But perhaps the argument I've given is open to a parallel objection.

[17] I.e., we need not suppose that 'benighted persons can in this sense even hunt unicorns', Quine contrasts this sentence with 'Tabby eats mice' in which opacity is not the point; and I cite the cases below (and the transparent use of 'hunt') just because they are not obviously open to an interpretation like "Tabby is regularly disposed to eat mice given certain favorable and not exceptional conditions" (134). But Quine's emphasis on the fact that "... there is no simple correlation between outward forms of ordinary affirmations and the existences implied," (242) – where opacity need not be involved – is enough for present purposes, given that immodified plurals and mass noun constructions are susceptible of uniform treatment.

Reverting to the view suggested in Section (6), one might say there is a certain kind of creature Tabby is disposed to eat; there are various kinds of things or stuff which Ernest and John breed or produce or grow. As a singular term in an opaque construction 'lions' (or 'gold') is no more problematic than 'the Holy Grail'. Strawson's 'Snow is falling' can be added to (1) and 'Leaves are falling' to (2) on this view. But the present suggestion – that we are dealing with something less than a singular term – is in any case intended to apply to all such cases.

[18] 'A lion is a carnivore' ('Man is a carnivore') says no more nor less I think than 'Lions (men) are carnivores', though it invites a reading, not explicitly discussed above, according to which something is claimed to be true of lions in general, or typically, or 'by nature'. The superfluous use of 'some' I intend is unstressed and does not regularly occur with singular count nouns. Its significance has been a matter of dispute, and in 'Heraclitus and the Bath Water', Section (3), the claim that 'some' gives rise to an ambiguity resolved by stress (the ambiguity of Quine's 'some apple'), is defended at length.

RICHARD SHARVY

THE INDETERMINACY OF MASS PREDICATION*

Mass terms, in their predicative use, suffer a kind of indeterminacy. Their indeterminacy is in some ways like the indeterminacy that Quine has shown affects count nouns, but it occurs for distinct and independent reasons. I will not rehearse the details of Quine's arguments; I intend only to show that mass terms satisfy the required hypotheses. I will show this in two ways: (1) there are mass terms which have distinct extensions, yet which have the same fusion, and (2) there are mass terms which have distinct extensions and distinct fusions, yet whose fusions occupy indiscernible regions of spacetime.

The narrow significance of this is to dispute Quine's own view (*O.R.*, p. 31; *W. & O.*, §19) that mass terms are not subject to any indeterminacy and can be learned by ostension, and that it is with terms that "divide their reference" that indeterminacy in ordinary language arises.

The broad significance of this indeterminacy is that we will see exactly how the application of mass terms as predicates belongs to physical theory rather than to observation alone. So the indeterminacy of such application is an instance of Quine's more inclusive views on the under-determination of theory by observation ("Reasons"). Furthermore, we revive philosophical problems that exercised Aristotle and his prede-cessors. For the indeterminacy of mass predication occurs specifically with the application of mass terms to combinations of quantities of stuff to which other mass terms apply, to quantities qualified by being portions of such combinations, and to quantities qualified in other ways. Accord-ingly, this raises the presocratic problem of determining which kinds of stuff are elementary (gold?), which are combinations of other kinds (salt = sodium chloride), and which are qualified subkinds of more inclusive kinds (ice = frozen water; diamond = crystalline carbon).

1. DISTINCT EXTENSIONS, IDENTICAL FUSIONS

Define

x is *C-succotash* iff$_{df}$ x is (a quantity of) corn that is mixed with lima beans

47

F. J. Pelletier (ed.), Mass Terms, 47–54. All Rights Reserved.
Copyright © 1979 by D. Reidel Publishing Company, Dordrecht, Holland.

x is *B-succotash* iff$_{df}$ x is (a quantity of) lima beans that are/ (is) mixed with corn

x is *KCB-succotash* iff$_{df}$ x is (a quantity of) corn and lima beans mixed together

x is *SCB-succotash* iff$_{df}$ x is a sum of some C-succotash plus some B-succotash

x is *ACB-succotash* iff$_{df}$ x is C-succotash *or* x is B-succotash *or* x is SCB-succotash.

Some informal comment on these artificial predicates seems due here.

Anything that is C-succotash is a quantity of corn. Being C-succotash is like being dirty water; the beans in my succotash are not a portion of my C-succotash, and the dirt in my water is not a portion of my dirty water, because it is not a portion of my water. A little water added to my dirty water becomes dirty water; a little corn added to my succotash becomes C-succotash.

Being KCB-succotash is like being macaroni-and-cheese, like being whiskey-and-water, and perhaps like being sodium chloride. The water in my whiskey-and-water is not whiskey-and-water; the corn in my KCB-succotash is not KCB-succotash. If I add a little water to my whiskey-and-water, it becomes *a portion of* a new quantity of whiskey-and-water, but it does not become whiskey-and-water. If I add a little corn to my succotash, it becomes a portion of some KCB-succotash, but it does not become KCB-succotash.

Finally, the corn in my succotash is ACB-succotash, and so is the quantity of lima beans in it. If I add a little corn to my succotash, it not only becomes a portion of some ACB-succotash, but it also becomes ACB-succotash. Being ACB-succotash is like being unseparated egg or being mixed nuts: unseparated egg yolk is unseparated egg, and so is unseparated egg white, and so is any sum of quantities of unseparated egg; the cashews in my mixed nuts are mixed nuts, etc. Notice that the corn in Lucy's succotash is ACB-succotash, and so are the beans in Benjamin's succotash, and so is the sum of these two quantities. The sum is also SCB-succotash.

In fact, all five of these predicates satisfy Quine's semantic condition on mass terms (*W. & O.*, p. 91): they *refer cumulatively*. Any sum of quantities which are, for example, ACB-succotash is itself ACB-succotash. And nothing seems to bar using any of these artificial terms in any of the nounlike ways associated with the syntax of mass terms.

Now the last three mass predicates have *distinct extensions*. The corn in my succotash is ACB-succotash, but it is neither KCB-succotash nor SCB-succotash. The sum of that corn and the beans in Benjamin's succotash is SCB-succotash and ACB-succotash, but this sum is still not KCB-succotash. However, these three predicates have the *same fusion*. The world's ACB-succotash = the world's SCB-succotash = the world's KCB-succotash. The ACB-succotash in my bowl = the SCB-succotash in my bowl = the KCB-succotash in my bowl, etc. And so the terms 'ACB-succotash', 'SCB-succotash', and 'KCB-succotash' have the same *stimulus meaning* (*W. & O.*, pp. 32–5).

When we last saw our field linguists, they were stuck in an unresolvable debate over 'rabbit', 'rabbit stage', and 'undetached rabbit part' as English translation of their native's 'gavagai'. The indeterminacy arose from the fact that the world's rabbits, its rabbit stages, and its undetached rabbit parts each add up to the same scattered portion of the spatiotemporal world (*O.R.*, p. 32), together with the underdetermination of spatiotemporal spread by pointing, and the consequent identity of stimulus meaning of the three English terms.

Imagine now that our field linguists encounter a tribe using the word 'succotash' in the presence of mixed corn and lima beans.[1] Imagine further that our linguists are trying to decide among 'KCB-succotash', 'SCB-succotash', and 'ACB-succotash' as its translation. The trouble is that whenever they point to different quantities of ACB-succotash, even to bits of corn, perhaps screening the beans, they are pointing also each time to a quantity of KCB-succotash and to a quantity of SCB-succotash (*cf. loc. cit.*).

Our linguists might attempt to decide the issue by asking the native in his own language if the corn in his succotash is succotash. This experiment would require, among other things, that the native have a word determinately translatable from our 'corn'. For even being ACB-succotash is not necessarily a *dissective* property. The nitrogen in my succotash is a portion of the succotash; is it even ACB-succotash? Well, first we must decide if the nitrogen in the corn is corn, and the same problem arises again. The experiment also requires that there be an objective matter to settle. I have asked a large number of people if the corn in their succotash is succotash, and have received nothing much better than blank stares. It does seem possible to determine that the yolk in my egg is egg, but that the cheese in my macaroni-and-cheese is not macaroni-and-cheese. But the partial determinacy here depends on factors not available in the pure succotash case.

These considerations also show that Quine's account of mass terms is definitely mistaken. Quine holds that when mass terms are used as *predicates* they are *almost dissective:*

a mass term in predicative position may be viewed as a general term which is true of each portion of the stuff in question, excluding only the parts too small to count (*W.&O.*, p. 98).

This will exclude a subatomic particle of a gold atom. But the corn in my KCB-succotash is a *portion of* the KCB-succotash, and is a large enough portion of the stuff to count as KCB-succotash, yet it is not KCB-succotash. The cheese in my macaroni-and-cheese is a portion of the world's macaroni-and-cheese, and is enough stuff to count as macaroni-and-cheese, yet it is not macaroni-and-cheese; the sodium in my sodium chloride, etc.; the water in my beer, etc.

We might try restricting Quine's condition to mass terms that apply to *elementary* kinds of stuff, forestalling such counterexamples. Since this procedure requires that first we decide what the elements are, we might reverse the order of procedure and use Quine's condition of being almost dissective as a *test* of elementhood, citing Anaxagoras as our precedent. F. Jeffry Pelletier pointed out to me that if two predicates refer cumulatively and have the same fusion, then if they are both dissective they will also have the same extension. Hence the sort of indeterminacy I have been discussing so far would not arise with such Anaxagorian elements.

But as a condition on *all* mass terms in predicate position, Quine's account fails. Parsons (1970) has noted that Quine's account of mass terms used as nouns in *subject* position fails as well. Quine's view is that in such uses a mass term such as 'water' denotes a single scattered object or quantity such as the world's water. This has the result that 'succotash', 'ACB-succotash', 'SCB-succotash', and 'KCB-succotash' all denote the same thing, that is, that succotash = KCB-succotash = SCB-succotash = ACB-succotash. But Parsons states that such an identity statement "cannot be true, since there are quantities of [ACB-succotash] which are not quantities of [KCB-succotash]" (pp. 376–7).

2. DISTINCT EXTENSIONS, DISTINCT FUSIONS, INDISCERNIBLE RECEPTACLES

Pointing underdetermines spatiotemporal spread intended, and so our field linguist had no way to separate 'KCB-succotash' from 'ACB-succotash' by ostension. He could, however, rule out 'C-succotash' as a translation of the native's 'succotash' by carefully pointing to lima beans in his succotash and noting the native's affirmation of 'succotash'. Such affirmation does not decide among 'ACB-succotash', 'KCB-succotash', and 'B-succotash', since quantities of each have been pointed to. However, similar careful pointing to corn, also accompanied by the native's affirmation of 'succotash', will allow our linguist to rule out 'B-succotash'.

But now imagine that all the world's succotash is mashed up into succotash baby food, which appears as a homogenous yellow-green kind of stuff. Then at our macroscopic level, we cannot point carefully enough to make such discriminations. Therefore, we will have an additional point of indeterminacy: we will be unable to rule out even 'C-succotash' and 'B-succotash' as translations of the native's 'succotash'. Here, the world's C-succotash is *discrete from* the world's B-succotash; they have no stuff in common. But they virtually occupy the same space at the same time. At least they come close enough to inhibit macroscopic linguists.

Less artificial examples can be found. Does salt water have the salt as a *part*, or is the salt merely *in* it, like the dirt in dirty water? Equivalently, is the salt water salty water, and hence water, or is it the salt + the water? If the language itself lacks an analytic clue, there appears to be no way to decide. Such a clue determines the difference between 'whiskey *with* water' and 'whiskey *and* water'. That whiskey with water is whiskey is a truth of analytic metachemistry, but not of observation. But if our native assents to 'grog' when stimulated by quantities of mixed rum and water, we cannot do much to decide among 'rum which has water mixed in', 'water which has rum mixed in', 'rum-and-water', etc. as the translation of his simple 'grog'.

3. OBJECTIONS

(A) The so-called mass terms employed here are completely artificial, unreal, spurious, perverted, and not true mass terms of English or any other sensible language.

I reply that they are at least adjectival and cumulative, and recall Quine's remark that "Adjectives that are cumulative in reference even double as mass substantives – as when we say 'Red is a color' or 'Add a little more red' " (*W. & O.*, p. 97). Furthermore, the varieties of being succotash are each of a logical sort corresponding to more mundane mass terms, such as 'dirty water', 'sodium chloride', and 'unseparated egg', as I have already discussed in §1. Many of the terms used here are compound *syntactically*, such as 'whiskey-and-water'. But mere syntactic simplicity or complexity is not relevant to any of the philosophical problems involved here. Whether a given mass term such as 'water' or 'H_2O' is *semantically* simple or compound can only be determined relative to a background of chemical theory that tells us what the elements are.

(B) These arguments show nothing beyond what Quine has already shown for count nouns. For one might just form the artificial mass terms 'stuff composing one or more rabbits' and 'stuff composing one or more undetached rabbit parts' and then just repeat Quine's argument, adding the fatuous claim that this shows something about mass terms. The result is nothing more than Quine's own argument made obscure.

I reply that the terms mentioned in this objection are not mass but rather *plural*. Plural terms such as 'cats' refer cumulatively also: any sum of (numbers of) cats are cats. Helen Cartwright argues that many terms which are syntactically plural are semantically mass ('mashed potatoes'), and that many terms which are syntactically mass are semantically plural ('luggage', 'furniture'), and that the *semantic* distinction between mass and plural is that plural terms are *atomic*, while mass terms are *nonatomic* (*CQNSR*, pp. 237–42, 275–83, 307–13).

Something is an *atom of* a predicate F just if it satisfies F and has no proper portion satisfying F. A predicate F is *nonatomic* just if there are no atoms of F. A predicate F is *atomic* just if anything satisfying F is itself an atom of F or else has an atom of F as a proper portion.

Being men is a plural property, belonging to e.g. the men in Oregon, and its atoms are individual men[2]; being men and women is a plural property, belonging to e.g. the people in Oregon (they are men and women), but not to the men in Oregon (they are not men and women). The atoms of the property of being men and women are the unordered pairs consisting of one man and one woman. Being people is a distinct plural property with distinct atoms and true of distinct items, such as the men in Oregon. However, the world's people = the world's men and women. Being stuff composing one or more rabbits is then plural also, since it is atomic. Its atoms are the quantities of stuff composing individual rabbits. Similarly, being the stuff of a number of undetached rabbit parts is atomic, and hence is a plural property rather than a mass property.

(C) Modify the objection then, and consider the *mass* property of being rabbit-stuff and the plural property of being the stuff of one or more rabbits. These two properties then have the same fusion, and the change in the example is slight. The point remains that the so-called indeterminacy of mass predication is implicit in Quine's own arguments.

I reply that this example is now equivalent to the one given by Parsons (*loc. cit.*), yet still somewhat different from mine. We have here two properties, one mass, the other plural, with the same fusion and stimulus meaning. But these examples in objections (B) and (C) belong to a discussion of indeterminacy and the *plural*. However, being succotash is not a plural property, nor is being corn nor being lima beans. Corn occurs in kernels (and in ears, rows, acres, etc.), but even kernels of corn are not atomic quantities of corn. Now 'lima beans' does have uses as a true semantic plural, on which something is a number of lima beans, and individual beans are atoms. But it also has a use as a nonatomic mass term, on which e.g. the stuff in the northern half of a lima bean is a quantity of lima beans. Such was its use here. The indeterminacy of mass predication is different from and independent of the referential indeterminacy of singular and plural count nouns.

4. CLOSING REMARKS

One way of viewing the difference between the latter three ways of being succotash is to note that all of the following seem to be equivalent views: that 'succotash' denotes a kind of stuff *more elementary than* corn or lima beans, that C-succotash is a subkind of succotash rather than an *ingredient* (as egg white is a kind of egg), and that succotash is the same as ACB-succotash. These contrast with another set of views: that corn is more elementary than succotash, that succotash is a compound and C-succotash is an ingredient, and that succotash is the same as KCB-succotash or perhaps SCB-succotash.

But this is the type of conflict which seems not to be determined by observation. Rather, each side of the issue deserves to be called an "analytical hypothesis" (*W. & O.*, §15). The theoretical aspect of what is undetermined includes the choice of which kinds of stuff are more elementary than others. This is true of mass terms in plain language ('water', 'succotash') as well as those of technical chemistry ('H_2O', 'dichlorodiphenyltrichloroethane').

The Avondale Institute

NOTES

* This paper is part of a longer work on mixture and combination, some of which was read at California State University/Northridge in 1974, and to the American Philosophical Association, Pacific Division, in 1976. I have benefited from the comments of F. Jeffry Pelletier and discussions with Lucy Carol Davis, Mark Nixon, and R. K. Hsueh. This work was supported by a grant from the California Employment Development Department.

[1] In fact the word is used by certain North Americans when stimulated by kernels of corn and lima beans cooked together. The *American Heritage Dictionary* gives a Proto-Algonquian, specifically Narraganset, etymology.

[2] Or perhaps their unit classes. I include singular as plural, so that being men is a property of Socrates as well as of the men in Oregon.

BIBLIOGRAPHY

Aristotle, *De Generatione et Corruptione* I 1, 10; II 6–8. *De Caelo* III 3–7.

Cartwright, Helen Morris, *Classes, Quantities, and Non-Singular Reference*, University of Michigan dissertation, 1963 (Ann Arbor: University Microfilms 64–6661), Chs. X, XI.

Cartwright, Helen Morris, 'Quantities', *Philosophical Review* **79** (1970), 25–42.

Cartwright, Helen Morris, 'Amounts and Measures of Amount,' *Noûs* **9** (1975), 143–64; reprinted in this volume, pp. 179–198.

Parsons, Terence, 'An Analysis of Mass Terms and Amount Terms,' *Foundations of Language* **6** (1970), 362–88; reprinted in this volume, pp. 137–166.

Quine, W. V., *Word and Object*, (Cambridge, Mass.: MIT Press, 1960), Chs. II, III.

Quine, W. V., 'Ontological Relativity,' in *Ontological Relativity and Other Essays* (New York: Columbia Univ. Press, 1969): 26–68.

Quine, W. V., 'On the Reasons for Indeterminacy of Translation,' *Journal of Philosophy* **67** (1970), 178–83.

Sharvy, Richard, 'Maybe English Has No Count Nouns: Notes on Chinese, Semantics,' *Studies in Language*, forthcoming.

FRANCIS JEFFRY PELLETIER

SHARVY ON MASS PREDICATION*

The property of being a mixture, the concept of mixture, the predicate
'is a mixture', and the physical mixtures themselves present complicated
and confusing mixtures of conflicting linguistic data, conflicting conceptual intuitions, and conflicting physical analyses of the stuffs. For
example, we can find question-begging definitions in chemistry texts
such as "A solution of x in y has x uniformly distributed in a continuous
medium of y", we find Quine and H. Cartwright have different intuitions
on whether 'furniture' and 'luggage' are mass terms, and we find that
people divide on whether the one cc. of water we add to a cup of coffee
becomes coffee, or is coffee, or is a part of a quantity of coffee, etc.
Sharvy also has no qualms about holding that two empirically distinct
predicates can pick out the same region of space-time.

There is, says Sharvy, something special about mass terms in the way
the following conclusions of his paper hold. (1) Predicates with different
extensions might have identical mereological fusions, (2) Predicates with
distinct extensions might pick out the same region of space-time.

Conclusion (1) is perhaps ambiguous. It might mean that, in the actual
world, our two predicates with distinct extensions have identical fusions.
This we should not find surprising: any predicate which describes
something which can be broken into parts will yield cases of predicates
with this feature, regardless of whether the predicate in question is mass
or count, whether it indicates a mixture or not. Let $F_1 : x$ is a physical
part of Richard Sharvy; $F_2 : x$ is Richard Sharvy. The fusion of F_1 and F_2
are identical, at least in the actual world. (In some world we might want
to say that F_2 is true of a certain amputee, but not of that amputee plus
his ex-limbs; and we might also want to say that those limbs satisfy F_1).
We can invoke mass terms and construct easier examples than ones
involving succotash. Let F_1: is a 1 cc. quantity of water; F_2: is a 2 cc.
quantity of water. Both fusions are all the world's water. (But in some
possible world there is only one cc of water, and hence F_1 and F_2 would
have different fusions there). And perhaps more naturally: $F_1 : x$ is one
of the (continental + Alaska) United States or x is the District of
Columbia or x is a Canadian province or x is a Canadian territory; F_2:

55

F. J. Pelletier (ed.), Mass Terms, 55–61. All Rights Reserved.

x is North American; F_3: x is North America. The fusions of F_1 and F_2 are identical, viz., all the land in North America; but F_2 is true of various patches of land that F_1 isn't. The fusions of F_1 and F_3 are identical, viz., a certain continent; but F_1 is true of some parts of the continent whereas F_3 is true of it only as a whole.[1] I therefore conclude that if this is what is meant by Sharvy's conclusion (1), it is without interest, for there is nothing special here about mass terms: all the examples constructed use at least one count term (even the ones which "invoke" mass terms are not themselves mass terms, since they are not cumulative in their reference). The crucial feature is rather that we can construct different ways of describing objects – and this means only that we need have some physical object so that it has parts.

So perhaps we should consider whether (1) means that there could be predicates which have distinct extensions in some worlds but for each possible world their fusions are identical. It is obvious that no two *independent, empirical* predicates have this property. For, if they were independent and empirical, there would be some possible world in which the extension of one predicate but not the other is empty, and so the fusions would be distinct.

Relaxing the requirement that the predicates be empirical will allow cases where the denotations of the predicates exist in all possible worlds. Let $F_1: x = \{1\}$ or $x = \{2\}$; $F_2: x = \{1, 2\}$. Their extensions are different: the extension of F_1 is a set containing the two singletons, $\{1\}$ and $\{2\}$; that of F_2 is a set containing the doubleton $\{1, 2\}$. Yet the fusions are the same, namely $\{1, 2\}$. So once again we see that there is nothing special here about mass terms. What is important for these kinds of cases is the property of empiricalness.

Relaxing the requirement of independentness, we can have cases like F_1: x is either the first half of a book or x is the second half of a book; F_2: x is a book. Or again, F_1: x is a husband or x is a wife; F_2: x is a married couple. Note that the extensions of the F_1's and F_2's are different: a half a book will satisfy F_1 but not F_2. A whole book will satisfy F_2, but the sense in which it satisfies F_1 is that "there are two of them". The notion of "independent" is not perfectly defined, but its general intent is clear: Whenever the one predicate's being true of something entails (in some suitable vague "relevance" sense) that the other predicate is true of something and vice versa, they are not independent[2]. In the examples given, the existence of something which is F_1 entails the existence of something which is F_2 and conversely. Furthermore, in constructing the examples so that the fusions are identical, we guaranteed that the two disjuncts are dependent on each other. Finally, we note that the examples here given are count; being a mass term is not crucial to the "distinct extensions, identical fusions" conclusion. What *is* essential is that the predicates not be independent.

It is clear that Sharvy's succotash examples for conclusion (1) depend upon non-independence. The existence of B-succotash entails the existence of C-succotash; the existence of these entails the existence of SCB-succotash (since it is only the mereological sum of any B- plus C-succotash). The converse implications all hold also. The existence of any one of these entails the existence of ACB-succotash; and the existence of ACB-succotash entails the existence of at least one of these and hence of all of them. Note though, that just as in the count case, it is different stuff that these predicates are true of. The lack of independence amounts to the fact that the predicates are defined in such a way that in order for one to have an extension they all must. In this respect KCB-succotash is different: 'KCB-succotash' is true of a sub-portion of what 'SCB-succotash' is true of – KCB-succotash is just a special kind of SCB-succotash, namely that kind which has the corn and beans *actually* mixed together. The fusions of KCB-succotash and SCB-succotash are identical, however; therefore, the third disjunct in the definition of 'ACB-succotash' could have been "*x* is KCB-succotash" – or (in light of the remarks made above) a third disjunct could have been eliminated, since the predicate "*x* is C-succotash or *x* is B-succotash" would have the same fusion as SCB-succotash without any other disjunct. So why did Sharvy add the third disjunct of "*x* is SCB-succotash"? Merely to make "*x* is ACB-succotash" be a mass term, for with only the two disjuncts this would not be a mass term (it would not be cumulative in its reference); and with the addition of "*x* is KCB-succotash" as a third disjunct it is still not cumulative in its reference and so not a mass term. (The beans on my plate plus the corn on your plate satisfies neither of the first two disjuncts nor does it satisfy 'is KCB-succotash'). But this just shows how irrelevant the mass term is in establishing the indeterminacy-of-fusion-reference thesis. In order to even make up examples of such mass-indeterminacy, Sharvy needed to invoke the machinery of mereology (with his 'is SCB-succotash'). The moral of this should be that the indeterminacy of reference is there, but that it's there for the very reasons Quine suggested for count terms. There is no special indeterminacy of mass predication to be found here.

Is there anything to conclusion (2) – that predicates with distinct extensions and distinct fusions can be indiscernible – other than the fact that pointing underdetermines spatiotemporal spread intended?[3] Sharvy would have us consider cases such as (macroscopically) homogenous succotash baby food, salt water, grog, etc. Isn't this merely a case of being unable to "carefully point to" the relevant parts of the mixture? It may be true that the parts, while being discrete from each other, "virtually occupy the same space at the same time" and that "at least they come close enough to inhibit macroscopic linguists." But that is surely just a case of the indeterminacy of pointing. Rather than saying that the parts occupy the *identical* region of space-time, we would be happier with an account of mixtures which took into account a notion like concentration. Surely the result obtained by adding a little water to a lot of pure alcohol is alcohol and perhaps more of it; but it isn't more *pure* alcohol. Adding a tablespoon of salt to 200 litres of pure water will yield 200 + litres of impure water. For some mixtures, certain concentrations have special names. For 43% (by volume) alcohol, 56 + % water, and other traces we call it 86-proof scotch. A *little* more water added, and it is still scotch, but not 86-proof scotch. For mixtures of water and scotch between 1/4 and 3/4, we call it scotch 'n' water. Add a *little* more water and we have more scotch 'n' water. In the former case you *might* be tempted to say (before reflection) that the water became part of a quantity of scotch; in the latter case that the water became part of a quantity of scotch 'n' water (but not of scotch). But let me enter here a plea for common sense: after reflection it is clear that talk of concentration and atoms is preferable. And I don't think this is merely a parochial, 20th century, North American prejudice. It is part of what we mean by "mixtures".

I think that the underlying reason Sharvy believes conclusions (1) and (2) is this: he thinks that a mereological-like logic is appropriate for describing the "logical form" of mass predication (or rather: of sentences invoking mass predications). If this is not antecedently believed, one can hardly even state conclusion (1). And if one takes mereology seriously, one will take mass terms as (completely) dissective. This leads directly to a view that atomism is false (not of course in the sense that there aren't what we call atomic particles, but rather in the sense that even their parts can be truly characterized by the mass term; I think the problems with this view are obvious). And this leads one naturally to a view of mixtures that holds that language does not rule out the possibility of finding mixtures such that, no matter how small a volume one picks, there is each element of the mixture in that volume (i.e., to conclusion (2)).

These consequences ought by themselves to dissuade one from thinking mereology appropriate to mass predication, but there are other compelling reasons also.

Let us therefore briefly consider what Sharvy takes to be the usefulness of mereology. The scope of his inquiry which explicitly invokes mereology is circumscribed indeed: it is of sentences wherein (a) the predicate is a mass term, and (b) where the subject is a "quantity" or a variable ranging over "quantities". Sentences like 'This electron in the third orbit is gold', 'My ring is gold', and 'This puddle is water', etc., are excluded from the enquiry on the grounds that the subject is not a "quantity". I shall not raise any of the obvious issues here (of how we ever can tell), but do wish to question the wisdom of separating the role of the general term 'gold' as it occurs in the aforementioned sentences and as it occurs in sentences like 'The metal in my ring is gold', 'The fluid in this puddle is water', etc. It is not by any means obvious that the principle of compositionality of denotation or even of meaning can be maintained if we have to antecedently know that in 'Gx' the 'x' ranges over quantities or objects.

Quine had said that a mass term in predicative position is true of each portion of the stuff in question excluding only the parts too small to count. Sharvy perversely interprets this as meaning that there is some *volume* for which any smaller part cannot count as an instance of the mass term and for which any larger part does count. Clearly Quine has some notion that every stuff described by a mass term is composed of some smallest *naturally occurring* part (or something like that), and that the parts of such a part are not truly described by the mass term nor is just *any* arbitrary combination of parts of these parts truly described by the mass term. So, for example, Quine thinks water has water molecules as smallest naturally occurring parts, and the oxygen parts of the molecules are not water nor is a combination (or sum) of the oxygen parts truly described as water. The idea is that 'part', in the relevant sense, means 'part with such-and-so structural properties'. A mereological-like logic with this notion as primitive was given by Julius Moravcsik. However it seems that it is impossible to give an adequate account of such a mereology.[4]

Some final, perhaps idiosyncratic, objections to mereology are these.

Suppose we do find some way to allow a transcription of 'There is some mucus in my nose' in terms of an existential quantifier whose values are quantities. It would seem that allowing quantifiers and quantities would give legitimacy to

$$(\exists!x)(x \text{ is mucus in my nose})$$

And yet such a sentence would be necessarily false, given Sharvy's understanding of 'quantity'. A related difficulty with quantities is that 'quantity', by itself, seems to have no amount function associated with it: you can't simply measure quantity A and compare it in amount with quantity B. You have to know first what kinds of stuff A and B are. If they're both the same, then (perhaps) the comparison goes through, but if they're different kinds of stuff we need some other convention (like volume or weight) to measure the amounts. Consider, for instance, whether a bucket of sand and a bucket of mucus are the same in amount – the answer is that it depends on whether amount is being measured by weight, volume, etc. Or consider whether a cup of flour directly out of a bag is the same in amount as a cup of sifted flour. This seems to imply that quantification over quantities (simpliciter) is improper; yet mereology assumes that it can be done.

For these reasons, it seems best to me to reject mereology as a way of accounting for mass predication. I have no alternative to offer, but am firmly convinced that one will have to be found.

University of Alberta

NOTES

* The present paper revises my comments made on Richard Sharvy's 'Mixtures', which were read to the Pacific APA in 1976. My thanks go to Richard Grandy both for his help in formulating the comments and for reading the paper at the meeting.
[1] This example is for those of us who think that Mexico, Central America, Hawaii, Greenland, and the Carribean are not North American. Those who think otherwise can construct their own examples.
[2] I add the "suitably vague" qualification, because I do not want "is F or not F" and "is G or not G" to be dependent even though if the one is true of something then so is the other. I have in mind something like "*essentially* entails".
[3] In introducing this problem, Sharvy claims that the linguist could rule out "C-succotash" and "B-succotash" as translations of the native's 'succotash' by "carefully pointing to [the relevant part of the stuff] and noting the native's affirmation of 'succotash'." He claims that this procedure cannot decide among "ACB-succotash", "KCB-succotash", and "SCB-succotash". This claim depends for its truth upon our

not being able to find the native's term for 'mereological sum' (and upon our not being able to teach it to him). For, if we have the term (say that it is 'sulp'), then we can "carefully point to" the corn on Lucy's plate and "carefully point to" the beans on Benjamin's plate and ask whether the one sulp the other is succotash. If he denies it, we can rule out both "ACB-succotash" and "SCB-succotash" as translations of the native's 'succotash', and hence 'succotash' is to be translated by "KCB-succotash". If he affirms it, then we can rule out "KCB-succotash" as translation of the native's 'succotash'. We are then left with "ACB-succotash" and "SCB-succotash" as possible translations. We can do no better; since, under the assumption that 'succotash' does not translate as either "B-succotash" or "C-succotash", it follows that "ACB-succotash" and "SCB-succotash" have identical extensions. (I.e., the first two disjuncts in the definition of "ACB-succotash" are otiose – it isn't because the stuff is B-succotash or C-succotash that it is ACB-succotash). So, if we can be careful enough in our pointing to rule out B-succotash and C-succotash, and if the concept of mereological sum is a legitimate enough concept for the native to have or be taught, then we can also be careful enough in our pointing to rule out all Sharvy's predicates (except the ones which are logically equivalent).

[4] Julius Moravcsik, 'Mass Terms in English' in Hintikka, Moravcsik, and Suppes (eds.), *Approaches to Natural Language* (Reidel, 1973). For criticism, see Richard Grandy 'Response to Moravcsik' in the same volume and F. J. Pelletier 'On Some Proposals for the Semantics of Mass Terms', *Journ. Phil. Logic*, 1973.

EDDY M. ZEMACH

FOUR ONTOLOGIES

In this paper I wish to describe four ontologies, all of which are derivable from one basic principle. I shall suggest that ordinarily we employ, in somewhat mixed fashion, terms that designate entities recognized by each of these ontologies. I shall further suggest that one must therefore realize that the ontology presupposed, or implied, by one group of ordinarily used terms may be very different from the ontology pre-supposed, or implied, by another group of such terms. Yet my thesis is not essentially concerned with ordinary-language analysis. My main claim is that each one of these ontologies is complete and self-sufficient and that it *need* not be used in conjunction with any other. Our reason for ordinarily using all of these ontologies (though some of them are used *much* more frequently than others) is not that any of them is, in itself, deficient or faulty. The reasons are pragmatic and historical, and have to do with naturalness, ease and simplicity of expression rather than with essential adequacy.

All the ontologies here to be considered can be called, roughly, 'nominalistic,' since none of them is capable of handling such non-spatiotemporal entities as classes, numbers, universals, or gods. If this is a deficiency, then these ontologies are indeed all of them deficient. I believe, however, although I shall not go into this matter in the present paper, that no ontology *should* be able to accommodate such Platonic entities. At any rate, in what follows I shall assume that all the entities an ontology should ever accommodate are spatiotemporal. The point is, however, that recognizing that the domain of ontology should be the spatiotemporal world, is *not* tantamount to having an ontology. A spatiotemporal world can be 'cut' into separate entities in several *radically* different ways.

The four ontologies I shall discuss result from the possibility of referring to spatiotemporal entities qua spatiotemporal, that is, as extended in time and in space. An ontology may construe its entities as either *bound* or *continuous* in time and in space. An entity that is continuous in a certain dimension is an entity that is not considered to have *parts* in the dimension in which it is continuous. It can be said to

63

F. J. Pelletier (ed.), Mass Terms, 63–80. All Rights Reserved.
Copyright © 1970 by The Journal of Philosophy.

change or *not to change* in this dimension, but what is to be found further along in this dimension is the *whole* entity *as changed* (or unchanged) and not a certain part thereof. The opposite is true of an entity's being bound. If an entity is bound in a certain dimension, then the various locations along this dimension contain its parts, not the whole entity *again*. It is possible that two locations on this (bound) dimension will contain, each of them, the *whole* entity only if there also is between these two locations a distance in a dimension in which the said entity is continuous. Thus, if a certain entity which is an *F* is found at a certain spatiotemporal location *i* and if another spatiotemporal location *j* is also *F*-ly filled, then one may say that it is the same entity, *x*, which inhabits, all of it, both *i* and *j* iff there is between *i* and *j* a distance in a dimension in which *F*s are not bound. If, however, there is no distance between *i* and *j* in a dimension in which *F*s are continuous, then we must say *either* that *i* and *j* contain *different parts* of the same *F or else* (e.g., in case the concept of being an *F* precludes having two such parts as are contained in *i* and in *j*) contain *two different F*s.

In order to define 'continuous with respect to a certain dimension', let us refer to the entire spatiotemporal area occupied by a given entity *a* ('throughout its life,' so to speak) as *A*. Now,

(1)   If *a* is continuous with respect to a certain dimension *x*, then there are several cross sections of *A*, perpendicular to *x*, such that each of them contains *a* as a whole.

Let us refer to each such section of *A* as *B*. We may now proceed to define 'bound with respect to a certain dimension' as follows:

(2)   If *a* is bound with respect to a certain dimension *y*, then there are several cross sections of *B* perpendicular to *y* such that each of them contains a part of *a*.

If an entity has no dimension with respect to which it is continuous, then $A = B$. This entity can be given the following simple definition (which is stronger than what can be derived from (1) and (2) only):

(3)   If *a* is bound with respect to all its dimensions, then each section of *A* contains a part of *a*.

One would probably like to have the reverse of this simple definition as a definition of an entity continuous with respect to all its dimensions, i.e., something like

(4′)   If a is continuous with respect to all its dimensions, then each section of A contains a as a whole.

However, as we would see in section (4), this definition is too narrow. Therefore we shall go back to a strict conjunction of (1) and (2) to get

(4)   If a is continuous with respect to all its dimensions, then there are several cross sections of A perpendicular to some of a's dimensions $(x,y,\ldots)$ such that there are several cross sections of *those* sections, perpendicular to x's *other* dimensions $(z,u\ldots)$ such that each of them contains a as a whole.

An ontology carves its entities as either bound or continuous in time and space. Hence, four kinds of ontology: an ontology whose entities are bound in space and in time, an ontology whose entities are bound in space and continuous in time, an ontology whose entities are bound in time and continuous in space, and an ontology whose entities are continuous in space and in time.

I

Entities bound both in space and in time can be called *events* or *noncontinuants* (NCs). They are entities defined by their spatiotemporal extension. An entity whose boundaries are given in all four dimensions is an event. An event is an entity that exists, in its entirety, in the area defined by its spatiotemporal boundaries, and each part of this area contains a *part* of the whole event. There are obviously indefinitely many ways to carve the world into events, some of which are useful and interesting (e.g., for the physicist) and some of which – the vast majority – seem to us to create hodge-podge collections of no interest whatsoever. Any filled chunk of space-time is an event. Since the term 'continuous' has a special meaning in this paper I shall use the term 'contiguous' to stand for what 'continuous' normally means, i.e., being uninterrupted and unbroken. Events, then, although absolutely noncontinuous, can have either contiguous or noncontiguous parts. An event does not endure – it cannot be (all of it) either at many places or at many times.

When philosophers and physicists talk about spatiotemporal worms, about points-events, or about world-lines, when they describe material things as 'lazy processes' and refer to spatial and temporal slices of entities, they are using the language of this first ontology. Their substances, i.e., the entities out of which they say the world is composed, are *events* (NCs). Events are the *only* substances of this ontology. Only they can have genuine proper names and be the subjects of predication. A description of the world in the language of the first ontology is a description of four dimensional entities, their properties and relations.

The language of this ontology is relatively new. Although I am not sure about it I think it came into existence only with Minkowski and his space-time diagrams. There is no essential connection, however, between the ontology of events and Relativity Theory. Newton could have used it as well as Quine, Goodman, Williams, or Taylor. The concept of a thing, or a substance, as any chunk or chunks bound in space and time (and which, therefore, has spatiotemporal parts and can be sliced both spacewise and timewise) can be accommodated by various systems of thought. I have nothing to add to the various proofs that this ontology is adequate for describing the world, formulating laws of nature, etc., and since most contemporary philosophers do not doubt that the language of events is at least as adequate as any other language that might be used to categorize reality, I shall conclude that the possibility of the first ontology has already been granted.

II

The second ontology is the one we use most and that comes almost naturally to us. If it were not for the first ontology, which lately becomes more and more entrenched in our language, we would not have felt at all that this second ontology is just one particular ontology, based upon a certain way of handling the spatiotemporality of objects. The entities it recognizes are continuous in time and bound in space. We may call them *continuants in time* (CTs) or, simply, *things*. We normally regard almost every object we come across as a CT: this chair, my pencil, my friend Richard Roe, the tree around the corner, the fly that crawls on the page. This is not to say that all these cannot be re-categorized and regarded as events. They certainly can be. 'This chair', e.g., can be used to name an NC, and some philosophers do use it in this way: they say that they see a temporal slice of the chair and sit on another temporal slice of it. But this is not the most common way of using 'this chair' or 'Fido'. Normally we *do not* regard chairs and dogs as NCs. We consider them to be not events but a very different kind of entity, and the names we give them, in our language, obey a grammar which is fundamentally dissimilar to the grammar of names of events.

A thing, I said, is bound in space. My desk stretches from the window to the door. It has spatial parts, and can be sliced (in space) in two. With respect to time, however, a thing is a continuant. When I look at my desk tomorrow, I will not say that I see a new part of the desk – a new temporal segment of it. No, what I would say (talking the language of the second ontology) would be that I now see the desk *again*. Note: what I see (according to this ontology) is not a *part* or a *slice* of the desk, but the *whole* desk. I saw the desk yesterday, and here it is, all over again, today. To say (in this language) that, strictly speaking, what I have today is only part of the desk, would be ridiculous and downright misleading; that would mean that I have lost part of the desk – its legs, maybe, or its top – so that now I do not have a complete desk, only a part of one. The concepts *chair, house, my friend Roe*, etc , which we normally use, are *not* concepts of events (although it has been granted that they could be *translated* into the event language). When you introduce me to Richard Roe, you say, "Please meet my friend Mr. Roe." and both of us will tend to say that what we see is Mr. Roe *in his entirety*, and not a slice or a part of him.

The concept of a CT is the concept of something that is *defined* (bound) *with respect to* its location in space, but is *not defined with respect to* its location in time. The definition of a pin specifies that whatever is a pin must have a certain characteristic *spatial* shape, but it says nothing about the kind of career a pin should have – it can be momentary or eternal. We can regard two (identically) pinshaped entities as one and the same *only* if there is a temporal distance between their respective locations. But if they co-exist, and there is no temporal distance between them, we say that these are two different pins. Difference in spatial location has, thus, an individuating role with respect to CTs, which difference in temporal location completely lacks. The fact that a and b are man-shaped and are simultaneously at different places is enough to decide that a and b are different men; but the fact that a and b are man-shaped and are at the same place at different times counts neither for nor against their being different men.

It will be superfluous, if not ridiculous, for me to try to "defend" here the ontology of things. Ordinary language and the languages of most sciences provide extant proof of its effectiveness and self-sufficiency. Moreover, it has been shown by several philosophers (most clearly, probably, by Wilfrid Sellars[1]) that the ontology and the language of events can be defined by using the language of things only: in other words, that every fact that can be expressed by using names of NCs can in principle be expressed by using names of CTs only.

III

The third ontology is used very infrequently by us, and when it is used its terms are often confused with those of the first ontology. However, terms like 'this noise', 'the Industrial Revolution', 'the heat', 'the rain', 'the Roosevelt era', 'the Great Famine', etc. are not generally used as names of events (i.e., of NCs). Also, some of the more frequent uses of terms like 'the present inflation', 'this tide', or 'World War II' show that these terms sometimes serve as names of substances of the third variety, i.e., entities that are bound in time but continuous in space. We may artificially expropriate the term 'process' to designate those substances, the *continuants in space* (CSs).

The logic of processes constitutes a highly interesting mirror image of the logic of things. A partial description of this logic was given by Bernard Mayo[2], who tried to show that what he calls "events" (i.e., in the terminology of the present essay, processes, or CSs) are ontologically the exact reverse, with respect to time and space, of material objects. However, Mayo's defense of the thesis of parallelism between space and time is, I think, nonsystematic, and it cannot get off the ground at all without making several paramechanical hypotheses which are far from obvious and which, in the following discussion. I shall try do do without. What I try to do in the present section is *not* to prove the parallelism thesis. i.e.. that whatever can be said about space can be said about time and vice versa. (It seems to me that, in this naive form, the thesis is so ambiguous as to be neither true nor false; it has no precise meaning at all.) I shall, rather, try to show that whatever *one* ontology can do with CTs as basic substances, *another* ontology can do with CSs, and do it in the same way. Hence these two ontologies will be formally (qua calculi) indistinguishable from each other

Let us, then, take Fido as our example of a thing (CT) and the French Revolution as an example of a process (CS). and note the following two points of comparison between them:

(a) Fido cannot be at the same time in many places, but he can be in the same place at many times. In contrast, the revolution can be at the same time in many places. but it cannot be in the same place at many times.

This point, I think, is fairly clear. We say that the revolution, or the Great Famine, or this rain, or that noise, are in place x as much as they are in place y. Our language seems to establish here a logical pattern that is radically different from the pattern usually followed when it treats things. If we are told that Jack and John, who do not live in the same place, heard a certain explosion (or live under Nazi occupation) we would not normally say that Jack heard part of the explosion and John heard another (or that Jack lived under one part of the Nazi occupation while John lived under another part of it). To say that would mean something entirely different, e.g., that John heard the beginning of the noise whereas Jack heard only the end (and similarly with life under the occupation, its beginning and its end). Thus while Fido must be at any one time at one place only, a typical CS like the French Revolution can be, as a whole, at many places at the same time. On the other hand Fido can be, as a whole, at many times. He can be in London in 1969 and in New York the year after. He can even return to a place that he inhabited before and thus be, as a whole, at two times in the same place. All this is impossible for a CS. If the revolution is in Lyon between 1798 and 1812, then we would say that in 1798 Lyon witnessed the beginning of the revolution whereas in 1812 it experienced its end. Now if in 1848 there is another beginning of a revolution in Lyon, we would not normally say that it was the same French Revolution which returned to Lyon, but rather that another, new revolution is now ravishing the city. The individuating role that space plays with regard to CTs is played by time with regard to CSs.

(b) Fido need not have all his parts in every place he occupies, but must have all his parts at any time he occupies. In contrast, the revolution must have all its parts in every place it occupies, but need not have all its parts at any time it occupies.

This too, I think, is intuitively clear. We would not say that Fido existed at time t if it were not the case that all his parts (head, legs, heart, lungs, etc.) existed at time t, occupying, each of them, a different place in space. In contrast, the French revolution can very well exist at time t although at this time some of its parts (e.g., its last degeneration into an imperialistic dictatorship) do not exist at any place yet. Although it is possible that at a certain time the revolution shall have its different stages present in different cities, these segments of the revolution *need* not (although they may) be all present at different locations at any given time. Coming now to the second half of this comparison, it is true

that Fido *may* behave in such a way that a certain place that was previously occupied by his left hind leg will be later occupied by his right
front leg, and then by his head, etc., such that this place will eventually
have contained all of Fido's parts. But this kind of behaviour is surely not
necessary for Fido in order for him to be what he is, and does not normally
occur with respect to most of the places that contain one or other of
Fido's parts. The revolution, on the other hand, must have each of its
parts present at every place it occupies, or else we would not say that
this particular revolution was really present at that place. If a city *a*
underwent only two of the five stages that characterized this particular
revolutionary process (or this particular plague, or this explosion, etc.)
we would normally say that *a* had undergone only part of the revolution,
not the revolution (the explosion, inflation, etc.) as a whole.

The comparison between a CS and a CT will probably be clearer if we
unpack the above points (a) and (b) into eight different propositions,
arranged in two groups. Note that the negation of each of the propositions
A_1-A_4 is true of any CS, whereas the negation of each of the propositions
B_1-B_4 is true of any CT.

A.   1. At one time a thing *cannot* be as a whole in different places.
      2. At different times, a thing *can* be as a whole in one place.
      3. At any time, a thing *must* have *all* its parts in different
         places.
      4. At all times, a thing *need not* have *all* its parts in one place.
B.   1. In one place, a process *cannot* be as a whole in different
         times.
      2. In different places, a process *can* be as a whole in one time.
      3. In any place, a process *must* have *all* its parts at different
         times.
      4. In all places, a process *need not* have *all* its parts at one
         time.

The structure of propositions A_1-A_4 is identical with that of propositions
B_1-B_4. The only way in which they differ is that wherever we have 'time'
in A_1-A_4 there is 'place' in B_1-B_4, and vice versa. This, finally, leads to a
general definition of an entity bound with respect to one dimension and
continuous with respect to another:

(5)   With respect to any entity *a* and any dimensions or groups of
       dimensions *x* and *y*, *a* is continuous with respect to *x* and
       bound with respect to *y* iff:

1. At one x-location, a cannot be in many y-locations.
2. At many x-locations, a can be in one y-location.
3. At any x-location, a must have all its parts in many y-locations.
4. At no x-location must a have all its parts in one y-location.

(where 'location' is to be understood as 'location occupied by a'.) Symbolically, these conditions can be presented as follows:

1. $\quad \Box \sim (a,x,y_1 \ldots y_n)$
2. $\quad \sim \Box \sim (a,x_1 \ldots x_n,y)$
3. $\quad \Box\, (Pa_1 \ldots Pa_n, x,y_1 \ldots y_n)$
4. $\quad \sim \Box\, (Pa_1 \ldots Pa_n, x_1 \ldots x_n,y)$

Unlike Cassirer, Whitehead, Bergson, or Schopenhauer, I do not claim that Process Ontology is *the* correct ontology. But I do claim that, if the world can be seen as the totality of things, it can also be seen as the totality of processes. A society that prefers the language of CSs will probably slice the world into chunks that differ greatly from the entities we now discern. However, to prove the self-sufficiency of the CS ontology there is no need actually to construct a language of processes. All we have to do is to realize that processes, like things, are nothing but dynamic slices of events. The self-sufficiency of ontologies I and II logically entails the self-sufficiency of ontology III: if ontologies I and II are self-sufficient, then every sentence in a language of completely bound entities can be translated into a language of partially bound entities. This translatability is due to purely formal considerations, and has nothing to do with either space or time. It makes no difference in which dimensions the partially bound entities are bound, and there is nothing that makes entities bound in any one dimension, or group of dimensions, intrinsically more self-sufficient than entities bound in other dimensions. The point is, rather, that a complete description of an occupant of a certain spatiotemporal area *can* be given in a language whose substantives denote dynamic slices of this occupant. Just as we can say that Kant has never left Koenigsburg, so we can remark that certain processes which together can be called 'Kanting' never occurred before 1724 or after 1804; as we say that Kant lived 80 years, so we can say that the processes of Kanting occurred in an area of about four square miles, the area of Koenigsburg. If it is true that Kant was fond of his cat, Max, then it also must be true that Kanting included being-fond-of*Maxing; if Max sometimes sat on the mat, then surely at some of the places where Maxing occurred it bore the relation of sitting* to a certain matting.[3]

I V

Last we come to the fourth ontology. The substances recognized by this ontology are bound neither in space nor in time. They are, hence, *pure continuants* (PCs) or *types*. Types have been, for a long time, the Cinderella of ontology. They were considered to be universals, abstract entities, forms, classes, or whatnot, For example, expressions like 'The common elm is a green tree' or '(The) Dog is man's best friend' were construed as containing not names of the entities The Common Elm, (The) Dog, Man, etc., but names of classes. This interpretation, I believe, is counterintuitive. The Common Elm, we said, is a green tree, and Man has a friend, Dog. But the class of elms neither is a tree nor is green, and the class of men cannot befriend the class of dogs. A class cannot be persistent or evasive, and yet we do say that The Enemy is both. The parrot can talk and the letter V has the shape of a wedge. But do classes talk, or have they shapes and forms?

The Frege-Russell approach to types is even less sympathetic than the previous one. On this view, expressions containing type names are completely analyzable into expressions that include bound variables and general terms only. Given this analysis, 'The African Lion is ferocious', e.g., is not a subject-predicate sentence of the form, 'S is P'. Rather, this sentence is an "unperspicuous" way of expressing the quantified statement, 'Whatever is an African Lion is ferocious'. [In the jargon of *Principia*, $(x)(Ax \supset Fx)$.] Thus, quite paradoxically, the institutional 'the' (the expression is Langford's[4]) was seen as a universal quantifier of sorts. The proponents of this view have not felt that what they offered under the innocuous title of 'analysis' was as a matter of fact a suggestion for linguistic revision, an attempt to force language into the straight-jacket of one and only one ontology. Since Frege, Russell, and their followers believed it impossible to construe this use of 'Woman', 'The Taxpayer', or 'The African Lion' as naming genuine individuals, they concluded that the singular form of predication (. . . is . . .) used with these terms must be a linguistic aberration!

There are many other difficulties with this reduction. (The) Chrysler is a good car, although not all Chryslers are good. The letter Q occurs twenty times on this page, but it is not true that all the tokens of Q occur twenty times in this page. *War and Peace* was concluded by Tolstoy in 1869, but it is not true that all the tokens of *War and Peace* were concluded by Tolstoy in 1869. The African Lion weighs no more than 500 pounds, but it is not true that all African lions (put together) weigh less than 500 pounds. The Enemy took hill 69, but it is not the case that, for every x, if x is an enemy, x took hill 69 (nor, for that matter, is it true that *part* of the enemy took hill 69). I shall not go into any of these examples in detail. I am sure that, with enough logical ingenuity, we could analyze away all these problematic expressions (although each of them would require a different kind of analysis), so that in the final re-writing we named only entities of the kind favored by the reductionist – most probably, either things or events. The question is, however, why should we do so? What's more, even if there is a good reason for the reduction, the reductionist should realize that what he is doing is not just clarifying the sense of an obscure expression; rather he is stamping out an ontology, a whole way of carving out reality, which can, on its own, classify, categorize, and account for the world we live in. True, The Taxpayer, The Lion and their ilk are not *things*; i.e., they are not CTs. Substances or objects, however, they are – since types, i.e., PCs are objects. I contend, then, that types like The Letter A, or The American Woman, are material objects (*not* abstract entities) recurrent both in space and in time.[5] They are every bit as material, or "primary", entities as CTs are.

I have tried to argue that in everyday language we often use terms that name PCs and exhibit the peculiar kind of logic that is typical of these entities. My sole example has hitherto been the use of the institutional 'the', either explicitly (as in 'The Union Jack') or implicitly (as in 'Man is mortal'). But this is by no means the only example of everyday use of type names. The most common example of such use is the group of terms known as *mass nouns*, which, I contend, behave like names of PCs and should be regarded as such.[6]

Historically, masses have fared much better than (straightforward) types. Although the institutional 'the' has almost never gained recognition as a genuine singular-term functor, mass nouns ('water', 'sand', 'food', 'leather', 'grass', etc.) have had several advocates who refused to dismiss them as freak linguistic phenomena, as degenerate plural forms, or as class-names, recognizing their status as genuine singular terms. W. V. Quine, e.g., has tried several times[7] to interpret mass nouns as full-fledged names of individuals. His attempt, however, failed (one of the strange results he gets is that Triangular may be, e.g., square), and the reason for this is that he misidentified the *kind* of object named by a mass noun. For Quine, mass nouns name scattered individuals; 'water' names the aqueous part of the universe; 'red' (or 'red-stuff') names the red-looking part of it. The main difference between water and mama is that mama is spatially contiguous while water is spatially scattered (*Word and Object*, p. 51). Now it is in keeping with Quine's general approach to view every object as a four-dimensional section of the world (i.e., in my terminology, as an event). But this approach cannot do justice to masses (i.e., to types). The distinctive feature of continuants is that, with respect to the dimension in which they are continuous (and in the case of Pure Continuants with respect of all dimensions) they are considered to be present in their entirety at all the places they occupy in this dimension.[8] Herein lies a major difference between *the river Cayster* and *Water*, between *Mama* and *Red*. It is not only the case that Cayster and Mama are not scattered whereas Water and Red are. I agree with Quine that this is an inconsequential point. The crucial logical difference, however, is that, wherever water is present, *water* (and not a certain water-part) is present, and that whatever is red is *red* (and not a segment of red). This is not the case with the river Cayster, Mama, Fido, or London. Although we may say, when in Chelsea, "This is London," and then say again, "This is London," when we point to Piccadilly, we are ready to admit that what we mean is that London has many parts, so that we have first pointed to one part of London and then pointed to another part of the same city. This goes for Fido (pointing to his ears and then to his tail saying, on both occasions, "This is Fido"), for Mama, for Cayster, and for any entity which is a CT or an NC. On the other hand, if the director of the Bronx Zoo says "I will now show you the polar bear, the african lion, the gorilla, . . . ," he would not be ready to admit that what he shows us is not really the polar bear but only a part thereof. If Jones tells me that he heard Beethoven's *Missa Solemnis* last night, he would probably be very insulted if I responded, "You mean, of course, that you heard a *part* of the *Missa* – you could not have heard it all!" He would rightly protest that he did hear the whole *Missa* indeed (i.e., he did not leave in the middle). If I insisted that in order to hear the whole *Missa* one has to hear *all* its occurrences, including its past and future ones, he would probably believe that I had gone completely out of my mind. Now if 'red' is learned as a mass noun (i.e., 'red stuff') it also behaves in a similar manner, and so, of course, do 'water', 'wheat', 'paper', and all other mass nouns. If I want water and you bring me a cupful I cannot object saying, "You brought me only part of water, not water itself," but I am likely to make this objection if I want Fido and you bring me his ear. When the geologist says he has found gold in Alaska, we would not say that this is impossible since gold is found in California, too. *Gold* (not a part thereof) is found in California *and* in Alaska, just as the Fifth Symphony (not a part thereof) can be heard in California and in Alaska, too. Mass nouns in our language thus follow the grammar of types. "Milk is healthy" is, then, a genuine subject-predicate sentence, and so is "Man is mortal"; and what they refer to are Milk and Man, respectively.

One of the most important works on the issue of mass nouns is to be found in Strawson's *Individuals*,[9] where it is argued that an ontology of masses (PCs) that does not recognize the concept of *a thing*, is perfectly possible and in fact is absolutely sufficient for all our needs. Strawson argues that

All that is required is the admission that the concept of the naming-game is coherent, the admission that the ability to make identifying reference to such things as balls and ducks includes the ability to recognize the corresponding features, whereas it is logically possible that one should recognize the features without possessing the conceptual resources for identifying reference to the corresponding particulars.

I believe this line of reasoning is absolutely sound. Strawson, however, insists on keeping the honorific term 'individuals' for those entities which fall under genuine sortal terms – i.e., for dogs, cats, houses, and men – and consistently refuses to acknowledge anything else, e.g., the entities referred to by mass nouns, as individuals. Mass nouns and other type-nouns are called by him 'feature universals' or 'feature concepts', and he evades the question of what the entities are which the "feature concepts" designate, by using only the formal mode of speech when discussing this level of language and reverting to the material mode of speech only when he reaches the level where the "conceptual innovation" of the introduction of *things* is finally made. One may answer that what type-names (Strawson's "feature-placing concepts") denote is simply *things* – cats, dogs, houses, etc. That is, that in using either the feature-placing statement 'cat here' or the sortal-using expression, 'this is a cat', we refer to this cat. This answer would be true, but it is not the whole truth. It elevates *one* of the ontologies to the pedestal of *the* ontology, in enjoining that whenever one wishes to discuss not modes of referring but the entities referred to themselves, one must use the terms of the one chosen ontology. Such a decision *can* be made, but it is clearly arbitrary. We could similarly say that by both 'cat here' and 'this is a cat' we refer to The Cat (the type entity). Strawson, then, has made a discovery but has explicitly turned his back on it. Instead of recognizing that, since we have several co-equal ontological languages, there must be a plurality of kinds of individuals, he cherished one kind (CTs), turning a deaf ear to the claims that he himself had so brilliantly formulated for some of their conceptual rivals (the PCs).

Strawson's discussion is also helpful in answering one of the objections that may be made against the thesis of the self-sufficiency of the language of types. The objection is that, although type names can be used with uniform masses such as water or wood, they cannot do the work of sortals like 'cat' or 'apple'. "For particulars such as heaps of snow could be physically lumped together to yield one particular mass of snow; but we could not lump particular cats together to yield one enormous cat" (*Individuals*, p. 205). But, as Strawson points out, as long as we use the language of types *only*, i.e., as long as we say "Snow – more snow" and "Cat – more cat," the analogy is preserved. The pile of snow is "much snow," the pile of cats, "much cat."

This point, however, needs some further elaboration. The difference between types and masses seems to be that, with blood, cotton, red-stuff etc., we can point to *every* place the said stuff occupies and truthfully say "This is blood," "This is cotton," etc., *without* having to qualify these statements by saying, "Strictly speaking, this is only a *part* of blood (cotton, etc.)" But type names like 'The Cat' (in Strawson's terminology, 'cat' as a feature-placing universal) behave somewhat differently. We can say "This is (The) Cat" only when we point to the whole area occupied by what is called in the language of ontology II a single cat. One cannot point to the head, saying "Cat" and then to the tail, saying "More cat." This might lead one to believe that type names are not independent of thing names. But this would be incorrect. In the case of 'dirt' 'blood', 'water', etc. we also put limitations on the size of the area that can qualify as containing the entity in question. A molecule of H^2O is not water, and a white corpuscle is not blood. That is, even the denotata of classical mass names are not present (as a whole) in *every* spatial location they occupy, if we put no restrictions on the term '*every* spatial location'. But if we do introduce those restrictions, the difference between 'water' and 'The Cat' vanishes. One can now say that the entities denoted by these terms are present, as a whole, in every place they occupy – where the term 'every place' carries the rider that this place must be of a certain minimal size, *determined by the type-name in question.* Thus the place where the gestalt *cat* may be found must be bigger than the place where the (simpler) property *barley* can be instantiated, which in turn is still bigger than the place where *water* can be. If only a cat's tail is here (The) Cat is not here, and if we ground up a heap of cats the resultant mess would not be the reference of the type-name '(The) Cat'. But then, if we took a heap of barley and ground it, we would not get anything that would be called 'barley' (it would be flour).

The above liberal interpretation of the demand that a PC be wholly present at all the places it occupies has one immediate result. According to it, all proper names, which were hitherto considered to be names of CTs, can qualify as names of PCs too. Lyndon Baines Johnson could be a type, since if we demand only that Lyndon Baines Johnson be wholly present at every place large enough to allow the instantiation of the complex property (or the disjunction of properties) *Being LBJ*, then the person LBJ can also qualify as the type The LBJ. The same goes for names of larger entities, e.g., 'Jerusalem' or 'Uruguay'. The only difference that might be detected between 'LBJ' as naming a PC and 'LBJ' as naming a CT is the singularity condition which limits the employment of the second use of 'LBJ'. That is, in the notorious puzzle case (made famous by B.O.A. Williams' story of the two brothers who "became Guy Fawkes") of, say, LBJ disappearing and two (or more) people, who qualify equally well for being, each of them, LBJ showing up, the grammar of 'LBJ' the type-name will part ways with 'LBJ' the thing-name. The type name would apply to both LBJs; that LBJ (i.e., The LBJ) is now present at two distinct places at the same time would be completely unproblematic; conceptually, it would be similar to discovering oil, or the Bubonic Plague, in a new location. However, if 'LBJ' is used as a thing name we would not be able to use it with respect to both contenders. As Williams suggests, we would probably refuse to use it with respect to either one, and declare LBJ lost or dead.

The same solution is applicable to similar philosophical problems. Many terms are successfully used in normal circumstances without our having to specify whether we mean them as type-names or as thing-names. However, in border-line cases, or in puzzle cases specifically manufactured by philosophers, we seem confused, because the term in question now tends to behave in two different ways, depending on whether we construe it as a PC name or not. These puzzles abound especially in the philosophy of mind and in aesthetics, where the ordinary use of a term does not give us any clue as to what ontology is presupposed by the use of this term. For example, does 'thought' name a PC, a CS, or a CT? Is 'mind' a type name, a thing-name, a process-name, or an event-name? Is *War and Peace* a type or a thing, and is the *Eroica* a type or a process? Ordinary language does not give us many clues, and often the clues it does give go in different directions. The philosopher, therefore, is often trapped in bogus problems when he does not realize what the ontology presupposed in a given locution is and what the precise logical structure is of that ontology. Take, e.g., the problem of the ontological status of works of art. Many philosophers have claimed that works of art *cannot* be material things, because when we discuss the aesthetic merits or demerits of a certain poem, painting, or musical composition, we are talking about a *type*, which is realizable (at least in principle) in many tokens. Thus the said philosophers conclude that the work of art must be a universal or a group of universals. On the other hand, those who find this solution too strange to adopt have tried to claim (no less strangely) that an exact reproduction of a work of art cannot (logically) ever be made, or, alternatively, that to talk about the merits of a work of art, e.g., Beethoven's Fifth, is just to talk imperspicuously about the merits of every performance of the said work. However, all these forced ontological revisions become redundant the minute we realize that types are perfectly legitimate material objects, and that pronouncements about their properties need not be construed as presupposing Platonism or else reduced to statements about things.

Of course, the philosopher may refuse to accept our untidy ordinary language, which makes constant use of four different ontologies. He may, rather, adopt an ideal language, trying to use everywhere the ontology he favors most. In principle there is nothing wrong with this strategy, as long as the philosopher who adopts it realizes that the English phrases he "analyses" into the ontological framework of his choice can also be differently construed. That is, he should remember that the resolutions he offers for such philosophical puzzles can be matched by (at least three) other solutions, which, given the whole ontology they presuppose, can handle those problems equally well.

The Hebrew University of Jerusalem

NOTES

[1] Wilfrid Sellars, 'Time and the World Order' in Herbert Feigl and Grover Maxwel (eds.) *Minnesota Studies in the Philosophy of Science*, Vol. III (Minneapolis: University of Minnesota Press, 1962), pp. 527–618.

[2] Bernard Mayo, 'Objects, Events and Complementarity,' *Philosophical Review*, LXX, (July 1961): 340–361.

[3] Terms from thing-languages are not automatically transferable into process- or event-languages. 'Being fond of' or 'sitting on' are relations that take place between two *things*, and one cannot expect them to obtain in an ontology of events or processes. Rather, the corresponding process-terms 'being-fond-of*' and 'sitting on*' may be learned, e.g., ostensively, at occasions similar to those at which 'being fond of' and 'sitting on' are learned in our society.

[4] C. H. Langford, 'The Institutional Use of *The*,' *Philosophy and Phenomenological Research*, X, 1 (September 1949): 115–120.

[5] The most detailed and meticulous examination of the logic of types I know of is to be found in John B. Bacon's unpublished dissertation (Yale University, 1965) *Being and Existence*. Bacon also investigates the view that types are genuine singular entities. However, after a long examination he finds the idea untenable, and reaches the conclusion that "Institutional phrases *cannot* be names; types *cannot* be objects" (p. 240). His main argument is the antinomy that, if Man is an object, "you would be I, since we both embody Man. In fact, each thing would be everything else, since all would betoken the Thing. In particular, X is $\bar{X}$" (p. 239). This argument, however, is based upon a category mistake. 'Zemach' and 'Bacon' are names of *things*, and "Zemach is Bacon" is a *false* statement in the language of the ontology II. The closest one can get to this, in the language of types, is "Man is here, and Man is there." Now it is true that Man is there blond (in the language of CTs, Bacon is blond) and here black (again, in the language of things, Zemach is black). But the fact that Man is blond here and is not blond there is no more contradictory, or puzzling, than the fact that Bacon is blond now, but may not be blond ten years from now. "Bacon is blond and is identical with something not blond" is puzzling only if one fails to recognize the language of things here used and misconstrues it as a statement about events. On this (mis-) interpretation, the statement made would be that X (Bacon's blond stage) is identical with $\bar{X}$ (Bacon's nonblond stage), which is a flagrant contradiction. Bacon's mistake is, then, his failing to realize that the language of types is an *alternative* to, rather than an *extension* of, the language of things. The incongruities that can be discovered between the two languages do not discredit one or the other. They only demonstrate that terms of two different ontologies cannot always be simply juxtaposed without either of them being translated or reinterpreted in terms of the other ontology.

[6] Again one may find in Bacon, *op. cit.*, a most helpful discussion of the relation between masses and types. Bacon's conclusion is that masses can, indeed, be regarded as types.

[7] Most lately in *Word and Object* (Cambridge, Mass.: MIT press, 1960), pp. 90–110. Earlier in 'Speaking of Objects,' in J. A. Fodor and J. J. Katz (eds.), *The Structure of Language* (Englewood Cliffs, N.J.: Prentice-Hall, 1964), pp. 446–459, and in his own *From a Logical Point of View* (New York: Harper & Row, 1963), pp. 65–79.

[8] This formulation is not precise. It will be corrected and amplified later on.
[9] P.F. Strawson, *Individuals* (London; Methuen, 1959), pp. 202–213.

EDDY M. ZEMACH

ON THE ADEQUACY OF A TYPE ONTOLOGY

In this note I shall try to answer two counter-arguments (the first of which consists of two separate objections) against one of the theses advocated in my 'Four Ontologies'.[1] The thesis is that an ontology of types (types, on my view, include masses) may be self-sufficient and quite adequate for all our descriptive and theoretical needs.[2] Types (and, thus, masses), I argued, are fully real *particulars*: The Polar Bear,[3] The Taxpayer, Man, Dog, Oil, Gold, Sand, Blue Stuff, etc. are neither universals, nor classes, but material particulars which are continuous (i.e., repeatable) in both time and space. Just as Mr Jones (Mr Jones himself, not a part of him) may be found to exist at two distinct *temporal* points, so can gold (gold itself, not a part of it) be found to exist at two distinct *spatial* points.[4] Jones (a temporally continuous *thing*) is bald *now* and nonbald *then*; Man (a spatially continuous *type*) is bald *here* and nonbald *there*. Exactly as we say (when we speak about masses) that Sugar is expensive *here*, but cheap *there*, we can say that Cat is running *here*, and simultaneously is asleep over *there*. Another analogy to the logic of types is to be found in the logic of trans-world (e.g., Kripkean) individuals: the same individual, Jones, is a tall sailor in W_1 and a short lawyer in W_2. Similarly the same particular, Woman, is servile in the east and rebellious in the west.

Now, the objections. It was claimed that, contrary to what I have just said, an ontology of types can never be self-sufficient; it must presuppose the ontology of ordinary, spatially bounded, *things*. The most fundamental concept of the ontology of things, which is completely missing in the ontology of types (or masses) is the concept of the possibility of a numerical multiplicity of qualitatively identical particulars. E.g., while the ontology of types recognizes only entities like Chair or Rabbit, the ontology of things can countenance many numerically distinct chairs or rabbits. But (the objector continues), without this notion of pure numerical multiplicity the type-language cannot get off the ground.

In explaining how Man (or Oil) can be both e.g. black and non-

81

F. J. Pelletier (ed.), Mass Terms, 81–87. All Rights Reserved.
Copyright © 1975 by D. Reidel Publishing Company, Dordrecht, Holland.

black I have relied on the notion of a multiplicity of spatio-temporal locations. I have argued that sentences which simply attribute properties to types are not well formed. Instead, a sentence attributing a property to a type must consist of a predicate alleged to be true of the type in question and an expression denoting an ordered pair, the first member of which is a type and the second a spatiotemporal point or region *at which* the said type is supposed to satisfy the said predicate. But spatio-temporal points and regions are not types. When we say that this spatio-temporal point is non-identical with that spatiotemporal point we do not claim that they are qualitatively different, but rather that they are numerically different. If our ontology is limited to types only, the sentence 'Black (Man, P_1T_1)', e.g., is unavailable to us, because 'P_1T_1' does not name a type. At best, we can say 'Black (Man, The Spatio-temporal Location)'. But this expression is of course completely unhelpful. It results in the same contradiction we intended to avoid, i.e., that x is both F and not F *simpliciter*.

At first it seems that one can get around this objection by denying the premise that spatiotemporal locations are not qualitatively distinct and hence do not constitute distinct types. E.g., if a Newtonian absolute space is postulated, one may perhaps claim that spatiotemporal locations are, as such, qualitatively distinct. I must agree, however, that this answer is very poor indeed. We have no idea what property the *location* P_1T_1 as such can have that another location, P_2T_2, has not. On the other hand it seems that we cannot use such differences as the presence at these locations (or at certain distances from these locations) of certain particulars, since 'The location at which Water is present' would not characterize any location; in a type-ontology, Water (itself) may be present at many locations.

It may be suggested that *Being P_1T_1* is itself a quality of P_1T_1 only, and hence P_1T_1 *is* the type, The P_1T_1. But, again, this ploy seems quite dishonest. *Being a*, I think, is not a property which can, all by itself, differentiate *a* from the otherwise exactly identical *b*. The ontology of Types is precisely the ontology which results from a full endorsement of the so-called 'Leibniz Law'. One cannot, then, have one's cake and eat it too: one cannot first adopt a policy of recognizing only qualitative differences as entity-distinguishing factors, and then recognize a difference between entities (i.e., $=a$ and $\neq a$) *not* arrived at through the procedure enjoined by this policy as a qualitative difference.

A second objection is that a type ontology cannot account for *measurement*. Measuring spatial and temporal distances between locations is absolutely essential for the type ontologist; he needs it in order to identify the various locations at which types are said to have certain properties. But measuring involves the concept of a unit of measurement. To say that *a* is three yards away form *b* is to say that an object one yard long can fit three times over in the said interval. But can the type ontologist express the idea of an object fitting three times over in a certain interval? He can say that The Yard is in *this*, in *this*, and in *that* location. What he has to explain, however, is the idea of one object being *three times* the length of another. But how can this idea be expressed if not through pointing out the *numerical* difference between the first, second and third yard-long stretches which exhaust the said three-yard-long interval?

I shall now try to give an answer to these objections. First, the differentiations of locations in a type-ontology. Assuming for the moment that he can afford measurement, what the type ontologist needs is less than 'Leibniz's Law'. The 'Law' of the discernibility of non-identicals requires that *every* object be qualitatively different from any other. But even if there is one spatially bounded thing which is qualitatively different from any other it can also be identified as the type The *F* ('*F*' being a conjunction of all the predicates true of it) and the location at which it is can also be characterized as a type, The Location of The *F*. And once this location is available to description in type-language, all locations are so available, being uniquely characterizable, each of them, as The Location at Distance d*x* d*y* d*z* d*t* from The Location of The *F*.

Now I think it can be shown that there *must* be at least one qualitatively unique thing in the world. The only world in which there are no qualitatively distinct things is a symmetrical universe. But, as argued by Reichenbach and Swinburne[5], we may, in this case, claim that the geometry of space is non-Euclidean (e.g., closed). For example, that what is seen 'beyond' the axis of symmetry in this universe is not a set of objects qualitatively identical though numerically distinct from the other set on the other side of the axis but the same set of objects all over again. This description of the symmetrical universe, which is also available and optional for a thing ontology, is mandated for a type ontology, which does not have the concept of entities which are only numerically distinct.

Thus type ontology is again shown to be self-sufficient and completely adequate for the description of any empirically given world.

The second objection, concerning the possibility of measurement in a type ontology, can be answered thus. It is surely possible for the speaker of the type-language to learn mathematics as an uninterpreted calculus. It is also possible for him to recognize and identify the following types: The Yard, The Two Yards, The Foot, The Mile, etc. In other words, he can (because he distinguishes The Yard from, e.g., The Mile) correctly say what is the distance between a and b – i.e., whether it is The Yard, The Foot, or The Mile which encompasses the entire distance between them. Now the only additional step required for making this recognitional ability into measurement *proper* is to apply to the entities thus identified the mathematical calculus which was independently mastered. E.g., it would be stipulated that one may substitute in the uninterpreted equation $1+2=3$, the expressions 'The Mile'. 'The Two Miles' and 'The Three Miles' for '1', '2', and '3', respectively, and get a true statement. The same procedure will work for counting. By hypothesis, a speaker of a type-ontology language would be able to recognize and identify The Horse, The Couple of Horses, The Triad of Horses, etc. The fact described in thing-oriented languages by saying that when you add one horse to two horses you get three horses, would be expressed by the type-ontologist thus: If we apply the calculus of mathematics to the types identified according to the key of interpretation mentioned above (e.g., replacing '1' by 'The Horse', '2' by 'The Couple of Horses', '+' by 'added to', etc.) we get the coveted result, i.e., that The Horse added to The Couple of Horses will be, together, The Triad of Horses.

The procedure in question is essentially that of assembling, say, a radio receiver by putting together certain components in a certain way. The specific way of assembling is clearly of crucial importance here; the F may be a very different sort of particular than the G although both consist of the same components (e.g., The H, The I and The J). Thus mathematical operations may be seen as ways of combining and relating any specified types. 'Assembled' in different ways, The Couple of Horses and The Triad of Horses can constitute very different entities: e.g., The Single Horse (by subtraction), The Minus One Horse (by another way of subtraction), The Fivesome of Horses (by addition), etc.

The other argument against the ontology of types was expressed mainly by John Bacon, in a number of papers.[6] The gist of Bacon's argument is that there is no formula of the form $F(\text{The } G) \equiv F \,\&\, H(Gs)$ relating predication over types to predication over things which preserves meaning and yet does not beget hopeless contradictions and outlandish consequences. (For example, Bacon shows that if we adopt the formula suggested by Twardowski, $F(\text{The } G) \equiv (x)(Gx \supset Fx)$, we shall get as a consequence that there is only one thing in the world!) There is no reason for me, however, to go into Bacon's argument in any detail, or to consider the various candidates that he examines in order to see whether any of them will do. I am ready to grant that there may be no one way of translating sentences about types into sentences about things. Indeed I believe that correct translation depends, in each case, on the predicate involved. To me this seems quite natural, since there is no single or standard way of translating sentences of the form $F(\text{The } G)$ into sentences of the form $F(\text{The } G, pt)$ which I regard as canonical for a type ontology. For example, we might be inclined to follow Twardowski in saying that 'The Lion is tawny' is equivalent to 'all (normal) lions are tawny' and hence translate 'Tawny (The Lion)' into '(pt) [The Lion is at $pt \supset$ Tawny (The Lion, pt)]'. But universal quantification seems quite inappropriate when we deal with other predicates.

Sometimes, existential quantification seems more appropriate, as in 'The Lion was sighted in Virginia this year' which we would probably formalize by using a sentence like '$(\exists pt)$ [$pt = $ Virginia this year) & Sighted At (The Lion, pt)]'. These are by no means the only possibilities. In 'The Lion is extinct', e.g., we seem to say something which is not directly about The Lion; it would be better if we construe this sentence as saying, more directly, something about all the locations in which The Lion exists (i.e., that they all antecede now). Thus it would be appropriate to translate 'The Lion is extinct' by a sentence having the logical form (pt) [The Lion is at $pt \supset F(pt)$].

The same form should probably be used in the translation of 'The Lion is rare'. Here, too, we do not say of each lion, or of some lion, that it is rare. Rather, we say something like this: there are only *few* locations, pt, such that t is now and The Lion is at pt. In short, the correct formalization of sentences about types depends, in each case, on the predicate attributed to the type in question. But if this is the rule about translation of ordinary language sentences *about types* into canonical sentences about types, I see no reason why we should expect that the situation will be so much simpler when we attempt to translate ordinary language sentences about things into sentences (whether in the ordinary, or in some formalized, language) about types.

One might be tempted to argue that this absence of uniformity in translating sentences about types into sentences about types-at-locations is itself an indication of the dubious ontological status of types. This, however, is definitely wrong. If this were the case then ordinary material things would not really exist, since there is no uniform way of translating sentences about material things into sentences about material-things-at-certain-locations. Here, too, it is the predicate employed which determines the correct translation in each case. 'Jones is a murderer', so it seems, may be true even though Jones has murdered only once in his life. Thus if we have to formalize this sentence by quantifying over locations, an existential quantifier would seem to be called for: '$(\exists pt)$ (Jones murdered at pt)'. But if we wish to translate 'Jones is a teacher', it would not be enough to say that at least on one occasion Jones has taught. Here we would need something of the form '$(\exists pt)$ (Jones taught at pt and $F(pt)$'. Other sentences will call for universal quantification (e.g., 'Jones is human'). There simply is no single formula for translating sentences about things into sentences about things-at-locations, and into sentences about events, regardless of the predicate attributed to the thing in the sentence. Why, then, should there be one formula for translating sentences about types into sentences about things, regardless of the predicates involved? If absence of a single way of translating sentences about entities continuous in a certain dimension into sentences about entities bounded in this dimension is tantamount to the non-existence of the former, then ordinary material things (which are bounded in space and continuous in time) do not exist. If this is so, I ask no more; all I claim is that types exist just as much as ordinary material things do.

I have not given in this article, or in the previous one, anything like a systematic semantics for type names, but this is a flaw which is easily rectified. Any standard possible world semantics will do, with type names taking the place of proper names and names of locations replacing names of possible worlds (or model sets).

The Hebrew University of Jerusalem

NOTES

[1] *The Journal of Philosophy* **67** (1970) 231–247.

[2] In the said article I have argued that ordinary materialistic and nominalistic language uses four distinct and mutually incompatible ontologies, resulting from four distinct methods of 'carving up' the world into sundry particulars. But I have claimed that, in principle, *any* of the ontologies can suffice for all our needs; the plurality of ontologies is a matter of convenience only.

[3] For easy identification. I shall from now on capitalize the first letter in names of types.

[4] Mr Jones is continuous in time, but bounded in space. *Aïda* is bounded in time, but continuous in space. Water is continuous in both space and time, and four dimensional 'worms' are bounded in both space and time. (Theoretically there can be not four but sixteen kinds of entities, since there are three spatial dimensions, and we *could* regard our entities as either continuous or bounded in *any* dimension.)

[5] H. Reichenbach, *The Philosophy of Space and Time*, New York 1957, Chapter 1, §12; R. Swinburne, *Space and Time*, Macmillan, London, 1968, pp. 130–132.

[6] Cf. John Bacon, 'Do Generic Descriptions Denote?', *Mind* **82** (1973), 331–347, and 'The Untenability of Genera', *Logique et Analyse* **17** (1974) 197–208.

HENRY LAYCOCK

THEORIES OF MATTER

"Matter" may be defined, according to the *Oxford English Dictionary*, as "The substance, or the substances collectively, out of which a physical object is made or of which it consists". And while the *O.E.D.* is not the ultimate authority on words, nor is it, I believe, far wrong in this particular case. The definition is, as I shall argue in this paper, in substantial harmony with a tradition of some antiquity, according to which material objects do not constitute a somehow 'fundamental category' for ontology; and it is in conflict with a more contemporary view which maintains precisely that they do.

According to the older kind of view, material objects are in fact derivative from or dependent upon a more fundamental category of material stuff or matter, exemplified by the ancient 'elements': earth, air, fire and water. "Most of those who first philosophised", says Aristotle at *Metaphysics* 983b, supposed that "that from which all things come, that from which they first arise and into which at last they go... is elemental and primary in things". But serious obstacles have long appeared to confound the plausible development of this kind of view, and it is with an examination of some of these that I shall primarily be concerned in what follows.[1]

My plan will be to make (i) a preliminary identification of a general doctrine, which (ii) seems incompatible with an understanding of the concept of matter; to support this identification by showing that (iii) while the doctrine presupposes that what there is must be countable, (iv) matter is not countable, and thus that (v) and (vi) attempts to understand matter which presuppose the doctrine will inevitably go wrong. Finally, I suggest (vii) reasons why the concept of matter may fail to be distinguished from the concept of an object.

1. THE ONTOLOGY OF OBJECTS

It would seem that there exists a curious and elusive but nonetheless widely accepted doctrine, which I propose to call 'the ontology of

F. J. Pelletier (ed.), Mass Terms, 89–120. All Rights Reserved.

objects'. The historical origins of this doctrine are obscure, although it may perhaps be traced to certain Eleatic teachings. Nor is the doctrine always clearly or explicitly formulated – nor even clearly recognised – when it is employed. Instead, it often tends to function as an implicit or unstated framework for enquiry; and its influence does not seem to be confined within philosophy, at least within philosophy more narrowly construed. In fact, however, the ontology involves a single essential belief: a belief to the effect that our world is (or must somehow be conceived by us as being) quite generally a world of 'objects' or 'individuals' or 'things', no matter whether concrete or abstract, whether particular or universal.[2]

"We are prone", Quine (1958) has written, "to talk and think of objects ... for how else is there to talk?" (p. 1). And where Quine speaks of "objects", Strawson (1959) for his part speaks of "individuals": "So anything whatever can appear as a logical subject, an individual. If we define 'being an individual' as 'being able to appear as an individual', then anything whatever is an individual" (p. 227). Which is just to say, as Strawson (1950) once put it, that the world is the "totality of things" (p. 198).[3] And Strawson here appears to echo Leibniz (1697), who speaks of "the world or aggregate of finite things" (p. 32). Another of the many who assume a 'world of individuals' is the (self-styled) nominalist Nelson Goodman: but this doctrine is shared by 'nominalists' and 'realists' alike. Thus in his 'Universals and Metaphysical Realism', Alan Donagan (1963) remarks that one of the fundamental metaphysical questions about the world is the question "what sorts of individuals does it contain?" (p. 157). Locke's particularism is a specific form of this same doctrine, as are, I am inclined to think, doctrines which may be discerned in at least some of the writings of Hobbes and Aristotle. I have chosen to label the doctrine 'the ontology of objects', though it might just as aptly have been labelled 'ontological individualism', had we thought fit to ignore the fact that some have preferred (on account of Russell's paradox) to reserve the term 'individual' for objects of the lowest 'type' – so that, e.g., objects which are classes of individuals are not themselves counted as individuals. On the other hand, little of any substance can be made to hang upon the choice of labels.

The ontology of objects is a puzzling doctrine. Thus on the one hand, the doctrine is presented as placing no restrictions *whatsoever* upon what in general there may be. It is not, for example, presented as requiring that objects be material or physical or concrete or particular, though such requirements might be added to it. In this respect, in fact, the doctrine is presented as assuming that there is no more to the idea of an object than there is to the idea of a *logical subject*. Strawson and Russell, for example, are quite explicit about this. For Strawson (1959), "anything whatever can appear as a logical subject, an individual"; and the phrase "one object", Russell (1903) writes, "seems to mean merely 'a logical subject in some proposition'" (p. 136). But if this opinion is right, and the doctrine does exclude precisely nothing, then to say we speak only of objects will be to state a purely *trivial* truth. And this surely *is* puzzling, for on the other hand, the doctrine also *seems* to be supposed to be substantial. It seems at any rate thought to be sufficiently significant to be worthy of repeated emphasis. There are the makings of a dilemma here, one which Quine (1958) appears to dimly sense when he remarks that to say we speak of objects "seems *almost* to say nothing at all" (p. 1, italics mine). Unfortunately, Quine does not specify in what way the doctrine may not indeed be (quite) empty, apart from making some obscure remarks about its relationship to "our present Western conceptual scheme" (p. 25).

2. A PROBLEM WITH THE DOCTRINE

I want to argue that these intimations of substantiality are well-founded, and that the doctrine is indeed far from trivial. Pervasive though it seems to be, the ontology of objects would nonetheless appear to be quite fundamentally mistaken. For suppose that we consider the implications of this doctrine, for our conception of the spatio-temporal constitution of our world. Evidently, it is a consequence of the ontology of objects that there can be nothing which substantially occupies space, nothing which is bulky or material, apart from material *objects*, and paradigmatically, such things as sheep and statues, moons and planets, rocks and trees and tables. In speaking of "that aggregate of all bodies, the universe", Hobbes (1651, 111, 34) articulates succinctly just such a picture of the world; and it is a picture which many others have embraced, both before, and especially after Hobbes. But there would seem to be good reason for believing that this Hobbes-like consequence of the object ontology is simply not defensible, and thus, that the object ontology itself must be rejected.

The Hobbesian world-picture appears, in fact, to be open to an extremely elementary yet quite decisive objection. It looks very much as if this view of the material world as a world of nothing but material objects or 'bodies' – a view which is, and must be, at least as widespread as the general ontology of objects, and which often appears to be regarded as the very epitome of 'common sense' – is *necessarily* false or incoherent.

For in the first place (as the dictionary has it) material objects are precisely those objects that consist of *matter*, stuff which may in fact persist, while the objects that it constitutes decay, disintegrate, or otherwise cease to be.[4] Lumps of gold, to take a simple case, consist of nothing but gold, impurities apart; and human beings consist largely of water (and whereas a lump of gold cannot continue to exist if it is used to make e.g. a pair of earrings, the gold of which it consisted can, and will persist, present in the pair of earrings).

And secondly, if we pose the question of wherein the concepts of matter and material object differ, the answer would appear to be that they differ *precisely* with respect to the concept of objecthood. For if it is a truism that materiality or space-occupancy is what the concepts have in common (and indeed material objects occupy space just *because* they consist of matter, of space-filling, material stuff – that is why they are *material*), it is surely just as much a truism that objecthood, pure and simple, is what distinguishes them.

Thus it would seem that while the advocates of Hobbes' concept of the universe, or of the ontology of objects quite generally, suppose themselves to be at home in recognising the existence of sheep and rocks and planets, they are nonetheless incapable of recognising the existence of those very substances, like water, carbon, oxygen, and so on, of which these objects are composed: a rather curious predicament.

As an objection not only to the picture of the world portrayed by Hobbes, but also to the overall ontology of objects, the point – simple though it is – is still I think decisive; and if it is, then any attempt to comprehend matter within the framework of the object ontology is doomed to certain failure.

But this may seem a somewhat sweeping claim, and in the remainder of the paper I shall be concerned to do little more than just defend it and explain its basis, so that we may hope to be a little clearer as to why matter should be, as I claim it is, so refractory to those analyses which presuppose the adequacy of the object ontology.

3. THE MEANING OF THE DOCTRINE

Now it may well be that, in some unspecified sense of 'analysis', the notion of an object is "too simple to admit of analysis", as Frege once remarked: but simple though the notion be, it is not as if there is just nothing *at all* that can be said about it. For we can at the very least say of the idea of an object or individual or thing that it is, precisely, the idea of *an* object or individual or thing – that it is the idea of a single item, of *one* among possible others. Correlatively, we may say that the idea of a world of objects (individuals, things) is at the very least the idea of a *plurality* or *multiplicity* of existents. 'Objects', 'individuals' and 'things' are themselves plural terms; objects may be many, few or none, and each object singly must be counted as one.

These may seem to be resounding truisms, and perhaps they are; but they give us just the purchase on the notion of an object that we shall need. 'Object' is indeed a dummy count noun, supplying no principle of counting for the things to which it can apply, and standing in instead for determinate species terms e.g. like 'dog' or 'star'; but it remains true that whatever can be counted as an object must still be counted as one, whatever its kind may be, physical or otherwise.

There is in this connection a curious idea, unfortunately all too common, that "a number cannot be uniquely ascribed to a physical object", as Geach (1951, p. 213) puts it. The idea appears to rest on an unaccountable confusion between the fact that 'object' is a dummy count noun, and thus supplies no principle of counting, and the falsehood that when we refer to some *specific* object as a 'this' we may *still* lack any principle of counting. Thus Geach continues "A pile of playing cards has a definite weight but not a definite number; 'How heavy is this?' makes sense as it stands, but 'How many is this?' does not make sense without some added word, expressed or understood – 'how many packs?' or 'how many cards?' or 'how many suits?'". Apart from the fact that in such cases the question ought to have been 'how many are these?' and not 'how many is this?', the pile of cards of which Geach speaks is clearly *one* – one *pile*, and if we know that 'this' refers to the pile (the 'added word, expressed or understood'), there can be no *question* of the number of its reference. Any physical object must be of some kind, and we cannot even know which is the object that is talked about unless we know the kind. Geach's odd remarks on this may have some connection with his thesis on the "relativity of identity"; yet very similar remarks abound in other writers. Thus Barrington Jones (1974) writes that "the terms 'everything' and 'anything' are not genuine sortals but 'dummies'. One cannot even begin to count every *thing* in the room, since one has no principle of individuation" (p. 497, italics in original). And so far, we may think, so good. But Jones continues, as if it were a consequence, "Is *a table* one thing or several?" (italics mine). The required rejoinder to this (apparently) rhetorical question with its (implicitly) indefinite answer would be a definite '*one*': the table is (that is, is *identical* with) one object, viz., a table, though it may *consist of* ever so many different things (legs, screws, nails, fibers, molecules or what-have-you).

Jones also uses an example which perhaps he finds in Frege: Frege (1884) claims that one pair of boots may be the very same "physical and tangible phenomenon" as two boots (p. 33e). But 'physical and tangible phenomenon' is just as much a dummy term as 'object', and if we are to ask: what *kind* of phenomenon might this be? (what general term covers the identity relationship alleged between the one pair and the two boots), we will be hard put to find an answer. In fact, I suggest, two boots cannot be *a* physical or tangible phenomenon, for they are *two*; and in the ordinary sense of 'pair', the two boots may well outlive the pair. Thus if I give one to Mr. A, who lacks a boot, and the other to Mr. B, who also lacks a boot, are we not inclined to say that while my boots (which still indeed exist) have contributed to these two (*new*) pairs, there exists no third pair of boots which they alone still constitute?

In the hope of obviating such confusion, then, our point may be expressed more formally as follows. We may say that if some concept **F** is indeed the concept of an object, then if and when we speak of this *F*, that *F* or the other *F*, we speak in each and every case of *just one F*. In precisely this sense, a world of objects or individuals or things can be none other than a world of countables. In just this sense, countability must be a necessary condition of objecthood.[5] Whether it must be sufficient, on the other hand – whether five blows on the head, for example, must be counted as five objects – is far from clear, and would even seem intuitively unlikely, but need not in any case concern us here.

This, then, it would seem, is the basic significance or presupposition of the ontology of objects; and assertions of this basic presupposition are not themselves uncommon in the literature. Thus Locke (1690) remarks that amongst "all the ideas we have, ... there is none more simple, than that of *unity*, or one ... every idea in our understanding, every thought in our minds, brings this idea along with it ... For number applies itself to ... everything that either does exist or can be imagined" (pp. 121–122, italics in original). Likewise Russell (1903): "Whatever ... may occur in any true or false proposition ... I call a *term*. This, then, is the widest word in the philosophical vocabulary. I shall use as synonymous with it the words unit, individual and entity ... anything ... that can be mentioned, is sure to be a term ..." (p. 43, italics in original). So too it is with Geach (1951), for whom number "applies to everything thinkable" (p. 213). Leibniz (1687), remarks with similar force that being and one are convertible terms: "I do not conceive of any reality at all without genuine unity" (p. 80).

The question of whether we must always speak of objects – whether there is some unshakeable connection between the notions of object and logical subject – seems therefore to reduce to or to presuppose the question of whether everything we speak of can be counted. Now we have already cited evidence of a most general and schematic character indicating that the concepts of matter and material object differ precisely with respect to objecthood; and it would appear that we may now add as confirmation of this claim the fact that while we may indeed speak of matter, of e.g. the water in some glass – that is, while (some) matter may appear as the logical subject in some proposition – it does not *seem* that matter can be counted.

It is not at any rate good English to speak of 'one water' or 'two golds', and the basis of this fact would appear to be that matter simply lacks the oneness or unity of objects. (If I throw the water from a glass and scatter it, that water is not thereby 'broken' or 'destroyed'. But if I throw the glass itself and 'scatter' – or shatter – it, that glass *is* thereby broken or destroyed.) If this point on counting can be shown more formally, then, we shall have some independent confirmation of our claim that matter is not comprehensible within the framework of the ontology of objects.

4. MATTER AND COUNTING

We have at this point to record the fact that it has been supposed quite explicitly that matter *can* be counted, and is not thereby in conflict with the object ontology, even though, as it would seem, we have no ordinary count noun with which to do the job. Helen Cartwright (1965, 1970), most notably, has argued in effect that if we have e.g. two distinct glasses of water, then there *must* be some concept '*F*' such that the water in one glass will be one *F* and the water in the other glass another *F*. Equally, she has argued that if the gold of which a certain ring is made is the same gold as the gold of which some other ring was made, then there must be one G which that gold is (on the inverse Quinean principle, perhaps, of no identity without entity – a principle which is, I would argue, false). The concept Cartwright introduces here is the concept of a *quantity*, technically construed. It is obviously not enough, therefore, to simply point to the fact that expressions like 'two waters' and 'one gold' are not good English: that matter is not thus countable stands in need of proof.

Such a proof does I think exist, and it can be best presented in the form of a *reductio*, by starting with the assumption that matter can indeed be counted. The assumption, then, is that any phrase of the form 'this water', 'that bronze', 'the gold in my ring', etc., can be replaced by (and will be thus equivalent to) a phrase of the form 'this *F*', where '*F*' represents some (possibly technical) count noun. 'Quantity of matter' ('quantity of water', 'quantity of gold') is the count noun suggested by Cartwright, but one might equally suggest a noun like 'instance of matter', so that e.g. the water in this glass could be supposed to be countable simply as one instance of water. All we actually need, however, is the purely formal assumption that phrases of the form 'this water' can be replaced by phrases of the form 'this *F*', where '*F*' represents just some count noun or other.

On this basis, then, let us suppose that we have two statues *X* and *Y*, both of which consist of bronze. The bronze of which *X* is composed will, on our assumption, be countable as one *F*; and the bronze of which *Y* is composed as another *F*. Let us suppose further that we proceed to melt the statues down, with a view to making one larger statue *Z*. The bronze constituting *Z* will then have come from *X* and *Y*. Now to say that the bronze constituting *Z* has come from *X* and *Y* is, on our present assumption, to say that the *one F* constituting Z has come from X and Y; and to say this is to commit oneself to the view that there *is* only one F constituting Z. However, it is plain that in reality, Z may just as well be said to consist of the bronze from X and the bronze from Y, and these are, on our same assumption, *two other F*s. (The physical fusion is in fact quite inessential to our point: if X and Y were, let us suppose, in region R, then we could refer simply to the bronze in R, and this would generate precisely the same difficulty, implying that there was only one F in R.)

We seem thus clearly obliged to conclude that our original assumption was illegitimate, leading as it did to contradiction. The bronze of some statue (the water in some glass, etc.) *cannot* be an F, whatever count noun 'F' may be, for the very notion of such a thing is incoherent. The bronze of some statue is not an F of any kind, not e.g. a 'quantity' or 'instance' of bronze: rather, it is just *bronze* – a certain amount or quantity of bronze, to be sure, but then we might have the very same amount or quantity of bronze in a different and co-existing statue.[6]

The bronze of some statue is not an F of any kind, and hence, not an object or individual or thing of any kind, and our original claim would seem confirmed. We have argued that the bronze can be no such thing, since to count it as one, as a unity, is to invite incoherence. And this is not a purely 'abstract' point, a point of 'mere' conceptual significance. On the contrary, it has a profoundly concrete meaning.

An object, we have argued, must have unity. An object of any kind must consequently have the kind of unity appropriate to objects of its kind, and a *material* object must therefore have a *material* unity. The loss of an object's unity – in the case of a material object the loss of its material unity – must therefore involve the loss of its objecthood. Specifically, for example, a unitary chunk of bronze cannot persist if it is broken into a plurality of pieces. And here, needless to say, it is the unitary *chunk* that is destroyed, not the *bronze*; for the bronze has no such unity to *be* destroyed. It is all the same whether it exists in a unitary chunk or in a plurality of pieces, for it is perfectly capable of persisting through such changes. It can persist through being broken, divided, dissolved, scattered, or ground to dust.

Another way of putting this would be to say that whereas the notion of a material object of any kind involves some notion of built-in limitation or essential boundary – essential to the identity and unity of objects of its kind – the notion of matter of any kind does not (it is, as the tradition has it, 'formless'). As Quine (1960) puts it in the jargon of semantics, full-fledged general terms like 'apple' and 'rabbit' must have "built-in modes of dividing their reference" (p. 91). Objecthood or individuality presupposes oneness or unity, which in the case of physical objects must be physical oneness or physical unity: an obvious point, perhaps, but one that is sufficient in itself, when recognised and understood for what it is, to disqualify matter's purported claims to objecthood.[7]

It is because e.g. this bronze is not a unity, that we cannot think of this, that and the other bronze as a plurality of 'bronzes', distinct entities; and only objects composed of bronze may be so-called. The distinctness that some bronze may have from some more bronze is, as I shall argue in due course, a purely *contingent* affair, and may thus be contrasted with the essential distinctness between objects.

In formal terms, what the attempt to construe phrases like 'this bronze' as phrases like 'this *F*', where '*F*' represents some count noun, actually amounted to, was an attempt to classify *mass* nouns as *count* nouns of some kind, i.e., to deny the difference; but since the difference is all too real, such an attempt was bound to end in incoherence.

Objection. It may be felt that our conclusion is in some respect wrong-headed; that it should not have been that matter is not *countable*, in the sense that the bronze of which some statue is composed cannot be counted as one, but rather that there must be some fundamental arbitrariness about *how* matter is to be counted – that mass nouns supply no one determinate principle or procedure for counting that to which they are applied, so that whereas our statue might indeed have been said to consist of just one *F*, from (as it may be put) a certain arbitrary standpoint, from another such standpoint it might equally well have been said to consist of two, three, or ever so many *F*s. The thought behind this vaguely-formed objection may perhaps be brought out as follows (and here I introduce an example drawn from Wiggins (1967)).

Wiggins argues that although 'crown' is an individuative term, still there may be no determinate way of counting the number of crowns in a certain region. He writes: "The Pope's crown is made of crowns. There is no definite answer, when the Pope is wearing his crown, to the question 'how many crowns does he have on his head?'" (p. 40). The suggestion is, perhaps, that when something of a kind has things of the same kind as parts, indeterminacy of the required sort may exist for counting – and so, the thought may go, it is with bronze, since 'parts' of bronze may well be bronze.

Now we might in any case have doubts about the Wiggins-type example: the larger squares upon a sheet of graph paper, for instance, can be viewed as consisting of the smaller squares, but it is unquestionably possible to go about determining the total number of squares in any given region of the sheet. The seeming indeterminacy of Wiggins' question has a different source, I think: the rather uninteresting indeterminacy or vagueness of 'on his head'. However, examples of this kind are fundamentally un-helpful for the case at issue, and to find them in any way relevant is to miss the essential force of our argument. That is, were Wiggins right about his 'crown' example, it would be clearly impermissible to speak of *the* crown on that pious person's head, since the use of the definite article would imply, contrary to Wiggins' stated multiplicity, quite unambiguous *uniqueness*. In the case of some statue, however, we can and do speak of the bronze of which the statue is composed; and this would mean, were 'bronze' indeed replaceable by some count noun, that there would have to be just one 'bronze' of which the statue were composed, questions about the applicability of principles of counting notwithstanding.

It is only fair to point out here that Cartwright has attempted to incorporate just such a point into her thesis. For she attempts, at least in (1965), to define an F such that it will be a 'totality' of bronze (to be explained); and this attempt deserves some scrutiny.

The idea is that for e.g. some statue, there *will* be just one thing which is the totality of gold of which that statue is composed. We must note in the first place that in (1970) Cartwright introduces quantities by analogy with sets. We are supposed to be able to proceed from 'the gold of which my tooth is made ...' to 'the quantity of gold of which my tooth is made ...' in the way that we are supposed to be able to proceed from 'the cats we had in Harlem ...' to 'the set of cats we had in Harlem ...'. But it is clear that this latter move cannot be exactly as it seems; for there is no such thing as *the* set of cats we had in Harlem. That is, corresponding to a given number of cats there is a rather larger number of sets of cats, not just one (for n cats there are $2^n - 1$ non-empty sets of cats). Clearly, the move thus represented must actually be a move from 'the cats we had in Harlem ...' to 'the set of *all* the cats we had in Harlem ...'; and analogously, the move from 'the gold of which my tooth is made ...' must really be a move to 'the quantity of *all* the gold of which my tooth is made ...' (or more perspicaciously, perhaps, to 'the totality of gold in my tooth').

As Cartwright notes in (1965), what "the water Heraclitus bathed in yesterday" requires is a variable x "such that x is *all* of the water Heraclitus bathed in yesterday" (p. 481), for we *cannot* go from that referring expression to a variable x for which there is "exactly one x such that x is some water, and Heraclitus bathed in x yesterday" (p. 481), since, as Cartwright points out, even if Heraclitus took only one bath yesterday, he "bathed in most of what he bathed in as well as all of it; he bathed in all but a quart and all but a pint ..." (p. 481).

The point of these manouvers, then, is clear: but it may be doubted whether they can achieve their purpose. For one thing, the effective move from 'the gold of which my tooth is made ...' to 'all the gold of which my tooth is made ...' is one which involves a shift in meaning, indeed the importation of an additional concept, that of totality. Just as we cannot move from 'Tigers have four legs' to 'All tigers have four legs' (since some may unfortunately have lost their limbs, even though a normal and uninjured tiger has four legs), or from 'Water is good to drink' to 'All water is good to drink' (since some of it may be poisoned or polluted, even though ideally it is just what we need), or from 'Snow is white' to 'All snow is white' (since in our cities it is often dirty), so in the non-generic cases we have no license to move from 'This stuff is G' to 'All this stuff is G'. If, for example, this gold is tarnished, we cannot conclude that all this gold is tarnished (whatever that may mean, if anything). A closely analogous block exists between 'the Hs ...' and 'all the Hs ...' (where 'H' is some count noun): thus the fact that I can see the leaves in such-and-such a pile does not mean that I can see all the leaves in that pile. Consider also the difference between what happens if we prefix 'the cats' and 'all the cats' with 'the set of'. There is such a set as the set of all the cats we had in Harlem; but there is no such set as the set of the cats we had in Harlem, for suppose our cats were a, b, c and d. Then those cats are contained in various sets, for example in the sets $\{a, b\}$ and $\{c, d\}$, as well as $\{a, b, c\}$ and $\{d\}$, and $\{a, b, c, d\}$.

And secondly, the proposal that there is just one thing which is the quantity of all the gold in my tooth will not in any case avoid the earlier *reductio*, appearances notwithstanding; for what exactly *is* it that we are claiming there is only one of in my tooth? – of what concept is this object an instance? What, in other words, is the general term corresponding to the definite referring expression 'the quantity of all the gold in my tooth'? It can only be 'the quantity of all of *some* gold in my tooth' – '*the* quantity', since there can be only one totality; and this in fact reduces simply to '*a* quantity of gold in my tooth'. Clearly, the expression 'the quantity of all of some gold in my tooth' does not *denote*: there are many such things, if there are any. The only way a denotation can be secured is by the use of such expressions as 'the quantity of all of some gold which is *this* gold'. And the quantity of all this gold, which is what the expression denotes, is just one of the many (if any) quantities of (all of some) gold which are in my tooth – which one, depending on the reference of 'this'.

To recapitulate. It follows from the logic of Cartwright's 'quantity' that if there is one glass of water on the table, there must be (indefinitely?) *many* quantities of water on the table. But the logic of the definite article 'the' is such as to require that if 'the water in that glass' is equivalent to 'the quantity of water in that glass', there can be only *one* quantity of water in the glass. Quantities, then, are *entia non grata*.

5. THE PROPER CONCEPT OF A QUANTITY

Although Cartwright's proposal is therefore not coherent as it stands, the proposal is by no means without interest, and there are some worthwhile lessons to be learned from it. Although there can be no object which some matter *is*, Cartwright's proposal may best be understood as a proposal that there will be just one object which all of (and only) it will constitute, so long as it continues to exist, and no matter how dispersed or scattered it may become. Thus construed, the proposal would not, of course, amount to the view that all of it will constitute a certain material object, something like a chunk of matter, since such objects are precisely not capable of persisting through dispersal, and they are capable of persisting through change or loss of substance. The proposal would be analogous rather to the proposal that for some objects (e.g. the pigeons on our roof), it is possible to conceive of an object – in this case a set – which all (and *only*) those things will constitute, so long as they continue to exist, and no matter how dispersed or scattered they might become. The set in question will be the set of *all* the birds on our roof, since 'the set of birds on our roof' denotes nothing; corresponding to n birds on our roof there are $2^n - 1$ non-empty sets of birds. There is no one set which contains those birds, but there is one set that contains them all. Just as, for pigeons, we may posit a set containing all those pigeons, so, perhaps, for some gold (e.g. the gold in my tooth) we may posit a _____ containing all that gold. 'The quantity of gold in my tooth' then will denote nothing, since corresponding to so much gold in my tooth there will be ever so many quantities of gold in it, if there are any; but 'the quantity of all the gold in my tooth' will denote at most one thing.

Unfortunately, Cartwright is driven to suppose that the gold in my tooth is *identical* with this object, rather than that all of that gold *constitutes* it. Among other things, she fails to make, or rather fails to make explicitly and consistently, the crucial distinction between the notions of constitution (or its converse, containment) and identity; and she in fact equivocates on whether some matter is identical with a quantity of matter (as she would like to maintain), or whether it merely constitutes such a thing. A set cannot be identical with its members, for they may be many, few or none, while the set itself must be one; and so we adopt the device of saying, rather, that it *contains* them or that they *constitute* it. (As Geach (1953) notes, "the ideas of a class as many" is "radically incoherent" (p. 225).) Analogously, a quantity of matter cannot be identical with, but rather constituted of, the matter it contains (which will be all of such-and-such matter, e.g. all of the gold in my tooth), for the quantity must be one, while its matter can be neither one nor many. (To assume relationships of identity either of these cases, instead of relationships of constitution or containment, would generate the kind of incoherence pointed up in the *reductio*.)[8]

(i) Cartwright's explicit thesis in 'Quantities' is that what a phrase like 'this gold' denotes is identical with what a phrase like 'this quantity of gold' denotes. Identities like

> The gold of which my ring is made is the same gold as the gold of which Aunt Suzie's ring was made

are, Cartwright argues, "*equivalent* to identities like

> (5) The quantity of gold of which my ring is made = the quantity of gold of which Aunt Suzie's ring was made" (p. 28, italics mine).

(ii) On the other hand, there are other occasions when Cartwright is, no doubt unwittingly, equivocal as to whether the relationship is indeed one of identity as against constitution; she remarks that given the truth of the former identity, "there is *one* thing which that gold *is or constitutes*' (p. 28, first italics only in original), and that what "it *is or constitutes* is a quantity of gold in a quite special sense of the word" (p. 28, italics mine).

(iii) Furthermore, there are numerous occasions on which she either tacitly or explicitly, but at any rate quite unequivocally, acknowledges that the relationship in question must be one of constitution and not one of identity. Thus she says of 'gold' that it "does not individuate gold, but it *does* ... individuate" (p. 27, italics in original). What Cartwright is suggesting here, of course, is that 'gold' individuates not gold but quantities of gold – thereby implying that there is a difference. And she goes on: "Suppose now that I have before me a cup filled with coffee. My claim is that there is a non-empty set, Q, of quantities of coffee, each of which *contains* some of the coffee in my cup and one of which *contains* all of it" (p. 31, italics mine). In general, it would seem that we must conclude that the relationship that Cartwright would like to see between matter and quantities of matter – the relationship of identity, essential in this context to a defender of the object ontology – is not the one that she does in fact see.

Now there remain some reservations about the concept of a quantity, even when not inconsistently construed, as containing, rather than being identical with, some matter.

(i) There would seem to be no determinate principles for counting quantities: just how, for example, would we go about counting the number of quantities of bronze in a single statue? (Bronze being a mixture, it even lacks those 'smallest units' which might otherwise serve as some kind of basis here.)

(ii) It is not at all obvious what the identity-criteria of quantities could be. With sets there is no problem: their identity-criteria are a function of the identity-criteria of objects they contain. Likewise, the identity-criteria of a quantity would have to be a function of the identity-criteria of the matter it contained. But in what could this latter consist? The answer to this question – a question to which I shall return – is far from being clear.

(iii) Even if the concept of a quantity were in all respects legitimate, it would nonetheless be an artificial or fabricated concept. It certainly does not *in fact* follow, if what I have is some gold, that I have a quantity of gold. (Indeed no more does the existence of a certain set follow, I should think, from the existence of some pigeons on our roof.) The existence of quantities could at best be taken seriously if it could be shown that the concept were not only coherent but also had some genuine explanatory value, and was not merely a case of multiplying entities beyond necessity; so far as I can see, however, it has none. (To say that there is, e.g., some bronze which is the bronze of some particular statue's torso, is not to say that there is some object in the world which is that bronze. Such talk, in contrast with talk of 'quantities', does not generate potentially indefinite and indeterminate sets of countables – it generates no sets of countables at all.)

Finally, and what is perhaps of most importance, there is a fundamental oddity in Cartwright's intended thesis in 'Quantities'. Cartwright proposes that matter must exist in the form of objects she calls 'quantities', which are by her own account analogous to those paradigmatic non-concrete objects, sets. It must surely seem extremely queer that something than which nothing could be more *concrete* should be conceived to be, or to be very like, a kind of *abstract* entity. However, this is no mere eccentricity of Cartwright's theory. Rather, it is an inevitable consequence of accepting the ontology of objects, that one cannot so much as recognise a *distinction* between the concepts of matter and material object, so long as one also recognises matter to be what it trivially is, that is, substantial or material. (We might expect the orthodox ontology to be embraced by any Bishop Berkeley.)

I argued earlier that theories of matter which presuppose the ontology of objects must be doomed to failure, and if this is right, there will be just three general alternatives open to one who would understand the concept of matter, two of which are wrong. Each of these alternatives can in fact be found in recent literature, and this may perhaps be counted as a further confirmation of our basic thesis.

(i) If on the one hand one does recognise matter for what it trivially is, as material, and also understands the concept as the concept of an object, then it cannot be distinguished from, or must be 'reduced' to, the concept of a material object. This is perhaps the most common misconception, and may be found in Hobbes and Quine (to mention but two): the assumption that 'matter' is somehow synonymous with 'body'.

(ii) If on the other hand one recognises matter to be distinct from material objects, as it is, while not distinguishing it from objects altogether generally, then one must conceive of matter as somehow non-material. This is Cartwright's approach (though needless to say, this aspect of her thesis is one that she is not concerned to emphasize).

(iii) Finally, one may recognise the concept of matter to be distinct from that of material object, and simply *reject* the ontology of objects, thus laying the basis for a suitably 'materialistic' and non-reductionist theory of matter. Such an approach can be found, perhaps expressed obscurely and certainly not consistently, in the work of Strawson – whose work thus represents, if somewhat falteringly, a major breach in the received ontology.

6. THE OTHER TWO ALTERNATIVES

We have already studied (ii), and it is time to turn to (i) and (iii). (a) Quine's reductionism. Throughout his writings, Quine appears to make much of the fact that words for matter are 'pre-individuative'; that they do not involve talk of objects. Quine (1958) speaks specifically of 'water' as pre-individuative (pp. 7, 8, 10, etc.). Such pre-individuative terms do not involve talk of objects: it is only when one uses "*individuative* terms like 'apple' that he can properly be said to (be) speaking of objects" (p. 8, italics in orginal). Curiously enough, however, nowhere does Quine *identify* a pre-individuative use of mass nouns. Although this is a category of noun "ill fitting the dichotomy into general and singular", nevertheless the "philosophical mind sees its way of pressing this archaic category into the dichotomy" (p. 10), and nowhere is it explained why, if mass nouns can indeed be "smoothly reconstrued" (p. 10) as general and singular, the category should be one ill fitting that dichotomy.

Quine's concession to the 'pre-individuative' character of talk of matter is thus no concession at all; this character is not to be understood, but to be dismissed as 'infantile' or 'immature' or 'archaic'. As is well enough known by now, Quine views mass nouns in their role as 'singular terms' (that is, before the copula, in grammatical subject-position) as the proper names of scattered objects. Thus "In 'Water is a fluid' ... the mass term is much on a par with the singular term of ... 'Agnes is a lamb'. A mass term used thus in subject position differs none from such singular terms as ... 'Agnes', unless the scattered stuff that it names be denied the status of a single sprawling object" (Quine (1960), p. 98).

In their role as 'general terms', on the other hand, mass nouns are viewed as applying to those things that are bodies or bits of matter. Thus, "After 'this', as after 'is', we do best to view a bulk term as a general term. 'Water' so used amounts to the general term 'body of water' conceived as applying equally to a river, a puddle, and the contents of a glass" (*ibid.*, p. 101).

These bodies or bits of matter, furthermore, are said to be related to the overall scattered object as parts to whole: "There remain, besides the world's water as a total scattered object, sundry parts which are lakes, pools, drops and molecules ..." (*ibid.*, p. 98).

Thus Quine locates matter squarely, if somewhat foggily, within the framework of the object ontology. Now his theory will not in any case withstand close scrutiny. It is not, for example, at all plausible to say that after 'this', 'water' amounts to 'body of water'; for it is compatible with supposing that this body of water (which may for example be a lake) will be here tomorrow, to suppose that this water (which presently constitutes it) will not, and will perhaps be in the sea.

What, on the other hand, of the status of Quine's scattered object and its name? And what of its relation to its 'parts'? Although the underlying structure of Quine's ideas cannot be said to be translucent, nonetheless it is not difficult to see that for Quine, the difference between matter and bodies, bits of matter, is a difference with no real difference – the merely superficial appearance of a difference, designed to seem to do justice to what Quine is acute enough to recognise as a troublesome difference between mass nouns and count nouns. There are perhaps two rather different strains in Quine's thinking here, and we shall deal with them separately. (I am less concerned to criticise the errors and inconsistencies in Quine's view, however, than to show how it exemplifies what I have claimed to be the inevitable consequence of producing a theory of matter based upon the object ontology.)

(i) The 'physical' conception. Quine's 'Water', if so we may refer to it, is supposed to be in some way a 'sum' of parts which are bodies of water. Now since Quine remarks that "any sum of parts which are water is water" (*ibid.*, p. 91), and since he also holds that 'water' after 'is' may be construed as a general term of the form 'body (or bit) of water', we may conclude that any sum of parts which are *bodies* of water will be a *body* of water – much, perhaps, as all the seven seas together constitute a single mass of water. So Water must itself be just another sprawling mass or body of water, the biggest one there is; and in support of this we may point to Quine's (1960) much-favoured analogy between 'water' and 'red' (pp. 91–121), and his (1950) idea that Red is "the largest red thing in the universe" (p. 72). Such scattered masses need not boggle us, since as Quine reassures us, even the 'tightest' objects have a scattered substructure. The only mystery about all this, then, concerns the reasons for dignifying the largest mass of water – which could just be the water in a certain bottle, if that were all the water in the world – with a *proper name*; but while this may help to save appearances, it cannot be of any consequence, since it follows from a well-known doctrine of Quine's that names can be 'eliminated'.

All there really are, we may conclude, are bodies of water large and small, and the largest one being honorifically, but quite superfluously, labelled 'Water'. (The fact that the seas of Earth and Venus, if such there be, do not in fact constitute a single larger mass of water, and the fact that there is not in fact – although perhaps there might be – one all-inclusive mass of the world's water, need not concern us here, since I was primarily interested in showing that for Quine, matter and body are not distinct.)

(ii) The 'logical' or 'mereological' conception. It is clear enough from a number of Quine's (1960) remarks – pp. 52, 54, 61, 98n, 181–2 – that he conceives his scattered object as the 'fusion', in Goodman's sense,[9] or the mereological sum or whole, in Lesniewski's original sense, of those objects of which 'water' as a general term is true, i.e. (for Quine) of all bodies of water. (In fact, the relationship of 'Water' as singular term to 'water' as general term is just analogous to the relationship of 'gavagai' to 'rabbit' when, as Quine proposes, 'gavagai' is construed as "a singular term naming the fusion, in Goodman's sense, of all rabbits: that single though discontinuous portion of the spatiotemporal world that consists of rabbits" (*ibid.*, p. 52).)

And whatever we may think of the idea of a Lesniewskian sum in general, it is clear that since 'water' as a general term (as in 'this water') does not in fact apply to objects, the mereological fusion of what it *does* apply to cannot be an object *either*. In addition, the whole idea that such a 'singular' term as 'water' used before the copula functions as a definite referring expression is misleading. For in the kinds of cases emphasized by Quine, 'water' has an essentially generic significance, comparable to that of 'rye' in 'Rye is made in Canada' or to that of 'man' in 'Man is an animal'. In 'Water is a fluid', 'Water' names (if we may put it so) the kind. And Quine is not altogether unaware of this, for he remarks that 'water' in this context has the "air of the abstract singular" (*ibid.*, p. 120), a remark which is re-inforced by the close analogy between 'lions' in 'Lions are numerous' and 'lamb' in 'Lamb is scarce'; since Quine remarks that 'Lions' here "does the work of an abstract singular term designating the *extension* of the general term (i.e. the class of all the things of which the general term is true)" (*ibid.*, p. 134, italics in original), even though 'lamb' is used as a "singular term to name that scattered object which is the world's lamb meat" (*ibid.*, p. 99).

Further, it is no more incompatible with water's being concrete that 'water' before the copula be an abstract singular term, in Quine's sense, than it is incompatible with lions being concrete, that 'lions' before the copula be an abstract singular term; and it may just be that Quine is mislead by his own terminology here. For although the characterisation 'abstract singular' may not be wholly inappropriate for terms like 'roundness' or 'humility', it goes against the grain perhaps for the generic use of common nouns with such obviously *concrete* significance as 'water'.

Unfortunately, however, it is possible for Quine's somewhat equivocal views on the significance of mass nouns before the copula to co-exist together in a framework which is tailor-made to accommodate such contrary conceptions – I have in mind Quine's thesis of the 'indeterminacy of parsing terms' with respect to 'stimulus meaning'. The intersection of this thesis with Quine's vacillation over mass nouns is clearly represented in the following:

A further alternative likewise compatible with the same old stimulus meaning is to take 'gavagai' as a singular term naming the fusion, in Goodman's sense, of all rabbits: that single though discontinuous portion of the spatiotemporal world that consists of rabbits. Thus even the distinction between general and singular term is independent of stimulus meaning. The same point can be seen by considering, conversely, the singular term 'Bernard J. Ortcutt': it differs none in stimulus meaning from a general term true of each of the good dean's temporal segments, and none from a general term true of each of his spatial parts. And a still further alternative in the case of 'gavagai' is to take it as a singular term naming a recurrent universal, rabbithood. The distinction between concrete and abstract object, as well as that between general and singular term, is independent of stimulus meaning. (*ibid.*, p. 52).

Again, I am less concerned with questions of consistency or error here, than with the general structure of Quine's view. According to the mereological conception, the 'rabbit-fusion' and 'Water' are constructs defined in terms of their parts, which are rabbits and bodies of water respectively. ('Water' is defined in terms of 'body of water'.) Thus apart from Quine's (1960) thesis on the elimination of names, 'Water' as much as 'Socrates' (see pp. 181–182 especially) being capable of being eliminated, 'Water' is in any case introduced via 'body of water'. Thus Quine, whose primary inclination – indeterminacy notwithstanding – is to treat his water as concrete, presents us with an analysis (or analyses) in which talk of water actually evaporates, or equally, boils down to talk of bodies of water, even though on the surface there is the appearance of a difference. In so far as Quine (as with all reductionists) does not even really recognise the special status of that which he purports to recognise, it is dubious whether we can say that he has a theory of matter at all. And this, as I have argued, is the inevitable consequence of accepting the ontology of objects, while rightly recognising the concreteness of such stuff as water.

(b) Strawson's partial breakthrough. Recent work upon material stuff, in the form most commonly (though not exclusively) of work on concrete mass nouns, has seen the beginnings of what may well become a break with the ontology of objects. For it is a consequence of accepting that ontology, as I have argued, that the production of internally coherent theories of matter must be precluded from the start. And it is I think fair to say that the more perceptive among contemporary theorists of matter have expressed their qualms, wittingly or otherwise, about the status of the object ontology.

Thus in 'Heraclitus and the Bath Water' Cartwright remarked that given the truth of

> Heraclitus bathed in some water yesterday and bathed in the same water today,

"one would *not* have supposed that Heraclitus bathed in a thing – still less that he bathed in an object or individual" (p. 474, italics mine); and this, in spite of her final, though still somewhat hesitant, conclusion to the contrary. And Quine, as we have seen, appears to be quite explicit about the 'pre-individuative' character of mass nouns, though he goes no way at all to showing what this might involve, and is indeed primarily concerned to refute his own suggestion.

But there is one writer (so far as I am aware he is the only one) who has advanced beyond expressing qualms about the status of the object ontology, and who, in so far as he has recognised a distinction between the concepts of matter and material object – for he has not done so consistently – has recognised the necessity for outright rejection of the object ontology. This writer is Strawson, and unlike Quine or Cartwright, he has laid the basis for a both coherently 'materialistic' and non-reductionist theory of matter.

According to Strawson (1959), when we make a 'feature-placing' statement by the use of some such sentence as 'There is water here', we are not speaking of any 'particular', and hence any material object, at all. Such sentences

neither contain any part which introduces a particular, nor any expression used in such a way that its use presupposes the use of expressions to introduce particulars. Of course, when these sentences are used, the combination of their use with the tense of the verb and the demonstrative adverbs, if any, which they contain, yields a statement of the *incidence* of the universal feature they introduce. For this much at least is essential to any language in which singular empirical statements could be made at all: viz. the introduction of general concepts and the indication of their incidence (p. 203, my italics).

Similarly, Strawson (1954) remarks elsewhere that feature-placing sentences contain

the material-name of a general thing ... but none contains any expression which can be construed as serving to make a definite or indefinite mention of individual *instances* of those general things (p. 38, my italics).

Now there is more perhaps than just a single strand to Strawson's thinking in these passages; but their central thrust, I suggest, is clear. It is essentially that assertions of the existence of matter – or indefinite references to its 'incidence' – are *categorially distinct from any talk of objects*. Although a concept must of course be 'satisfied' if we are to say that something of the kind exists, this does not in the case of material stuff involve the notion of an *instance* of the concept. Strawson (1959) remarks that it is easy to find "convincing cases where we operate, not with the notion of particular instances of, e.g., gold or snow, but merely with the notion of the universal feature itself and the notion of placing" (p. 205).

(The talk of 'general things' and 'universal features' is best construed as talk of *kinds* of stuff or matter *concepts*, and not – though this is certainly one strand in Strawson's thinking – as talk of murky 'concrete universals';

for Strawson does after all speak in the same breath of 'feature-universals or feature-concepts', and of snow, water, coal and gold as "general kinds of stuff" (p. 202)).

And if Strawson is right about all this, as I have argued in effect that he is, then of course when we make definite reference to the incidence of matter – when we move from 'There is water here' to 'the water that is here' – we do not refer to individual instances or objects either. 'The water that is here' cannot serve to designate an object.

This crucial step, however, is one that Strawson feels unable to take, and it is here that Strawson does *not* consistently recognise a distinction between talk of matter and talk of objects. For expressions making definite reference to matter, when they are considered at all (which is infrequently) are considered to be elliptical for definite references to objects; and Strawson not only speaks of the incidence of feature-concepts, but also of their *instances*, which are characterised by him (for such is the logic of 'instance') as instances of things. Thus Strawson (1954) mentions such expressions as "This (patch of) snow" (p. 38) and "being (a piece of) gold" (p. 29); and pools of water and pieces of gold are said to be precisely instances of water and of gold (p. 38). And if a pool of water is an instance of 'water', then 'water' is not mass but count, and stands in for determinate count nouns such as 'pool of water', 'drop of water', and the like – which is to say, expressions like 'this water' are just elliptical for expressions like 'this pool of water' (even though we may not know exactly *which* count noun the mass noun *is* elliptical for).

The tension between rejection and acceptance of the object ontology would seem most acute in Strawson's conception of the move from talk of 'features' to talk of 'particulars'; for it is central to his theory that *more* is involved in the idea of an instance of water, than is involved in the idea of water itself. The move to instances involves the adoption of 'criteria of distinctness and identity', it involves the introduction of 'particularising divisions'; yet it is clear that there *can* be nothing more to instances of a concept than is contained within the concept itself.

Strawson's theory lacks the *consistent* recognition of a distinction between the concepts of matter and material object that we find in Cartwright's; but in so far as it does involve a recognition of that distinction, it also involves a rejection of the object ontology itself, and thus makes possible an adequate conception of matter as concrete – a 'material-listic' theory of matter, impossible within the framework of the object ontology.

7. DISTINCTNESS AND CRITERIA OF DISTINCTNESS

(a) *Identification*

The temptation to objectify matter or to 'entify' it, to assimilate talk of matter to talk of objects, seems at its strongest when one is confronted with the role of mass nouns in definite reference. This at any rate is indicated by the theories we have just considered: for in those it was just the cases of *in*definite and *generic* 'reference' (Strawson's "There is water here" and Quine's "Water is a fluid") which were recognised to be perhaps distinct from talk of objects in some way – which were recognised indeed *as* talk of matter.

Now there is I think a simple explanation for these facts, and it concerns a misconception about what definite reference must involve. For it is just definite reference that is most closely associated with the idea of *particularity*; definite reference, unlike generic and (perhaps) indefinite reference, is always reference to something in particular – that is why there is something definite about it. And particularity, to the philosophical mind, tends to be associated firmly with objecthood. In fact, however, 'particularity' is just another word for 'thisness', distinctness or discreteness, the basis of our ability to identify,[10] and hence to definitely refer. Thus particularity – the condition of being something in particular – is such that not only objects, but also matter, may well possess particularity. We may speak of 'this particular stuff' as well as of 'this particular thing', without in any way compromising the ontological contrast. Particularity is no exclusive feature of 'particulars', of concrete objects. Thus it is quite wrong to suppose that one can always move from 'this particular _____' to 'this particular' simpliciter, since the latter carries a connotation of thinghood or individuality which the former, if I am right, does not. To have 'thisness' is not necessarily to be *a* 'this'. (There is a correlated conflation on the formal level of definite reference, reference to something in particular, with *singular* reference, reference to something countable, and a failure to recognise that the latter is a narrower notion than the former. The result is the ontologically loaded characterisation of dcfinite referring expressions as 'singular terms'.) Thus the misconception that mass nouns in definite reference apply to objects, in brief, results from the assumption that particularity brings with it objecthood.

Now though not only objects, but also matter may be particular, matter and objects relate to particularity in quite different ways. That is, whereas objects are *essentially* particular, matter itself is just *contingently* so. To put the point in terms of identifiability, we may say that so long as objects continue to exist we *must* be able to identify then; but with matter this is simply not the case. (Another and more traditional way of putting these points would be to say that whereas objects have '*criteria* of distinctness (identification)', matter, as I mean to argue, has none.)

Consider then the contrast between the following two thought-experiments. Suppose firstly that there is an enclosure A, whose population at $t1$ consists of two pigs (two material objects of a kind). At $t2$ these pigs are herded out of A, one of them entering enclosure B and the other entering enclosure C. We may suppose that it is not known, at $t1$, *which* pig will enter which enclosure, only that one must enter one and one the other. Now the population of A at $t1$ *in fact* consists of the pig that will end up in B at $t2$ and the pig that will end up in C at $t2$, even though we do not know at $t1$ which one of these is which. The pig that will be in B at $t2$, like the pig that will be in C at $t2$, can thus be *denoted* (in the Russellian sense) at $t1$, even though we are not able to refer to it or identify it *as such*.[11] We are not able to identify it as such, that is, as the pig that will be in B at $t2$; but the fact remains that we most certainly *are* able to identify it. It is obvious, that is, that there is a unique and specifiable procedure for dividing up the population of A into discrete parts, such that one of these will in fact be the pig that ends up in B, and the other will be the pig that ends up in C, even though *ex hypothesi* we cannot know which one is which. And this of course is because pigs, along with material objects quite generally, have a built-in structure or integrity or 'form', in virtue of which each one is distinct from every other, and can be picked out or identified at any time in its career.

Contrast this sort of case, now, with a case involving matter of some kind. Suppose that at $t1$ we have a jug A' containing water; and suppose that at $t2$ we pour this water into two glasses B' and C'. (And, on the assumption that it makes sense to suppose that we might have known, we may suppose that we do not know, at $t1$, which water is to be poured into which glass). Now at $t1$, A' in fact contains the water which will be in B' at $t2$ and the water which will be in C' at $t2$; thus the water that will be in B', like the water that will be in C', can be denoted at $t1$. But it is plain that not only cannot we identify the water that will be in B' *as such*, we are unable to identify that water *at all*. For there is no specifiable procedure whereby the water in A' can be divided into discrete parts, such that one of these parts will consist of the water that ends up in B' and the other will consist of the water that ends up in C'.

Of course, to say that we are *unable* at $t1$ to identify the water that will end up in B' does not mean that we might not have *happened*, at $t1$, to identify that water. If we had dipped a cup into A' at that time, it is I suppose conceivable that the water we would collect in the cup might by accident be the very same as the water we later pour into B'. But there is an obvious difference between the ability to identify something, grounded in its intrinsic distinctness, and the accidental identification of something grounded in no intrinsic distinctness; and it is the former we are guaranteed with objects, so long as they exist, and that we are in no way guaranteed with matter.

This, then, is the difference; water, along with matter altogether generally, has no built-in structure or integrity of 'form', in virtue of which there is a guarantee that we will be able to pick out and distinguish some of it from some more of it. And to lack such built-in form or structure is to lack essential or intrinsic distinctness – it is to lack the traditional *criteria* of distinctness or identification.

(b) *Re-identification*

Criteria of re-identification, I shall argue, quite trivially presuppose criteria of identification, and thus since matter lacks the latter, it must also lack the former. But the idea of re-identification should not be confused with certain other ideas with which it may very well *be* confused, and finally, therefore, I shall draw the necessary distinctions. We must distinguish the *possibility* of identifying and re-identifying from the possession of *criteria* of identification and re-identification, and we must distinguish all of these from the possession of criteria of *identity*.

Firstly, although we must distinguish criteria of identification from criteria of re-identification, the former criteria are presupposed by the latter. For to *re*-identify something must involve (i) identifying it, and (ii), judging on some basis that what has been identified is the same as what was identified on some earlier occasion. Criteria of re-identification thus involve both criteria of identification and criteria of identity, if the latter are understood (in the normal way) as constituting the basis for judgements of sameness over time. On the other hand, criteria of identity may be understood in such a way as *not* to presuppose criteria of identification or re-identification.

The identity of anything is intimately bound up with its existence; so that for something of kind *F* to lose its identity is not to be distinguished from that *F*'s ceasing to *be*. Now in the case of material objects, for a thing to cease to be is not to be distinguished from our ceasing to be able to identify it; but with matter this is not the case. Some matter may persist between times $t1$ and $t2$, but this does not mean that we are automatically entitled to ask questions of the form "what are the necessary and sufficient conditions for the F ('F' being here a mass noun) identified at $t1$ to be the same F – if it is the same F – as the F identified at $t2$?"; for we need not be able to independently identify the stuff identified at some one time at any *other* time.

A question such as the above runs together criteria of re-identification and criteria of identity (which in the case of material objects come to the same thing, since to be is to be identifiable for them), and in the case of matter these kinds of criteria must be clearly distinguished, for it is not incompatible with matter's lacking criteria of re-identification, that it should have criteria of identity. That is, though there is no *guarantee* that we may be able to identify and re-identify some matter, nonetheless, in the right circumstances, we may *in fact* be able to do these things. The water in the green jug may be the water I purchased in a bottle yesterday; and we may ask in virtue of *what* that water is the same. (And it is here that criteria of identity come in.) On the other hand, it is far from clear what such identity criteria might be. With material objects we (think we) have a clear enough criterion in spatio-temporal continuity, but such a criterion is inapplicable to matter, which may persist through being crushed, ground up, scattered, dissolved and so on. We could perhaps attempt to pin the identity of matter upon the identity of constituents (grains, flakes, molecules or what-have-you); but, as Cartwright (1965) has pointed out, there are grave difficulties about any such attempt. We may have the same salt but not the same molecules of salt, for example, since molecules are capable of dissociating and re-associating in different ways. On the other hand, if we cannot pin the identity of matter on the identity of constituents, it is difficult to see what *else* is left to pin it on, and we may find ourselves in sympathy with Quine's (1964) claim that a mass term like 'water' does not "primarily admit 'same'", and that when it does, "some special individuating standard is understood from the circumstances. Typically, 'same sugar' might allude to sameness of shipment" (p. 102).

I mention the question of identity criteria for matter, however, only to distinguish it from the question of criteria of re-identification, for an examination of the former question would not be central to our present concern, and would indeed take us far beyond it.

Re-identification must be distinguished from identity, then, and it must also be distinguished from two other notions with which it is particularly likely to be confused. Suppose we have two pieces of iron V and W; and suppose that these are ground up and the resulting heaps mixed together. Now we cannot expect someone to be able to pick out or identify within this larger pile, the iron of which V consisted, and distinguish it from the iron of which W consisted (let alone to identify the iron from V *as* the iron from V) – unless of course the iron from the one lump was of a somehow different kind from the iron from the other lump. The iron from V, like the iron from W, cannot be *identified*, and thus cannot be re-identified. I have belaboured the obvious here in order to distinguish it from two other points alluded to before. Our inability to identify or re-identify should not be confused with (i) an inability to *trace*, nor with an inability to (ii) *d*-identify, as I shall call it; for there may be no such inabilities.

(i) The point does not imply, then, that we cannot do what we obviously *can* do, that is, to trace the iron (or at any rate the constituents of the iron) from V, say, through its dissection and intermingling with the iron from W. We can clearly trace all the bits from V, and thereby trace the iron of which V consisted. But such tracing is very different from re-identifying. It does not involve (a) picking something out and (b) judging that it is the same as something independently identified earlier. It is in fact dependent upon the one original act of identification alone; it is essentially tied to that act. (Whether we must always be able to trace constituents in this general way is a question which concerns the identity of matter, and cannot be considered here.)

(ii) Nor does the point imply that we could not, on the basis of identifying such constituent bits or grains of the iron from V, re-identify those bits at a later date, and thus identify the iron from V once more. But in the first place, I think that we should be extremely reluctant to call this procedure a case of re-identification. For again, it is not as if what we do is firstly, to pick out some iron, and secondly, to identify that iron *as* the iron originally in V, on the basis of identifying the constituent bits. For there is no question here of an *independent* identification of the iron from V. We can *only* identify it as: the iron with the same constituents as the iron which was in V – and such an identification would be parasitic or dependent in a direct way upon its original identification as the iron in V. It would not, for example, be possible to ask any non-question-begging questions about whether the stuff we had picked out on such a basis *was* the same as the stuff originally identified; for a condition of picking it out at all would be the supposition that it was. The case would thus not be a case of re-identification, as we have understood that term: it would be a quite special and parasitic form of identification. I'll call it d-identification to distinguish it from cases of genuine and independent *re*-identification. *D*-identification would of course involve information in addition to the information necessary to perform an original or independent identification, information about constituents. (To have identified some iron does not imply to have identified constituents; the former is a necessary condition of the latter, but in doing the latter we go beyond what is necessary for the former.)

I conclude then that the original claim that matter lacks criteria of identification and thereby criteria of re-identification is justified; and these facts do not preclude the possibility of either tracing constituent parts and thereby tracing matter or re-identifying constituent parts and thereby d-identifying matter. (On the other hand we should not I think too readily assume that such tracing and re-identifying of parts is always possible). This lack of criteria of identification is the material ground of the differences between material objects and the stuff of which they are composed, and once it is properly recognised, the basis for confusion in this area is gone.[12]

Queen's University

NOTES

[1] The paper is intended as a further development of certain ideas in Laycock (1972); and a familiarity with that paper, while not essential to the reading of this one, may nonetheless be of some help in understanding what I am about.

[2] It might be objected that to talk of a single doctrine here would be at best misleading, since there are surely certain differences between the notions of object and individual and thing. But we can admit the possibility of such differences, and still maintain (as I argue presently) that there is a central core that all these notions – and not only these, but also such other general notions as those of 'entity', 'item' and 'existent' – have in common, something in virtue of which we are justified in speaking of a common doctrine in all these cases.

[3] In fairness to Strawson, however, and in spite of his outspoken advocacy of the object ontology (in its more general and also more particular forms), it should be said that he has in fact come closer than any other writer I am aware of to outright rejection of this ontology – a point to which I will return in due course.

[4] In general agreement with the O.E.D., I mean by 'matter' just those various natural kinds of substances of which the various kinds of material objects are composed. These substances are designated by mass nouns, and are nowadays the subject-matter of chemical enquiry.

[5] Knowing what counts as one object of a certain kind, and what as another, may just conceivably not involve knowing how to go about determining the number of such objects in a given region of space. Such at least is Wiggins' (1967) claim; and if this claim were justified (which is itself by no means clear), then there would be another and more exacting sense of 'countable' in which countability would not even be a necessary condition of objecthood.

[6] Thus that way of speaking of existence which employs the jargon of 'instantiation' – for something of a kind to exist is for the concept of that kind to have instances – is wholly inadequate as a general way of speaking of existence.

[7] cf. Aristotle at *Metaphysics* 1016a. Frege (1884), quite incomprehensibly in my view, opposes 'one' and 'unity' in physical objects. 'Unity', he says, is associated with 'being united' or 'undivided'; but not so 'one'. For when we say that 'Earth has one moon', he insists, "we do not mean to point out that our satellite is ... undivided" (p. 43e). But if our satellite *were* divided – and how else but into separate chunks of matter? – then we would just not *have* one satellite any longer, but instead a number of them corresponding to the number of the separate chunks.

[8] Although the argument against construing a reference to some matter as a reference to a single thing (a 'quantity') would apply equally against construing a reference to some objects as a reference to a single thing (a 'set'), it would I think be seriously mistaken to assimilate the former type of reference to the latter. The arguments in Cartwright (1970) against any such assimilation are much superior to those in Laycock (1972) in favour of it; and though there are undoubtedly analogies between mass and plural count nouns, mass nouns are I now believe more fundamental than *any* kind of count noun, singular or plural.

[9] Goodman (1951) defines the sum of Dalmatians, for example, as 'that individual which overlaps all and only those individuals which overlap some Dalmatian' (where 'overlap' can be roughly construed in the context as 'has as parts').

[10] I use the term 'identify' in the favoured philosophical sense, as belonging to that cluster of notions which includes 'single out', 'mark off', 'point to', 'recognise', 'pick

out', 'discriminate', 'separate out' and 'distinguish'. In this use the term is to be distinguished from its use in, e.g., 'Smith was identified as the murderer' and 'The insect was identified as belonging to such-and-such a species'.

[11] For an account of this extremely valuable distinction see e.g. Donnellan (1966).

[12] The fact, if such it really is, that matter is not countable, does not mean that matter cannot be *quantified*, at any rate in the ordinary sense of that term: for it is obvious that although matter cannot be counted, it can still be measured, and indeed 'quantification' in the ordinary sense is tied more intimately to measuring than it is to counting. On the other hand, it appears to be often assumed that the concept of number can be somehow introduced into first order quantification theory merely by adding identity, so that e.g. the statement that there are at least two things of kind *F* can be represented by

$$(Ex)\,(Ey)\,(Fx\ \&\ Fy\ \&\ x \neq y).$$

But it should be clear that unless we have already *introduced* the concept of number in some way, this will not do. That is, we must already have supposed either that the predicate letters stand in for *count* nouns exclusively (an extremely restrictive supposition, ruling out such terms as 'red' and 'heavy'), or that variables cannot be placeholders for just any referring expressions – not e.g. for 'this water' – but only for referring expressions designating *objects;* for the fact that this water and that water are distinct does not, if our arguments are sound, that mean there are at least two objects in the world.

BIBLIOGRAPHY

Note: page numbers given in text refer, where applicable, to reprints listed below.

Aristotle, *Metaphysics* (transl. by R. Hope) Ann Arbor, 1960.

Cartwright, H., 'Heraclitus and the Bath Water', *Philosophical Review* 74 (1965), 466–485.

Cartwright, H., 'Quantities', *Philosophical Review* 79 (1970), 25–42.

Donagan, A., 'Universals and Metaphysical Realism' (1963), reprinted in M. J. Loux, *Universals and Particulars,* New York 1970.

Donnellan, K., 'Reference and Definite Descriptions', *Philosophical Review* 75, (1966), 281–304.

Frege, G., *Grundlagen der Arithmetik* (1884), (transl. J. L. Austin as *The Foundations of Arithmetic*), Oxford 1959.

Geach, P. T., 'Frege's *Grundlagen*' (1951), reprinted in Geach, P. T., *Logic Matters,* Oxford 1972, pp. 212–222.

Geach, P. T., 'Quine on Classes and Properties' (1953), reprinted in same volume, pp. 222–226.

Goodman, N., *The Structure of Appearance,* Cambridge, Mass. 1951.

Hobbes, T., *Leviathan* (1651), Molesworth edn. (Oxford 1961).

Jones, B., 'Aristotle's Introduction of Matter', *Philosophical Review* 83 (1974), 474–500.

Laycock, H., 'Some Questions of Ontology', *Philosophical Review* 81 (1972), 3–42.

Leibniz, G. W., Letter to Arnauld (1687), reprinted in *Leibniz: Philosophical Writings* (transl. by M. Morris) London 1934, 77–83.

Leibniz, G. W., 'On the Ultimate Origination of Things', (1697) reprinted in same volume, pp. 32–41.

Locke, J., *An Essay concerning Human Understanding* (1690), Pringle-Pattison edition, Oxford 1924.

Quine, W. V. 'Speaking of Objects' (1958), reprinted in *Ontological Relativity*, New
    York and London 1969, pp. 1–25.
Quine, W. V., *Word and Object*, Cambridge, Mass. 1960.
Quine, W. V., 'Identity, Ostension and Hypostasis'. (1950), reprinted in Quine, W.,
    From a Logical Point of View, New York 1963, pp. 65–79.
Quine, W. V., 'Review of Geach's *Reference and Generality*', in *Philosophical Review*
    73 (1964), 102.
Russell, B., *The Principles of Mathematics*, London 1903.
Strawson, P. F., 'Truth' (1950), reprinted in *Logico-Linguistic Papers*, London 1971,
    pp. 190–213.
Strawson, P. F., 'Particular and General' (1954), reprinted in same volume, pp. 28–52.
Strawson, P. F., *Individuals*, London 1959.
Wiggins, D., *Identity and Spatio-Temporal Continuity*, Oxford 1967.

KATHLEEN C. COOK

ON THE USEFULNESS OF QUANTITIES*

There are problems about the relation between material objects and the matter of which they are composed. This can be illustrated by the following well-formed sentences of English: 'The bronze of which the statue is made is the same bronze that was a lump yesterday' and 'The gold of which my ring is made is the same gold as the gold of which Aunt Suzie's ring was made'. To understand just what we mean here and to understand why such sentences are true or false we need to know what 'the bronze' and 'the gold' refer to.[1] Helen Cartwright has suggested[2] that such expressions refer to 'quantities' of gold or bronze.

In this paper I will focus on the problem of determining the precise reference of these expressions and of others like them. We might construe these expressions as making some reference to matter and in particular to matter which can retain its own identity over time independently of the continued existence of any material object. To give support to such a construal, it is necessary to become clearer on what we mean by matter here, and on how such expressions make reference to it. This problem of reference is important for the project of giving an account of the relation between matter and material objects and also for the broader project of providing an account of what it is for different sorts of things to remain the same over time.

This paper is an investigation of the usefulness of the technical term 'quantity', suggested by Helen Cartwright, for solving this problem of reference for the expressions at issue. I will first set out her account of 'quantity', pointing out those features of her definition which embody conditions which must be met by any adequate referent of such expressions. I will then consider a few competing accounts of the reference of these expressions and show why they are inadequate. In addition, I will consider a difficulty to which quantity as a referent of our matter expressions might seem prone and will demonstrate that this difficulty can be overcome.

121

F. J. Pelletier (ed.), Mass Terms, 121–135. All Rights Reserved.

I. QUANTITIES

Cartwright (p. 28, 'Quantities') claims that identities like

(1)   The gold of which my ring is made is the same gold as the gold
         of which Aunt Suzie's ring was made

are equivalent to identities like

(2)   The quantity of gold of which my ring is made = the quantity
         of gold of which Aunt Suzie's ring was made,

and that (p. 39) "In a large and important class of cases when we talk of β
(where β ranges over kinds of stuff like coffee, gold, or water) we are
talking of quantities of β."

In general, Cartwright compares the entailment relation between (1)
and (2) with that between (3) and (4).

(3)   The cats we have in Boston are the same cats as the cats we
         had in Detroit.
(4)   The set of cats we have in Boston = the set of cats we had in
         Detroit.

The technical term 'quantity' which Cartwright employs is borrowed
from Russell (*Principles of Mathematics*, part III) and is defined by Cartwright as (p. 28) "anything which is capable of quantitative equality with
something else". "Two things are quantitatively equal if they are the same
quantity of something, where 'quantity' means 'amount'" (p. 28). She
gives a parallel definition of set: "anything which may be numerically
equal to something with which it need not be equal". Cartwright then
says that with one important qualification, "the sense in which a quantity
of something contains an amount of it is just analogous to the sense in
which a set of things contains a number of them".

Thus we can have definitions D_1 and D_2 where D_1 defines a set of A and
D_2 defines quantity of β.

D_1: x is a set of A if and only if, for some y, x and y are comparable
         with respect to the number of A each contains, and x contains
         nothing other than A.

D_2: x is a quantity of β if and only if, for some y, x and y are comparable with respect to the amount of β each contains, and x contains nothing other than β.[3]

(Note that 'A' can't be, e.g., 'things' or 'elements' but must be something like 'cats'. 'β' must be a term referring to some kind of stuff, like 'gold' or 'water'; mere 'stuff' won't do. This is because to count we need a kind of thing to count, and to measure we need a kind of stuff to measure. This last point will be further discussed later in this paper.)

The qualification which, according to Cartwright, must be put on D_2, though there is no analogous qualification on D_1, is

the range of β in D_2 is restricted to those cases in which Russell's axiom holds; that is to those cases in which without qualification, as a matter of necessity, amounts of β are identical or one is greater and the other less.

(Russell's axiom: "Necessarily, for every x and y, if x and y are amounts of β then x is the same amount of β as y or x is a larger or smaller amount of β than y". Russell's axiom doesn't hold in the case of 'stuff'.)

A set of A contains other sets. A quantity of β often contains other quantities. But, Cartwright wants to say, while the quantity of coffee in my cup is a set containing other quantities of coffee, it is not the set of all the quantities of coffee in my cup. This is true because we may not be able to determine that there is some quantity of coffee which is the smallest quantity of coffee in my cup. While we see that there are no quantities smaller than a few molecules of caffeine, we are not able to determine what size the smallest possible quantity of coffee might be. This problem would presumably arise for many kinds of substances. I will take up later in this paper the question of whether there might not be an alternative to Cartwright's solution to this problem.

Quantities, like sets, can be added and divided. The physical coherence of a quantity is irrelevant to its being the same quantity. Therefore, though, e.g., lumps of clay can be added and divided also, and thus differ from cats and (most) chairs, physical coherence is a necessary condition of being the same lump in a way that it isn't for quantities. We can divide a lump and get two lumps, but if we physically divide a quantity or set the original set or quantity still exists. It is also true that the sets and quantities contained in the original set or quantity exist whether or not a physical division takes place. This is not true in the case of a lump of clay though we may want to say that the two smaller lumps are there potentially.

The identity of a quantity of stuff over time is thus independent of the identity of the material thing or things in which it is contained. Therefore, although we can count quantities, they do not individuate physical objects. Many physical objects are made of, or constituted by, quantities of stuff (e.g., the gold in a ring or a lump is a quantity of gold), but each of these quantities contains a number of quantities of gold, and each, with one class of exceptions (the smallest quantities) is also a part of a number of larger quantities of gold.

To fill our needs for a referent for stuff which retains its identity over time, a term like 'quantity' must pick out something which retains its identity independently of the continued existence of any particular material object. It must do this in the sense that its conditions for retaining its identity over time are independent of the conditions for the identity over time of any particular material object. Also, although for any material object made from only one kind of stuff there is a quantity of matter of which it is composed, this quantity has an identity independent of that of the particular.

To fill our needs for a description of the referent of that which remains the same over time in cases (like that of Aunt Suzie's ring) in which there is a formal or substantial change an entity must have certain properties. It would seem that quantities have these properties.

For any ϕ, if the reference of 'same β' (where β, as before, ranges over kinds of stuff like gold and bronze) is to be 'same ϕ of β', ϕ will need the following properties:

(1)   It is not identical with a material object over time though it may occupy the same space with one at a time.

(2)   It has an identity over time independent of that of any material object.

(3)   It usually (unless it is the smallest ϕ of β) contains other ϕ's of β.

(4)   It is part of a number of other, larger ϕ's of β. (Unless, of course, it is the largest ϕ of β, and so contains all the β in existence.)

(5) ϕ's, like sets, 'overlap'.

Regarding condition (5), quantities or sets 'overlap' in the following sense: part or all of one set or quantity can be part of two other different quantities or sets at the same time. For instance, the quantity of clay in the handle of the pitcher is part of the quantity of clay in the left one half of the pitcher and part of the quantity of clay in the top one half of the pitcher. If conditions (1)–(5) are not met, a ϕ of β is not distinct from a material object made of β in the way necessary for the truth of our two original sentences (p. 443). Regarding conditions (1) and (2), although at a time a ϕ of clay may coincide with a vase, we can talk about its existence over time independent of that vase and, in fact, independent of other material objects as well. Regarding conditions (3)–(5), if ϕ did not meet conditions (3) and (5), there would be no reason to assert that if, e.g., a lump of clay which is constituted by ϕ_1 of clay is divided, the two smaller lumps of clay that are produced are composed of ϕ's ϕ_2 and ϕ_3 of clay. Furthermore, the truth of conditions (4) and (5) is what justifies our being able to say that a lump of clay which is made by joining two smaller lumps constituted by ϕ_4 and ϕ_5 of clay is itself constituted by $\phi_6 (\phi_6 = \phi_4 + \phi_5)$. Without conditions (3)–(5) a ϕ would be dependent for its coming into being on the coming into being of some material object which it constituted.

11. COMPETING ACCOUNTS – RIVAL SOLUTIONS TO THE PROBLEM OF THE REFERENCE OF 'THE GOLD' OR 'SAME BRONZE'

(A) Lump, piece, bit, etc.

Someone might argue that we need no such technical term as 'quantity' to explain the reference of these expressions. We mean, they might say, same 'lump' or 'piece' or 'bit of bronze'. However, the following problem arises with 'lump' and other such words: we want to be able to say that the clay in this vase is the same as the clay in the two lumps I had yesterday. But if 'the clay' and 'the same clay' refer to the same lump of clay we have the difficulty of 'The clay of which the vase is made is the same lump of clay as the two lumps of clay I had yesterday'. What does it mean to say that the two lumps are one lump? The most obvious way of making sense out of such a statement (that the clay of the two lumps is the *same clay* as the clay of an earlier or later single lump) is not open to us here since it is just such a use of 'same clay' that we are here trying to explain. The problem with trying to use 'lump' in this way is that we have an ordinary sortal use of 'lump' which is at variance with the use we are trying to put the word to here. A lump is solid and spatially distinct from other stuff. While its particular shape is unimportant, (squeezing it or flattening it will not usually affect its identity as the same lump) it does, however, have clear boundaries. As a consequence of these properties, lumps are counted in a certain way and if one lump is divided into halves we no longer have one lump but instead have two. Likewise, if two lumps are joined together we no longer have two lumps but instead one. And if we melt a lump we have no lump but a puddle.

So the way in which lumps are normally counted and individuated and identified over time is being called into question here by this attempt to claim that the reference of 'same bronze' is 'same lump of bronze'. We normally think that there is a difference between one lump of bronze and two, but here we are being told that on some level at least there is no difference, that in some sense our two lumps are one lump. Also on this view we would sometimes be forced to say that one lump is really two. If we object by saying that our ordinary notion of lump would lead us to believe that there are two lumps of clay here, not one, the defender of lumps may reply that what is meant by saying here that the two lumps are one lump is simply that there is some clay that you can talk about independently of shape, the identity of any material object over time, etc. It might then be agreed that this use of 'lump' (call it L_2) which differs from our usual use of 'lump' (call it L_1) needs to be further explicated and defined. When this is done, however, we will have a technical term 'L_2' which shares important features with 'quantity'.[4] This is true because the properties which L_2 will need in order to be the referent of, e.g., 'same bronze' are properties needed by any ϕ as enumerated in Section I.

So it seems that 'lump', 'piece', 'bit', or any other usual way of sortalizing stuff, i.e., ways that divide stuff into material objects or spatially coherent wholes, will not, in contrast to 'quantity', pick out an adequate referent for an expression like 'bronze' or 'same gold'. These sortal terms all have an ordinary usage in which physical coherence is required for their individuation and identity over time. But it is precisely the absence of this restriction which we need in a term which will pick out the referent of an expression like 'the bronze' or 'the gold' in our original sentences above (p. 121). If we create a non-ordinary usage for one of these terms which does meet conditions (1)–(5), we will then have a technical term like 'quantity' but which will conflict with its ordinary usage in a much more troublesome way than 'quantity' conflicts with its ordinary usage. Also it is difficult to provide a non *ad hoc* rationale for condition (5) in the case of a proposed technical term such as 'L_2' whereas there is no such problem with 'quantity'.

(B) *Chappell's solution – 'parcel'*

V. C. Chappell has suggested in his paper 'Stuff and Things'[5] that we talk about 'parcels of stuff'. He seems to intend 'parcel' here to be a technical term much like Cartwright's 'quantity' to which he compares it. He thinks, however, that it is preferable to 'quantity' because it does not have another common usage whereas 'quantity'[6] does (e.g., 'There is the same quantity of wine in my glass as there is in Mary's glass'.)

As Cartwright points out,[7] however, referring to (I)–(II′) below, Chappell seems to want 'parcel' to be substitutable not only in (I) in which 'quantity' can be substituted, but also in (II) in which 'quantity' is not substitutable and in (II′).[8] Now 'quantity' is substitutable in (II^c) which is in some way like (II). But it is not substitutable in (II′), and as Cartwright says,[9] it seems unlikely that anything which satisfies (I) should also satisfy (II). I would add that anything which satisfies (I) will not satisfy (II′).

(I)   The truth of 'This is the same gold as that' is necessary and sufficient for the truth of 'This _____ of gold = that _____ of gold'.

(II)   It is at any rate a sufficient condition of the truth of 'This is a _____ of gold' that 'This is a lump or piece or sack or coin or ring or… of gold' be true.

(II^c)   It is at any rate a sufficient condition of the truth of 'This is constituted by a _____ of gold' that 'This is a lump or piece or coin or ring or… of gold' be true.
(We need restrictions on what is included in the '…' here. 'Sack' is excluded, but 'sack', 'glass', etc., might be included if we said 'constituted by or contains a _____ of gold' or we could include 'sackful' or 'glassful' in '…'.)

(II′)   The truth of 'This is a lump or piece or sack or coin or ring or … of gold' is both necessary and sufficient for the truth of 'This is a _____ of gold'.

Some of the difficulty with 'parcel' seems to be that it is not clearly defined. But if it were so defined, the inconsistency between (I) and (II′) would be clear. According to (II′) every parcel of, e.g., silver, will be a lump or piece or ring or... of silver and every lump, etc., of silver will be a parcel of silver. But according to (I), the truth of 'The silver in my new earrings is the same silver as the silver that was in the top one half of the left handle of Uncle Harry's wrestling trophy' is necessary and sufficient for the truth of 'The parcel of silver in my new earrings = the parcel of silver that was in the top one half of the left handle of Uncle Harry's wrestling trophy'. But the parcel of silver in my new earrings would not seem to be a parcel according to (II′) and the parcel of silver in the top one half of the left handle of Uncle Harry's trophy would not seem to be a lump or piece or ring or... of silver though it should be according to (II′). Part of the problem can be put this way: a quantity often contains other quantities. A ϕ often contains other ϕ's (condition (3)). But *apropos* of Chappell's (II′), all the parcels that a parcel of β contains cannot be a lump or a piece or a ... of β.

As we saw above for a technical term ϕ to provide the reference we need it must be defined in a way that will insure that it is individuated independently of any particular physical boundaries or pattern of physical coherence so that its identity over time is independent of its partial or total spatial coincidence with any material object. Therefore, though it *may* spatially coincide with such an object at a time, it cannot be *necessary* that it do so.

Having explained the difficulties with (II′), I would now like to consider the weaker (II). A parcel, we have seen, cannot necessarily be a material object if (I) is to be true of 'parcel'. Can it even be identical at some times with such an object as (II) would imply? Like Cartwright, I do not think that 'quantity' or anything else substitutable in (I) is also substitutable in (II). Cartwright argues that not identity, but containment, is at issue. She argues correctly that a quantity of stuff and a thing cannot be identified because they may have separate histories and other non-shared properties such as atomic weight, value, the property of having been made by Smith in February of 1973, and so on.

In conclusion, it seems that 'parcel of stuff' as explicated by Chappell is too vague to serve our need for a referent of 'the bronze' and 'the gold' in our original sentences. When 'parcel' is made more precise it is shown to be inconsistent. It seems clear that the relationship of a quantity of stuff to a material object of which the stuff is made is not one of identity, but it is difficult to go beyond this. 'Containment', 'composition', and 'constitution' seem to capture the relationship in some cases but these terms seem to amount to little more than metaphors or to assertions that some relation other than identity is at issue. This problem is one on which more work must be done; it is hoped that the present paper may serve as a beginning.[10]

(C) *Laycock's Solution– m-elements*

So far we have defended 'quantities' against the competition of 'lumps' and 'pieces' and 'parcels'. Now we will turn to more serious competition: '*m*-elements'. Henry Laycock (in 'Some Questions of Ontology', *Philosophical Review*, 1972) talks of '*m*-elements of a stuff' as being 'the very small elements of which any kind of stuff consists and which themselves do not consist of that stuff, e.g., a molecule of water', (pp. 39–40). We can then talk about sets or collections of *m*-elements so that, for example, the gold in a lump of gold will be a certain set of *m*-elements of gold, and this will, of course, contain other sets of *m*-elements of gold.

In many ways sets of *m*-elements are like quantities (e.g., the subsets of a set of *m*-elements overlap as quantities do) and they seem to provide equally good referents for 'same gold' and 'the bronze' as do quantities. In spite of many similarities between quantities and sets, there are, as Cartwright has pointed out, important differences. I think that it is significant that we measure stuff rather than counting it as we do, e.g., material objects. *M*-elements are a way of trying to consider stuff as something to be counted, not measured. Laycock (p. 36) says he is

proposing actually to construe mass terms as plural sortal terms. This means we are to think of stuff as a plurality of things, each of the same kind for any given kind of stuff (we may call each of these objects an *m*-element of the stuff). In the formal mode, the proposal is to construe any mass term '*m*' as a plural sortal of the form *m*-elements. This can be understood as an hypothesis about language, as the postulation of a linguistic theoretical entity, justified to the extent that it illuminates the behavior of mass terms and the nature of stuff.

There seems to be the following difficulty for *m*-elements: if we can't specify what constitutes an *m*-element for a kind of stuff *S*, then we cannot talk about *m*-elements of *S*. Laycock seems to admit (p. 39) that there are cases in which we cannot determine whether or not there are *m*-elements of certain complex sorts of stuff like mud and beer which would be chemically categorized as mixtures. However, he then says:

Given our quite recent knowledge of the distinctions between (chemical) elements, compounds, and mixtures, we know that there is nothing in the case of mud which is *really* analogous to water molecules in the case of water. But of course it is just this knowledge which makes it possible to see mud as a complex mixture of elements and compounds, each of which *does* have smallest units, and thus we can think of the smallest units of mud as aggregates of the smallest units of each of its constituents (p. 39).

This does not seem to me to provide us with an adequate answer to the question of whether there really are *m*-elements of stuff like beer, mud, and coffee. It seems that if there are cases in which there are no *m*-elements there is then a difficulty, even if we can 'think of' the smallest units as aggregates of the smallest units of each of its constituents. How can there be sets of *m*-elements of *S* if there are no *m*-elements of *S*? So *m*-elements seem to fail to provide reference for a broad class of kinds of stuff. Quantities are able to provide reference in these same cases, however. We do not think of stuff as a plurality of things, and I think quantities do more than *m*-elements to illuminate the behavior of mass terms that refer to kinds of stuff and particularly kinds of matter and to illuminate the nature of stuff. I will try to buttress these remarks by considering a specific difficulty for *m*-elements which is not a difficulty for quantities.

The same difficulties about the existence of *m*-elements of certain stuffs arise concerning the existence of the smallest quantities of these same stuffs. Cartwright says (pp. 40–41) that there isn't necessarily a smallest quantity of *S* for certain stuffs, e.g., coffee. So the quantity of coffee in a cup can't be the set of all the quantities of coffee in the cup.

What has to be granted, I think, is that it can only be *some set or other* of quantities containing elements of *A* (an infinite set) large enough to be amounts of coffee – and, it may be added, quantities which differ from one another by quantities containing elements of such a subset of *A*. *Q* (the quantity of coffee in a particular cup) is one of various sets (p. 41).

So there are quantities of *S* in these cases even if there is no smallest amount of *S* and so no smallest quantities of *S*. Therefore quantities do not have the same difficulty as *m*-elements here. We can have quantities of *S* as long as *S* is measurable (though not necessarily in the smallest possible units). Quantities need only be measurable, while sets of *m*-elements require *m*-elements and not simply smaller sets of *m*-elements, since these too are dependent on *m*-elements.

Laycock thinks that:

A kind of atomic theory is implicit in the ordinary use of mass terms, based on our experience of the behavior of stuff; and science in extending our experience, is able to fill in the details with which ordinary experience does not provide us (p. 39).

While science may provide details, I think that no atomic theory (if that means one about small particles) is implicit in our ordinary use of mass terms. It seems rather that a theory involving measuring as opposed to counting is implied.

III. A DIFFICULTY FOR QUANTITIES?

Now I would like to consider another problem which seems to arise for quantities as well as for m-elements. It is a necessary condition for Q_1 and Q_2 to be the same quantity of β that they be the same amount of β. This might seem to rule out 'same quantity of β' as the reference of 'same S' in many cases. For instance, if even one very small quantity of gold gets lost when we make a ring from the gold that was in Aunt Suzie's ring, it would seem that it is then not true that 'same gold' in our original sentence ((1) on page 122 above) can have 'same quantity of gold' as its reference.

Let us consider the various solutions which might be offered to the trilemma we have posed.

> Trilemma: If 'quantity' is defined as it has been by Cartwright in such a way that two quantities of β must contain the same exact amount of β if they are to be the same quantity, then in many if not most cases in which we talk of 'same stuff' we do not have the same quantity of stuff. What are we to say?

I will consider three possible solutions to this trilemma.

(1)   'Quantity' should be defined as Cartwright defines it, but quantities are not what we refer to when we say 'same gold'. But then what *do* we refer to? Same what? We are back where we started.

(2)   We need to modify our definition of 'quantity' to make it less precise in order that the same gold can be the same quantity of gold in cases where a little gold is lost.

(3)   'Quantity' need not be redefined in cases in which a small
           quantity of stuff is lost; just as in non-problematic cases
           'same β' does refer to same quantity of stuff.

Solution (1) simply does not fit with the way in which someone would
react to the claim that they didn't have the same gold because a bit had
been lost. They would, I think, admit that if a bit had been lost, it was not
strictly speaking the same gold. This does not preclude their saying that
this fact is irrelevant in certain contexts. Often we need not be so precise.
If it is agreed that we do not really have the same gold it makes no sense
to try to find a referent for 'gold' of which it will be true in these cases that
we have the same ϕ. We do not *strictly speaking* have the same thing.
       Solution (2) advocates defining 'quantity' more loosely in order that we
may say that we have the same quantity of gold in cases where we do not
have exactly the same amount of gold. But of course if we do not actually
have the same gold, though we speak of 'same gold', it will not matter
that we do not have the same quantity of gold. I would, however, like to
point out a practical difficulty which would arise in any case if we tried to
define 'quantity' more loosely to accommodate the cases. How loosely
should it be defined? How much gold can we lose and still have the same
quantity of gold? As much as we could lose and still speak of 'same quantity of gold'? But surely that is arbitrary. Suppose I say we have the same
gold and you say it is not the same gold. Is it the same quantity of gold in
our new loosely defined sense of 'quantity'? There would seem to be no
answer. Solution (2) is not only misguided and unnecessary, but unfeasible,
It also seems as if we might under solution (2) have to give up the transitivity of 'same gold'. The amount of gold which is the difference between
A and B might be insignificant and the difference between B and C might
be insignificant, but the difference between A and C might be significant. So
according to solution (2), A would be the same quantity of gold as B and B
would be the same quantity as C. But A would not be the same quantity
as C. This seems like an additional reason for rejecting solution (2).
       Solution (3) seems to solve the trilemma in the following way. The
reason we say 'same β' in cases in which we do not have strictly speaking
the same quantity of stuff, is that we have an intuitive idea of quantity of
stuff and that what we mean by 'same β' is 'same quantity of β'. I am not
suggesting that ordinary speakers think of Cartwright's quantities. I mean

only that our ordinary ways of thinking and speaking imply a belief in something like quantities. In particular, the property of quantity most relevant to the present debate – that Q_1 and Q_2 are the same Q of β only if they contain the exact same amount of β – is a property also applied to same stuff. It is for this reason that when pressed in the gold ring case an ordinary speaker will admit that strictly speaking it isn't the same gold (this is because it isn't the same amount of gold and 'same stuff' implies among other things 'same amount of stuff').

This argument might be objected to in the following way: sometimes a person may talk of same β when he knows quite well that a bit has been lost, that it's not really the same stuff but it's enough the same for the context. Such a case seems unproblematic. But there is another much larger set of cases we need to concern ourselves with here. There are cases in which only a scientist using very delicate balances or strong microscopes can know that we do not have the same amount of gold. One might think that the observations and judgments of this scientist and of the philosopher who incorporates the scientist's precision into his definitions ought not to matter to the common person. But it seems that they do in the sense that they are recognized as bearing on the exact truth of what is said. They do not matter in that they do not keep people from talking in useful, though technically imprecise, ways. But why do the precise measurements of matter of the scientist matter? Because they are more precise *measurements*, more precise versions of something done by the ordinary speakers themselves.

In reply to such an objection I would like to suggest that quantities are in a much better position here than m-elements. Suppose we have one or two or a few less m-elements and we tell the ordinary person of our findings. We may get him to agree that we don't therefore have the same gold, but it will take a lot more steps. We must convince him that gold is really made up of a lot of small unobservable things which are not material objects. He might just say that that's not what he means by gold and that our findings are irrelevant to him. But if we say we do not have the same *amount* of gold he may react differently. It might be suggested that I am making irrelevant distinctions, but I do not think it is unreasonable to choose one candidate for the reference of an expression over another if the first is closer to the implied assumptions of the speakers using the expressions.

Does what I have said about 'quantity' with respect to the 'mistake' cases run counter to what Cartwright has said? I think not. She says that identities like (1) (p. 122 above) are equivalent to identities like (2). I have not contested this. I have merely pointed out that though many identities of type (1) are strictly speaking false they can still be seen as referring to quantities of β when they contain expressions like 'the β'.

V. CONCLUSION

I have argued that there is a philosophical problem posed by a need to determine the reference of expressions which seem to refer to kinds of stuff or matter and to make identity claims about it (e.g., 'the gold', 'the same clay'). Ordinary sortal expressions such as 'lump', and 'piece' have been shown to be inadequate to the task of providing reference for the expressions in question. What is necessary is an expression which does not have an ordinary sortal use and which meets certain other conditions which I have enumerated. There does not seem to be an expression in ordinary language which fits these conditions. The technical term, 'quantity', as defined by Helen Cartwright, meet the conditions. 'Parcel', suggested V. C. Chappell, fails to meet the conditions. Another technical term, 'm-elements', coined by Laycock, comes close to meeting the conditions, but has a number of difficulties. Mose of these difficulties stem from the fact that counting (rather than measuring, as with quantities) is behind the application of 'm-elements', and stuff is as a matter of fact measured, rather than counted, in most situations. I have also considered a possible difficulty with 'quantity' (that in most cases in which someone talks of 'same stuff' strictly speaking we don't have the same quantity of stuff) and shown it not to be a genuine difficulty.

Indiana University

NOTES

* I have benefited greatly from conversations with Richard Grandy and Adam Morton and from their comments on an earlier version of this paper.
[1] I think that a similar problem arises in trying to give an account of what it is precisely that, according to Aristotle, 'remains' when a new material object comes into being out of some matter (*Physics*, Book I, Chapter 7). I will not consider this problem of interpreting Aristotle in this present paper. I have done so, however, in 'Matter and Coming to Be', a chapter of my dissertation in progress, *Aristotle on Matter and Coming to Be*.

[2] In 'Quantities', *Philosophical Review* **79** (1970), 25–42, and 'Chapell on Stuff and Things', *Nous* **6** (1972), 369–377.

[3] It has been pointed out to me by Adam Morton that the further condition 'and x contains something' is needed here.

[4] I don't mean to suggest that there is no ground in ordinary usage for having 'lump' or 'piece' play this role. Descartes, as Cartwright mentions (p. 375, 'Chappell on Stuff and Things'), uses 'piece' in this way. But such a use of 'piece' does conflict in many cases with another, more usual, use of 'piece'. Those cases force us to see that we have two competing notions. I don't think that they compete equally, for I suspect that when pressed the ordinary speaker would admit that the L_2 use of 'lump' and Descartes' use of 'piece' were loose ways of talking. If Descartes' piece of wax were divided, and someone were asked how many pieces of wax there were, they would say 'two'. When we are under pressure to be precise, not Descartes' use of 'piece' (or L_2) but the ordinary (or L_1) use prevails.

[5] *Proceedings of the Aristotelian Society* **71** (1970–71) 61–76. Chappell has changed his view on this topic and deferred to Cartwright since this paper was written (in 'Matter', *Journal of Philosophy* **70** No. 19, fn. 1, p. 685).

[6] 'Stuff and Things', p. 66.

[7] In 'Chappell on Stuff and Things', pp. 370–373.

[8] *Ibid.*, pp. 3–5. He says (II) and implies (II').

[9] *Ibid.*, p. 4.

[10] It seems worthwhile to attempt to spell out a kind of formal relation between quantities and material objects. R. E. Grandy (in 'Stuff and Things', this volume, pp. 219–225) has done some work towards that end in defining material objects, such as rings and tables as relations between times and quantities of matter.

TERENCE PARSONS

AN ANALYSIS OF MASS TERMS AND AMOUNT TERMS[1]

I. INTRODUCTION

A mass term is a term like 'water', 'gold', 'information', 'green ink', 'green ink which has been diluted', etc. The first three of these, 'water', 'gold', and 'information' are simple mass nouns; the others are complex terms built up from mass nouns plus modifiers. Strictly speaking, it is occurrences of words, or something of the sort, which count as mass nouns, for the same *word* can occur both as a mass noun and as a count noun. For example, 'chicken' is a mass noun in 'I had some chicken for dinner', or in 'We had chicken for dinner'; it is a count noun in 'Our cat caught a chicken' and in 'Some chickens got into the garden'. In the sentence 'I looked, but I saw no chicken', the word 'chicken' is ambiguous between its count noun sense ('I didn't see any chickens') and its mass noun sense ('I didn't see any chicken (meat)'). The task of giving complete and explicit criteria for isolating out mass nouns is a detailed task which I will ignore here; I will assume enough competence at recognizing mass nouns to evaluate the analysis given below.[2]

It's not difficult to analyze single sentences containing mass terms – there's always some reconstrual available, say in terms of properties (e.g., analyze 'my watch is made of gold' as 'my watch has the property of being golden'). What is not so simple is to do this in a systematic, general way, and to see just what this accomplishes. I will try to give such a general account – ideally the analysis of each *individual* sentence entailed by this account should look obvious and trivial.

My 'analysis' will consist in showing how to translate sentences containing mass nouns into a 'logically perspicuous notation'. This requires several comments. First, ideally I should formulate explicit translation rules which would map English sentences onto sentences of the canonical notation. This, of course, is a Herculean task, and well beyond the scope of this paper. But it can be cut down to size by supposing that we already have a systematic way to translate *count*-noun sentences, and then by concentrating only on

F. J. Pelletier (ed.), Mass Terms, 137-166. All Rights Reserved.
Copyright © 1968 by Terence Parsons.

those difficulties peculiar to mass nouns. In the Appendix to this paper I sketch part of a more rigorous translation procedure.

I will take as my 'logically perspicuous notation' an enriched version of the ordinary predicate calculus with notation for set theory. But the 'enrichments' need not trouble us, for none of them are essentially due to mass nouns. For example, we will ultimately need some sorts of operators to represent sentences containing adverbs, both modal ('necessarily') and non-modal ('slowly'). But this has nothing to do with the difficulties of translation due to mass nouns as opposed to count nouns, and for most of our purposes we can ignore them. In fact, with few exceptions we can assume that our background 'logically perspicuous notation' simply is the first-order predicate calculus. Roughly speaking, then, the task is to paraphrase mass nouns in terms of names and count nouns – not because the latter are more basic, but rather because their logic, embodied in the predicate calculus, is better understood than that of mass nouns.

One more point – I count a translation into logical notation as *correct* if it relates sentences which are necessarily equivalent in truth-value. This is not a *clear* criterion for correctness; I mention it merely to exclude other criteria.[3]

In the next section I will lay out some sample problem sentences to guide our analysis; the analysis itself is given and discussed in Sections III–VII. W. V. Quine[4] has proposed an analysis of mass terms analogous to that in Sections III–V; I will indicate points of agreement and difference in footnotes to my proposals.

II. SOME PROBLEM SENTENCES

Any adequate characterization of mass terms must do at least the following things: first it must distinguish the seemingly various readings of 'is gold' in the sentences:

(a)   My ring is gold.
(b)   The element with atomic number 79 is gold.
(c)   The particular bit of matter which makes up my ring is gold.

On the surface it looks as if 'is gold' is predicated of three different kinds of thing here: objects (the ring), elements, and bits or quantities of matter; this suggests that it might be used in 3 or more different senses. Our analysis should illuminate this situation.

Second, our analysis must give a logical form to:

(d)   Blue styrofoam is styrofoam.

and must explain why (d) is logically true.

Third, our characterization must explain the logical forms of:

(e)   Water is widespread.
(f)   Muddy water is widespread.

And fourth, it must offer an analysis of:

(g)   Three teaspoons of gold weighs thirty ounces;

explaining the differences between phrases like 'thirty ounces', and 'three teaspoons *of gold*', and showing how they may be related as in (g).

When we try to express mass terms in the familiar idiom of names, predicates, quantifiers and connectives, a certain tension arises concerning whether we are to treat mass terms as *names* or as *predicates*.[5] Treating mass nouns as names (e.g., of elements or the like) seems natural and tempting, until we consider sentences like (d). How are we to treat *complex* mass terms in terms of names? If 'blue styrofoam' is a *name*, does it have logical structure, or not? If so, how can this structure be exposed with the resources at our disposal? And if not, how can we account for the analyticity of (d)? Further, we speak of '*some* water', '*all* blue styrofoam'; phrases which combine quantifier locutions with mass terms. But quantifiers do not normally combine with *names*; how then can we construe these expressions?

Suppose, then, we revert to treating mass nouns as *predicates*, in much the same way that we treat count nouns, like 'man', as predicates, like '*is a* man'. Then it is not clear what these predicates should be true *of* (sentences (a)–(c) suggest that there may be many answers to this). And it is not clear how we will analyze the complex predicates associated with complex mass nouns, such as 'blue styrofoam' and 'cheap metal'. Further if we do *not* represent mass nouns by names, then we may not be able to account for inferences like:

> x is made of gold
> *gold is the element with atomic number 79*
> x is made of the element with atomic number 79

On either view, the additional task of representing sentences like (g) will remain a problem. No analysis of (a)–(f) will be acceptable which does not allow of an extension to an analysis of (g); conversely, a successful treatment of (g) will be a strong point in favor of any analysis of (a)–(f).

III. THE ANALYSIS OF SENTENCES (a)–(c)

My policy throughout this paper will be to separate two problems: (1) the problem of giving an analysis which preserves the requisite logical relations and truth-conditions, and (2) the problem of giving a *nominalistic* analysis which preserves the requisite logical relations and truth conditions. I will be as Platonistic as I like in *producing* the analysis – on the grounds that this is usually the easiest way to proceed, and sometimes the only way to proceed. *Later* (Section VI) I will discuss the problem of producing a nominalistic analysis. It is my belief that even if one is firmly committed to some form of nominalism this is still the appropriate way to proceed. For it makes both problems easier. It is easier to produce an analysis if we don't overly concern ourselves with nominalistic strictures. And it is usually easier to nominalize an already given Platonistic analysis than to attempt a nominalistic analysis from scratch.

Adopting this procedure, we turn to sentences (a)–(c). We begin by supposing that we have a name, 'g', which names (refers to) the *substance*[6], gold. As a first pass we can analyze (a)–(c) as follows (our final analysis will be a logically equivalent variant of this). Sentence (a):

(a)   My ring is gold

becomes

(a_1) rCg,

where 'r' names my ring, and where 'C' means 'is constituted of', or 'is made of'. Thus (a_1) reads, roughly:

(a_2)   My ring is constituted of the substance gold.[7]

The exact sense of 'is constituted of' should be clear from the stipulation that (a_2) is to be the analysis of (a) – it is a relation between *objects* and *substances* which holds between o and s just in case o's matter (or an appropriate subpart thereof) is a quantity of s (I shall have more to say about both *substances* and *quantities* of substance below).

Sentence b:

(b)   The element with atomic number 79 is gold

is analyzed as

(b$_1$) $e = g$,

where '*e*' abbreviates the definite description 'the element with atomic number 79'. Thus, (b$_1$) reads roughly:

(b$_2$)   The element with atomic number 79 is identical with the substance gold.

Sentence (c):

(c)   The bit of matter which makes up my ring is gold

is analyzed as:

(c$_1$) mQg.

Here, '*m*' abbreviates 'the bit of matter which makes up my ring', and '*Q*' reads 'is a quantity of'. (c$_1$) reads:

(c$_2$)   The bit of matter which makes up my ring is a quantity of the substance gold.[8]

So far I have simply been following the suggestions that mass terms act as names, and spelling out the various ways in which the word 'is' must be construed so as to make this work.[9] But already we are involved in a fair amount of metaphysics – referring to substances (in the chemist's sense), objects, bits of matter, and quantities of substances. I will postpone a discussion of *substances* to Section V below; here I will say a little more about *bits* of matter and *quantities* of substances.

The notion of a bit of matter being a *quantity of* a substance (i.e., the notion expressed by '*Q*' above) is a primitive notion in my analysis. I can explain it roughly as follows: A substance, like gold, is found scattered around the universe in various places. Wherever it 'occurs' we will have a bit of matter which *is a quantity of* gold. This somewhat vaguely delimits the extension of the relation 'is a quantity of'. Another such delimitation is the following: if it is true to say of an object (a physical object) that it 'is gold', then the matter making it up will *be a quantity of* gold. *This* account must be qualified in various ways. I mean to exclude cases in which we say that the object 'is gold' because of its *color* (i.e., because it is gold-colored), and I also mean to exclude cases where the object is only 'partly gold' – e.g., a 'gold ring' with a diamond set in it. In this case only part of the matter of the ring (the *gold* part) is a quantity of gold. I also intend that the matter of *some subparts* of gold objects be quantities of gold – e.g., the matter of half of the band of the ring will be a quantity of gold. But not any old subpart will do – if we take sub-atomic sub-parts of the ring, say the neutrons of one of its atoms, then we do not have a quantity of gold (i.e., it is my intent to use 'is a quantity of' in this manner).

This should give us a fair idea of the meaning (or at least the extension) of 'is a quantity of' for quantities of *material* substances. I will return to 'non-material substances' at the end of this section. Now let me turn to the notion of a 'bit of matter'.

First, to resolve a potential ambiguity. Sometimes people distinguish between two entities: an object, and the matter which composes the object. Each of these are to occupy the same spatio-temporal region (for at least part of their duration), yet they are to be two distinct entities. I will discus this proposal further in Section VI. For the moment I will try to remain neutral on this issue of whether or not an object and its matter are two distinct entities, or one and the same entity. However, *if* the former line is taken, then I mean the locution 'bit of matter' to be true of the *matter of the object*, and not of the object itself.[10]

A second point needs to be made concerning bits of matter – this is that what will count as a 'bit of matter' is not to be restricted to bits making up 'ordinary objects'. For example, not only do we have the bit of matter making up this ring, we also have the bit of matter making up the lower half of this ring *and* the upper half of the nugget in the safe. More succinctly, bits of matter are to be 'Goodman individuals' – i.e., they are to obey the laws of the Goodman-Leonard Calculus of Individuals.

What this means in our case is, first of all, that we must have notions of (spatio-temporal) discreteness, overlapping, and a (spatio-temporal) part-whole relation (all of these being interdefinable in various ways). This much seems fairly straight-forward, given what has been said so far. In addition, we have some identity-conditions; where our variables range over bits of matter, we have:

$x = y \equiv (z) \, (z$ is part of $x \equiv z$ is part of $y)$.

And we also have conditions which compel us to treat amalgams of bits of matter as further bits of matter. In particular, when English letters range over bits of matter, and Greek letters over classes of bits of matter, we have:

$$(\exists x) \, x\varepsilon\alpha \, . \supset . \, (\exists y) \, yFu\alpha,$$

where $yFu\alpha$ ('y is the fusion of α') means that y is that bit of matter spatially coinciding with all of the members of α.[11] This exhausts most of the formal requirements on bits of matter – for the complete details see Goodman and Leonard.[12] Notice that there is no requirement that a bit of matter which is spatially extended have proper sub-parts which are themselves bits of matter. We might, for example, want to refrain from letting sub-atomic parts of atoms be bits of matter. What counts as a bit of matter is underdetermined at the sub-atomic level. This seems unobjectionable at this point – what we eventually want to count as a bit of matter cannot be determined until we have the whole analysis, and then it may depend on all sorts of scientific facts, facts about linguistic usage, etc.

So far I have discussed only cases where our mass term refers to *material substances*. But there are other sorts of mass terms; consider 'information', 'speed', etc. I see two possible ways of treating them.

First, recall that all that is required by my translations so far is references for simple occurrences of mass terms, plus meaningfulness of the locutions 'is made (composed) of' and 'is a quantity of'. The former locution will not occur with 'abstract' mass terms and we may ignore it. The latter, however, will be essential to the treatment of more complex sentences below.

Now one way to treat abstract mass terms would be to retain the translation procedure sketched so far, supposing that mass terms like 'information' and 'speed' (and perhaps sometimes 'goodness') name certain 'abstract substances', and supposing also that we understand what a 'quantity' of such a substance is. This would be a partial solution to our problems in that it would yield an analysis that would account for many valid inferences involving sentences with abstract mass terms. But we wouldn't really have a satisfactory interpretation of such sentences. Recall that the above explanation of our primitive terms dealt explicitly with material concepts, and does not carry over to the abstract case. We do not have a really clear notion of a *quantity of information*, and although we may have a notion of a *quantity of speed*, it is not clear that such quantities obey anything like the calculus of individuals. Similar remarks apply to quantities of goodness. So if we are to adopt this analysis, we must employ a rather ill-understood notion of 'quantity', a metaphorical extension of the spatio-temporal notion.

The second alternative involves construing sentences involving abstract mass terms and abstract property names as grammatically derivative from sentences without abstract mass terms, and to give a wholly different analysis of such sentences. For example, we might analyze 'The report didn't contain *much information*' as 'The report wasn't very informative'. This may be the most fruitful approach, but it awaits developments in grammar which are not expected in the near future.

In what follows, I will restrict myself to the analysis of 'concrete' mass terms, leaving the broader problem for future investigation.[13]

IV. MASS TERMS WITH QUANTIFIERS

We now turn to sentence (d):

(d)   Blue styrofoam is styrofoam.

To analyze this sentence we need to make two distinctions. First, we need to realize that (d) is inspecific; it can mean '*All* blue styrofoam is styrofoam', '*Some* blue styrofoam is styrofoam', '*Most* blue styrofoam is styrofoam', etc. These different readings of (d) will certainly have different analyses, for they are by no means equivalent.[14] Let us concentrate on the reading:

(d_1) All blue styrofoam is styrofoam.

The next distinction involves the reading of 'is styrofoam'. As we saw in the case of (a)–(c) above, this can be construed in at least three ways. However, having clarified the sense of (d) by adding *quantifiers* suggests that we take a reading of 'is styrofoam' which gives us something natural to quantify over. I suggest that we analyze (d_1) as:

(d_2) $(x) (Bx \ \& \ xQs \supset xQs)$,[15]

where '*s*' refers to the substance, styrofoam, where '*Bx*' means '*x* is blue', and where '*Q*' means 'is a quantity of', as above. Thus (d_2) reads:

(d_3) Every quantity of styrofoam which is blue is a quantity of styrofoam.

(d_2) displays the logical form of (d_1) in a natural manner, and its logical truth is seen to be a consequence of the ordinary rules of inference of the predicate calculus.[16]

This analysis, however, raises several problems. First, why not analyze (d_1) as:

(d_4) $(x) (Bx \ \& \ xCs \supset xCs)$,

i.e., as

(d_5)   Every object which is blue and which is made of styrofoam is made of styrofoam.

I don't believe that this is the correct analysis. For it confuses 'objects which are blue and made of styrofoam' with 'objects which are made of blue styrofoam'. These are not the same. If we make an ice chest out of blue styrofoam and then paint it pink, we have a pink (non-blue) object which is made of blue styrofoam.[17]

It may be, however, that there is *another* interpretation of (d), according to which we are not quantifiying over *quantities* of substance. This can be brought out by considering the sentence

(h)   Most gold is still unmined.

By analogy with (d_1) it looks as if we should analyze this as:

(h_1)   Most quantities of gold are still unmined.[18]

But this is a peculiar reading of (h). In the first place, it is not at all clear that it even makes sense, for, given unlimited means of isolating out quantities of gold, there might be an infinite number of them, and the notion of a majority of an infinite set is in general undefined. Yet no such difficulty seems to attend (h). Further, if we isolate out quantities of gold in some way that guarantees only a finite number of quantities, then (h_1) may differ in truth-value from (h). For example, if we only counted as quantities the bits of matter making up individual detached macroscopic nuggets or flakes, then (h) could be true, while (h_1) was false. (Just imagine that all of the unmined gold is in a single enormous nugget under a mountain in South Africa. Then only *one* quantity remains unmined, but if the nugget is large enough, *most gold* remains unmined.)

The correct analysis of (h) seems to be this:

(h₂)   The quantity of unmined gold exceeds the quantity of mined gold.[19]

We see that the quantifier 'most' preceding mass terms introduces certain complications. But fortunately no such complexity need attend our re-reading of the original (d). Remember that the point of considering sentence (h) was to illustrate the difference between 'Most (all, some, ...) gold' and 'Most (all, some, ...) *quantities of* gold'. In the case of 'most', these readings are *not* equivalent, but fortunately in the case of 'all' and 'some' they *are* equivalent, at least insofar as truth conditions are concerned. For, 'all gold is ____' is true if and only if 'every quantity of gold is ____', and 'some gold is ____' is true if and only if 'some quantity of gold is ____'. Thus our original interpretation of (d₁) (namely, (d₂)) is correct.[20]

Interim Summary: A: Sentences in which mass nouns stand alone, unmodified and unquantified, are analysed as if the mass nouns were names; B: Sentences in which quantifier locutions precede mass terms (either as they stand, or introduced in order to resolve ambiguity) are to be analyzed in terms of quantification over mass quantities. With few exceptions the analysis is quite straightforward (some exceptions in addition to 'most' are 'much', 'a lot of', 'a little'). We thus have a *partial* solution of the problem posed by complex mass nouns.[21]

V. COMPLEX NAMES OF SUBSTANCES

Now let us turn to sentences (e) and (f):

(e)   Water is widespread.
(f)   Muddy water is widespread.

It would be simple enough to write (e) as an assertion about the substance, water; we could write it as

(e₁) Sw,

where 'Sx' means 'x is widespread', and 'w' names the substance, water. But (f) is harder to treat this way, for (f) contains a *complex* term 'muddy water'.

We solved the problem of complex mass terms above by analyzing their use in terms of quantification over *quantities* of substance; perhaps something like that can be done here.

A clue to a possible analysis can be found by comparing (e) and (f) with similar assertions involving count nouns.

Consider:

(i)   Men are widespread.

(j)   Virtuous men are widespread.

(k)   Mankind is widespread.

(l)   The class of clever men is small.

(m)   The property of being a virtuous man is no longer held to be very important.

In each of (i)–(m) the subject-term must be treated in a special way; these subject-terms are taken to refer not to men, clever men, or virtuous men, but rather to the *class* of (clever, virtuous) men or the *property* of being a (clever, virtuous) man. The following analogy suggests itself: we compare individual quantities of water with men, the substance, water, with the class of men, and the property of being a quantity of water with the property of being a man.

Now, analogies are cheap, as are disanalogies. The point of *this* analogy is merely to suggest that, in general, to talk about substances, we need some sort of higher-order terminology like class terminology in the case of count nouns. Granted, we seem not to need such terminology in *some* cases; we already have names for substances like water, gold, etc. But likewise we already have the name 'mankind' for the class of men. Neither of these facts mitigates the necessity for a more complex terminology when we turn to *complex* terms. We have no simple names for the class of clever men who love their mothers, nor for the substance, muddy water (although we introduce such names when they are useful; e.g., for 'leaded tin' we have 'zinc'; for 'frozen water' we have 'ice', etc.).

I suggest, then, that we introduce a 'substance abstraction' operator, on a par with the class abstraction operator. Let us use $\sigma x[...]$ for the substance abstraction operator. Inside the brackets go formulas which are true of *quantities* of a substance (pursuing the analogy suggested above). The resulting term is to refer to that substance which has as quantities all and only things which the formula inside is true of; i.e., we are to have:

$xQ\sigma y[...y...]$ if and only if $...x...$[22]

We can then form the following substance terms:

(n)   muddy water: $\sigma x[Mx \ \& \ xQw]$
(o)   water: $\sigma x[xQw]$
(p)   leaded tin that has been annealed: $\sigma x[xQt \ \& \ Lx \ \& \ Ax]$[23].

Notice that (o) is no more peculiar than corresponding class terms; for example, if 'm' names mankind, then we can also write 'm' as '$\{x:x\varepsilon m\}$'. Possession of simple names for some classes merely makes part of our terminology redundant.

We can now analyze sentences (e) and (f). Sentence (e) can be written *either* as:

(e$_1$) Sw

or as:

(e$_2$) $S\sigma x[xQw]$,

and (f) is analyzed as:

(f$_1$) $S\sigma x[Mx \ \& \ xQw]$.

Roughly speaking, when mass terms do *not* appear with quantifiers, either explicitly or implicitly, we translate them as complex names referring to substances, forming these names in the natural manner with the operator $\sigma x[... x ...]$. (See Appendix for more explicit details.) The simplest *general* approach is now to revise our earlier translations of (a)–(c), to make them instances of our present general procedure. Thus (a):

(a)   My ring is gold,

which we formerly translated as:

(a$_1$) rCg

will now translate as

(a$_2$) $rC\sigma x[xQg]$,

which is logically equivalent to (a$_1$) (see next section).

VI. ONTOLOGICAL SIMPLIFICATIONS

We have talked, rather Platonistically, of three sorts of entities: physical objects, substances, and bits of matter. In this section I will digress momentarily, and consider two proposals for simplifying our ontology.[24]

A. Substances are bits.

The most plausible ontological reduction consists in identifying substances with the sum of the bits of matter making them up. Explicitly, this would mean adopting the identity:

$$\sigma x [\ldots x \ldots] = (\imath y)\, yFu\{x: \ldots x \ldots\}$$

for all substance-terms.

This proposal is independent of the translation procedure sketched in earlier sections, in the sense that we can adopt it without altering that procedure at all. The only advantage it offers us, so far as translation is concerned, is to replace the primitive '$\sigma x[\ldots x \ldots]$' with a definition, '$(\imath y)\, yFu\{x: \ldots x \ldots\}$'. But since the latter notation was only used in the informal explication of what is to count as a 'bit of matter', and not in the translation procedure itself, replacement of the former by the latter does not even reduce the number of primitives employed in the translation procedure.

Nevertheless, the proposal does yield a simpler ontology, it also makes it unnecessary to perform a 'philosophical abstraction' in order to distinguish a substance from its spatio-temporally coincident Goodman-individual, and it places stricter conceptual bounds on our notion of 'substance', presumably thereby making it clearer. Unfortunately, we might have to buy such advantages at the price of truth, for a case can be made that this move will get the identity-conditions of substances wrong. Let me explain. Sums of bits of matter are individuated spatio-temporally, in the sense that any two bits which spatio-temporally coincide are one and the same bit. Let us suppose, then, that all the salt (sodium chloride) in the universe is (and has always been) gathered together and piled up in a single room, r (non-counterfactual examples are possible, but more complex to describe). Now consider the two descriptions:

$$xQs$$
$$xQm,$$

where s = salt, and m = matter in room r. Since s and m coincide spatio-temporally, we have:

$$(\imath y)\, yFu\{x:xQs\} = (\imath y)\, yFu\{x:xQm\}$$

or simplifying:

$$s = m\,^{25}.$$

In summary, the principle at issue entails that any two substances that coincide spatio-temporally are identical. But this cannot be true, since there are quantities of m that are not quantities of s – just take any sodium ion. Or to take another two mass terms, consider 'wood' and 'furniture'. Even if all and only furniture were composed of wood, it would not follow that wood = furniture, since parts of chairs might be wood without being furniture.[25a]

I conclude that the first ontological simplification is quite dubious – it would be nice if it were true, but substance terms just don't behave that way.

B. A second proposal is to identify physical objects with the bits of matter making them up. Again this would have no effect on the translation procedure sketched above.

Such a move requires a certain amount of care. First of all, a physical object cannot be identified with just any old bit of matter with which it happens to coincide at a given moment. For at a later time, the object and that bit of matter might diverge. This possibility can be denied only by requiring that identity conditions for bits of matter coincide with those for ordinary objects – a requirement that I haven't imposed and which I see no reason for imposing (I have been presuming that any macroscopic, 'filled' spatio-temporal region defines a bit of matter).

However, a weaker thesis might be plausible – the thesis that any physical object is identical with that bit of matter which coincides with it throughout its duration. For example, let m_1 = that bit of matter consisting entirely of the atoms which at the moment make up object o. Presumably m_1 came into being when all of these atoms had been formed, perhaps long before o was around. Further, o may have been present before o and m_1 came to coincide (consider a person and the atoms now making him up – both he and they came into being long before they came to make him up). Now let

$m_2 =$ that bit of matter which coincides with o throughout o's duration.[26] Notice that at the present moment, o, m_1, and m_2 all coincide spatially, and that at other times o and m_2 will coincide with one another, but perhaps not with m_1.

Now we can, at *most*, identify o with m_2; in general, we might identify objects with the bits of matter which coincide with them *throughout* their duration. Even this view has its difficulties, but it is not clear that any of them are fatal.[27]

VII. AMOUNT TERMS: SENTENCE (g)

The remaining puzzles concern terms like '3 gallons', '21 ounces', '21 ounces of gold', etc. I will first propose a systematic treatment of these terms that will be overly platonistic for some tastes. I will then consider a nominalistic reconstrual.

We can distinguish two sorts of 'amount' terms, those containing merely a numeral plus a unit of measure (e.g., 'three gallons') and those containing, in addition, the word 'of' plus a mass term (e.g., 'three gallons *of water*'). I will call the first sort 'isolated amount terms' and the second sort 'applied amount terms'. Our sentence:

(g)   Three teaspoons of gold weigh thirty ounces

contains an isolated amount term as direct object of the verb, and an applied amount term as subject.

The platonistic account takes the simple-minded view that an isolated amount term names an abstract entity – an amount. For example, '3 gallons' names a certain amount: the amount, 3 gallons; 'one pound' names a different amount; '16 ounces' names the same amount as does 'one pound'.

We will represent isolated amount-terms as follows: for each unit of measure (e.g., 'gallon', 'quart', 'pound', 'heap'[28]) we introduce a relational predicate. For example, corresponding to 'gallon' we have 'xGy', where the first variable ranges over numbers, and the second over amounts. Filling in the first place with a numeral yields a term that specifies an amount. For example, corresponding to 'three gallons', we have the formula '$3Gy$' which is true of the amount, three gallons, and nothing else.

An *applied* amount term like 'three gallons of water' will be analyzed something like 'a quantity of water which (is not identical with, but) measures 3 gallons'. For example, the sentence:

Every bucket contains three gallons of water

would be translated as:

$$(x)\ (Bx \supset (\exists y)(3Gy\ \&\ (\exists z)\ (zQw\ \&\ zMy\ \&\ xCz)))$$

(where 'zMy' means 'z measures y' and 'xCz' means 'x contains z').

We see that the role of the word 'of' in 'three gallons *of water*' is taken in our symbolism by the primitive term 'M' (which we read as 'measures').

Our sentence, (g):

Three teaspoons of gold weighs thirty ounces.

(when construed as '*Any* three teaspoons of gold weighs thirty ounces.') now translates as:

$$(x)\ ((\exists y)\ (3Ty\ \&\ xQg\ \&\ xMy) \supset (\exists z)\ (30Oz\ \&\ x\ \text{weighs}\ z)).\ [29]$$

Sentences relating isolated amounts with one another are treated quite naturally; for example:

One pound equals 16 ounces.

becomes:

$$(\exists x)\ (1Px\ \&\ (\exists y)\ (16Oy\ \&\ xEy)).[29]$$

The foregoing treatment of amount-terms is platonistic in that it treats amounts as abstract standards against which to measure concrete quantities (for a catchy parallel, read 'x measures y' as 'x participates in y'). I will discuss two proposals for deplatonizing that account. The first makes the 'Forms' (our *amounts*) concrete; the second involves giving up their role as standards. The first is unworkable; I am not sure about the second.

The first proposal exploits a familiar parallel often used in explaining Plato's theory of meaning. The parallel is between Forms like the Good, the Virtuous, etc., and standards like the standard meter stick in Paris – these Forms are supposed to function in discovering goodness, virtues, etc., in (metaphorically) the same way that the standard meter is used to discover length. There is no *standard good man* anywhere, so the Form, the Good, cannot be a concrete object (i.e., a man) stored somewhere in Paris – instead, it must be an *abstract* entity. But in the case of measures, there *are* concrete standards available – the standard meter in Paris, the standard pound in Washington, etc. Why not replace our *abstract amounts* by those concrete objects which constitute the standards upon which our systems of measures are based? The only other alteration we would need would be to reinterpret 'measures' as 'measures the same as', 'weighs' as 'weighs the same as', etc.

There are several problems with such a proposal, at least one of which is fatal: although it is plausible for phrases like '*one* gallon', '*one* meter', it is unworkable for phrases like '3 gallons', '$7\frac{1}{2}$ meters'. For there is no *standard concrete object* which is $7\frac{1}{2}$ meters long, and no *standard concrete container* which contains exactly 3 gallons. We cannot replace our infinite array of amounts with a finite number of concrete standards *without* making drastic changes elsewhere in the theory. The second approach does this.

The second approach is analogous to Quine's disposal of meanings[30], where he paraphrases individual contexts which seem to involve quantification over meanings into unanalyzed predicates and relations. E.g., 'has a meaning' becomes 'is meaningful' (or 'is significant'), 'have the same meaning' becomes 'are synonymous', 'is true in virtue of meaning' becomes 'is analytic'. If we can do something similar for *all* contexts involving amounts, without loss of logical inferences, then we will have nominalized our treatment.

Our amount terms occur in two sorts of context: isolated and coupled with mass terms. The latter sort of context will always utilize a complex formula of the form:

$$(\exists y)\,(nGy \ \& \ xMy) \ \& \ \phi x,$$

where 'n' is a numeral, 'G' a relational predicate representing a unit of measure, 'M' the predicate we read 'measures', and 'ϕ' some condition on x (e.g., 'ϕx' may be 'xQg'). Suppose that for every unit of measure, 'G', we introduce another relational predicate '$\bar{G}$' which has the meaning:

$$n\bar{G}x =_{df} x \text{ measures } nG\text{'s},$$

e.g., for 'gallon' we would read '$n\bar{G}x$' as '(the quantity) x measures n gallons'. This term is to replace the '$(\exists y)\,(nGy \ \& \ xMy)$' above, and it by-passes quantification over amounts. Of course, the Platonist will insist on analyzing '$n\bar{G}x$' as '$(\exists y)\,(nGy \ \& \ xMy)$', just as he will also insist on analyzing 'x is meaningful' as

'$(\exists y)$ (y is a meaning & x has y)';

but the nominalist need not do this.

This device will work for applied amount terms. But now it is unclear how to treat *isolated* amount terms. These, in turn, occur in two sorts of problematic contexts. First we have contexts of the form 'x weighs n pounds'. Previously this expressed a relation between x and n *pounds*. But now, 'n pounds' no longer names anything. Presumably what we need to do here is to refuse to divorce the 'weighs' from the 'n pounds' – i.e., to treat 'weighs n pounds' as a unit, just as we did 'n pounds of –'. The required analysis seems to be that 'x weighs n pounds' be written '$n\bar{P}x$', where '$\bar{P}$' is our new analogue of 'pounds'. On this line, 'weighs' is just a dummy word which gets absorbed into the '$n\bar{P}x$'.

The second sort of problematic context is that in which amount terms appear as subjects of sentences like:

(i)   One pound equals 16 ounces.
(j)   Three pounds is a unit of measure.

We would *perhaps* analyze (i) in an *ad hoc* manner as:

(i₁) $(x)(1\bar{P}x \supset (y)(16\bar{O}y \supset xEy))$

i.e., as 'Every one-pound quantity is equal (in weight) to every 16-ounce quantity'. But I don't see how to give a *general* account along these lines. And I see no plausible analysis of (j) along these lines, or along any nominalistic lines at all.

APPENDIX[31]

The goal of this appendix is to describe in brief terms a procedure for translating a fragment of English into a canonical notation, and then to show how to extend this procedure to a larger fragment including mass terms and amount terms. First the fragment without mass terms.

Suppose we begin with those sentences of English that contain no English connectives, no attributive adjectives, no relative clauses, no pronouns which 'refer back' to preceding locutions, no prepositional clauses, infinitive clauses, or gerundive clauses (or other unspecified grammatically complex constructions). In the terminology of transformational grammar, we are beginning with sentences generated from simple phrase structure sentences, without recursive embeddings of sentences within sentences.[32] Even this is a relatively rich fragment of English, including sentences like 'some men might have been talking with Agatha under an arch during Lent'. Translated into canonical notation such sentences become conglomerates of quantifiers, connectives, operators, predicates, and proper names. Momentarily ignoring constructions that give rise to operators (i.e., ignoring 'might', 'have been ...-ing', 'with', 'under' and 'during') we are left with the transformational grammarian's *Nominals*: 'some men', 'Agatha', 'an arch', 'Lent', plus the verb: 'talk'. Notice that the *Nominals* are just those phrases that Russell called denoting phrases, and the key to their translation is essentially due to him.[33]

Each simple denoting phrase, or Nominal, consists of a quantifier locution (called by transformational grammar a *determiner*) plus a noun (count noun or proper noun, so far). The determiner may be unspoken as in 'Agatha', grammatically it is there however. In t-grammar it appears as the null morph, ϕ, preceding the noun.[34]

Our schema for translating Nominals is as follows: the determiner of the Nominal provides a matrix which has two places for predicates or formulas. The first place is for a predicate or formula provided by the noun of the Nominal, and the second place is for a predicate or formula provided by the rest of the sentence in question. I indicate these places by '$\textcircled{1}_x$' and '$\textcircled{2}_x$'. The noun portion of the Nominal translates as a one-place predicate, which, in translation, is inserted in the $\textcircled{1}$ place of the matrix provided by the determiner. Most verbs translate as one- or two-place predicates. The translation problem then is two-fold: to say what each particular sentential constituent contributes to the translation, and to say how these constituents are ordered in the resulting translation.

To take a simple case suppose we wish to translate 'Some man kicks John'. The matrix for 'some' is:

$$(\exists x)\,(\textcircled{1}x \,\&\, \textcircled{2}x);$$

the predicate associated with 'man' is:

$$M$$

(read 'Mx' as 'x is a man'). The verb 'kicks' yields the two-place predicate:

$$K$$

(read 'Kxy' as 'x kicks y'). Preceding 'John' we have the null morph determiner ϕ; its matrix (when preceding a proper noun) is also:

$$(\exists x)\,(\textcircled{1}\,x \;\&\; \textcircled{2}\,x).$$

The proper noun, 'John', yields the one-place predicate:

$$J$$

(read 'Jx' as 'x is John').[35]

Our simple sentence: 'Some man kicks John', has the grammatical analysis:

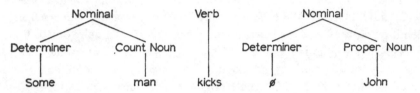

The rule for translation is simply to insert appropriate items in the matrices contributed by the determiners, continuing this process until we get sentences (we have to keep variables straight while doing this – I won't go into detail on that). For example, we can insert 'J' and 'K' into the matrix contributed by ϕ, getting:

(i) $(\exists y)\,(Jy \;\&\; Kxy)$

and then insert 'M' and (i) into the matrix contributed by 'some', getting as one possible translation:

(ii) $(\exists x)\,(Mx \;\&\; (\exists y)\,(Jy \;\&\; Kxy)).$

Alternatively, we could have started with the 'Some' matrix, in which case we would have ended up with:

(iii) $(\exists y)\,(Jy \;\&\; (\exists x)\,(Mx \;\&\; Kxy)).$

(ii) and (iii) are the only two translations of the sentence in question, and they turn out to be equivalent. This doesn't always happen; the translations of 'Some man dates every girl' are:

(iv) $(\exists x)\,(Mx \;\&\; (y)\,(Gy \supset Dxy))$

and

(v) $(y)\,(Gy \supset (\exists x)\,(Mx \;\&\; Dxy)).$

(The matrix associated with 'every' is: '$(x)\,(①x \supset ②x)$'.) These are not equivalent but that is appropriate – since the English sentence being translated is ambiguous.[36]

Operators: Many other sentential constituents contribute operators as their translations. Adverbs and modals do this. For example, in 'John may write slowly', both 'may' and 'slowly' translate as operators which operate on predicates to produce more complex predicates. The whole sentence translates as:

$$(\exists x)\,(Jx \,\&\, \Diamond\,(S(W))\,x),$$

where '$\Diamond$' represents 'may' and 'S' represents 'slowly'.[37] Prepositions also behave like operators, although they add argument-places to the verb phrase. For example, 'ran into' is represented as '$I(R)$', where '$I(R)\,xy$' means 'x ran into y'; the extra variable, y, being contributed by 'into'. Prepositional objects, e.g., 'the church' in 'John ran into the church', are denoting phrases, and are analyzed as sketched above.[38]

Relative Clauses: A first natural step beyond the simple sentences we have considered so far is the addition of restrictive relative clauses.[39] These are sentential-like constituents which are inserted into Nominals immediately following nouns. They provide predicates or formulas which, in translation, are conjoined with the ① place in the matrix contributed by the determiner in the original Nominal. For example, 'Some man is dead' is translated by inserting 'M' and 'D' into '$(\exists x)\,(①x \,\&\, ②x)$'; then 'Some man who shot a giraffe is dead' is translated by conjoining '$(\exists y)\,(Gy \,\&\, Sxy)$' (i.e., '$x$ shot a giraffe') with 'Mx' before inserting it in ①. The result is:

$$(\exists x)\,(Mx \,\&\, (\exists y)\,(Gy \,\&\, Sxy) \,\&\, Dx).[40]$$

Adjectives: Adjectives in attributive position (immediately preceding nouns) are best translated uniformly as operators on the predicate contributed by the noun.[41] In some cases, these operators can be further analyzed in terms of conjunction with a predicate. For example, 'Some red box ...' can be translated as '$(\exists x)\,(R(B)\,x \,\&\,...)$', and then '$R(B)\,x$' can be further analyzed as '$R'x \,\&\, Bx$' – i.e., we further analyze 'x is a red box' as 'x is red and a box'. But 'Some fake gun ...', which will be translated as '$(\exists x)\,(F(G)\,x \,\&\,...)$' cannot be further analyzed as '$(\exists x)\,(F'x \,\&\, Gx \,\&\,...)$', since 'fake' has no determinate extension apart from a 'filler' like 'gun'.

More Complex Constructions: I have sketched barely enough of a procedure to account for the sentences that have been treated in this paper. But there is no reason to suppose that mass nouns present problems in grammatically complex constructions (such as propositional, infinitival or gerundive clauses) which they do not already present in the simple constructions discussed here.

Mass Terms: One advantage of the treatment of mass terms sketched in the main body of the paper is that it can be assimilated into the present translation procedure with a minimum of effort. We need only say what predicates are contributed by mass terms, and what modifications are necessary in the translations of determiners when they precede mass terms. The predicates are easy: associated with *every* simple mass noun, m, is the predicate 'xQm'. (Complex predicates due to complex mass terms like 'muddy water' or 'bronze that has been annealed' are formed automatically by the translation rules for attributive adjectives ('muddy') and for relative clauses ('that has been annealed').) Further, most determiners translate in exactly the same way, whether they precede mass nouns or whether they precede count nouns. The only cases that need special treatment are the zero morph, ϕ, and a few determiners like 'most' and 'much'.

As for the zero morph, recall that:

ϕ-men-are-clever

is ambiguous, meaning 'all men are clever', 'some men are clever', 'most men are clever', etc. That is, the null morph, ϕ, when it precedes count nouns, can produce all of the matrices:

$$(x)\,(① \supset ②)$$
$$(\exists x)\,(① \,\&\, ②)$$
$$(\text{Most } x)\,(①, ②)$$
etc.

Excluding 'most', there is no difference between these cases and the mass noun cases – cf. Section III. The difference comes in contexts like:

ϕ-men-are-widespread

where the null morph contributes the matrix:

$$(\exists x)\,(x = \{y: ①y\} \,\&\, ②x).$$

This yields the translation:

$$(\exists x)\,(x = \{y : My\}\ \&\ Sx)$$

(which is equivalent to $S\{y : My\}$ – i.e., 'the class of men is widespread').

For corresponding contexts with mass terms, the matrix contributed by the null morph must be: [42]

$$(\exists x)\,(x = \sigma y\,[\textcircled{1}y]\ \&\ \textcircled{2}x).$$

For example, 'water is widespread' translates:

$$(\exists x)\,(x = \sigma y\,[yQw]\ \&\ Sx),$$

which is equivalent to

$$S\sigma y\,[yQw]$$

(which is in turn equivalent to 'Sw'; cf. Section V).

Except for treatment of determiners like 'most' [43] and 'much' our procedure now grinds out all of the translations discussed in Sections I–VI of the paper – or equivalent variants thereof. [44]

Amount Terms: These terms appear in two sorts of contexts: embedded within complex determiners, as in 'two *quarts* of', 'several *pounds* of'; and outside of determiners, as in 'one *pound* equals 16 *ounces*'.

First, the applied amount terms (embedded within determiners). I'll give the platonistic account; its nominalistic reconstrual is discussed in Section VII above. The usual cases are those in which the amount terms occur with numerals. Let 'n' be a numeral, and let 'G' be a sample amount-term, say 'gallon' (then 'nGx' means 'x is the amount, n gallons', as in Section VII). Then the phrase 'n gallons of' contributes a formula which, in translation, is to be conjoined with the noun predicate contributed by the noun which follows it. The phrase it contributes is:

$$(\exists z)\,(nGz\ \&\ xMz)$$

(where 'M' reads 'measures'; cf. Section VII above).

When nothing else is present in the determiner, the whole matrix is $(\exists x)\,((\exists z)\,(nGz\ \&\ xMz)\ \&\ \textcircled{1}x\ \&\ \textcircled{2}x)$.

For example, in the sentence

(g)   Every bucket contains three gallons of water.

the Nominal 'three gallons of water' translates as (filling in the noun predicate):

$$(\exists x)\,((\exists z)\,(3Gz \ \& \ xMz)\ \& \ xQw\ \& \ ...\ x\ ...).$$

Inserting this in the part contributed by 'every bucket', and adding the predicate for 'contains', this yields

$$(y)\,(By \supset (\exists x)\,((\exists z)\,(3Gz\ \& \ xMz)\ \& \ xQw\ \& \ yCx))$$

as in Section VII.

Occasionally an explicit determiner occurs before the amount term; in such cases, that determiner fixes the containing matrix. For example, in 'Every three gallons of water ...' the word 'every' tells us that we are to conjoin the amount-term phrase with the noun predicate within the normal matrix for 'every', namely '$(x)\,(\textcircled{1}x \supset \textcircled{2}x)$'. Thus 'Every three gallons of water ...' translates as '$(x)\,((\exists z)\,(3Gz\ \& \ xMz)\ \& \ xQw \supset \textcircled{2}x)$'. When an explicit determiner occurs before the amount term, but no numeral appears, the number 1 is understood. For example, 'Every gallon of water weighs 62.4 pounds' translates as '$(x)\,((\exists z)\,(1Gz\ \& \ xMz)\ \& \ xQw \supset ...)$'.[45]

Isolated amount-terms are the easiest to translate. Their noun-predicates are all of the form 'nGx', and their determiners translate as '$(\exists x)\,(\textcircled{1}x\ \& \ \textcircled{2}x)$'. Thus 'One pound equals sixteen ounces' translates as '$(\exists x)\,(1Px\ \& \ (\exists y)\,(16Oy\ \& \ x=y))$'.

Chicago Circle

NOTES

[1] I have benefited particularly from discussions with Fred Feldman, Kathryn Pyne Parsons, Brian Skyrms, Paul Ziff and other faculty and students at Chicago Circle. Research on this paper was partially supported by NSF grant GS 2087.

² As a rough guide, a noun is being used as a mass noun if it is being used in a sense in which it would make sense to precede the word, as used, by 'much' (this suggestion is due to Rita Nolan). Another hint is that, with few exceptions, mass nouns do not have plural forms. Thus 'chickens' is always a count noun. (The exceptions I know of are some uses of 'potatoes' and 'beans'.) Some abstract nouns seem to have mass noun uses. For example, in 'There isn't much goodness in him', 'goodness' seems to be a mass noun (this point is due to Ruth Marcus). On the other hand, 'goodness' *seems* to be a proper noun in 'Goodness is a property'. Grammatically, abstract nouns closely resemble mass nouns; but I have reservations about whether I can analyze them – see the end of Section III.

³ For example, I am not concerned that the translation and the original sentence should be 'about the same things', if this is not reflected in their truth-conditions.

⁴ W. V. Quine, *Word and Object*, Wiley, New York, 1960, esp. Sections 19–21.

⁵ Quine treats mass terms "before 'is' " as names and "after 'is' " as predicates (cf. p. 97). For discussion of this proposal see notes 7, 8, 15, 21, 22 below.

⁶ I use the word 'subtance' in the chemist's sense – to stand for any *material*.

⁷ Quine does not analyze mass terms following 'is' as names; rather he analyzes the whole predicate (including 'is') as a single atomic predicate. For example, he would analyze (a) as:

(a') *Gr*.

But his explanation of such predicates cannot apply to sentences like (a). For these predicates are to be "true of each portion of the stuff in question, excluding only the parts too small to count" (*op. cit.* p. 98). Presumably this means that '*G*' is to be true of each portion of gold. But for (a') to be true, '*G*' must be true of the referent of '*r*' – namely my ring. This causes two difficulties:

(i) it is not clear that my ring, a physical *object*, is a portion of stuff at all (see Section VI for a discussion of this point);
and
(ii) if it is a portion of stuff, it is not a portion of gold, but rather a portion of gold plus a portion of gem (a portion of gold-gem?).

⁸ Quine objects to this analysis. He says: "... the idea suggests itself of ... treating mass terms thus as singular terms ... after the copula. It may seem that this can be done by reconstruing 'is' in such contexts as 'is a part of'. But this version fails, because there are parts of water, sugar and furniture too small to count as water, sugar, furniture. Moreover, what is too small to count as furniture is not too small to count as water or sugar; *so the limitation needed cannot be worked into any general adaptation of 'is' or 'is a part of'*, but must be left rather as the separate reference-dividing business of the several mass terms, conceived as general terms" (*op. cit.* p. 99) (my italics).

I take it that my 'is a quantity of' is an adaptation of Quine's 'is a part of'. It does not, of course, mean 'is a part of', for the reasons Quine gives. But Quine's objection to *any* such adaptation does not hold. Which 'parts' of *x* are quantities of *x* depends on *x*, and not just on some abstract notion of 'part'. See my discussion below.

⁹ I.e., in terms of a general translation procedure into canonical notation, the suggestion so far is that for sentences like (a)–(c) we merely treat mass terms as names (of substances), bearing in mind the ambiguities of 'is' exposed by comparison of (a)–(c).

¹⁰ This phrase, 'bit of matter', is a technical one. Ordinarily a locution of the form '– of –', e.g., 'nugget of gold', is used to refer to an *object*. It is only by a non-ordinary-language philosophical abstraction that we acquire the notion of the matter of an object; thus the technical jargon.

Many of my remarks about bits of matter parallel Quine's remarks about the references of mass terms. Cf. pp. 95, 98–99 *op. cit.*

[11] It's strict definition is:

$$yFu\alpha =_{df} (z) \ (z \text{ is discrete from } y \equiv z \text{ is discrete from every member of } \alpha).$$

[12] Nelson Goodman and Henry S. Leonard, 'The Calculus of Individuals and Its Uses', *Journal of Symbolic Logic* **5** (1940), No. 2. Goodman and Leonard take the relation of (for our purposes, spatio-temporal) *discreteness* as primitive. The part-relation is defined as:

$$x \text{ is part of } y =_{df} (z) \ (z \text{ is discrete from } y \supset z \text{ is discrete from } x).$$

In addition to the two axioms cited, they have, for any x and y:

$$(\exists \ z) \ (u) \ (u \text{ is discrete from } x \lor u \text{ is discrete from } y \supset u \text{ is discrete from } z) \equiv x \text{ is not discrete from } y.$$

We may or may not want to add a requirement that bits of matter have atomic parts (i.e., parts which themselves have no smaller parts which are bits of matter). Cf. A Tarski, Appendix E of Woodger, J. H., *Axiomatic Method in Biology*, Cambridge University Press, Cambridge, England, 1937.

[13] I have omitted mention of certain non-concrete but spatially extended 'materials' such as shadow, shade, room (in the sense of 'there wasn't much *room* between them'), etc. These should probably be treated on a par with material substances, expanding our notion of 'bit of matter' to cover these as well (if we do this we should then give up the word 'matter'; I don't know of a good substitute for it).

[14] This is no peculiarity of mass nouns; the same phenomenon occurs with count nouns – cf. 'Men are clever'.

[15] Quine says that in sentences like (d₁) 'blue' "must be treated as a mass term" (*op. cit.* p. 104). I don't know why he says this; he gives no reason why one might object to analyses like (d₂). Adjectives like 'blue' in attributive position *can* be treated as mass terms, but the resulting analysis would be more complex than that given here. It's not clear what Quine would say about phrases like 'styrofoam which has been pressure molded'; i.e., whether he would treat 'has been pressure molded' as a mass term, on a parallel with *his* treatment of attributive adjectives, or whether he would treat it as a normal predicate, on a par with *my* treatment of attributive adjectives.

[16] It might be maintained that it is incorrect to analyze 'All blue styrofoam …' as 'All quantities of blue styrofoam …' and then to analyze *this* as 'All quantities of styrofoam which are blue …', on the grounds that the next to last phrase does not mean the same as the last phrase. A proposed counterexample might be 'All fake styrofoam is styrofoam', which cannot be analyzed in the way we have sketched, since 'All quantities of fake styrofoam …' doesn't mean 'All quantities of styrofoam which are fake …'. In fact, the sentence 'All fake styrofoam is styrofoam' is not even true, let alone logically true – although our analysis would seem to indicate that it should be logically true.

The 'solution' to this problem is to point to the corresponding phenomenon in the case of *count* nouns. We unhesitatingly represent 'All clever doctors are doctors' as the logically true '$(x) \ (Cx \& Dx \supset Dx)$', in spite of the fact that 'All fake doctors are doctors' is not logically true. Words like 'fake' interfere with our ordinary modes of translation. The best way to treat such adjectives is to translate them as *operators* which precede the predicates they modify. Thus 'All fake doctors are doctors' would be represented as '$(x)(F(D)x \supset Dx)$' which will not be logically true. And our problem sentence will be handled the same way: 'All fake styrofoam is styrofoam' will translate as '$(x)(xF(Q)s \supset xQs)$'.

Phrases like 'white gold', 'fool's gold' represent another sort of case; these *can* be treated as just described, but it seems more in accordance with usage to treat them as *simple* mass nouns, whose meanings are not simple functions of the meanings of their constituents (i.e., as idioms).

[17] This alone does not show that we would get the truth-values of any sentence wrong if we amalgamate 'all blue styrofoam' to 'all blue objects which are made of styrofoam'. An example which *does* show this is the following: Suppose all blue styrofoam is granular, while pink styrofoam is not. And suppose there are objects made of pink styrofoam which have been painted blue. Then it is *false* that 'all blue objects which are made of styrofoam are granular' (or perhaps '... are made of something which is granular'). But this is the suggested analysis of our sentence 'all blue styrofoam is granular', which we assumed to be true. So the suggested analysis is incorrect.

[18] In symbolic notation (h_1) is: (Most x) $(xQg, -Mx)$. I write 'Most A's are B's' using the quantifier '(Most x)' which governs *two* sentences, instead of one. I.e., we write 'Most A's are B's' as '(Most x) (Ax, Bx)'. John Wallace first called my attention to this quantifier. (Cf. J. Wallace, *Philosophical Grammar*, doctoral dissertation, Stanford, 1964.)

It is possible to write 'All A's are B's' in this form also – i.e., as '(All x) (Ax, Bx)'. We do not do so because *this* locution can be analyzed in terms of the universal quantifier 'Every x is such that' plus the connective 'if ... then ...'; i.e., '(All x) (Ax, Bx)' is analyzed as '$(x) (Ax \supset Bx)$'. However, 'most' can*not* be analyzed in terms of any one-placed quantifier plus connectives, and we must leave it expressed as above.

[19] This shows another way in which (h) is inspecific; it does not specify whether the quantity of unmined gold exceeds that of mined gold in *weight*, in *volume*, in *number of pieces*, or what.

Even spelling out the analysis (h_2) requires a certain amount of complication. The simplest formula seems to be:

$$(\exists x) (\exists y) (xFu\{z:zQg \& Uz\} \& y = g - x \& xEy),$$

where 'Uz' means 'z is totally unmined', where $x-y$ is the Goodman-individual got by removing y from x, if it exists, and where "xEy" means "x exceeds y".

('x is totally unmined' can be defined in terms of 'x is totally mined' as follows:

$$Ux =_{\mathrm{df}} (y) (y \text{ is part of } x \supset -My).)$$

[20] The only reservation we might have here concerns sentences like:

(e)   Water is widespread,

which, in a sense, is about all water (and does *not* mean 'Every *quantity* of water is widespread'). But (e) is irrelevant to the *present* issue, as is evidenced by the peculiarity (ungrammaticalness?) of

(e′)   All water is widespread.

Sentence (e) is *not* construable as containing an implicit quantifier, and is thus not relevant to the present discussion. Sentence (e) is discussed in the next section.

[21] Interim comparison with Quine:

Quine says that "after 'is'" a mass term is to be construed as a predicate and not as a name; my analysis contradicts this – see discussion in notes 7 and 8 above.

He says that "before 'is'" mass terms are to be construed as names. This is unclear. The mass term 'styrofoam' precedes 'is' in 'Some styrofoam is purple', yet it is unclear in what sense 'styrofoam' can be written as a name here and then combined with 'some'. We can, of course, write 'styrofoam' as a name and then rewrite 'some' as 'some quantities of'. This produces the analysis I have given, but I doubt if Quine would want to rewrite quantifiers in this way. Another interpretation is that we only test to see if a word comes before or after 'is' when the sentence has been partially translated into canonical notation. We might then treat 'styrofoam' as coming *after* 'is' because of its position in "Something is such that it is styrofoam and it is purple". Then perhaps Quine's analysis and mine converge again (overlooking our disagreements about how to construe 'is styrofoam'). But again this interpretation is very speculative.

[22] This is similar to Quine's account of the references of complex mass terms functioning as singular terms. For points of disagreement with his view see Part A of Section VI.

[23] Again we have a problem as to how to symbolize 'x is a quantity of leaded tin'. As we have symbolized it, this has the form 'x is a quantity of tin & x is leaded'. But it is not clear that we want to say that leaded tin is tin (that every quantity of leaded tin is a quantity of tin). Our language is vague here, and we can take either of two lines:

(a) We suppose that 'xQt' is true only of quantities of *pure* tin, and we symbolize 'leaded' as an operator rather than as an independent predicate. (See note 16.) In this case 'x is a quantity of leaded tin' is written '$L(xQt)$'.

(b) We suppose, in accordance with ordinary usage, that 'tin' has a broader meaning than 'pure tin'. If so, we *may* symbolize 'x is a quantity of leaded tin' as in (p), i.e., as 'xQt & Lx'. Then, if we want to refer to quantities of *pure* tin, we do so with an operator representing the adjective 'pure': '$P(xQt)$'.

[24] I believe that Quine's presentation of his views presupposes both of these simplifications.

[25] This simplification is gratuitous; the argument goes through without it. I am assuming throughout that

$$(\exists x)\ xQy \ \& \ (\exists x)\ xQz \ \& \ (x)\ (xQy \equiv xQz) \supset y = z.$$

This gives us a sort of principle of extensionality for non-empty substance terms. The principle probably doesn't apply to 'empty' substance terms. For example, the element with atomic number 130 may not be identical with the element with atomic number 131, even though both of them have the same quantities of matter making them up – namely none at all.

[25a] I am indebted here to Quine, *op. cit.*

[26] This requires that bits of matter, like physical objects, may persist through time while losing and gaining atoms. We *could* restrict our notion of 'bit of matter' so as to disallow this. But I see no reason in favor of doing this. Further, this would constitute a peculiar dependence of a logical analysis of language on a particular physical theory, which seems undesirable.

[27] Cf. David Wiggins, *Identity and Spatio-Temporal Continuity*, Blackwell, Oxford, 1967.

[28] Certain words are ambiguous between amount terms and physical object terms. For example, 'three cups' may refer either to three drinking objects, or to a single amount. Likewise, 'three cups of coffee' may refer either to three cups, each containing coffee, or to a quantity of coffee which is three-fourths of a quart in volume. In either case it is the latter interpretation that is being analyzed here.

[29] For a more precise account of the general treatment of amount terms, see the Appendix.

[30] W. V. Quine, *From a Logical Point of View*, Harper & Row, New York, 1969, pp. 11ff, 22, 48ff.

³¹ Some of the terminology and details of this Appendix are now (1978) out of date.
³² Cf. Noam Chomsky, *Syntactic Structures*, Mouton, The Hague, 1965.
³³ Bertrand Russell, 'On Denoting', reprinted in *Logic and Knowledge* (ed. by R. Marsh), Allen and Unwin, London, 1956.
³⁴ Actually there are several 'null morphs' – i.e., unvoiced syntactical units that frequently figure importantly in word order. I am only concerned with the null morph that precedes proper nouns, singular count nouns and mass nouns.
³⁵ Our translation of proper nouns could be varied in several ways. For example, we could analyze 'Jx' as '$x = j$', where 'j' is a logically proper name. Translating it as the predicate 'J' assimilates the translation of proper nouns to that of count nouns thereby making the procedure simpler. The matrix I have selected for the null morph causes proper nouns to have 'existential' commitment; this could be avoided by selecting instead '$(x)\,(\textcircled{1}x \supset \textcircled{2}x)$'.
³⁶ In general sentences have a surprisingly large number of translations. Some logicians and some grammarians would like to cut this down, by insisting for example that (iv) is the only correct translation (cf. exercises in many books on symbolic logic). But the sentence *is* used in both senses in everyday language. Perhaps there is some sense in which (iv) is preferable to (v); if so it is probably an interesting problem to say how and why. But I am concerned only to produce all grammatically possible translations; not to sort out the preferred ones. Indeed, there is reason to believe the latter task impossible; cf. Paul Ziff, 'About What an Adequate Grammar Couldn't Do', *Foundations of Language* 1 (1965) 5–13; also Gilbert Harman, 'About What an Adequate Grammar Could Do', *Foundations of Language* 2 (1966) 134–141.
³⁷ Not only do matrices intermingle in various ways in translation; operators do also. An alternate translation of the sentence in question is:

$$\Diamond \ (\exists x)\,(Jx \ \& \ S(W)x),$$

where '$\Diamond$' has moved to the outside. But adverbs of manner, like 'slowly', never move outside the subject matrix.
³⁸ The original sentence, 'Some men might have been talking with Agatha under an arch during Lent', will have as one translation (leaving predicates and operators in English):

$(\exists x)\,(x$ is a man $\& \ (\exists y)\,(y$ is Agatha $\&$ might $((\exists z)\,(z$ is an arch $\& \ (\exists u)\,(u$ is Lent $\&$ with (under (during (have been (talks)))) $xyzu)))))$.

There are several other possible translations, got by interchanging the order of matrices and by moving the 'might' operator around.
³⁹ These are relative clauses as in

(a)   The man whom you saw is a doctor.

as opposed to

(b)   The man, whom you saw, is a doctor.

To consider non-restrictive clauses would take us too far afield in a matter not relevant to problems concerning mass nouns.
⁴⁰ In transformational grammar these clauses are generated by inserting a sentential-like structure just after the main noun. This sentential-like structure will have the main noun in it, preceded by a special determiner, '*wh-*'. A transformational rule turns this structure

into a relative clause. In general the rule is:

$$\text{Noun} - (\underline{\quad} wh\text{-} \text{Noun} \dots) \Rightarrow$$

$$\text{Noun} - \left\{ \begin{array}{l} \text{who} \\ \text{whom} \\ \text{which} \end{array} \right\} - \underline{\quad} \dots.$$

E.g., the rule transforms 'man (John saw *wh*- man shooting a bear)' into 'man whom John saw shooting a bear'.

To get the formula to conjoin with the main noun, translate the determiner '*wh*-' as the redundant matrix:

$$\textcircled{2}x.$$

Thus the example 'Some man who shot a giraffe is dead' is a transformation of 'Some man (*wh*- man shot a giraffe) is dead'. The translation of '*wh*- man shot a giraffe' is just 'shot a giraffe' – i.e., '$(\exists y)\,(Gy\ \&\ Sxy)$', and the whole sentence translates as in the text.

(Sometimes matrices from within a relative clause may come outside the whole sentence; thus 'Every boy who dates a certain girl will be bored' has as one of its translations:

$$\text{'}(\exists x)\,(Gx\ \&\ (y)\,(By\ \&\ Dxy \supset y\text{ will be bored}))\text{.'})$$

[41] This is in simple adjective-noun constructions. When there are strings of adjectives, or adjectives plus intensifiers (e.g., 'very') a more complex treatment is necessary.

[42] This alteration is unnecessary if we want to 'reduce' substances to classes of their quantities. This might be desirable for some philosophical purposes, but I see no reason to adopt it in general.

[43] The matrix for 'most', as sketched in Section IV, is:

$$Fu\{x:\textcircled{1}x\ \&\ \textcircled{2}x\}\ E(Fu\{x:\textcircled{1}x\} - Fu\{x:\textcircled{1}x\ \&\ \textcircled{2}x\}).$$

[44] For example, our procedure yields '$(\exists x)\,(x = \sigma y[yQw]\ \&\ Sx)$' instead of '$S\sigma y[yQw]$', and it frequently yields '$\dots\sigma x[xQm]\dots$' instead of the simpler '$\dots m\dots$'.

[45] Including the translation of the object of the verb the complete translation is

$$\text{'}(x)\,((\exists z)\,(1Gz\ \&\ xMz)\ \&\ xQw \supset (\exists u)\,(62.4Pu\ \&\ Wxu))\text{'},$$

where 'P' is the predicate corresponding to the amount-term 'pound', and 'W' means 'weighs'.

If the extra word in the determiner is 'several', then normally the matrix is '$(\exists x)\,(\textcircled{1}x\ \&\ \textcircled{2}x)$', and 'several' behaves like a vague numeral. E.g., 'Several gallons of water ...' becomes

$$\text{'}(\exists x)\,((\exists z)\,(sGz\ \&\ xMz)\ \&\ xQw\ \&\dots)\text{'}.$$

[46] *Added in proof:* I have just discovered two articles related to this paper, to which the interested reader should be referred: Helen Morris Cartwright, 'Heraclitus and the Bath Water', *Philosophical Review* 1965, and 'Quantities', *Philosophical Review* 1970.

TERENCE PARSONS

AFTERTHOUGHTS ON MASS TERMS

Since the publication of 'An Analysis of Mass Terms and Amount Terms' (hereafter 'MT & AT') there have appeared various criticisms of the theory it presented, as well as various alternative theories. I have little to say about many of the issues that have been raised (e.g., 'how' mass terms 'divide their reference'), but I will here comment briefly on four issues that are particularly relevant to the theory proposed in MT & AT.

1. ARE SUBSTANCES ABSTRACT?

Some authors have claimed that the theory of MT & AT requires that substances such as gold, water and salt be abstract entities,[1] and one author even attributes to the theory the consequence that salt does not occupy space.[2] I seem to have encouraged this interpretation by calling the basic theory 'rather Platonistic',[3] a locution that I now regret. For in fact the theory is quite neutral on this point. It allows interpretations which make substances be abstract entities, but this is only an option; it is not forced by the theory. The only consideration that might tempt one to conclude that the theory entails the abstractness of substances is the argument I gave to the effect that two different substances may occupy exactly the same space without being identical (see point 3 below). But this by no means entails that they are abstract entities, and it certainly doesn't entail that they do not occupy space at all.

2. EXCESS PRIMITIVES?

I proposed symbolizing sentences like 'Water is widespread' as 'σx [x is water] is widespread', The subject of the sentence was supposed to refer to the substance, water. It is composed of the predicate, 'is water', plus what I called the substance abstraction operator: 'σx[... x ...]'. The latter I took as primitive, and the theory has been criticized for this.

Were I to rewrite the paper, I would *not* attempt to eliminate, replace or

167

F. J. Pelletier (ed.), Mass Terms, 167–171. All Rights Reserved.

define the substance abstraction operator. I would even move to make it 'more primitive', by eliminating or modifying my footnote 25 which suggests constraints on its interpretation. The reason is this: My intent in MT & AT was to formulate a *semantical* theory which is as neutral as possible on controversial philosophical issues. All of the proposals that I know of for defining or replacing the substance abstraction operator run a strong risk of falsehood (cf. MT & AT, p. 376). For example, here are several proposals for the correct treatment of the word 'water' in a sentence like 'water is widespread':

Moravcsik$_1$, pp. 281–82	$\{x$: in some possible world x is that spatiotemporally scattered individual whose parts are all the water that was, is and will be in that world$\}$
Moravcsik$_2$, pp. 281–82	the mereological individual that is made up of all the members of the class described in Moravcsik$_1$
Montague, p. 298	the property of being a body of water[4]
Grandy, p. 297	$\{x$: x is water$\}$[5]
Burge, p. 279	the fusion of $\{x$: x is water$\}$[6]
Pelletier, p. 106	the predicate 'water'

Ignoring the suggestion of note 25, the theory of MT & AT is compatible with each of these[7], but they are all incompatible with each other. In addition, every one of them strikes me as implausible. And in general I see no reason why the notion of a substance should be definable in terms of notions that have already become entrenched in our philosophical tradition;[8] if all such definitions are incorrect then it is a virtue rather than a defect to treat the substance abstraction operator as primitive.

3. 'QUANTITY OF'

In the Appendix of MT & AT I sketched a general systematic treatment of English sentences (of a relatively rich though restricted class) containing mass terms. According to that treatment, every use of a mass term in English analyses into a complex of quantifiers and a predicate, plus sometimes the substance abstraction operator. If we ignore questions concerning the proper analysis of the predicate and the substance abstraction operator then we have a format for representing English sentences containing mass terms that I think most writers would not take serious issue with.[9]

Most disagreements will center on the analysis of the primitive terms. Most authors want there to be one predicate per mass term, and they want simple mass terms in English to give rise to *primitive* monadic predicates. Corresponding to 'water' will be a primitive predicate, 'W'. It is to be read variously as "is water" (Quine, p. 97), "is a portion (quantity) of water" (Burge, p. 275), "is *sm* water" (Pelletier, p. 95); but the complexity in the latter two readings is merely a gesture towards English syntax, and does not reflect any complexity in the corresponding canonical predicate.

The theory of MT & AT instead has this predicate being logically complex; in place of 'is water', represented as '$W-$', it has 'is a quantity of water', represented as '$-Qw$', where 'w' is a primitive name of the substance, water.[10] Were I to redo the paper now I would follow the majority and leave the predicate unanalysed. This is not because I think that the way I originally did it is incorrect, but rather because analysing the predicate in the way that I did tends to beg a philosophically controversial question concerning the identity conditions for substances. Specifically, I argued (MT & AT, pp. 376–77) that two substances might coincide in space without thereby being identical. Burge (p. 269) correctly points out that in the case I imagined the proof that the two substances were not identical exploits the relational analysis of the predicate in question. I still think that substances should be allowed to coincide in space (throughout time) without thereby being identical (this is true on all of the theories mentioned in Section 2 above, with the exception of Burge's), but I don't believe that a *semantical* theory should legislate an answer to this question.

4. EXTENSIONALITY AND EMPTY SUBSTANCES

Pelletier (p. 100) claims that the theory of MT & AT utilizes a non-extensional canonical language. My intent was to remain neutral on this point. Surprisingly, the issue of whether the theory *must* be non-extensional turns on whether you take seriously my comment in footnote 25 concerning 'empty' substance terms. I proposed there that there might be two non-identical substances (say, elements 130 and 131; call them F-ium and G-ium) neither of which is manifested anywhere in the universe. If so, the substance abstraction operator is non-extensional. For we will have two predicates, 'is F-ium' and 'is G-ium' which are coextensive (since nothing is F-ium and likewise nothing is G-ium) but which are not intersubstitutible *salva veritate*; for this is true:

$$\sigma x \,[x \text{ is } F\text{-ium}] = \sigma x \,[x \text{ is } F\text{-ium}]$$

and this is false:

$$\sigma x \,[x \text{ is } F\text{-ium}] = \sigma x [x \text{ is } G\text{-ium}].$$

This is probably just a particular version of a standard problem about 'empty' singular terms that has nothing specially to do with mass terms[11] (compare 'Pegasus = Zeus'). Extensionality could be preserved by either giving up empty substances, or else going Meinongian (so as to invoke unactualized manifestations of the substances in question). Or extensionality could be given up only in the case of 'empty' terms (this is what you get by taking footnote 25 completely literally).

University of Massachusetts

NOTES

[1] T. Burge, 'Truth and Mass Terms', *Journal of Philosophy* 69 (1972), 263–82; J. Pelletier, 'On Some Proposals for the Semantics of Mass Nouns', *Journal of Philosophical Logic* 3 (1974), 87–108. Moravcsik seems to imply this in J. M. E. Moravcsik, 'Mass Terms in English,' in K. J. J. Hintikka, J. M. E. Moravcsik, and P. C. Suppes (eds.), *Approaches to Natural Language*, D. Reidel, Dordrecht and Boston, 1973, pp. 263–85.
[2] Burge, p. 269.
[3] MT & AT, p. 376. I never said, though, that substances are abstract entities.
[4] From R. Montague, 'Comment on Moravcsik's Paper', in Hintikka, Moravcsik and Suppes, *op. cit.*
[5] From R. Grandy, 'Comment on Moravcsik's Paper', in Hintikka, Moravcsik and Suppes, *op. cit.* This was also suggested in MT & AT, footnote 42.
[6] This may also be Quine's view; cf. W. Quine, *Word and Object*, M.I.T. Press, Cambridge, Mass., 1960, p. 98. Burge's 'fusion' is a mereological individual in the sense of N. Goodman and H. Leonard, 'The Calculus of Individuals and Its Uses', *Journal of Symbolic Logic* 5 (1940), No. 2. However, Moravcsik's 'mereological individuals' are different; cf. discussion of identity conditions in Moravcsik p. 281.
[7] Except for Burge's proposal; but adopting the change discussed in point 3 below makes the theory also compatible with his proposal.
[8] Some of Frege's most important contributions to modern semantics (e.g. the notion of second-level concept, and the notion of sense) would have been impossible if he had been obliged to define them in terms of already available (and 'respectable') notions.
[9] Cartwright would probably disagree with at least some parts, Moravcsik would complicate the treatment of adjectives, and Pelletier has reservations about my analysis of

'Gold is the element with atomic number 79' (Pelletier pp. 105–06). I am skipping over the issue of potential agreement or disagreement concerning what kinds of thing the predicates are true of. Footnote 17 of MT & AT contains an argument which, if good, rules out Ontological Simplification B of that paper. I now have reservations about the argument, because of the possible unclarity of application of predicates like 'is blue' to things whose surface color diverges from their interior color.

[10] MT & AT, p. 386. Some authors have asked how the theory can provide for the equivalence of 'x is water' with 'x is sm water'. The answer lies not in the canonical symbolism, but rather in the principles governing how English is to be represented therein. I would treat 'sm' before mass nouns just like 'a' before count nouns. There are alternatives here. The simplest device is to treat these as small-scope existential quantifiers, to treat unadorned mass nouns as containing the null determiner (this is required; cf. MT & AT p. 382), and to analyse 'is' preceding noun phrases as '='. Then 'x is water' and 'x is sm water' both translate identically as '$(\exists y)(yQw \ \& \ x = y)$'.

[11] Brian Skyrms advocated this view when I was writing MT & AT.

THE PROPER TREATMENT OF
MASS TERMS IN ENGLISH

The basic problem is to determine what concrete mass nouns denote and how one is to give truth conditions for sentences containing them. I ignore for the most part 'abstract mass nouns' and 'mass adjectives', but see below.

I speak within the normal intuitive framework, according to which ordinary proper nouns denote individuals, ordinary common nouns and intransitive verbs denote sets of individuals, infinitives of ordinary intransitive verbs denote properties of individuals (that is, functions from possible worlds to sets of individuals), and so on; and not within the elaborately inflated framework of my paper at the present workshop. The more elaborate framework is introduced in order to accommodate intensional verbs and the like. The present proposal could be made to fit in with that development by a rather obvious inflation in type, but for clarity it is better to avoid such complications and accordingly to renounce intensional verbs here.

Moravcsik has very usefully set out the main proposals so far advanced, and has presented arguments and examples sufficient to show all but one of them inadequate; the single exception is not his own but Parsons'. Thus I need not consider alternative proposals (apart from Parsons'; see below) but simply give the one that appears to me right.

Concrete mass nouns should basically be taken as denoting properties of individuals. For instance, **water** should denote the property of being a body of water, and **iron** the property of being a piece of iron. In general, a mass term will denote that function on possible worlds which takes as its value for a given world the set of all samples (or, to give synonyms, portions or quantities (in the sense ascribed to Parsons) or "parts with the correct structural properties") of the substance in question in that world. (It would be irrelevant to object that there may be no *minimal* portions;

173

F. J. Pelletier (ed.), Mass Terms, 173–178. All Rights Reserved.

the proposal applies equally to the unusual case in which every part of a portion of the substance is itself a portion of the substance.)

This much is sufficient to account for occurrences of mass nouns standing alone in normal substantive positions – for instance, in **portion of** α, which should clearly denote the extension (in the actual world) of the property denoted by the mass noun α, or in α **is a liquid**. (**Liquid** should clearly be taken as a higher-order common noun, that is, as denoting a set of properties of individuals.) Other contexts, however, must also be explained. A mass noun α standing alone in predicative position should be regarded as synonymous with **a portion of** α. If a quantifier (for example, **some**, **all**), a demonstrative, or an adjective phrase accompanies a mass noun, then the mass noun should in that occurrence be taken as denoting the extension of the property usually denoted. (In this connection notice that **water is wet** should be taken as elliptical for **all water is wet**; notice that this sentence is quite different from **water is a liquid**.)[1] In those exceptional cases in which a mass noun is used as an adjective (as in **iron bed**) the denotation of the adjective (which must as always be a function) can be easily obtained in terms of the extension of the property denoted by the mass term. (To be more explicit, if ζ is a common noun phrase and hence denotes a set A, then **iron** ζ denotes the intersection of A with the extension of the property denoted by **iron**.)

Notice that it would not be good to treat a mass noun as denoting the **set** of portions of the substance in question. For consider the example brought up in the September workshop session of two never-to-be-realized (but describable and realizable) substances called Kaplanite and Suppesite. The two sets in question would then be identical, but **Kaplanite is a liquid** might be true and **Suppesite is a liquid** false.[2]

So far I have said nothing about such phrases as **the gold in Smith's ring**. Let me give what now appears to me the best treatment, though I may be on shakier ground here than in the foregoing. In the first place, **in Smith's ring** is an adjective phrase; hence, in accordance with what was said above, **gold** should here be taken as denoting the set of portions of gold, and it would be natural to take **gold in Smith's ring** as denoting the set of portions of gold that are 'in' Smith's ring. In the second place, I would take **the** in **the gold in Smith's ring** as the ordinary singular definite article, so that **the** ζ has a denotation if and only if ζ denotes a unit set, and in that case **the** ζ denotes the only element of that set.[3] But is there not a conflict here? It would seem that there are many portions of gold in Smith's ring. For while not all parts of portions of gold are portions of gold, still many are; and these would appear to be in Smith's ring. Yet for **the gold in Smith's ring** to denote, it is necessary for **gold in Smith's ring** to denote a unit set.

The solution is I think to regard **in** as in one sense (and indeed the prevailing though not altogether unique sense when accompanying mass nouns) amounting to **occupying** or **constituting**. Then **gold in Smith's ring** comes to **gold constituting Smith's ring**, denotes the set of maximal portions of gold that are 'in' (in the more inclusive sense) Smith's ring, and hence denotes a unit set.

It seems more or less arbitrary whether to assume that the set of portions of a given substance is always closed under physical composition, but I prefer to make this assumption, inasmuch as it appears to simplify the treatment of such compounds as **much** α and **more** α, where α is a mass noun. Then, for instance, it is not unreasonable to treat **much α F's** as synonymous with **some large portion of α F's**, and **more α F's than G's** as synonymous with **there is a portion of α that F's and is larger than any portion of α that G's**. (The word **larger** is of course ambiguous, and the linguistic or extralinguistic content must be considered to determine whether it is to mean **greater in volume**, **greater in weight**, or something else. **Large**, besides sharing the ambiguity of **larger**, is in addition vague; but the vagueness and ambiguity of these two words is fairly accurately reflected in **much** and **more**.)

The question naturally arises whether portions of substances are full-fledged physical objects like tables and rings (together with physical compositions of these). Perhaps. At least, I see no clear-cut argument to the contrary. If this is so, then under appropriate conditions (for instance, that Smith's ring is made entirely of gold) the sentence **Smith's ring is the same as the gold constituting Smith's ring** could very well be true. This may appear strange, and indeed seems to contradict the intuitions of Cartwright (1970, especially the first sentence on p. 28); but I cannot find any good argument for rejecting it.

There is, however, a *bad* argument. Suppose that Jones had an all-gold ring, but that it was melted down and made into a ring for Smith. Then, given our understanding that portions of gold are full-fledged physical objects, it would be reasonable to assert the following:

   (1)   **Smith's ring is the same as the gold that constitutes Smith's ring,**
   (2)   **Jones' ring was the same as the gold that constituted Jones' ring,**
   (3)   **the gold that constitutes Smith's ring is the same as the gold that constituted Jones' ring.**

At first glance these three sentences might appear to imply the rather clearly false conclusion,

   (4)   **Smith's ring is Jones' ring;**

but the appearance would be deceptive. The supposed inference would amount to one involving substitution on the basis of an identity sentence within the scope of a tense operator; and as everyone knows (cf. Cocchiarella's UCLA dissertation), that is invalid. (Of course,

       Smith's ring is the same as the gold that constituted Jones's ring

does follow from (1) and (3), but this is unobjectionable. And if we were to change *was* to *is* in (2), (4) would follow from (1)–(3); but then (2) would be false.)

At the moment, then, I should recommend regarding portions of substances as full-fledged physical objects, or physical compositions of these. But if some strong argument were found for not doing this, and indeed for distinguishing between Smith's ring and the gold constituting Smith's ring, my general proposal for treating mass terms would not thereby be overturned. It is perfectly possible to construct an ontology allowing for physical objects of different sorts, objects that may coincide without being identical. The construction was sketched in a letter I wrote in June 1968 to Dana Scott, and corresponds, I believe, to Hume's outlook. Let us for present purposes suppose that our *basic objects* have no temporal duration, each of them existing only for a moment; they are accordingly what we might regard as temporal slices of 'ordinary objects', and might include such physical slices as heaps of molecules at a moment, and possibly such additional objects as instantaneous mental states. Then *ordinary objects* or *continuants* (for instance, physical objects, persons) would be constructs obtained by 'stringing together' various basic objects – or, more exactly, certain functions from moments of time to basic objects. Two continuants f and g may be said to *coincide* at a moment i just in case the function values $f(i)$ and $g(i)$ are the same.

To quote from my letter:

Now most pairs of ordinary objects are such that if they coincide at one moment, then they do so always.... But this is not true of all pairs of ordinary objects. There *are* different ways of stringing basic objects together.

For instance, we are told that we change our bodies completely every so often. It follows that some living organisms 'correspond' at different times to two or more different heaps of molecules. Yet suppose we are materialists and do not believe in 'souls' or 'transcendent unities' or 'entelechies'. We should seem to be faced with an identity crisis.

The solution is of course obvious. Both heaps of molecules and organisms are continuants made out of heaps-of-molecules-at-a-moment (Homaams). But they are pieced together in different ways: each heap of molecules consists of Homaams related in simple ways describable in physics, while organisms consist of Homaams related in certain functional or biological ways. Thus it may well be that no organism is a heap of molecules, but that materialism is nevertheless true in the sense that every organism coincides with a heap of molecules.... It may also be (though butterflies, caterpillars, and divisions of protozoa give one pause) that whenever two *organisms* or two *physical objects* coincide, they are also identical. And indeed this may give some clue to *natural kinds*. For a set (or property) to be a natural kind it is probably necessary (though not sufficient) that for any two of its members, if they coincide, then they are identical.

Full-fledged physical objects and substance-portions could be similarly distinguished, though I do not at the moment recommend it. For instance, Jones' ring might be identified with a certain function defined just for that interval of time I_1 during which Jones' ring existed, and having as its value for a moment i in I_1 the Homaam which is its temporal slice at i; Smith's ring might be identified with a similar function defined for the later interval I_2 during which that ring exists; and the gold-portion constituting Jones' ring during I_1 and Smith's ring during I_2 might be identified with a function defined over a much longer interval of time (including both I_1 and I_2), always having Homaams as its values, and coinciding with Jones' ring and Smith's ring throughout I_1 and I_2, respectively.

Abstract mass nouns (correctly delimited; some of Moravcsik's examples, like **vagueness,** are unfortunate) would be treated in exactly the same way as concrete mass nouns. For instance, **information** would basically denote the property of being a piece of (that is, portion of) information. Of course, this leaves much unsettled: what sort of object is a piece of information? But that is a problem independent of the analysis of mass nouns and would arise even if we were to renounce mass nouns, treat **piece of information** as an unanalyzed common noun, and avoid using **information** in any other context. Such problems must be solved before we can expect a completely definite treatment of 'abstract mass nouns'.

Now some words that are *basically* adjectives (primarily and perhaps exclusively color words) have a derivative use in substantive positions; and in those positions they should be taken, like concrete mass nouns, as denoting properties of individuals. For instance, **red** in **red is a color** should denote the property of being red (or of being a red object). One could, if one liked, call such adjectives mass adjectives; but observe that there are few of them and that they definitely do not include Moravcsik's examples **sweet** and **heavy**.

I promised to say something about Parsons' treatment of mass nouns. It appears to be completely correct as far as it goes, and is I think completely compatible with my treatment. In fact, my treatment can be regarded simply as an amplification of Parsons', consisting mostly in saying what sort of thing 'substances' are (properties of individuals) and in consequence giving an analysis of Parsons' **quantity of** (that is, **portion of**).

University of California, Los Angeles

NOTES

[1] It should also be pointed out that **blue water is a liquid** turns out meaningless, but I think that on reflection this will be found compatible with intuition. ("How many liquids are there, and how many metals?" "Umpteen and phumpteen." "Did you count water?" "Yes." "How about blue water?" "Oh, I forgot." "And red water, and green water, and ...") Of course **heavy water** is different; **heavy** is here syncategorematic and **heavy water** an unanalyzed mass noun.

[2] It would not be good to maintain that **Kaplanite is a liquid** might involve a nonextensional context and for that reason might not, together with **Kaplanite is the same as Suppesite**, imply **Suppesite is a liquid**. No context is more paradigmatically extensional than those of the form **is a** ζ, and to rule such contexts nonextensional would require supplying a meaning for them other than the obvious and natural one.

[3] In a comprehensive treatment it is perhaps best never to assign a denotation (or at least one that is an individual) to a phrase of the form **the** ζ, but rather to treat such phrases syncategorematically; see Montague (1970a) and my paper in the present volume. Nevertheless, it will cause no harm to speak, for intuitive purposes, of such phrases as sometimes denoting; then the 'intuitive denotation' of the phrase will be genuinely involved in arriving at the 'real denotations' of longer expressions containing the phrase.

HELEN M. CARTWRIGHT

AMOUNTS AND MEASURES OF AMOUNT

1. Anything specified in response to the question, 'How much?' may, I suppose, be properly called an amount. But the amounts I want to discuss are those only which are amounts of such things as water or gold, objects designated by what Terence Parsons[1] has called 'applied amount terms' – phrases like 'ten pounds of water' or 'three teaspoons of gold', the result of concatenating a numeral, the name of a unit of measurement, and a word or phrase with the grammatical syntax of a mass noun.

The syntax of mass nouns is sometimes described in such a way that it would seem that anything has it if it simply lacks the features of a count noun, a noun which regularly takes the indefinite article in the singular, 'many' and 'few' in the plural and, among other things, numerical modifiers. If mass nouns constructions are in this sense simply non-count, they need not be regarded as nominal at all; and in fact they share some important features with adjectives.[2] But to avoid confusion for present purposes, I shall say that a word or phrase has the syntax of a mass noun only if, in addition to its appearance in applied amount terms, it regularly occurs where 'water' appears in sentences like

(1)   I'll have some (*Sm*) more water,
(2)   This is as much water as that,
(3)   That water is some of this,
(4)   This is the same water as that.

Something may be more or less wet or heavy or elastic, much more elastic, ten pounds heavier and as wet as something else, but 'some (*Sm*) more elastic', will not do, nor 'as much heavy as', nor 'the same wet as'.

It is of some importance, I think, that 'more' in (1) seems not to express the converse of *less*; 'some less water' is no better than 'some more' with an adjective; and no doubt this has something to do with the fact that the '-er' suffix of comparative adjectives always has the force of 'more'. No doubt also (2) is a near relative of 'This is as heavy as that', or for that matter, 'This weighs as much as that'. And in any case the criteria I have

179

F. J. Pelletier (ed.), Mass Terms, 179–198. All Rights Reserved.
Copyright © 1975 by Noûs.

suggested so far fail to exclude hosts of nouns which would make what I shall have to say most implausible.

In particular, I mean to exclude nouns like 'weight', 'volume', 'length' and the like – names of 'dimensions of measurement' or 'quantities' in any sense of the term in which 'quantity' is to be contrasted with 'quality'. But it might be argued that the oddity of 'ten pounds of weight' and 'one gallon of volume' is due only to their redundancy; and there is, I think, a tendency in some of the literature on measurement – for example, in discussions of what is sometimes called 'physical addition' – to assimilate the logical behavior of the names of amounts of such things as weight to that of applied amount terms more narrowly conceived.[3] I shall have little to say about the thorny issues here involved; and I mention the matter only to cast doubt on the assumption that nominalistic criticism of some theories of measurement[4] extends to a realistic account of applied amount terms. For I mean to defend and discuss the limitations of one such account, and the primary importance of what follows lies in whatever light is thereby shed on the logical significance of the syntax of mass nouns. I shall suggest that there are at least two important sources of confusion with respect to the semantics of sentences of the relevant sort, both involving varieties of nominalism.

2. 'A quantity' according to Russell, "is anything which is capable of quantitative equality to something else".[5] And I have, in effect, assumed the legitimacy of something like the theory I mean to explore in defending the ontological status of things which are, for example, quantities of water in this sense.[6] (1) through (4) are to be so understood that the referrents of 'this' and 'that' are quantities of water. If the request expressed by (1) is met, it does not follow that I am given something which is more water – or wetter – than something I have or have had. What does follow is that I am given some water which is *other* than something which I have or have had; namely, *another* quantity of water. And if X is what I shall then have had altogether, it follows from

(5) X is some water,

that

(6)   Something is some water which is some (or all) of X.

That is, part of what is meant by saying something is a quantity of water is that it has a *sub-quantity* which is a quantity of water.

But further, it is after all natural to suppose that if something is some water, it must be a certain *amount* of it – 10 pounds or a gallon of water. In fact, this seems to me to be the crucial insight behind Russell's definition of a quantity; and I should like now to suggest quite explicitly that the syntax of (5) can be so described that one reasonable semantic interpretation of it is that of

(5′) $(Ey) Wxy$,

where the two-place predicate 'W' is assigned what I shall call an 'amount function', a function from some set of quantities into a set of applied amounts of water.

Roughly, y is to be whatever amount of water x is; and the uniqueness of the values of a function which is at any rate formally analogous to the sort of function I have in mind is guaranteed by the fact that Russell's 'quantitative equality' is an equivalence relation. Given that 'as much water as' means 'at least as much' – as is surely proper, if x is as much water as z and z is as much water as x, then they are (by abstraction) the same amount of water.

(6), then, can reasonably be assigned a semantic interpretation in accordance with that of

(6′) $(Ez)(Ey)(Wzy \cdot zqx)$,

where the two-place predicate 'q' represents quantity inclusion, a relation which is transitive and anti-symmetric; and (6′) not only follows from but is (informally) equivalent to (5′), because quantity inclusion is reflexive in any set of quantities of water. I am assuming (1) through (6) can be so understood that (2) follows from both (3) and (4), and that if x is a sub-quantity of something, z, and x as much water as z as well, then x and z are identical.

(5′) can be assumed to be the analogue of a formula representing a reasonable way of handling sentences containing adjectives like 'wet' or 'watery'; and a function analogous to an amount function can be associated with 'as wet as' or 'as much wetness as'. But it is very hard to see in such cases what sense could be made of claims analogous to those I have made about (1) through (6), and such a function will not be an amount function.

In saying that 'W' represents an amount function then, I mean to say that the domain of that function is a set of quantities of something – water in particular – and to say further that the values of that function, applied amounts of water, are *linearly ordered by size*. That is, 'as large an amount of water as' represents a transitive, anti-symmetric relation which is reflexive in any set of applied amounts of water and which is such that every member of such a set bears that relation or its converse to every other. And the relation represented by 'as large an amount of water as' has these features in virtue of a one-to-one correspondence between amounts of water and the values of another function of a sort very like an operation which, if I understand the term, serves in 'extensive measurement'.[7]

The general claim I mean to defend then can be put by saying that, where π is one of a large and interesting class of words and phrases with the syntax of a mass noun, the schema

(A) X is some (*Sm*) π

represents an amount function for π – a function, **f**, which is such that for every x and y in a set of quantities for which an instance of the schema is true, two conditions are satisfied:

(i) x is as much π as y iff $\mathbf{f}(x)$ is as large an amount of π as $\mathbf{f}(y)$;
(ii)   the relation represented by ⌜as large an amount of π as⌝ linearly orders the values of any function for which (i) is satisfied.[7]

3.   Suppose now that we have ten buckets, and that

(7)   Every bucket contains as much water as every other.

Then the water in each bucket is a quantity in Russell's sense; and if we are allowed to abstract with respect to quantitative equality among them, we shall have the amount of water all the buckets *share*. (7) can then be assigned the interpretation of something like

(7′) $(x)(y)(Bx \cdot By \rightarrow (Eu)(Ev)(Cxu \cdot Cyv \cdot (\imath z) \, Wuz \geqslant (\imath z) \, Wvz))$,

'For every x and y, if x and y are buckets then for some u and v, x contains u and y contains v and the amount of water u is as large an amount of water as the amount of water v is'. The 'greater than or equal to' sign here represents the purported linear order relation for amounts of water; and my claim that it is so would be trivial if its field did not extend to *all* of those things which are amounts of water in one or more of the buckets – *all* of the values of an amount function for water in those buckets. The principle problem, then, is to try to say what one such function is; and to do this I shall first define a real valued function which can reasonably be supposed to be a measure of amount for those things in the buckets to which 'water' applies.

Let us begin by assuming that there is a set Q whose members are the contents of each of the buckets, and then defining a measure function on the set of its subsets. That is, let us assume that

$$Q = \{x : x \text{ is the water in one of the buckets}\}.$$

Then we can define a function **m** from the set Q' of all subsets of Q into the set of non-negative real numbers as follows: For each singleton of an element of Q, the value of **m** is one. For each pair set, each element of Q' which is the union of a pair of singletons of distinct elements of Q, the value of **m** is two and in general, for the union of any number of singletons of distinct elements of Q, the value of **m** will be the sum of the values of **m** for each. Every subset of Q but for the empty set is the union of such a set of singletons; so we may say that for every pair of non-empty subsets of Q, A, and B,

$$\mathbf{m}(A \cup B) = \mathbf{m}(A) + \mathbf{m}(B)$$

just in case A and B have no elements in common. **m** is thus additive, and if for the empty set we say the value of **m** is zero, we may conclude that **m** is a measure on the set Q', and the set Q and each of its subsets is measureable in one standard sense of the term.[8]

Now all that **m** does so far is count singletons and add them up to the number of elements of Q; and this small exercize in measure theory would be of no interest at all if it were not for the happy accident that, for example, given any element a of Q, the fact that

$$\mathbf{m}(Q) = 10 \text{ times } \mathbf{m}\{a\}$$

can be taken to reflect the fact that, according to our story, the amount of water in all the buckets is ten times the amount of water in any one of them. But we can do somewhat better than this.

At some risk of confusion, let us define the *fusion* of a set, A, as the object included in all and only those things which include every element of A. Then, if it is assumed that inclusion here is set-theoretic inclusion and that A is a set of sets, the fusion of A is simply the union of its elements. This assumption serves to bring out a quite straight-forward analogy between the union of a set of sets and the fusion of a set of *individuals*. But there is good reason to make it plain that it is the latter notion we are after; the inclusion relation in terms of which the fusion of a set is to be defined is not set-theoretic but mereological – for our purposes, it is quantity inclusion.[9]

Let us say then that

$$FuA = (\imath x)(y)(z)(z \in A \rightarrow z\mathbf{q}\,y) \leftrightarrow x\mathbf{q}\,y)$$

that is, the fusion of A is the quantity of water which is a sub-quantity of all and only those quantities of water which have every element of A as a sub-quantity. If A is empty, its fusion has no sub-quantity which is a quantity of water; so we cannot assume the fusion of the empty set is a quantity of water. But if we now redefine $\mathbf{m}$ by putting elements of Q for their singletons in its domain and replacing non-empty subsets of Q by their fusions, the *mereological union* of a pair of elements of this new domain will be their fusion. And, wherever two such elements x and y include no common sub-quantity, we have, by an argument just analogous to that given above,

$$\mathbf{m}(Fu\{x, y\}) = \mathbf{m}(x) + \mathbf{m}(y),$$

so that $\mathbf{m}$ is additive. Moreover we can preserve the fact that

$$\mathbf{m}(x) \geqslant \mathbf{m}(y) \text{ iff } x \text{ is as much water as } y$$

for every pair of elements in the domain of $\mathbf{m}$, by saying that wherever x is not a sub-quantity of y, there is an element in the domain which is a sub-quantity of x exclusively; that is, by saying that in any such case the *mereological difference*, $x - y$, is an element of the new domain of $\mathbf{m}$, where

$$u\mathbf{q}(x - y) \leftrightarrow u\mathbf{q}x \cdot \sim(Ez)(z\mathbf{q}u \cdot z\mathbf{q}\,y).$$

This assumption guarantees that every element of the domain of $\mathbf{m}$ is a quantity of water; we can suppose the values of $\mathbf{m}$ are all positive, and fairly conclude that **m** is a measure function, not on a set of sets, but on a *mereology* or *calculus of individuals*.[10]

4. Now as Tarski and others have pointed out, the notion of a mereology can be based on a single primitive, a 'part-whole' relation analogous to set-theoretic inclusion which, relying on this analogy and my claims about (1) through (6) and (7), I have here interpreted as quantity inclusion among quantities of water. But it might be objected, even by one who finds set-theoretic notions unproblematic, that the part-whole relation stands in need of further explanation or elimination; and Goodman has suggested a way of defining it by, in effect, assigning to the notion of an *atom* the role played by membership in the usual definition of set-theoretic inclusion – by saying, that is, that an individual A is part of an individual B just in case every atom of A is an atom of B.[11]

In the terms thus far introduced, an atom of something is a minimal sub-quantity; that is, x is an atom of A just in case it is a sub-quantity of A which has no sub-quantities other than itself. And given this, the atoms of all of the elements of the domain of our function **m**, as presently defined, are just the elements of Q. For the only elements of the domain of **m** which are not sub-quantities of some other element are the members of the set Q; it is just these, the contents of each bucket, that are their own sole sub-quantities; and since the elements of the domain of **m** are all fusions of subsets of Q, we have, for every pair of such elements, A and B; A is a sub-quantity of B, just in case every atom of A is an atom of B.

But now if, in accordance with Goodman's suggestion, this equivalence is taken as, a *definition* of quantity inclusion in the domain of **m**, what is again of crucial importance is the happy accident that made the specification of **m** of any interest in the first place; namely, the fact that the elements of Q happen to be quantitatively equal. **m** has just been defined in such a way that its value for every atom in its domain is the same. But there is nothing in the specification of Q that guarantees that the value of **m** for every atom has anything at all to do with the amount of water in those buckets. If (7) were false, **m** could not be supposed to add up amounts of water at all.

Moreover, of course, the elements of Q are atomic quantities of water relative only to the domain of **m** as presently defined. Given (7), **m** does measure amounts, but it is incomplete in an obvious way. We need to add to its domain quantities of water for which the value of **m** is, for example, one half. And having noticed this there are two ways in which, as it seems to me, one might go wrong.

5.   By further burdening the notion of a sub-quantity, we can amplify the domain of **m** by adding to it sub-quantities of elements of Q; and relying on the notion of the difference between a pair of elements, the result of 'subtracting' y from x, we can say that if $x-y$ is in the domain of **m**, $\mathbf{m}(x-y)$ is one half just in case x is an element of $Q - a\ unit$ element, and $x-y$ is quantitatively equal to y. It might now be suggested however, that we can define quantity inclusion in Goodman's way by *beginning* with atomic quantities. An atom of water will be water from which no water can be subtracted; the domain of **m** will be the set of fusions of subsets of the set of atoms of water in those buckets. And this suggestion invites shades of Eleatic criticism.

If **m** is to remain a measure of amount, atoms of water in its new domain must be *minimal in amount* relative to the fusion of every set of quantities of water in the buckets. So it is fair to ask whether the fusion of for example, Q, is infinitely divisible. If it is – if subtraction of quantities from elements of Q has no lower limit, *and* it is the fusion of atoms of water, then an atom will be assigned a value no greater than zero, unless we sacrifice the assumption that **m** is additive – and we must also assume (among other things) that a non-zero quantity of water, one for which the value of **m** is not zero, contains an uncountable infinity of water atoms.

And the alternative is not much more attractive. It is true that (pure) water has a molecular structure; if we say that the elements of the new domain of **m** are *not* infinitely divisible, molecules of water are natural candidates for their atoms – minimal quantities of water. But it is by no means obvious that molecules of water are minimal in *amount*; if they are, we can assume the value of **m** for each is *one*, and then every amount of water will measure an integral number of units – unless, again, we sacrifice additivity. But the value of **m** for fusions of subsets of Q was assumed to be an integral number of units only because of the truth of (7); if (7) is false, I for one find it quite unbelievable that any such result can be depended upon.[12]

We might in the interests of science perhaps, simply *lay it down* that a measure of amount for water is only as good as one which counts moleculcs.[13] Measuring amounts of water by the bucketful or gallon would then be like counting pennies by measuring their weight. But I am not sure that we could claim in this case to be measuring what, in English, we call 'water'. We could not, for example, speak of a given amount of impure, poisoned or chlorinated water.

6. Quantity inclusion cannot, I think, be defined by recourse to atoms; and in fact what Q represents is simply a choice of unit quantities. Given that choice, it is the order among values of $\mathbf{m}$ that determines the relation of quantity inclusion in its domain rather than the other way around, and there is no natural least unit quantity of water other than none.

But now it is not altogether implausible to assign to $\mathbf{m}$ a domain with the topological structure of the space occupied by elements of Q. Quantities of water are the occupants of regions of space about points inside the space occupied by the water in the buckets. Or better, to accommodate the fact that water retains its identity whether it is in one or more of the buckets or not, we can suppose the elements of the domain of $\mathbf{m}$ are the occupants of spatio-temporal regions about points of space-time. And with some refinement, quantity inclusion can be defined in terms of set-theoretic inclusion among occupied regions.[14]

According to this proposal, we need not suppose there are water atoms. If the domain of $\mathbf{m}$ is extended to include every region included in an occupied region, its values may be assumed to represent amounts of spacetime and amounts of water just in case a region is occupied by water; and this is again I think enough to show that the set of quantities of water in the domain of $\mathbf{m}$ – if there is such a set – is measurable.[15] We shall now say that, given any quantity of water, for example, the water in one of our buckets, its measure of amount is just that of the amount of spacetime it occupies.

But the trouble is that *that* amount of space-time is affected by such things as temperature. At a given time $\mathbf{m}$ may well assign a larger number to one element of Q than it assigns another – since it occupies more space; and this despite the truth of (7). And if it is assumed that the proposal can be salvaged by making $\mathbf{m}$ a measure of amount only under some more or less precisely specified set of standard conditions with respect to temperature pressure and the like, consider the case of a door which sticks in humid weather because it is a wooden door and the wood expands –that is, it becomes larger. Is humid weather non-standard? Perhaps so, if the size of the door is the size it has when it opens properly. But we can suppose the wood was cut to fit in humid weather and, instead, will not stay shut when the weather is dry. It seems plain that the door – and its wood – really do have two sizes. A measure of amount for 'wood', defined in accordance with the present proposal, will assign it two values; and we shall have to say we have two different amounts of wood.

Now it might be suggested that this is the best we can do. If an amount of wood or water cannot be identified via the amount of space-time it occupies, so it might be said, this is just because there is no *one* thing which is that amount. What I have called a measure of amount can only be a measure in some dimension – ultimately spatio-temporal; there are no amounts of water but only amounts by volume or by mass or the like; so the truth of (7), in particular, depends on a suppressed qualification. It can only mean that we have as much water *by volume* or some other quantitative property measured in accordance with some set of conditions, however *ad hoc*.

And I know of no quick way of countering this last suggestion except by appeal to a sort of conservation principle for those things for which I should maintain my initial claim about the schema (A). Without losing its identity, the wooden door might be made larger or smaller by adding or subtracting wood; but given that there *is* some one object which is the quantity of wood of which the door is made; adding or subtracting wood can only result in substitution of *another* object for that one – something which is more or less wood. And according to the story about humidity, that object does *not* lose its identity just because it does *not* become more or less wood.

7.   It seems we constantly make such judgments, and (7) is quite intelligible without qualification. It is to be so understood that its truth is enough for a reasonable measure of amount for those things to which 'water' applies – or at any rate enough to get such a function off the ground. Given the existence of a set of unit quantities of water, we have in the fusions of subsets of that set an operation analogous to the addition of weights or lengths which, however, is independent of methods and conditions of measurement. If we can assume that **m** is a function whose values really do represent the amounts of water in fusions of subsets of Q,

we can suppose it is based on nothing other than the nature of the water in those buckets – pure or impure, chlorinated or not. And sub-quantities of elements of Q will simply be assigned values in accordance with this requirement. In particular, where A is a set of such sub-quantities whose fusion is quantitatively equal to an element of Q, $\mathbf{m}(FuA) = 1$.

There is a real problem, of course, in specifying the *full* domain of $\mathbf{m}$ with any precision. We can preserve the assumption that it includes a mereology, and that in particular either $x - y$ or $y - x$ is in the domain of $\mathbf{m}$ if and only if x and y are distinct quantities of water. For a pair of elements of the domain of $\mathbf{m}$ are identical just in case they are the same water; and if x is a sub-quantity of y, $x - y$ is no water – i.e., not a quantity of water.[16] But without resorting to atomism, we cannot assume that there are quantities of water which can serve as a base for the domain of $\mathbf{m}$, a set of things such that every element of $\mathbf{m}$ is the fusion of some subset of that set.

Nor is it at all obvious that, having granted that the existence of the set of *all* quantities of water in one or more of those buckets is open to question, we can extend the domain of $\mathbf{m}$ beyond the set of fusions of sub-sets of Q in the way proposed earlier in accordance with the suggestion that quantity inclusion be defined in terms of spatio-temporal occupancy; for we cannot now assume any sense can be made of 'x is a subquantity of y' where x and y are not quantities of water.

We can, however, conclude that *some* set of sub-quantities of the fusion of Q, which, together with quantity inclusion, constitutes a mereology *is* the domain of $\mathbf{m}$; and although we have no guarantee that there is any one such set, $\mathbf{m}$ on the present proposal does not suffer from the defects of assuming it is based on a spatio-temporal metric or measurement in some dimension. What is crucial is the assumption that there are unit quantities of water, however arbitrarily selected, an assumption taken for granted in understanding sentences like (7). The existence of $\mathbf{m}$ as a measure of amount depends on that of Q, and the only difference between $\mathbf{m}$ and any other reasonable measure of amount for those things in the domain of $\mathbf{m}$ lies in the choice of another set of unit quantities. The fusion of such a set must have the fusions of subsets of Q among its sub-quantities; but it might be a set of half gallons or teaspoons or tons of water.

Again, then, to put the matter quite explicitly, I shall assume that D is a reasonably large set of sub-quantities of the fusion of Q such that $(D, \mathbf{q})$ is a mereology; and, where the domain of **m** is D, **m** is a measure of amount for 'water' if and only if its values are numbers such that for every x and y in D,

(i) $\mathbf{m}(Fu\{x, y\}) = \mathbf{m}(x) + \mathbf{m}(y)$ iff x and y have no common sub-quantities,

(ii) $\mathbf{m}(x) \geqslant \mathbf{m}(y)$ iff x is as much water as y,

(iii) $\mathbf{m}(x) > 0$.[17]

And my major claim can be put in part by saying that an amount function for 'water' is defined by what I shall call a *unit function* for the values of any such reasonable measure, **m**. We can say that whenever x is a quantity of water in the domain of **m**, the amount of water x measures in **m**-units is $u(\mathbf{m}(x))$. And (5′) is satisfied just in case the amount of water x is it the value of the **m**-unit function for the number assigned x by **m**.

In fact, since on the present suggestion we are still assuming that the value of **m** for every element quantitatively equal to an element of Q is *one*, where the elements of Q are the quantities of water in the buckets with which we began, if **m**′ is any *other* measure of amount for 'water' with the same domain as **m**, and the value of **m**′ is some number n, for every quantity of water quantitatively equal to an element of Q, then given any element x in the domain of **m**, $\mathbf{m}'(x) = n$ times $\mathbf{m}(x)$. And what this means is that **m**-units are simply water units; if, for example, each of the buckets contains two pounds of water, we can assume the values of the unit function for water in pounds are all just half the values of the **m**-unit function. And, in accordance with my claim, we need only say that for every x in the domain of **m**, x satisfies (5′) just in case it satisfies

(5″) $(Ey)(Wxy \cdot (En)(y = \mathbf{u}_w(n)))$,

that is, where the water unit function, $\mathbf{u}_w$, is the product of the **m**-unit function and the measure **m**, there is an amount of water which is the value of $\mathbf{u}_w$ for some number n; and (5″) says 'x is some number of units of water.'

8. Of course there is an obvious sense in which (5″) does not tell us what amount of water x is, but neither does (5′) nor (5); what is involved is an indefinite reference to an applied amount of water; and what is of prime importance about this formula is that anything which satisfies it satisfies the result of replacing 'units' by 'pounds' or 'gallons'. For in this, 'water' is *like* 'weight' or 'volume' in determining the analogues of *scales* of measurement. But measures of amount for quantities of water cut across dimensions of measurement, and I shall say that the linear ordering which a set of applied amounts of something inherits from a measure of amount applies only to amounts *of a kind*. 'Water', so I am supposing, designates a *kind*.

The sceptic lately considered will say there is no important difference between

(8)   Every bucket contains one gallon of water,

and

(9)   The water in every bucket measures one gallon.

Certainly there is room for confusion here. Carnap, for example, in illustrating "the operations by which extensive magnitudes are combined", says,

After partially filling a bathtub, we discover that the water is too hot, so we add some cold water. The total *volume* of water in the tub will be the sum of the *amounts* of hot and cold water that came through the faucets.[18]

And this way of using 'volume' may be one source of the assumption that, at any rate, (8) and (9) are to be interpreted the same way. Perhaps, then the present point may be clarified by insisting they are *not* to be so interpreted. (9) may be ambiguous; but while (7) plainly follows from (8), we can infer from (9), I think, and *not* (8) that

(10)   The volume of the water in every bucket is as large as the volume of the water in every other,

and, again, (7) does not follow from the likes of (10).

In accordance with the claim I am defending, (8) involves a definite explicit reference to an applied amount of water, and it can reasonably be assigned a semantic interpretation in the manner of

(8') $(x)(Bx \rightarrow (Ey)(Cxy \cdot (\imath z) Wyz = \mathbf{g}_w(1)))$.

'Every bucket contains the amount of water, one gallon'; $\mathbf{g}_w$ is a water-unit function defined via a function which, like $\mathbf{m}$, is a measure of amount for those things to which 'water' applies. In fact we can assume that $\mathbf{g}_w$ is

$\mathbf{u}_w$; and nothing follows about the volume occupied by the gallons of water concerned. And while (7′) is deducible from (8′) given the logic of identity, (9) is to be assigned an interpretation in accordance with something like

$$(9') \qquad (x)(Bx \rightarrow (Ey)(Ez)(Cxy \cdot Wyz \cdot (\imath v)\, Vyv = \mathbf{g}(1))).[19]$$

Here read 'Vyv' as 'y has the volume v'; the symbol for the unit function $\mathbf{g}$ need not be flagged since its values can only be the volume of something, regardless of the kind of thing it is; (9′) says the volume of the contents of a bucket is the value of the (pure) gallon function at one, and nothing follows about the amount of water in the buckets.

Now of course the truth of (8) – hence (8′) – depends on some agreement as to what is to count as a gallon of water. According to the *American Heritage Dictionary*, "In 1824 the British Imperial gallon was defined as the volume of 10 pounds of water at a temperature of 62° Fahrenheit".[20] That is, we can assume

(11)   The British Imperial gallon = the volume of 10 lbs. of water at 62°F.,

at least, as of 1824, and if the gallons of (8) are British Imperial, then no doubt at 62° Fahrenheit, they ought to measure one gallon. But to admit this is not yet to give way to the sceptic. Even if the definition is hedged with further qualifications as to pressure, the purity of the water to be measured and the like, it can only be understood if we have independent means of identifying 10 pounds of water. (11) can only be understood if it can be interpreted in the manner of something like

$$(11') \qquad \mathbf{g}(1) = (\imath x)(Ey)(Vyx \cdot (\imath z)\, Wyz = \mathbf{p}_w(10) \cdot y \text{ is at } 62°F\ldots)$$

One gallon (British Imperial) is the volume of something the amount of which is ten pounds of water – and it is at 62°F, etc. If reference to the applied amount, 10 pounds of water, is to be eliminated in favor of reference to a quantity of water weighing 10 pounds – without circularity or some sort of viscous regress – we shall be left with nothing to talk about. Perhaps, then, the best response to one who would say an interpretation of something like (9′) is all that is available for (8) – that, again, (7) depends on a suppressed qualification as to a dimension and conditions of measurement, is to say that the intelligibility of (9) – hence (9′) – depends on that of (8′). It may be conceded that the domain of any amount function for 'water' is not very tidy; but the elements of such a domain – the quantities of water in those buckets – are just those values of the variable 'y' for which (9′) is true – or, non-trivially, false. In order to draw any conclusions about the volume of some water which may or may not happen to be in a bucket, we need to be able to assume that there is something which *has* the volume in question and which might, under other circumstances, have another volume. But if there is any such thing, its identity depends upon the amount of water it is.

9. I have said that 'water' designates a *kind*, and my general claim about the schema (A) may be regarded as an explanation of what I mean by an amount of a given kind. There is an amount function for a word or phrase π, which provides a linear ordering for any set of amounts represented by some measure of amount for π, just in case π designates a *kind*. Thus, in particular, if in (7) 'water' is replaced by 'stuff' its truth certainly does depend on some unspoken qualification. If there is as much water by volume in one bucket as there is, say, sand in another bucket, presumably there is not as much water as sand by weight. There is no one linear ordering for amounts of stuff, nor in general for mass nouns like 'liquid' and 'metal' unless in a given context there is another sort of unspoken qualification as to what *kind* of liquid or metal is under consideration; again, 'as much water as sand' is like 'as much weight as volume'. Russell put the point somewhat unfortunately by saying, "We cannot first settle how much we will have, and then decide whether it is to be pleasure or mass".[21] I am not claiming that there is an amount function for 'pleasure' nor for some words, e.g., 'smoke' or 'fog' which seem to be the names of stuff. So it may be that, in some contexts, an amount of stuff is not the value of an amount function at all, though this seems to be true in just those cases in which there is no one object identifiable as an element of the domain of *any* function.

But now a final cautionary note is called for. In defending my claim about the schema (A), I have restricted myself to an easy word, 'water', and a simple story. It might now be argued that (7) depends after all on an unspoken agreement about the nature of the contents of the buckets. I hope I have made a convincing case for the difference between sentences like (2) in which 'much' occurs and sentences like 'This weighs as much as that' or 'This is as heavy as that'. Consider however, 'This is as muddy as that'. I should like to say that the truth of (7) is unaffected by differences in the purity of the elements of the set Q. But if we suppose that the water in one of the buckets is very much muddier than that in any of the others can (7) still go unqualified? One might say that in this case 'water' does not designate a kind; (7) depends on an unspoken qualification as to what *kind* of water – muddy or not – is in question.

Now I think the plausibility of this suggestion depends at least in part on nothing more than the vagueness of the distinction between muddy water and watery mud; as long as we are agreed that the former is in question, there is no problem about (7). Surely Aristotle was right to suppose that the result of adding a little wine to a lot of water is water – though not, as he seems to have claimed, *more* water.[22] The point at which the result of adding wine – or mud – to water ceases to be water is fuzzy; but it is at this point that we would cease to call it 'water with wine in it' or 'muddy water'. On an obvious reading (2) follows from

(12)   This is as much muddy water as that.

If (2) is interpreted in the manner of

(2′) $(\imath z)\,Waz \geqslant (\imath z)\,Wbz$,

and (12) is assigned an interpretation in accordance with something like

(12′) $(\imath z)(Waz \cdot Ma) \geqslant (\imath z)(Wbz \cdot Mb)$,

then (2′) follows simply because 'Wxy' represents an amount function for 'water'. In fact (12′) is equivalent to

$$Ma \cdot (\imath z)\,Waz \geqslant (\imath z)\,Wbz \cdot Mb,$$

'this is muddy and it is as large an amount of water as that, which is muddy too'.

Again, it is just possible that (12) suffers from an ambiguity similar to one which is familiar in recipes which, for example, call for a cup of sifted flour. One does not know whether to measure in flour units and then sift, or sift and then measure in sifted flour units. And if (12) is understood in the latter sort of way, it is not implausible to suppose it may be interpreted in the manner of something like

(12″) $(\imath z)(Waz \cdot Mz) \geqslant (\imath z)(Wbz \cdot Mz)$.

'The amount of muddy water this is is as large as the amount of muddy water that is'. The truth of (12″) depends upon the existence of an amount function for 'muddy water'; but if we assume that muddy water is water, (2) follows, (7) needs no qualification, and we can interpret sentences like

(13)   A gallon of non-muddy water is a larger amount of water than a gallon of muddy water,

by way of an interpretation of

(13′) $(\imath z)(Ex)(Wxz \cdot \sim Mz \cdot z = g_w(1)) > (\imath z)(Ex)(Wxz \cdot Mz \cdot z = g_w{}'(1))$,

'The amount of non-muddy water something is which is one gallon of it is larger than the amount of muddy water something is which is one gallon of *it*.' The difference between an amount of muddy water and an amount of non-muddy water is then due to a difference in choice of a water unit function; (13) is like 'A gallon of water is a larger amount of water than a pound of it'; and any linear ordering for amounts of water is a linear ordering for amounts of muddy water.

This is scarcely the end of the matter, however. The result of adding a little air to flour (by sifting) is flour, though not more flour; and the same may be said of whipped butter and the result of adding salt to salted nuts and, I think, salted water – one will have something saltier, but if it is still salted water and not some sort of slush, one will not have more water or more salt water or more of anything else. But it just possible that the result of adding mud to water, though not more water, *is* more of something else. And in this case an amount of muddy water is not an amount of water; the use of the predicate '*Wxy*' in (12″) and (13′) is just misleading.

The problem here involved does not affect the unqualified status of (7), since muddy water, if it is not water, is not a kind of water. But it does affect my general claim about the schema (A) where π is complex. Just what phrases permit an interpretation like that of (12″)? The problematic cases might be dealt with as idioms or assimilated to whatever treatment seems best for 'wooden indian', 'child who has grown up', 'heathen converted to christianity' and other problematic cases involving modified *count* nouns. What gives the question special interests here, however, is that 'muddy water' (or 'salt water' or 'soda water'), unlike 'fool's gold' or 'water which has turned to wine', raises issues concerning Aristotelian 'modes of combination'; and although I do not think the question in such cases is to be settled by chemistry, I am not at all sure how it *is* to be settled.

Tufts University

NOTES

[1] In 'An Analysis of Mass Terms and Amount Terms', *Foundations of Language* 5 (1970). It will be obvious to anyone familiar with that paper that much of what I have to say especially in Sections 8 and 9, was inspired by his treatment of applied amount terms. Sentence (8), in particular, is a variation on an example of his. I have profited as well from discussion with a number of people, in particular Richard L. Cartwright and C. Wade Savage.

[2] For an interesting theory which emphasizes these similarities, see Samuel C. Wheeler, 'Attributives and their Modifiers', *Nous* 6, No. 4 (1972). I think Wheeler's treatment of mass nouns in that article is at least consistent with what follows, though I am not entirely sure.

[3] Thus Russell's discussion of quantity in *Principles* of Mathematics (1903), Part III (especially, Sections 151–158 and 163), is much better suited to applied amount terms which are not the names of properties than it is to his professed subject; and that is why I have appropriated his word 'quantity' and contrasted it with 'amount' instead of his 'magnitude'. Norman Campbell couches his discussion of measurement in terms of properties, but in speaking of the 'physical addition' of weights, he says, "We say that the *body* C is 'added to' the *body* A, when A and C are placed in the same pan of the balance; ..." (*Physics the Elements* (1928), reprinted by Dover as *Foundations of Science* (1957), p. 279, my emphasis). Since we apparently do *not* add weights, it is at least tempting to suppose that, according to Campbell, we add amounts of something having weight. And this way of talking is perpetuated in, e.g., Morris Cohen and Ernest Nagel, *Introduction to Logic and Scientific Method* (1934), pp. 297–8. See also the quotation from Carnap below.

[4] For example, Brian Ellis, *Basic Concepts of Measurements* (1968); "... generally speaking, quantities are thought to be 'properties' of objects – characteristics which things must possess to some *specific* degree or other, even if we have no way of measuring or determining this degree" (p. 2). Ellis attributes this view to positivists and realists alike, and it is the general target of attack in his book. Parsons is a realist with respect to quantities in this sense, at any rate he gives a realistic account of 'isolated amount terms,' expressions which designate such things as one pound, and he seems not to be a realist with respect to applied amounts.

[5] *Principles of Mathematics*, Section 152.

[6] 'Heraclitus and the Bath Water' (1965) and 'Quantities' (1970), both in *The Philosophical Review*.

[7] Thus 'Wxy' represents an amount function for 'water' iff there is a function f whose values are applied amounts of water, and which is such that for every x and y in a set of quantities of water,

(i) x is as much water as y iff $f(x) \geqslant f(y)$
(ii) $\geqslant$ linearly orders the values of any function which satisfies (i).

It is to be understood here and throughout that in a context like this '$\geqslant$' means 'as large an amount of *water* as' and that the field of **q** is restricted to some set of quantities of *water*.

[8] Paul Halmos, *Measure Theory* (1950), p. 30, p. 73. **m** is a 'set function'. I am beginning with the notion of a measure on a set of sets because of the way additivity is defined; more generally, I am beginning here to emphasize the similarity, as well as the differences, between applied amounts and what might be called 'applied numbers' (objects designated by, e.g., 'ten rocks'). Though I shall not pursue the matter here, if (7) were 'Every bucket contains as many rocks as every other,' the second of the atomistic variants of **m** discussed below could reasonably be said to be a measure of the number of rocks in one or more of the buckets.

[9] The relation in question has the formal properties of the 'part-whole' relation in Lesniewski's mereology (A. Tarski, 'Foundations of the Geometry of Solids', *Logic, Semantics, Metamathematics*, trans. by J. H. Woodger (1956)), an algebraic structure equivalent to the calculus of individuals of Henry Leonard and Nelson Goodman ('The Calculus of Individuals and Its Uses', *Journal of Symbolic Logic* **5** (1940)), in which the notion of the fusion of a set is introduced.

[10] Here I am relying in part on D. H. Krantz, R. D. Luce, P. Suppes, A. Tversky, *Foundations of Measurement* **1** (1971). I am defining an abstract mereology as follows: Where M is a non-empty set which is the field of a relation **R** that is transitive, anti-symmetric and reflexive in M, the ordered pair $(M, \mathbf{R})$ is a mereology just in case

(i)   if A is a non-empty subset of M, then M contains an element x such that $(y)((z)(z \in A \rightarrow z\mathbf{R}\,y) \leftrightarrow x\mathbf{R}\,y)$;

and

(ii)   if x and y are elements of M such that $\sim x\mathbf{R}\,y$, then M contains an element z such that $\forall u(u\mathbf{R}z \leftrightarrow u\mathbf{R}x \cdot \sim (Ev)\,(v\mathbf{R}u \cdot v\mathbf{R}y))$.

Thus, where R is q, (i) requires that fusions of non-empty subsets of Q are quantities of water, (ii) rules out the fusion of the empty set, and (i) and (ii) require that for every pair of distinct quantities of water, x and y, either $x-y$ or $y-x$ is a quantity of water.

This definition, though perhaps less elegant, is equivalent to Tarski's; and it has the virtue of making a mereology look as much like an algebra of sets (Boolean algebra) as possible. Where B is a set of sets, $(B, \subseteq)$ is a mereology just in case it is closed under fusions (unions) and *non-empty* set-theoretic differences. The only mereology of sets which is an algebra of sets is $(\{\phi\} \subseteq)$, and if $B \neq \{\phi\}$ and $(B, \subseteq)$ is a mereology of sets, it would be an algebra of sets but for the empty set. There is no 'empty' individual in a (non-trivial) mereology.

[11] 'A World of Individuals' (1956), reprinted in *Problems and Projects* (1972). Goodman puts the suggestion in terms of a 'generating relation' which, unlike quantity inclusion, is asymmetric; but this is a minor difference. I do not mean to suggest that Goodman holds any version of the atomism discussed below, but generating relations are defined in this article only for systems based on sets of atoms.

[12] A variation on this view of the matter would be to suppose **m** assigns one only to the largest (or smallest) atoms of the same size; but since atoms have no sub-quantities in common $\mathbf{m}(x-y) = \mathbf{m}(x)$ for every pair of atoms, x and y, and it is hard to see how non-integral values are to be assigned to them without invoking a spatio-temporal metric in something like the manner discussed below.

To the extent that I understand him, Henry Laycock has recently expressed views which would seem to commit him to some version of atomism in 'Some Questions of Ontology', *Philosophical Review* **81** (1972).

[13] And in fact this seems not even to be sound science in view of such phenomena as ionization.

[14] This is pretty clearly the view of W. V. Quine (in *Word and Object* and elsewhere) and, less clearly, that of others. It is also Parsons' view in the article cited above; see pp. 366, 368. R. E. Grandy expresses justified discomfort at the introduction of a 'new primitive' (our quantity inclusion) in 'Comments on Moravcsik', *Approaches to Natural Language*, Hintikka, Moravcsik, and Suppes, eds. (1973). And he has recently expressed a view which suggests the scepticism discussed below.

[15] Here I am relying on Halmos, *op. cit.*

[16] It follows that if x and y are distinct elements of the domain of $\mathbf{m}$, and $y\mathbf{q}x$, there is an element z of the domain of $\mathbf{m}$ such that $x = Fu\{x, y\}$; z is $x - y$, and $\mathbf{m}(x) = \mathbf{m}(y) + +\mathbf{m}(x-y)$. It does *not* follow that for *every* pair of distinct elements of the domain of $\mathbf{m}$, there is an element z such that if x is as much water as y, x is quantitatively equal to $Fu\{y, z\}$ *unless* y is a sub-quantity of x; and the difficulty for the variants of atomism discussed in note (12) remains. Where x and y are distinct atoms, neither is a sub-quantity of the other, and there are elements u and v in the domain of $\mathbf{m}$ such that $\mathbf{m}(x) = \mathbf{m}(y) + (\mathbf{m}(u) - \mathbf{m}(v))$ only if x and y are sub-quantities of unit quantities; but there need be nothing in the domain of $\mathbf{m}$ such that its fusion with y is quantitatively equal to x (unless, again, quantity inclusion is defined in terms of spatio-temporal occupancy).

[17] Given the added condition that if $\mathbf{m}'$ is a function that satisfies (i) and (ii), there is a number n such that $\mathbf{m}'(x) = n\mathbf{m}(x)$, for every x in the domain of m (see below), I take it that according to Krantz, *et al.* cited above, m represents a 'positive closed extensive structure', the structure $(D, \gtrsim, \circ)$, where '$\gtrsim$' means 'as much water as' and $\circ$ is an operation such that $a \circ b = Fu\{a, b\}$, if a and b have no common sub-quantities, and, if they do, $a \circ b = Fu\{a, b\} - Fu\{u : u\mathbf{q}a \cdot u\mathbf{q}b\}$.

[18] *Philosophical Foundations of Physics*, Martin Gardner, ed., p. 71, my emphasis. Compare 'volume of business' or '... work'; surely 'volume' here just means 'amount'.

[19] This is roughly Parsons' rendering of the analogue of (8), given that '... we have the formula '$3Gy$' which is true of the amount three gallons and nothing else' (p. 379 of the article cited above). Thus, '$3Gy$' represents a function, and we may put '$y = g(3)$' instead.

[20] Under 'measurement'.

[21] *Principles of Mathematics*, Section 156. I think my use of 'kind' is in fact his (in more favorable cases), and my explanation of its use may be regarded as an attempt to interpret what he says in sections 155–57 about "the absolute theory".

[22] *On Generation and Corruption*, Bk. 1, Ch. 10. This Passage and that problems here involved were most recently called to my attention by Richard Sharvy and Lucy Carol. As a matter of chemistry there *may* be more water in the case in question; but surely not as a matter of semantics. Compare adding color or clay to some water or adding water to whiskey.

TYLER BURGE

MASS TERMS, COUNT NOUNS, AND CHANGE*

From early childhood we learn to distinguish compact, enduring things from the stuffs of which they are constituted. We count the former and measure the latter. We treat things as stable points of reference for action and experience; stuffs we think of as amorphous and protean.

Traditionally, philosophers have confronted these intuitive distinctions with categories like form and matter, substance and substrate, mode and extension. A linguistic analogue of these category pairs, albeit a rough one, is the distinction between physical-object count nouns and mass terms. Mass terms are nouns like 'water', 'wood', 'calcium', 'gravel' which under the relevant reading may be modified by the phrases 'how much' and 'very little' and which resist pluralization, the indefinite article 'a', and modifiers like 'how many' and 'quite numerous'. Physical-object count nouns under the relevant reading tolerate the listed syntactical modifications which mass terms exclude and exclude those which mass terms tolerate. From a semantical viewpoint, if a mass term applies severally to two isolated objects (portions of stuff), it usually also applies to the result of lumping them (or, better, considering them) together. Physical-object count nouns, on the other hand, tend not to apply cumulatively. Mass terms are typically used to measure the masses – count nouns, to number the multitudes.

The match between our rough linguistic distinction and the intuitive thing-stuff distinction is not exact. Not all mass terms are intuitively true of stuffs. 'Fruit', 'clothing', 'apparatus', 'hardware' are not. Some expressions which intuitively do, at least sometimes, apply to stuffs are not mass terms – 'quantity', 'aggregate' and perhaps 'part' and 'piece'. Still, the parallel between the distinctions is close enough to warrant the view that by giving a formal theory of sentences containing typical count nouns and mass terms, one will also be clarifying the logical and ontological content of the intuitions about stuffs and things which we have inherited from childhood and our philosophical tradition.

My plan in this paper is to develop two formal accounts of some sentences

199

F. J. Pelletier (ed.), Mass Terms, 199–218. All Rights Reserved.
Copyright © 1975 by D. Reidel Publishing Company, Dordrecht, Holland.

about change which crucially involve relations between mass terms and count nouns. A formal account will consist in showing how to represent the relevant natural-language sentences, or at least the relevant components of them, in a language whose syntax and semantics we clearly understand. For present purposes we will need little more than quantification theory supplemented with predicate constants. The point of a formal account is not to explicate the 'force', 'sense' or application conditions of particular natural-language words or phrases. Rather it is to render more evident the logical implications and ontological commitments of the unanalyzed sentences by exhibiting the formal roles of the parts of the sentences and explicating their contributions to the truth conditions of the wholes.

What criteria enter into choosing a best formal account is a complicated and vexed issue. But roughly, we take as evidence certain intuitions of native speakers that seem to bear on interpreting the sentences, such as intuitions about paraphrases, ambiguity, grammatical form, truth conditions, obvious implications. And we try to represent the natural-language sentences in such a way as to account for our evidence with as simple a logic and primitive predicate basis, and with as simple and clear an ontology, as possible. These requirements apply not only to the logic and the ontological commitments of the semantical theory, but also to the logic and ontology that the theory attributes to the natural object-language sentences. The aim is not to prohibit attributing baroque logics or ontologies to sentences of natural languages. It is merely to discourage doing so (ceteris paribus) if a simpler attribution is available. The reason for this stricture is the broad methodological principle that we should avoid attributing unnecessary complication or irrationality to the beliefs or presuppositions of those (here, native speakers) whose utterances we are trying to interpret. The attempt to simplify one's formal representations of natural-language sentences should be carried out with an eye on a theory of syntax for those sentences. Whereas the formal representations are to provide the basis for semantical interpretations of the natural-language expressions, they should not be such as to complicate transformation rules that connect 'deep' representations with surface sentences. We shall return to methodological issues near the end of the paper.

Although we shall develop our two accounts as *linguistic* theories, their development will bear on traditional philosophical questions. One of the approaches resembles the sort of reductionism about physical objects that takes only a few sorts of objects as basic and 'constructs' all others in terms of them. The other resembles a more 'common sense' viewpoint. I shall be pushing the 'reductionist' view as far as it can go as a representation of natural discourse in order to throw light on one-place predication as applied to physical objects – or more materially and narrowly, on what it is to be a physical object, whether a thing or some stuff, of a certain *kind*. Of course, arriving at a best representation of natural discourse about stuffs and things does not determine a best account of stuffs and things themselves. There is room for argument over whether natural discourse should be revised, discarded, or reduced. But the linguistic investigation is a long first step toward dealing with the metaphysical issues.

Two very old problems about change will provide the bulk of the intuitive, linguistic evidence with which our formal accounts are designed to deal. One of them is the Aristotelian problem of how to talk systematically about physical changes that occur in the form of some stuff or in the matter of a thing. The other is the problem, associated with Heraclitus, of explaining formally why from the premise that rivers are water we do not conclude that successive bathings in the same river are successive bathings in the same water.[1]

1. Changes in matter and form

The matter of which a given thing is constituted often changes without that thing's ceasing to exist. Proverbially, a ship may be rebuilt plank by plank until it is completely reconstituted. A river changes its water continually. The flesh and bone of a person's body is entirely replaced every several years. Moreover, in the case of many things, the kind of stuff of which they are made may change. A lake of water may become a lake of oil, yet remain the same lake. By replacing parts of a given engine over a period of time, one might change it from being made of steel to being made of aluminum.[2]

These considerations might lead one to adopt one of two representations of sentences describing changes in the matter of an object. On one approach, one might hold that the sentence,

(1)   That engine was once steel, but it is now aluminum

should be represented as

(2) $(\exists t)$ (Steel (that engine, t) & Aluminum (that engine, now)
           & Is-before (t, now)),

where 't' ranges over times and 'Steel (that engine, t)' is read 'that engine
is steel at t'. On this approach, mass-term predicates are relativized to a
time. Mass terms like 'steel' and 'aluminum' are on this view regarded
intuitively as expressing temporally relative properties of sortally identified
things.[3] Let us call the approach to sentences like (1) which (2) typifies
'*the Relational Approach*', the distinguishing feature being that mass terms
(and later, other common nouns) are consistently represented as relational predicates.

A second way of handling (1) is to represent it as treating a certain
relation between the engine and some steel at one time and between the
engine and some aluminum at another. Thus:

(3) $(\exists t)$ $(\exists y)$ $(\exists z)$ (Steel (y) & C(that engine, y, t) &
           Aluminum (z) & C(that engine, z, now) & Is-before (t, now)),

where 'C' is read, '_____ is constituted of _____ at ...'. Alternatively (and
non-equivalently), 'C' could be read, '_____ (spatially) coincides with
_____ at ...'. On either reading 'C' is true of ordered triples consisting of
two physical objects (e.g. some steel and an engine) and a time. Let us
call the type of analysis illustrated by (3) '*the C-Approach*'.

A possible reason for preferring (2) to (3) is the desire to maintain the
principle that no two physical objects can as wholes occupy the same
space at the same time. If (1) is true and (3) represents (1), then the principle is violated; for 'C' purports to express a relation between physical
objects which are spatially indistinguishable at time t, but which are not
identical because only one (the engine) is later constituted of some
aluminum. By treating mass terms themselves as relational, (2) does not
yield this consequence. Although the principle is a fruitful topic for
discussion, I shall not linger over it in the present context because it can
be shown implausible without recourse to mass terms. For example, a
rope and a hammock (woven from the rope alone) may be spatially
indistinguishable at a given time, and not be identical.

Before discussing further what is at stake between the two approaches,
we should bring into view another class of sentences which are relevantly

similar to (1). These are sentences which intuitively describe changes in the form of some given stuff. Focus, for instance, on

(4)   Once this gold was a ball, but now it is a statue.

The Relational Approach as we have so far characterized it will have difficulty with (4). A possible representation is

(5) $(\exists x)\,(\exists y)\,(\exists t)\,(\text{Ball}\,(x)\ \&\ \text{Gold}\,(x, t)\ \&\ \text{Statue}\,(y)$
           $\&\ \text{Gold}\,(y, \text{now})\ \&\ \text{Before}\,(t, \text{now})\ \&\ S\,(x, t, y, \text{now})),$

where '$S\,(x, t, y, \text{now})$' is read 'x is made of the same stuff at t as y is now' or 'x at t is same-stuffed with y now'. The primitive 'S' must be understood to express not just sameness of *kind* of stuff, but sameness of actual stuff. The problem with the representation is that despite the reading it gives 'S', it does not imply (as (4) intuitively does) that there is something which at both times exists, or that something at the earlier time is re-identified at the later time – namely the very gold which takes on the two different shapes. Other relational predicates besides 'S' are possible, but they raise the same difficulty.

Sentences like (4) seem to be mirror images of sentences like (1). Re-identification of the gold via (4) is analogous to reidentification of the engine via (1); change in the form of the gold is analogous to change in the matter of the engine. *These considerations tend to undermine attempts to distinguish count-noun predicates from mass-term predicates on the basis of the number of their argument places.*

A proponent of the Relational Approach to (1) can respond to this situation by extending its relativization strategy to (4). We shall henceforth construe the Approach more broadly than we have so far characterized it. Earlier only mass terms were relativized; now, count nouns themselves go relational:

(5') $(\exists t)\,(\text{Ball}\,(\text{this gold}, t)\ \&\ \text{Statue}\,(\text{this gold}, \text{now})$
            $\&\ \text{Is-before}\,(t, \text{now})).$

We shall postpone for a while the problem of how the Relational Approach is to construe the singular terms 'this engine' and 'this gold' in (2) and (5'). The C-Approach, which we applied to (1), can be utilized without substantial revision to represent (4). On this view, (4) goes into

(6) $(\exists y)\,(\exists z)\,(\exists t)\,(\text{Ball}\,(y)\,\&\,C\,(y,\,\text{this gold},\,t)\,\&\,\text{Statue}\,(z)$
         $\&\,C\,(z,\,\text{this gold},\,\text{now})\,\&\,\text{Is-before}\,(t,\,\text{now})).$

The differences between the two approaches may now be given initial
generalized characterizations from both linguistic and ontological points
of view. Linguistically, both approaches recognize that the 'is' in sentences
like (1) and (4) is not the 'is' of identity. The Relational Approach interprets it as the 'is' of tensed predication; the C-Approach represents it by a
non-logical primitive like 'constitutes' or 'coincides with'. Ontologically,
the Relational Approach takes ordinary stuffs and things to be phases of
something more basic (or less cautiously, as changeable properties of a
substratum); the C-Approach construes stuffs and things as fundamental
kinds of objects. A common impulse is to want to reject the Relational
Approach out of hand, claiming that the 'is' in (1) and (4) just *means* 'is
made of' or that stuffs and things are obviously not mere modes of a
substratum. Although such intuitions, especially those about predication,
have some force, uncritical acceptance of them tends to prevent one from
understanding a philosophically interesting network of considerations
underlying them.[4]

It should be noted that (4) does not involve what are ordinarily
thought of as phase sortals. The usual examples of phase sortals are
count-nouns like 'sapling', or 'boy' which are applicable to organisms at
only one phase of their growth, or like 'pauper' or 'banker' which are
closely related to adjectives or verbs and which may apply to an object
during only a stage in its history. From the usual examples one receives
the impression that phase sortals are a pretty restricted lot. 'River', 'ball',
'statue', 'molecule', 'engine', 'pebble', 'animal', 'dog', 'tree', and so forth
would certainly seem not to be included among them. A test often relied
upon for distinguishing phase sortals from 'permanence' sortals is that
the latter but not the former will truthfully substitute for 'F' in the schema

(NP) $(x)\,(x$ is an F at some time t & it is not the case that x is
         an F at some other time $t' \rightarrow x$ does not exist at $t')$,

where the first and third occurrences of 'is' are intuitively read as predicative copulation.[5]

The Relational Approach to sentences like (4) is unusual in that it suggests that according to this test the vast majority of count nouns should be represented as phase sortals. Thus something (the gold) is a ball at one time and is not a ball at a later time without ceasing to exist. So the test shows 'ball' to be a phase sortal. Similar arguments could be applied to most other count nouns, including those which have seemed to apply to natural kinds. To put the matter in a more traditional way: the Relational Approach holds that there are very few sorts of individuals or substances. Objects that we often think of as such are on reflection seen to be phases of something more basic.

What is it then that is more basic on the Relational Approach? In representing the sentences about change that we shall discuss, the Approach will nowhere be forced to be explicit about its ontology. A necessary condition for a theory to be explicit about its ontology is for it to contain primitive, *one-place* predicates which must be satisfied in order for the sentences of the theory to be true. The condition focuses on one-place predicates as opposed to relational predicates because we may always ask of the latter what kind of things are the relata. Among one-place predicates, those which represent common nouns are intuitively most informative about a theory's ontology. A proponent of the Relational Approach could simply claim that since virtually all common nouns in ordinary empirical assertions are represented by relational predicates, such assertions are not explicit about their ontology, except perhaps in trivial cases in which they contain a predicate like 'is a physical object'. The *sorts* of physical objects presupposed by ordinary asserions about change, on this view, would not be determinable on the basis of formal representations of those assertions.

Now it is no objection to a theory to say that it is not explicit about its ontology. Set theory in its usual formulations is not. But in evaluating the Relational Approach, it will be important to understand what ontological consequences it regards as implicit in ordinary discourse. The only predicates which the Approach can ultimately exempt from its temporal relativization strategy are those like 'is a physical object' whose generality prevents their applying to an object during only a stage of its history, and either those like 'is an elementary particle' that apply to objects which never coincide with other objects, or those like 'is a space-time thread of maximal duration' (or 'is a maximal world line') that apply to objects always underlying but never undergoing change.[6]

In its acknowledgement of very few sortal predicates, the Relational Approach bears a distant kinship to a long line of reductionist ontologies (from the pre-Socraties and Democritus to Sellars) which have held that only atoms in the void, or only matter, is fundamentally real and that the objects of ordinary experience are either 'mere appearance' or should be explained as modifications of the more basic entities. The Relational Approach differs from its elders in resting its case on an analysis of non-technical empirical descriptions rather than on an interpretation of sophisticated scientific theory. But it shares with them a certain aura of revisionism. Ordinary language-users do not tend to think of molecules, engines, or trees as phases of something more basic. According to the Relational Approach, however, a general analysis of ordinary discourse shows that that is what language-users have committed themselves to.

The ordinary phaseal-nonphaseal distinction is on this viewpoint a product of temporal near-sightedness. The reason why the phaseal character of most count nouns is overlooked is that when one uses a count noun, one typically intends to apply it to some object which is phenomenologically, structurally, or functionally similar to other objects of recurrent human interest. Suppose that some wood constitutes a table at a given time. The general term 'table', on this account, applies truly to both the wood and the table at that time. When the wood is broken up and used for some other purpose, the table ceases to exist; and one's interest in the table distracts one from tracing the continuing history of the wood. If in numerous such uses of 'table' one were more interested in the table than in its relatively protean constituents, it would be easy to conclude that if 'table' is true of an object at any given time, it is true of that object throughout its existence. Thus, according to the Relational viewpoint, arises the illusion that 'table' will substitute truthfully in (NP).

The anti-essentialist character of the Relational viewpoint should be clear. What is once a dog, or table, or molecule is not always a dog, table, or molecule – much less necessarily one. The intuition that 'table' applies more essentially to tables than to wood, however, need not be counted *entirely* groundless by the Relational Approach. It has both unitemporal and transtemporal significance. 'Table' is true of all tables but only some quantities of wood relative to a given time. 'Table' is true of a given table at every time during which it exists, whereas the term tends to be more fickle with respect to a given portion of wood. By using these points, it is possible to define an unrelativized predicate 'Table' in terms of the relativized one:

(UR) $\text{Table}(x) =_{df} (t)(x \text{ exists at } t \rightarrow \text{Table}(x,t)) \& (\exists t)(\text{Table}(x,t))$.[7]

(UR) utilizes the intuition behind (NP) to define phases of 'something more basic' which can play many of the roles of the ordinary objects of experience. (The phases are plausibly temporal stages of space-time threads or successions of time-slices of elementary-particle aggregates.) The relational predicate in the definiens is still fundamental for the Relational Approach because, given that 'is' in (1) and (4) is construed merely as the tensed copula, the one-place predicate is useless in representing contexts like these. But the defined predicate does fairly well in representing many other natural language sentences. And this partial adequacy, according to this approach, contributes further to the misconception that most physical-object count nouns substitute in (NP).

Remarks analogous to those made in the previous paragraph can be directed at predicates derived from mass terms. Definitions like (UR) are constructable for them as well. On the Relational Approach both concrete count nouns and mass terms are fundamentally time-relative – and for mirror-image reasons.

I should note that even definitions like (UR), which give us some one-place predicates to apply to approximations of the ordinary objects of experience, do not take the edge off the anti-essentialism of the Relational Approach. To be a Table (with capital 'T') one must be a space-time thread (an occupied space-time region) that is a table throughout its existence. But that space-time thread could have been 'filled' with matter, other than the wooden matter, that would have been unsuitable for use as a table. If time-slices of elementary particle aggregates are taken as basic, an analogous point may be made.

Traditional replies to the reductionisms kin to the Relational Approach have often resorted to vague denigrations of the ontological status of stuffs. Feeling that the objects which we ordinarily refer to with count nouns are 'basic', philosophers have fixed upon mass terms as the source of their uneasiness. (Cf. (5).) I shall not detail here why these moves seem to me misguided. In brief, reflection on sentences like (4) suggests that individuation of quantities of stuff is an integral element in our descriptions of the world. Stuffs do tend to have different sorts of individuation and reidentification conditions than ordinary things have. But this difference does not give ground for calling stuffs less real, less actual, or less physical than things.[8]

The C-Approach need not ally itself with these replies to reductionist ontologies. In fact, by treating ordinary count nouns and mass terms as primitive one-place predicates, it clearly commits itself to quantifying over both stuffs and things.

2. MATTER AND FORM AT A TIME

So far we have centered our attention on sentences dealing with changes in the matter or form of a specified object. I wish now to consider a class of true sentences in which singular terms denote objects which differ but which are spatially indistinguishable during a period in their histories. These sentences introduce the problem of how to give formal representation to our individuation of stuffs and things. As an example of the sentences I have in mind, consider

(7)   The gold which was once a ball is now the statue which stands on yon pedestal.

which for our purposes can be shortened to

(7′)   The gold is the pedestaled statue.

The problem of representing (7′) is an acute one for the Relational Approach as we have so far developed it. The most immediately attractive way of handling the sentence would be to treat it as involving an identity sign flanked by two singular terms. One might call on one-place predicates 'Gold' and 'Statue' defined in the manner of (UR), thus:

(a)   (that x) Gold $(x) =$ (that z) (Statue (z) & Pedestaled (z)).

Since we assume that in asserting (7) the language-user is demonstrating an object (the relevant gold) which pre-existed the statue, that object is not identical with the statue. So (a) is false, whereas (7′) is, by hypotheses, true.

The Relational Approach might deny that a singular term occurs on the right side of (7) and continue to treat 'is' as merely the tensed copula. But experimentation with this claim will indicate that it is prohibitively complicated in its effect on the analysis of sentences other than (7). For example, imagine accounting for the inference from (7) and 'The statue which stands on yon pedestal is identical with Cellini's finest piece of sculpture' to 'The gold which was once a ball is now Cellini's finest piece of sculpture'.

The upshot is that the Relational Approach is forced to introduce a non-logical primitive. There are two plausible choices for the Relational Approach. One is to introduce the relational predicate 'is a temporal stage of', abbreviated 'T'. The resulting analysis of (7') would be

(8)   (that x) $(T(x,$ (that y) Gold $(y))) =$
          (that z) $(T(z,$ (that w) (Statue (w) & Pedestaled $(w))))$.

(There is, of course, a certain indefiniteness as to *which* temporal stage is meant. But this might be said to be derivative from the indefiniteness of the 'now' in (7).) A second choice open to Relational Approach is to attribute to the 'is' in (7') a sense other than that of identity or the copula. This choice is, I think, best implemented by borrowing the primitive of the C-Approach and representing (7') as

(9) $C(($that $z)$ (Statue (z) & Pedestaled$(z)),$ (that x) Gold $(x),$ now$)$

For future reference I shall assume that the Relational Approach chooses (9). The C-Approach agrees in representing (7') as (9), except that its one-place predicates 'Gold' and 'Statue' are primitive rather than defined.

3. THE PROBLEM OF HERACLITUS

The problem of Heraclitus arises from the following argument:

(10)   All rivers are water

(11)   Heraclitus bathed in some river yesterday and bathed in the same river today

∴(12)   Heraclitus bathed in some water yesterday and bathed in the same water today.

One might imagine situations in which (10) and (11) are true, but (12) is false. So in natural language the argument fails. But in its most natural formalization, the argument sails through:

(13) (x) (River (x) → Water (x))

(14) $(\exists y)$ (River (y) & Bathed-in $(h, y,$ yesterday) & Bathed-in $(h, y,$ today))

∴(15) $(\exists z)$ (Water (z) & Bathed-in $(h, z,$ yesterday) & Bathed-in $(h, z,$ today)).

On one possible reading of them, (12) and

(16)   There is some water which Heraclitus bathed in yesterday and which he bathed in again today

are true whenever (10) and (11) are. The aggregate of all currently existing water molecules is certainly some water. If Heraclitus takes water-baths on successive days, he bathes on both occasions in (within) that portion of the world's water that exists during both bathings. Many, however, will refuse to count (12) or (16) true under these circumstances. In some cases such refusal stems from denial that all the water in the world is some water. A more reasonable ground for resistance is the view that 'bathed in' is true of some water only if that water more or less immediately surrounds a bather.[9]

What is important for our purposes is that even if one regards (12) and (16) true whenever (10) and (11) are, that is not enough to establish the validity of (10)–(11)–(12) and thence the correctness of (13)–(14)–(15) as a representation. For the world's water could have been less durable than it is (perhaps if the process of reversible ionization occurred at a much faster rate). Suppose that after Heraclitus' first bath, all the world's water dwindles into oblivion and continuously synthesized water takes its place, the process of replacement being complete in time for the second bath. In such circumstances (10) and (11) would be true and (12) false.

Very roughly speaking, the C-Approach has pursued the strategy of introducing a non-logical primitive to represent 'is' whenever that word links mass terms and count nouns. Hence for it (10) will be the center of attention. In this light, (10) will be read not as (13), but as

(17) $(x) (t)$ (River (x) & Exists (x, t) → $(\exists y)$ (Water (y) & $C(x, y, t)$)).

('Every river is constituted of (coincides with) some water at every time during which it exists.') The reading shortcircuits the Heraclitean argument regardless of which of the construals of (12) is chosen.

The Relational Approach sees the problem differently. (13) is left unaltered as a reading of (10), with the provision that 'River' and 'Water' are defined in the manner of (UR). Alternatively, (10) could be read as '$(x)(t)$ (River $(x, t) \rightarrow$ Water $(x, t))$'. Either treatment follows the general plan of taking all occurrences of 'is' which attach directly to count nouns or mass terms as occurrences of the tensed copula. Whereas the C-Approach attributed the mistake in (13)–(14)–(15) to its representation in (13) of 'are water' as it occurs in (10), the Relational Approach naturally focuses on (15)'s construal of 'same water' as it occurs in (12). From the Relational viewpoint, (15) must be read: 'There exists something that throughout its existence is water and that Heraclitus bathed in yesterday and today'. (Recall that 'Water' in (15) is defined by the Relational Approach in a way illustrated by (UR).) The problem is that the something quantified over in (15) could as well be the river as a quantity of water. For given (13), both satisfy the defined predicate 'Water'; both are water (are 'in the water relation') throughout their existence. So if our man bathed in the river on successive days, (15) would be true even if (12) were false. This problem seems to force the Relational Approach into finding some way of expressing a distinction between an object's being water throughout its existence and being some water. Definitions of the form of (UR) can now be seen to be inadequate as expressions of the latter notion.

Tinkering with various alternatives will, I think, lead the reader to the view that no use of the resources that we have so far allotted the Relational Approach will produce an analysis that is both equivalent to (12) and syntactically plausible. What is needed for a relatively simple representation is the introduction of a predicate which distinguishes the sort of entity that the relevant water is from the sort of entity that the river is. The need seems filled by the following:

(18) $(\exists x)$ (Quantity (x) & Water (x) & Bathed-in $(h, x,$ yesterday) & Bathed-in $(h, x,$ today)).

In words, 'There exists a quantity which throughout its existence is water; and h bathed in that quantity yesterday and today.'

To explicate the general notion of quantity (or stuff) here would side-track us too far. But in the present instance, the idea is roughly that a quantity of water is a concrete aggregate of water molecules. Quantities of water are the same just in case they have at all times, respectively, the same water molecules as parts. Given this construal of 'Quantity', (18) distinguishes 'same water' from 'same river' and gives the wherewithal to block the Heraclitean argument.

The grammatical lesson of that argument has been that one cannot always take phrases of the form 'is MT' and 'is the same MT as' (where a mass term subs for 'MT') into the analyses traditionally given to general terms – '$M(x)$' and '$M(x)$ & $x=y$' respectively. The C-Approach alters the analysis of 'is MT'. The Relational Approach reconstrues 'is the same MT as'.

The Heraclitean argument suggests a more important lesson. We have seen that the temporal relativization of predicates representing mass terms and count nouns and the reliance on definitions like (UR) left the Relational Approach with insufficient means to individuate some water in such a way as to distinguish it from a river. But the Approach's weakness in individuating runs deeper. Definitions like (UR) are *always* too weak to provide unique correlates of the objects we intuitively associate with common nouns.

To see this, imagine the following sentence to be true:

(19)   Exactly one river extends through Heraclitus' home town.

To represent (19) the Relational Approach must invoke its one-place predicate 'River' defined in the manner of (UR). The resulting representation will imply that exactly one object which extends through Heraclitus' home town 'is' throughout its existence a river. But innumerable temporal stages of the (full-length) river 'are' a river throughout their existence and extend through the relevant town: 'River (x)' as defined by (UR) is true not only of rivers but also of all river-stages. The difficulty applies to all definitions of oneplace, physical-object count-noun predicates in the manner of (UR) and to all attempts to individuate quantities of stuff by supplementing (UR)-type definitions by the notion of quantity.

What recourses are open to the Relational Approach? One is to deny that river-stages satisfy '$(\exists t)$ (River (x, t))', claiming that only rivers and quantities of water satisfy it. Taken by itself, the positive claim virtually begs the question. For the claim occurs in a semantical metalanguage that uses the very words ('river', 'water') whose formal representation we have been discussing. If those words are not to be construed as the C-Approach construes them, they must themselves be understood in terms of relational predicates; but then the same question arises for these predicates as arose with respect to 'River (x, t)' in the analysis of (19). The problem is that it is questionable whether the Relational Approach construes 'river' in such a way as to distinguish its application from 'river-stage'.

To defend the view that river-stages do not satisfy '$(\exists t)$ (River (x, t))', one must either deny their existence or explain why they do not satisfy it. (Similar points will apply to relational stuff predicates.) The former alternative is, I think, extravagant and implausible. The latter is unpromising. The Relational Approach is based on allowing entities that are not rivers, such as quantities of water, to satisfy 'River (x, t)' relative to certain times. Presumably they do so because they have the appearance, constitution, and form of a river at a certain time. But river-stages meet these very requirements. So there seems to be no cogent reason for denying that they satisfy '$(\exists t)$ (River (x, t))'. In fact, they seem to be paradigmatic satisfiers. Attributing the presupposition that river-stages do not exist or that they do not satisfy '$(\exists t)$ (River (x, t))' to ordinary assertions would be attributing unnecessary irrationality to the asserters.

Another artifice available to the Relational Approach is to hold that there is no reason to try to find a unique correlate of the ordinary notion of river: a multiplicity of river stages (of various temporal durations) will do. It is a remarkable fact that for the purposes of representing many natural-language sentences, such a multiplicity will 'do'. In (2), (5'), and (9), the relevant stage (engine-stage, quantity-of-gold-stage, statue-stage) could be regarded as vaguely determined in the context by demonstrative reference. As for (13), (14), and (18), the interpretation of 'River (x)' as river-stage (and 'Quantity (x) & Water (x)' as quantity-of-water stage) will in no way upset the material equivalences between the representations and the sentences they represent. Despite all this, the rationale is implausible. Applied generally, it would amount to giving up (or failing to account for) the practice of counting ordinary physical objects. For the number of temporal stages of any given sort would always be the same: non-denumerably many. Since we do not count with mass terms, this difficulty would attach only to count nouns. But another difficulty would attach to both. The proposed view would require giving up generalizations about the age of things and of quantities of stuff of a given kind. (Consider 'All the gold on earth is over one-half billion years old'.) These problems make this strategy unattractive from both metaphysical and linguistic points of view. Counting and dating are the weak spots in the Relational Approach.

In a sense the dating problem – or more generally, the problem of failing to represent fully our reidentifications over time – is the more fundamental of the two. Although, as we have noted, reidentification is a difficulty apart from counting, the converse does not clearly hold. This can be seen by considering an attempt to solve the counting problem while ignoring the problem of reidentification. One might represent (19) as saying that there is one spatial volume such that all river-stages that now extend through Heraclitus' home town fully and congruently occupy it (and some do). But the analysis depends for whatever plausibility it has on the present tense of (19) and on a peculiar characteristic of rivers, their relative immobility as wholes. No such analysis would be even mildly plausible for

(20)   During the last year there were exactly twelve balls on the billiard table.

The reason is that the balls might have moved around on the table during the year: there would be more than twelve spatial volumes fully occupied by the various ball-stages. Unless we provide it with some means of tracing a line of stages in a way that parallels our apparent reidentification of objects, the Relational Approach will be unable to deal convincingly with such sentences.

The only remaining defense of the Approach would seem to consist in trying to strengthen definitions like (UR). One thinks immediately of introducing some relation of spatio-temporal continuity which would count a thing of a given sort as a maximal line of spatio-temporally continuous stages, all characterized by the relevant temporally relative predicate. But the prospects of rigorous definitions for each intuitive kind of stuff and thing are not very bright. Not only are there a number of well-known difficult cases (cf., for example, note 2), but it is hard to see generally how to make continuity principles both precise and consonant with facts about the micro-structure of the objects of ordinary experience.

One might shift from continuity principles to causal principles – or to some combination of the two. But the task of specifying the relevant causal chains in a way sufficiently rigorous to facilitate the needed reductive *definitions* is hardly promising.[10]

Our methods of reidentifying physical objects over time are developed only as far as our immediate practical and theoretical needs require. Such needs do not include an understanding of general principles which are necessary and sufficient for reidentification. Nor is there any reason to think that in the general case there *are* principles tacitly guiding our usage which are comprehensive enough to cover all possible (or even imaginable, or even, sometimes, actual) cases. Confidence in applying common nouns to physical objects derives from ostensive teaching, from illustrative statements larded with demonstrative references, from inculcated rules of thumb, and from our innate learning capacities. In short, counting and dating physical objects of a given kind presuppose not a general criterion of identity or criterion of reidentification, but an ability that rests on an exposure to paradigm cases (not necessarily of the given kind) and on a congery of inclinations, prejudices and truisms which help focus the exposures and project them.

Thus to represent sentences like (19) and (20) with defined one-place predicates, the Relational Approach would not merely have to formulate principles that are inexplicit and highly complicated. It would have to lay down principles of reidentification that in the ordinary use of common nouns are fundamentally undetermined. The advantage of using primitive one-place predicates, instead of relational predicates that apply to temporal stages, is that we may thereby presuppose an ability to reidentify objects instead of having to state a principle of reidentification. There are, I think, theoretical reasons why we do not lay down and adhere to such principles. But exploring the vagueness in the reidentification conditions of common nouns would take us beyond our present venture.

The difficulty that counting and dating present to the Relational Approach suggests that these activities are fundamental to one-place predication as applied to physical objects. Demonstrative reference and the activity of locating objects are no doubt our most familiar and pragmatically important means of discriminating members of a physical-object natural kind. But counting and dating, or reidentifying, are equally central to ordinary usage. For these latter activities seem to be our basis for distinguishing physical objects of a given kind from mere modes or stages of an underlying substratum.

4. POST MORTEM

The Relational Approach's difficulty with sentences like (19) and (20) provides the best ground for preferring the C-Approach as a representation of natural discourse. But other grounds are worth articulating briefly.

The real lure of the Relational Approach, as a linguistic theory as well as a metaphysical one, is the simplified ontology it appears to promise. But it is not committed to fewer entities than the C-Approach. Syntactically plausible representations of (11) and (12) demand definitions like (UR). And specifying the relata of the relational predicates in these definitions requires postulating phases of the basic objects which are at least as numerous as the physical objects postulated by the C-Approach. Whether the Relational Approach is committed to fewer *kinds* of entities is a question in need of a way of counting the kinds a theory recognizes. Clear ways are not easy to come by. But one might suspect that if the Approach were to explicate the conditions under which each common noun marks out a stage of a maximal space-time thread, it would thereby make distinctions which would demarcate 'kinds' of threads that correspond one-one to the kinds recognized by the C-Approach. In brief, the ontological advantages of the Relational Approach are dubious.

Whereas the Relational Approach provides no clear ontological simplification, it complicates an account of syntax pretty drastically. To obtain reasonably simple representations of sentences like (11), (12), (19), and (20), the Approach would have to formulate a definition like (UR) for each mass term and physical-object count noun in the vocabulary. The Approach also requires a significantly more complicated primitive predicate basis,[11] a multitude of irreplaceable two-place predicates. The same number of monadic predicates are utilized by the C-Approach to do more work: they make possible a plausible formal representation of our activities of counting and reidentifying physical objects – which the Relational Approach has so far failed to do.

From the point of view of the ordinary use of natural language, neither all stuffs nor all things are relations on, properties of, or segments of something more basic. Paradigmatic examples of stuffs and things are fully concrete elemental members of our physical ontology.[12] From the point of view of a reconstruction of scientific knowledge, however, our anti-essentialist Relational Approach may remain an instructive if methodologically exacting option.

The University of California, Los Angeles

NOTES

* I am indebted to many people – especially to Robert Adams, John Perry, Warren Quinn, and John Wallace.

[1] Good informal discussion of aspects of the Aristotelian problem may be found in David Wiggins, *Identity and Spatio-Temporal Continuity* (Basil Blackwell, Oxford, 1967). On the Heraclitean problem, see W. V. Quine, 'Identity, Ostension, and Hypostasis', *From a Logical Point of View* (Harvard U. P., Cambridge, Mass., 1953), pp. 65–70; *Word and Object* (MIT Press; Cambridge, Mass., 1960), pp. 116, 171; Helen Morris Cartwright, 'Heraclitus and the Bath Water', *Philosophical Review* **74** (1965), 466–485; John Perry, 'The Same *F*', *Philosophical Review* **79** (1970), 181–200. In what follows I shall use 'physical object' to apply to anything which (from some assumed point of view) may be an object of reference, which is physical, and which is not an event. On our favored account, the terms 'stuff' and 'thing' will be construed as having *roughly* disjoint extensions each of which is included in that of 'physical object'.

[2] There are cases in which gradual change of parts seems to involve change in identity. Imagine that smugglers gradually dismantle a valuable, historic steel engine, replace its parts one by one with aluminum ones (to fool the authorities), and ship the original parts across the border where they are reassembled. I shall assume that such examples do not show that in all cases of complete part replacement, the identity of the whole is altered.

[3] This handling of mass terms is perhaps suggested by Aristotle's paraphrase of them into adjectives, *Metaphysics* **IX**, 7. The Relational Approach may be fairly characterized as treating substantivals on the model of adjectives.

[4] A position between our approaches is that of D. Gabbay and J. M. Moravcsik, 'Sameness and Individuation', *The Journal of Philosophy* **70** (1973), 513–526. The position treats mass terms and count nouns as one-place predicates true of functions from times to a substratum. Thus, portions of gold, tables, animals, and mountains are taken to be abstract objects. The excuse for this view is the unelaborated claim that it helps explain the sense in which physical objects are 'constructions'. But it is left unclear why such explanation requires identifying physical objects with functions rather then merely holding that for each physical object there is a function from times to some substratum that mirrors the object in the appropriate way.

[5] The schema is an offspring of Aristotle's so-called logical criterion for substance. Cf. *Categories* **4a**, 10–11.

[6] I use 'thread' instead of 'worm' because stuff can be spatially scattered (unraveled). I do not intend 'thread' to rule out even temporal discontinuity, but metaphors that make such a possibility four-dimensionally picturesque are scarce.

[7] I shall not argue for my representation of tense since it has no very deep bearing on the main issues of the paper. (For the argument see my 'Demonstrative Constructions, Reference, and Truth' *The Journal of Philosophy* 71 (1974), 205–223.) If we had used a tense-logic to represent English sentences, the same issues could have been developed by focusing on the metalanguage. I am willing to take 'Exists at t' as primitive, although as applied to physical objects it could be defined as 'occupies some place at time t'.

[8] Cf. note 3. Richard Rorty in 'Genus as Matter' in *Exegesis and Argument: Essays in Greek Philosophy Presented to Gregory Vlastos*, Edward Lee *et. al.* (eds.), Van Gorcum, Assen, The Netherlands, speculates that Aristotle's physical criterion for substance and his treatment of stuffs as 'mere potencies' were partly motivated by a desire to block reductionist ontologies which result from pushing the logical criterion for substance (essentially (NP)) to the point of counting only ultimate substratum as substance, cf. *Metaphysics* VII, 16. For criticism of more recent moves analogous to Aristotle's, see Helen Morris Cartwright, 'Quantities', *Philosophical Review* 79 (1970), 25–42; Henry Laycock, 'Some Questions of Ontology', *Philosophical Review* 81 (1972), 3–42; and my 'Truth and Mass Terms', *Journal of Philosophy* 69 (1972), 263–282, esp. sections II-IV.

[9] Quine occupies this ground in Review of Geach's *Reference and Generality*, *Philosophical Review* 73 (1964) 102. I assume that everyone would agree that water which does not exist while Heraclitus bathes is irrelevant to determining what water he bathed *in*.

[10] This is equally a difficulty for attempts to reconstruct our practice of counting by appeal to some sort of equivalence relation among the relevant stages. The problem is to state the equivalence relation without relying on the monadic 'kind' predicate.

[11] Reasons for this claim stem from Nelson Goodman's work on simplicity. See *The Structure of Appearance* (Bobbs-Merrill, New York, 1951), 2nd edition, pp. 63–123.

[12] This paper has dealt only with account-types. A closer examination of stuffs suggests that some of them are plausibly construed on the model of phases of more basic stuffs. Cf. 'A Theory of Aggregates', forthcoming in *Noûs*.

RICHARD E. GRANDY*

STUFF AND THINGS

Metaphysical problems often concern the relation between various types of entities or putative entities. Philosophers at least since Aristotle have puzzled over the relation between particulars and universals, substances and things, movements and actions. Debate over the first of these issues still continues, but I think it is fair to say that there was an increase in clarity when, around the turn of the century, the notion of a set was made clearer and more explicit. For the purposes of logic, at least, the use of a set of objects as the analogue of a universal has been quite fruitful. Interpreting a predicate by means of a set of ordered n-tuples has provided a precise characterization of the semantics of the language which has led to interesting metatheoretical and philosophical consequences. There are still some problems which are not resolved by this approach. For example, it seems intuitively plausible that there could be two distinct universals with the same instances. Nevertheless, the approach at least gives an unproblematic theory of truth for sentences involving only particulars and universals. The issue about distinct universals with the same instances is a disputed one and in any case the set theoretic view enables one to give a sharp statement of the issue in dispute.

I would not want to argue that having a theory of truth or of truth conditions for a particular type of sentence resolves all philosophical problems about those sentences, nor even all problems about their meaning. However, I do think that we have made an important step toward understanding that type of sentence when we discover how to give such a theory of truth. Thus I think that even though the set theoretic construal of universals leaves some unresolved problems, we do have a clearer understanding of sentences involving only universals and particulars than we do of sentences involving mass terms, where the issue of how to give a theory of truth conditions is still open.

I once attempted to argue that there is no obstacle to treating mass terms such as 'gold' and 'water' as predicates that are true of all bits, lumps, chunks and so on of gold and the pools, puddles, rivers, and so on

219

F. J. Pelletier (ed.), Mass Terms, 219–225. All Rights Reserved.
Copyright © 1975 by D. Reidel Publishing Company, Dordrecht, Holland.

of water.[1] It now seems to me that the main point which I was defending, that mass terms can be treated uniformly as predicates, is correct. However, I now think that certain further puzzles require that the predicates must apply to something other than bits, lumps, puddles and their ilk. The complexities begin when we consider statements that involve the relation of mass and sortal terms over time. It seems that we must introduce a notion of identity at a time. For example, the bit of gold G that was a statue S yesterday may be a cube C today, in which case we want to be able to say $G = S$ at t_1 and $G = C$ at t_2, while denying that $S = C$, with or without temporal subscripts. There are, of course, alternative analyses which could be given in which the gold and statue are distinct entities which bear some relation such as 'constituting' or 'overlapping' at various times.[2] The approach which uses an overlapping relation is alien to the spirit of the original claims, however, for one of the motivations of my treatment was an ontological repugnance toward having two entities of the same type, the bit of gold and the statue, in the same place at the same time. The constituting approach suggests that the entities are of different sorts, for the relation is asymmetric, but in its usual forms it gives no analysis of the relation or of how the entities differ.

Unfortunately, there are other puzzles about the relation between stuff and things that I did not consider in the earlier paper, and which cause serious difficulties.[3] For example, the statue may be new at t, whereas the gold of which it is made is not. Or a ring may be broken, though we would not ordinarily say that the gold of which it is made is broken. Clearly some modification of the theory is necessary. The situation is a puzzling one in that I think that our natural inclination is still to say that the gold *is* the statue, even in the face of the predicates which apply to one but not the other at the same time. The difficulty is to find a suitable sense of 'is'.

I think it instructive at this point to consider another example where the same type of puzzlement seems to arise, but where the solution is somewhat clearer. We can generate puzzles involving the term 'temperature' which are similar in form to those involving mass terms and count nouns. For example, comparable to the gold which was a statue yesterday and is a cube today, we have the fact that the temperature was 75 degrees an hour ago and is 73 degrees now. And comparable to the difficulty about the same predicate seeming to both apply and not apply at the same time, we have the fact that the temperature is 73 degrees and the temperature is falling, but 73 degrees is not falling. Again, a temporalizing of identity would provide a way out of the first difficulty, since we could say that $T=75$ at t_1 and $T=73$ at t_2 but it provides no way out of the second difficulty.

This situation is less puzzling than that of mass terms, for it seems clear that the temperature is not identical with 73 degrees, but rather the temperature-at-t is equal to 73 degrees. That is, we do not assert a temporal identity between the temperature and a number, but rather a non-temporal identity between the temperature-at-a-time and a number. The temporal relativization attaches not to the identity itself but to the temperature. This naturally leads, if we want to associate an entity with the temporally unqualified temperature, to identifying the temperature with a set of ordered pairs consisting of times and numbers. This last entity, of course, can be thought of as a function from times to numbers.

Frege taught us that in order to understand predication we must understand the nature of functions, and I believe that in order to understand sentences about temperature we also need to use functions. The similarity between the puzzle about temperature and the one about mass terms suggests that the same treatment would be enlightening in the second case. So let us try treating a ring as a function from times to quantities of matter. In order to put things in a more familiar notation, we can take advantage of the fact that a function is a relation, and thus we can consider a ring as a relation between times and quantities of stuff (remembering, of course, that the relation must associate at most one quantity of matter with a time). The qualification 'at most one' is necessary because there will be times such that the relation does not hold between those times and any quantity of matter; these are the times at which we would say the ring does not exist.

We thus distinguish two senses of existence, the timeless sense appropriate to interpreting the quantifiers and the tensed one which is what is usually in question when we speak of the existence of physical objects. The latter is definable in terms of the former, and thus we can express that the ring R did not exist in 1970 by writing $-(\exists x)\, R(x, 1970)$. It is crucial to remember that specific rings are relations between times and matter, and thus the property of being a ring is a property of such relations. Thus we need a distinct predicate $\mathscr{R}$ that applies to relations just in case they are rings. With this notation, we can express the sentence which might sound rather problematic: There is (tenselessly) a ring which does not exist now, as $(\exists R)(\mathcal{R}(R) \ \& \ -(\exists x) \ R(x, \text{now}))$. (Note that the existence of an R that satisfies $\mathcal{R}$ will require, among other things, that there is some time t and some matter x such that Rxt.)

It is also possible to say in English that a particular piece of gold is a ring at t, but this presents no difficulties for that sentence can be paraphrased as 'There is some ring which the bit of gold is at t' which, of course, can be rendered as $(\exists R) \ \mathcal{R}(R) \ \& \ Rgt$, where g is a name of the quantity of gold. To further clarify the view I am advocating, let us consider the possible objection that rings cannot be sets because rings have spatial locations and sets do not. The reply is that the location of a ring is the location of the quantity of matter which is the ring at that time.

What I have argued above was that rings and other physical objects are best construed as sets or functions but this is neutral between a first order and a second order formalization. The reason for choosing the second order formulation is that we wish to be able to systematically represent locutions such as 'x is a bit of gold' or 'x is a puddle of water' where the phrase 'bit of' or 'puddle of' can be attached to any mass term to produce a sortal. Thus we want these phrases to apply syntactically to mass terms to produce sortal terms and this can be done only within a higher order logic. For example, we would introduce a constant relation expression $\mathcal{B}(F)$ which takes mass terms as values of F and produces the corresponding sortal 'bit of F'. Since we require this much apparatus from higher order logic, we can most naturally treat the remainder of the theory in a higher order logic as well.

I suspect that the claim that some English predicates such as 'is a ring' are second order predicates will meet with some resistance, especially from those who wish to treat all English predicates as first order predicates when translating English into formal notation. But note that the distinction I am drawing is reflected in English itself. The quantification which is made explicit in my rendering of 'The gold is now a ring' is indicated in the English sentence by the occurrence of the indefinite article 'a'. Thus there is a systematic difference between the grammar of 'x is a ring, a table, a statue,...' and that of 'x is gold, water, beef,...'. A second way in which English distinguishes between mass and count predicates is that 'a gold ring' can be transformed into 'a ring of gold' but not 'a gold of ring'. That it is the mass-count distinction which is reflected here can be supported by noting that when a word which has a mass sense is not being used in that sense the transformation does not work. Thus a mud puddle, in which 'mud' is being used in its normal mass sense, is also a puddle of mud, but a mud guard is not a guard of mud.

It is not surprising that the distinction of levels between mass and sortal predicates has not been noticed, for quantification theory was invented for the purpose of formalizing mathematics, where mass terms play no significant role. And philosophers since Frege have mostly tended to relegate mass terms to a category of unimportant, if problematic, types of expression. To avoid misunderstanding, it should be emphasized that the values of the first level variables in my theory range over *quantities* of matter, in a technical sense of the term. I have deliberately spoken of quantities rather than lumps, bits, parcels or some similar expression for these terms are all count nouns. It is true that they are in some respect unparadigmatic count nouns, for unlike chairs or persons, there is relatively little point to counting bits or puddles.[4] Nonetheless, the grammar of 'bit' and 'puddle' is analogous to that of 'chair' and 'person'. In using 'quantity' in this technical sense, I am following Helen Cartwright's suggestion,[5] though I do not want to make as strong assumptions about quantities. For her, quantities of stuff must be comparable as to amount, an assumption which is difficult to defend and for my purposes unnecessary. For me it suffices that a quantity be spatio-temporally coherent and consist uniformly of the same type of stuff. One difference between such things as lumps and quantities is that although a lump of gold may be divided physically into two lumps of gold it is, until divided, a single lump. A quantity of gold, on the other hand, already contains many other quantities of gold. The division of lumps and puddles is a physical one while the division of quantities is a conceptual one.

The position that I am advocating here is clearly different from a view of mass and sortal terms which suggests that the items referred to by such expressions stand in a relation of overlapping or coincidence at various times. And it is different from a view which suggests that the relation is that of identity at a time – I have tried to make clear that 'The ring is the gold which was on the table' does not assert a temporally qualified identity, but an untemporalized identity between the gold and the-ring-at-the-present-time. My view could be considered a version of the position that the ring is constituted of the gold, but I would emphasize the advantage of my version in that it is explicit about the nature of the constituting relation and the types of entities related.

This suggested answer might be resisted on two grounds independent of the question whether the details of the theory can be worked out in a fruitful way and integrated with a grammatical theory. First, it might be objected that physical objects could not be sets of bits of matter since sets are abstract objects and physical objects are, of course, concrete. I have suggested earlier a way of getting around some of the force of this objection, but I think it desirable to set out the general principle which I am assuming. I consider the question what 'table', 'chair' and so on refer to to be most profitably answered by the following method. Construct the best semantics for English that you can, where 'best' includes fitting with a grammar and explaining the inferences that we make. Whatever that semantics associates with 'table' is what 'table' refers to in English. Thus if in the best semantics for English 'table' is true of sets, then tables are sets. Metaphysical intuitions may be useful in deciding between alternative semantic theories, but they should not have so much influence as to rule out a semantic theory in the absence of competitors. Epistemological objections in the vein that one cannot see sets will have to be answered by the semantics en route since the best semantics will have to provide plausible truth conditions for such sentences as 'David sees a table'. [6]

A different objection would be that my theory collapses the abstract-concrete distinction and this is an important metaphysical distinction. I do think the distinction is an important one, but it can be drawn within my theory. If one distinguishes those sets such that their members or the members of their members or ... are concrete from those sets which do not have this property, then one can recapture the abstract-concrete distinction.

The final objection I want to consider is in a way the opposite of the first. Someone might grant that what tables are is a question of what our best theory tells us they are, but then point out that physics tells us that they are collections of molecules. This is not incompatible with the theory I have been sketching. I have said that a table is to be considered as a set of pairs consisting of bits of matter and times, but I have said relatively little about the quantities of matter themselves. If one wishes to build in the most recent physical theories, one could well take quantities of matter to be collections of molecules, elementary particles or whatever one thought correct.

University of North Carolina at Chapel Hill

NOTES

* I am indebted to Brian Chellas, Kathleen Cook and David Rosenthal for helpful comments on an earlier version of this paper which was read at the APA Eastern Division meetings in December, 1973.
1 'Comments on Moravcsik', in K. J. J. Hintikka, J. M. E. Moravcsik, and P. C. Suppes (eds.), *Approaches to Natural Language*, D. Reidel, Dordrecht and Boston, 1973.
2 For a thorough discussion of the cost of alternative theories, see T. Burge, 'Mass Terms, Count Nouns and Change', this volume, pp. 199–218.
3 I am indebted to Stephen Schiffer for insisting on the importance of this point.
4 There are some anomalous mass terms in English which apparently must be treated as higher than second order. Terms such as 'furniture', 'jewelry' and so on have as minimal units items which are already individuated by means of count nouns such as 'chair' and 'necklace'. Thus if we identify the furniture in a room with the set of chairs, tables, etcetera, then we will find that 'furniture' is a fourth order predicate. I doubt that such nouns are of any theoretical interest.
5 'Quantities', *Philosophical Review* 79 (1970), 25–42; see also K. C. Cook, 'On the Usefulness of Quantities', this volume, pp. 121–135.
6 I find Cartwright's arguments (p. 40, *op. cit.*) that a quantity cannot be a set of elements puzzling. The argument seems to show that we may have to make a rather arbitrary decision as to exactly which set, but this does not mean we could not make such a choice. Indeed her argument seems to show that ordinary intuitions are sufficiently vague that no harm is done by such a choice. For a more extended discussion of this issue see Henry Laycock, 'Some Questions of Ontology', *Philosophical Review* 81 (1972), 3–42.

BRIAN F. CHELLAS

QUANTITY AND QUANTIFICATION*

In [2], Richard E. Grandy proposes that the distinction between *mass* and *sortal* terms be understood as a difference in levels of predicates. Mass terms – like 'gold' and 'water' – are first-level predicates; sortal terms – like 'ring' and 'statue' – are second-level predicates. A natural language with terms of both sorts is to be regarded as a kind of second-order language, with quantifiers appearing at (at least) two levels.

Mass terms apply to *stuff*; sortal terms apply to *things*. First-level variables range over stuff – or *quantities* of stuff; second-level variables (first-level predicate variables) range over things.

Grandy proposes to analyze things as *relations* between quantities of stuff and points in time, subject to the condition that each such relation associates at most one quantity of stuff with each temporal point. The idea is that things are best thought of as functions – not always defined – from times to quantities of stuff. Thus a gold ring is identified with the function whose values are the quantities of gold that constitute the ring from molding to melting. Moreover, the spatial location of a thing is determined by the spatial location of the stuff that constitutes it; so the spatial location of the ring at any moment is the spatial location of its gold.

In this way, a difference emerges between the sentences 'There is gold on the table' and 'There is a ring on the table'. The first has the simple form

(1) $\exists x\, (G(x) \land O(x, now))$,

where G and O are first-level predicates for 'gold' and 'on the table', and x is a first-level variable ranging over quantities of stuff. The second sentence, however, is cast something like

(2) $\exists R(\Re(R) \land \exists x(R(x, now) \land O(x, now)))$,

where $\Re$ is a second-level predicate for 'ring' and R is a first-level predicate variable ranging over thing(-relation)s, appearing once in subject position and once in predicate position.

By rendering mass and sortal terms distinctly in this way, Grandy is able

227

F. J. Pelletier (ed.), Mass Terms, 227–231. All Rights Reserved.
Copyright © 1975 by D. Reidel Publishing Company, Dordrecht, Holland.

to resolve some familiar puzzles. How can we affirm 'The ring is the gold which was on the table' and 'The ring is new' without implying that the gold which was on the table is also new? The answer, essentially, is that the expression 'the ring' is ambiguous. The sentence 'The ring is the gold which was on the table' is of the form

(3) $\imath x\exists R(\Re(R) \land R(x,\ now)) = \imath x(G(x) \land O(x,\ then))$.

Here 'the ring' means the quantity of stuff that currently constitutes a ring – as in the description $\imath x\exists R(\Re(R)\land R(x,\ now))$. The sentence 'The ring is new', on the other hand, comes out as

(4) $\Re(\imath R\exists x(\Re(R) \land R(x,\ now)))$,

where $\Re$ is a second-level predicate for 'new'. In this case, 'the ring' refers to the thing itself, and not to the stuff of which it is constituted – as in the description $\imath R\exists x(\Re(R) \land R(x,\ now))$. Clearly, there is no inference from (3) and (4) to

(5) $N(\imath x(G(x) \land O(x,\ then)))$

– 'The gold which was on the table is new' – in which 'new' appears as a first-level predicate, N.

I agree with Grandy that both mass and sortal terms are best treated as predicates, but I do not share his conviction that they are predicates of different levels. Not that I believe them to be on the same level; it is just that I see little to prompt the alternative opinion. Given Grandy's views on the nature of the entities involved, the sentence 'There is a ring on the table' could as well be cast as

(6) $\exists r(R(r) \land \exists x(\langle x,\ now\rangle \in r \land O(x,\ now)))$,

where R here is a first-level predicate – unquantified – for 'ring' and r is a first-level variable (perhaps with its range restricted to things).

The point is that nothing in the metaphysics of Grandy's proposal requires second-order predication and quantification, as he remarks himself. Nevertheless, he argues that higher-order logic is already essential to the representation of sortal predicates like 'bit of gold', in which 'bit of' appears to apply syntactically to a mass term to produce a sortal. However, while one might agree about the utility – even the necessity – of representing 'bit of gold' as $\mathscr{B}(G)$, where $\mathscr{B}$ is a predicate-forming operator corresponding to 'bit of', Grandy lacks an independent argument to show that $\mathscr{B}(G)$ is second-level rather than first-level. (It only confuses the matter – and perhaps begs the question – to call $\mathscr{B}$ a "constant relation expression".) Grandy does note what seems to be a "systematic difference" in the grammars of the two sorts of term. But I fail to see how this entails a difference of level.

Indeed, there may be a reason for preferring a uniformly first-order approach. There are predicates, like 'new', that apply equally to both stuff and things. Granted, the newness of the ring may have nothing to do with the newness of the gold that constitutes it – the gold may well be old. But 'new' is anyhow *applicable* to both the ring and the gold. Thus on Grandy's analysis not only do expressions like 'the ring' turn out to be ambiguous, so also do certain predicates. These must be represented – as in (4) and (5) – by predicates of different levels, and while there may be no logical objection to the appearance of such duplicates, it will nevertheless be incumbent upon the semantic theory for such a language to account for the connection in meaning between them.

Let me conclude my remarks on the linguistic aspect of Grandy's proposals with the observation that – whichever syntactic analysis be chosen – a great deal of theory must be attributed to any language containing both mass and sortal terms. For, as already noted, corresponding to every thing-relation covered by a predicate there needs to be a statement to the effect that the relation is many-one. And Grandy indicates further axioms – for example, that to say that a thing is a ring is to say that it is sometimes instantiated. It is not clear, however, where such theoretical constraints are to appear. As axioms in the object language? As part of the metatheory? More needs to be understood of Grandy's conception of semantics for natural languages.

Now I turn to the metaphysical aspect of Grandy's paper.

Responding to the objection that his analysis obliterates the concrete-abstract distinction – the objection that things (anyway, physical objects) are concrete whereas relations are abstract – Grandy asserts that what sort of thing something is should be accounted for in terms of the best semantic theory for a language containing words for things of that sort: "Whatever that semantics [for English] associates with 'table' is what 'table' refers to in English." This reply is meager enough, of course, in the absence of any substantive account of how a semantic theory for a natural language might interpret sentences with mass and sortal terms in the way Grandy advocates. But, regardless of how well his theory of stuff and things meshes with this-or-that semantic theory for this-or-that natural language, it is clear that Grandy *is* offering a theory – what may be called a formalization of certain notions implicit in discourse containing mass and sortal terms.

It is sometimes said that sortal terms differ from mass terms in that sortal terms "divide their reference" whereas mass terms do not. According to Grandy, mass terms do, after all, divide their reference; they divide it among quantities of stuff. What is a quantity of stuff – of gold, for instance? Grandy declares the notion to be a technical one, akin to but not the same as that discussed by Cartwright in [1]. For Grandy, "it suffices that a quantity be spatio-temporally coherent and consist uniformly of the same type of stuff." He says further that "[a] quantity of gold... contains many other quantities of gold."

This last remark causes some perplexity. If a quantity of gold is indeed divisible into further quantities of gold, then although sentence (1) – 'There is gold on the table' – is intelligible enough, I do not know how to construe a sentence like

(7) $\exists!x(G(x) \wedge O(x, then))$

– 'There was exactly one quantity of gold on the table'. The point is not that (7) is false or that it is necessarily false. Rather, the idea that quantities are divisible in this way simply calls into question the very meaningfulness of quantification and identity in connection with mass terms and quantities of stuff.

The question raised here is important for Grandy. For he regards it as an attractive feature of his analysis that good sense can be made of sentences like (3) – 'The ring is the gold which was on the table'. But (3) seems likely always to be false, or meaningless, inasmuch as it implies (7).

The sensible thing might seem to be to give up the idea of divisibility. Still, sentences like (7) – and hence (3) – are puzzling. Any good-sized quantity of gold will contain other quantities of gold. But how many? Does it make sense to ask? Questions like this require resolution before quantity and quantification can be used successfully to explain the behavior of mass and sortal terms.

University of Calgary

BIBLIOGRAPHY

[1] Cartwright, Helen Morris, 'Quantities', *The Philosophical Review* 79 (1970), 25–42.
[2] Grandy, Richard E., 'Stuff and Things', this volume, pp. 219–225.

NOTE

* The present paper revises one I read as a reply to an earlier version of Richard E. Grandy's 'Stuff and Things' at the seventieth annual meeting of the American Philosophical Association, Eastern Division, in Atlanta, 27 December 1973. I thank Duane T. Williams for helpful criticism of this and my previous efforts.

D. GABBAY AND J. M. E. MORAVCSIK

SAMENESS AND INDIVIDUATION*

Is 'same' always used in the same sense? Do the truth conditions of statements of the form 'x is the same as y' remain constant throughout the variety of uses in which they may be embedded? These questions have been worrying linguists and logicians for some time. This paper is designed as a modest attempt toward the clarification of these issues. Its main claim is that we must distinguish the concepts of identity, persistence through time, and individuation: concepts which are interwoven in a variety of ways in our uses of 'same'. On the basis of these distinctions a rigorous semantics can be developed that clarifies the meanings of a number of key phrases in natural languages like English. It should also aid those who probe the depths of certain metaphysical and logical problems concerning identity.

1

Though philology does not recapitulate theology, certain phrases can be borrowed from theology to facilitate exposition in philology. With respect to phrases of the form:

(1) $x = y$

one can distinguish between the unitarian and the pluralistic analyses. According to the unitarian analysis, traced back at least as far as Leibniz, (1) is complete as it stands, is unambiguous, and entails the indiscernibility of its referents. As Quine has remarked, even if some may doubt the identity of indiscernibles, no one can doubt the indiscernibility of identicals. The contrasting pluralistic interpretation can best be illustrated by some recent writings of P. T. Geach.[1] According to Geach, (1) is incomplete as it stands. The expression of English that functions as the connector in the schema derived from (1), i.e., 'is the same as', needs to be completed to read 'is the same F as', where F is some general term. Furthermore, depending on different substitutions for F, (1) will be linked to different criteria of sameness. In other words, the full expanded form derived from (1) will read: 'x is the same F as y', where F not only

233

F. J. Pelletier (ed.), Mass Terms, 233–247. All Rights Reserved.
Copyright © 1973 by The Journal of Philosophy

helps to specify the referents of 'x' and 'y', but also determines their criteria of identity. In support of this view Geach claims that statements of the form:

(2) x is the same F as y, but not the same G as y.

are well-formed and in some cases true.

In a recent defense of the unitarian view, John Perry[2] has claimed that Geach's examples of instances of (2) can be given adequate interpretations that maintain the unitarian view of identity, while admitting the possibility that different analyses, resting on notions other than just identity, may apply to the variety of sentences in which 'same' is used.

One can separate the issue of the nature of identity from the issue of the possible ambiguity of 'same'. As the starting point of this paper we accept Perry's defense of the unitarian position on identity. At the same time, we intend to explore the possible ambiguities of the phrase 'is the same as', and look for uses that Geach's (2) might fit, though we agree that the formula does not fit statements in which *identity* is expressed.[3]

The need to distinguish different senses of 'same' arises when we consider statements like

(3)   The metal of which your toy is made is the same as that of which airplane engines are made.

This sentence can be interpreted in two ways, depending on whether or not one wishes to quantify over species and kinds. If we interpret the referring expressions on the two sides of 'is the same as' as designating actual pieces of metal, then the 'is the same as' must mean "belongs to the same kind (species) as." This notion is indeed distinct from that of identity, and it requires completion by some predicate 'F'. This can be seen by considering the fact that one would naturally go on, having made statement (3), and say something like: "namely, aluminum." Thus this use of 'is the same as' meets one of Geach's conditions, that of being in need of completion by some predicate 'F'. It does not, however, meet his other condition: that F determine the criteria for sameness. For the conditions for belonging to the same kind or species are quite general and do not vary from predicate to predicate, thus making formula (2) inapplicable. (This use will be given rigorous treatment in the appendix.) The use in question can be seen also in a statement like

(4)   They are the same metal, but not the same piece of aluminum.

This example also illustrates an interesting fact about terms like 'metal', 'liquid', 'animal', etc. These terms have a double use: on the one hand they are to be interpreted as denoting classes of animals, pieces of metal, etc.; on the other hand, in some contexts they denote classes of animal species, metal species, etc. The latter use seems to be related to what linguists call the "generic use" of certain terms, though it may not be identical with that.

One we have a representation for kinds and species, (3) can be interpreted as asserting the identity of the species to which the metal of the toy belongs with the species to which the metal of the airplane engines belongs. In other words, (3) – given the appropriate ontological assumptions – is equivalent to:

(5)   The species of metal to which the metal of the toy belongs is identical with the species to which the metal of the airplane engines belongs.

The relation between (3) and (5) helps to explain why the relation of belonging to the same species should be expressed by the same expression in English as that which expresses identity.[4]

Yet another sense of 'is the same as' is revealed by a certain set of statements that are about things enduring in time. Let us consider

(6)   The young woman I met eight years ago turned into the senior lecturer whom I met last year,

and

(7)   The prince whom I met eight years ago turned into the dragon I met last year.

These statements express processes of turning or changing into something, or becoming something. There is an important difference between the two. We can restate (6) as

(8)   The young woman I met eight years ago is the same as the senior lecturer I met last year.

But we cannot restate (7) as

(9)   The prince whom I met eight years ago is the same as the dragon I met last year.

The reason for this difference is that in (6) we have the same entity referred to through two of its temporal stages – or temporal properties – whereas in (7) we have the statement that one of two distinct entities succeeded the other. One is a case of change, the other a case of perishing and becoming. Aristotle construes the analysis of the difference between these notions as one of the key tasks of the philosophy of nature.

(6) and (7) are syntactically isomorphic – in the relevant respects. What, then, enables the competent speaker of English to recognize that two different relationships are expressed by the two statements? It is, clearly, the information that a prince and a dragon do not constitute temporal stages of a third entity, whereas being a young woman and being a senior lecturer can be stages in the life of the same entity, namely a person. In other words, attached to a certain set of properties are what might be called *persistence criteria*. Given, e.g., the property of being an animal, the understanding of this property involves knowing the criteria by which we can judge whether certain temporal stages are or are not stages of the same animal. The examples about women and princes show that there is no such thing as a persistence criterion *simpliciter*. Persistence criteria vary from one family of properties to another, and an entity has its persistence criteria through some of those properties which it has essentially.

Whatever enables us to tell the difference between (6) and (7), it is not Leibniz's law of identity. This is sufficient to show that persistence criteria are not to be assimilated to the notion of identity. Furthermore, since (6) is equivalent to (8), and (6) does not express identity, the 'is the same as' of (8) must be regarded as a distinct sense, and should not be assimilated to that of identity.

The following must hold for (6): it is true if and only if there exists a woman, and there are stages s' (being the young woman, etc.) and s'' (being the senior lecturer) such that s' and s'' belong to the same entity, namely the woman. The key notion here is that of distinct stages belonging to the same particular. Persistence criteria are, as one can see from the above, not conditions of identity, but conditions individuating chains of temporal stages, in accordance with essential properties of the particular in question. It follows from all this that there cannot be a particular whose essential properties are linked to incompatible persistence criteria.

It is easy to illustrate the differences between persistence criteria linked to various properties. The simplest persistence criterion is that of sameness of parts. It is attached to predicates like 'is a piece of iron', 'is a collection of body cells'. Much more complex criteria are attached to functional properties, such as that of being a human body – whose parts are replenished every seven years – or being an artifact like a chair. Though the notions of continuity and causal connection play important roles in many persistence criteria, they are neither necessary nor sufficient as persistence criteria for all types of particulars. For example, a mother dying at childbirth and her baby exemplify both continuity and causal connection, but are clearly not construed as temporal stages of a single entity. For countries and nations, continuity as a persistence criterion notoriously breaks down: countries or nations may be swallowed up by others, then reappear in history, etc. As for causal links, they do not seem to play any role in the reidentification of entities like nations, or rivers. Does one temporal stage of a river *cause* another?

This notion of stages belonging to the same entity – or *gen-identity*, as some logicians have called it – not only requires the kind of completion Geach talked about and is relative to families of predicates; it also satisfies formula (2). As an example we may consider

(10)   This is the same human body as that which I saw seven years ago, but not the same collection of body cells as that which I saw seven years ago.

This statement can be interpreted as being about stages. Stage (a) is both a stage of a human body and a stage of a collection of body cells. So is stage (b); but although stages (a) and (b) are stages of the same human body, they are stages of different collections of body cells. Both at (a) and at (b) a human body and a collection of body cells coincide. But there are two collections of body cells involved and only one human body. Even if we opt for an alternative interpretation and construe (10) as about a human body and collections of body cells rather than about stages, gen-identity will enter into the analysis anyway. For, on the alternative reading, (10) states that the human body I saw seven years ago is identical with the body I see now, but the collection of body cells I saw seven years ago is not identical with the collection I see now. But in the analysis of the truth conditions we are once more thrown back to chains of stages, since the ground for asserting the identity of the human body that has different temporal predicates is that the stages marked by the temporal predicates – and not all temporal predicates mark stages – constitute a single entity, whereas this is not true of the collections of body cells. (The difficulty, from a philosophical point of view, with the alternative reading is that we lose sight of the equivalence with statements of change and becoming.)

This analysis of persistence criteria suggests the representation of an individual as a function picking out a set of temporal stages, according to principles that are tied to its essential properties. Thus – as will be shown in the appendix – the persistence criteria can be expressed in a formal semantics as axioms governing the composition of entities out of their temporal stages.

This investigation also helps us to discover differences between the temporal and logical modalities. The persistence criteria linked to properties are not sufficient for identifying an object across possible worlds. Tracing an object back to the earlier stages through which it has changed is not the same as knowing what that object might have been, under all possible circumstances. It is notoriously difficult to state what makes transworld identifications possible. But in the context of this paper only the negative point need be made, namely that it is not solely persistence criteria.

Another point emerging here is that, since continuity and causal connections are not even sufficient to guarantee persistence in general, and since persistence criteria are not sufficient for transworld identifications, surely continuity and causal connections can be playing only a limited role in identifications across possible worlds. The logical and temporal worlds are in any case not isomorphic; for we trace an object through the temporal worlds by connecting its stages, but we do not construe an object as composed of stages represented by that object in various possible worlds. Things have careers and stages through time, but not through possible worlds.

The distinctions drawn here should also help us to see that all four combinations of temporal/omnitemporal and necessary/nonnecessary properties are possible. For example, being young may be necessarily true of a human, i.e., true in all possible worlds in which humans exist, but not true throughout the whole lifetime of a human. Again, the predicate of having a birthmark is true of a human through its lifetime, but not across possible worlds. The combination temporal and non-necessary is exemplified by being sun-burned; being rational is omnitemporal and necessary.

Returning now to (6) and (8), let us consider in detail their semantic interpretation. Since they are equivalent, substitution in one should have the same result as the same substitution in the other. If we substitute in (6) on the right side the expression we have on the left, and if we construe the expressions as simply referring to the woman, then we get

(11)   The young woman I met eight years ago turned into the young woman I met eight years ago.

which is false. Consequently, when we perform the same substitution in (8):

(12)   The young woman I met eight years ago is the same as the young woman I met eight years ago.

the result fails to be equivalent to (11), and thus we fail to preserve truth value. (12) taken naturally is a truism, but (11) is not. This shows that the 'is the same as' in (8) has a sense distinct from identity; it also shows the need for interpreting the referring expressions in (6) and (8) as denoting stages of entities instead of the entities themselves. Of course, once we construe the referents as stages, the sameness involved cannot be identity, since the stages are very discernible indeed and since Quine's dictum about the indiscernibility of identicals must not be violated.

This interpretation of statements of the form (6) and (8) does not commit us to interpreting definite descriptions like 'the young woman I met . . .' as always referring to stages. Indeed, there are very good reasons, brought out, e.g., by Chisholm,[5] why we should not so construe these expressions in certain types of normal subject-predicate statements. For the agent of an action is not a stage, but the individual himself; else there would be a conglomerate of agents, i.e., the various stages, involved in the performance of such a simple act as the singing of a song, and embarassing questions would emerge concerning the individuation of stages. Consequently, as our formal semantics will show, we interpret the particular itself as the agent *acting at a certain temporal stage*. This is in accord with common sense; e.g., as a teen-ager one does certain things, and at another stage, as an octogenarian, one does something else again. The agents are not the stages, even though the agent is composed of stages and acts at a given stage.

As an alternative, one might want the relevant definite descriptions not to be ambiguous – but then these have to be taken as a shorthand for something like 'the woman who was the young woman whom I met . . .' and again 'the woman who is the senior lecturer. . .'. The 'is' and 'was', respectively, will now have to be taken as expressing the relation between stages belonging to one entity; and, apart from losing the connection with the phrases of change, it is not clear why imputing ellipsis to ordinary language should have an advantage over the imputation of ambiguity.

II

So far we have said only that some terms are linked to persistence criteria. Further characterizations of this class are obviously desirable. One proposal is to claim that these terms will be a subset of those terms which designate individuating properties, and which have been called "terms with divided reference" by Quine and "count nouns" by linguists. Thus, e.g., 'man' and 'body' come with persistence criteria, whereas 'red' and 'water' do not, though 'body of water' does. Again, 'iron' does not, though 'piece of iron' does. It has been argued that even terms like 'iron' and 'water' carry persistence criteria,[6] but, even if this is so, the criteria are of the crudest sort, e.g., sameness of parts. We have seen already that there are more complex persistence criteria than this and that these criteria are linked to terms with divided reference. In any case, the interpretation of sameness of parts takes us back to the scientist, who, at various stages of history, has given us his answer in terms of such count nouns as 'molecule', 'atom', etc.

Individuating properties provide principles for the unambiguous counting of their instances through space and time. If the instances are abstract entities, then the counting principle is formulated without reference to spatiotemporal location.[7] Unambiguous countability is linked to the device of pluralization, though syntax and semantics do not always coincide in this connection. Furthermore, individuating properties underlie our ability to construct singular referring expressions by the utilization of definite descriptions. Thus there are a number of important linguistic and philosophic reasons for pressing toward a rigorous characterization of the difference between individuating properties and nonindividuating properties, to be expressed on the linguistic plane as the difference between $+$count and $-$count expressions. Intuitively, the key distinction rests on the fact that what can be counted unambiguously should not be referable at the same time as one F and as many F's, whereas the $-$count terms have denotation ranges with precisely this ambiguous countability condition. (Thus the difference is really not between countability and noncountability, but between ambiguous and unambiguous countability.) The condition for $+$count terms is:

C1.   A $^+$count term F is such that (i) there are some F's, e.g., F'
and F'', such that their union is itself not an F, *or* (ii) there
are no F' and F'' such that one does not contain the other
(with $F' \neq F''$), *or* there is only one F.

C1 is meant to apply to each possible world, thus including 'unicorn',
etc. The second part (ii) covers predicates like 'box-within-a-box in the
coldest spot of the world'; i.e., where there is only one collection of
instances in any given possible world and these are contained in one
structure. Note that such a collection falling under a $^-$count term could
not exist; 'gold-within-gold' would not qualify, since a $^-$count term *must*
have instances such that one does not contain the other. Finally, predicates that can have only one instance in any given possible world are
$^+$count.

Within the basic category of $^+$count, we can draw various distinctions.
A *strong* $^+$*count* term will be a $^+$count term whose instances are discrete;
no intersection of two F's is also an F. A further subdivision is the class
of those expressions which are linked to the weakest persistence criteria,
in the sense explained above.

For the other main category, predictably, the following condition
holds:

C2.   A $^-$count term F is such that (i) the union of any two F's is
also an F, *and* (ii) there are some F' and F'' such that neither
contains the other.

Within this class too, there are important subdivisions. Two of these
are important for the understanding of the structure of the language
required by scientific reasoning: the set of mass terms and the set of
dimension terms. Both of these are needed if we are to give quantitative
descriptions of the elements of the environment. The mass terms are
needed in order to raise questions about the constituents of objects
characterized normally by $^+$count terms. The stuff things are made of
will be characterized by terms such as 'air', 'water', 'iron', etc. – terms
that have been regarded as mass terms since pre-Socratic times. We
then need to introduce dimension terms such as 'weight', 'length', etc.
This allows us to make *quantitative comparisons*; thus the semantics of
expressions like 'much' and 'little' (as contrasted with 'many' and 'few')
and that of 'more' and 'less'. These expressions could not be introduced
without mass and dimension terms. Needless to say, when we move

from quantitative comparison to quantitative measurement, we need to introduce units of measurement (hence the further, abstract, $^+$count, use of 'length', etc. with plural forms), and thus we fall back once more on $^+$count terms.

Mass terms are those $^-$count terms which, with the addition of expressions like 'piece of', 'bit of', etc., form expressions that have persistence criteria linked to them. Dimension terms are different from any of the types considered so far, since their ranges of application are not spread out over space and time. Finally, there are $^-$count terms, such as 'money', 'help', 'footwear', etc. that are neither mass terms nor dimension terms.

This set-theoretic characterization of the $^+$ and $^-$ count distinction and the respective subdivisions apply only to nonabstract terms. For abstract terms a different characterization will be needed. The scheme, however, can be extended to adjectives. Adjectives have as their semantic objects functions that pick out sets of individual functions. They do this either by being evaluated at a time or by applying to individuals throughout their lifespan. An example of the former class is 'yellow', and of the latter 'mortal'. Adjectives like 'red' and 'fat' will be $^-$count; others like 'spherical' (Quine's example) will be $^+$count. The $^+$ $^-$ count distinction does not apply to quasi-adverbial adjectives such as 'tall', 'large', etc. These stand for functions that map subclasses onto denotation ranges of verbs or nouns. The extension of the $^+$ $^-$ count distinction to verbs is also a viable task.

Needless to say, a complete semantics and syntax will have to handle also the combination of $^+$ and $^-$ count terms within sentences. Thus, for example, the following sentences need to be given analyses.

(13)   This statue is bronze.
(14)   Ice melts.
(15)   My ring is gold.
(16)   The gold that is now my ring will become the gold of some coins.

The appendix to this paper will show how, with the help of the interpretations so far intuitively characterized, we can give formal analyses of these sentences. The need for analyzing such sentences prevents one from characterizing $^+$count terms simply as those that have unit sets as elements of their denotation ranges.

Let us briefly summarize the scheme developed so far. We start out by considering temporal stages of objects and construe these as sets with infinite number of elements. These elements are not objects of scientific or everyday experience. Rather, they are infinitesimal "parts" that underlie whatever construction determines a range of objects acknowledged in science or by common sense. In this way, this domain on the first level resembles Aristotle's prime matter. This is the domain that always underlies whatever constructs and objects science postulates and out of which ranges of objects with their temporal stages are constructed.

Individuals across time are construed as functions picking out sets of temporal stages. Persistence criteria are rules (e.g., sameness of parts, functional continuity, causal links, etc.) by which the various kinds of functions are computed. A general term, such as a common noun, selects in a given possible world a set of functions f', f'', etc. as characterized above. The principles involved in the methods of selection include the axioms that separate $^+$count from $^-$count terms, and their respective subdivisions. If we label the temporal stages as level 1, the individuals as level 2, and the extensions of general terms within one possible world as level 3, then one can characterize persistence criteria as conditions on the relations between levels 1 and 2, and the axioms determining the $^+$ and $^-$ count distinction and the subdivisions will be conditions on the relations between levels 2 and 3. For an adequate representation of the meaning of a general term, such as a common noun, we must move to level 4; i.e., we must associate with the term a function that picks out from each possible world the class (on level 3) that is the extension of the term in that world.

It might seem odd to construe individuals like tables and mountains as functions and classes. But the advantage of doing this is that it brings out certain important and often neglected facts. One of these is that the objects of science and everyday experience are *constructions*, and these constructions require the understanding of the general terms under which the objects are subsumed. As represented in our framework, particulars do not come "ready-made" as parts of the domain of discourse. These facts, and our attempts to represent them might help toward an understanding of the *constructive* aspect of the semantic component of linguistic competence, as well as helping to clear up metaphysical puzzles concerning the basic features of the human conceptual framework.

Stanford University

APPENDIX

We present here the formal semantics corresponding to our point of view We begin with a set $T = I \times J$ of possible worlds, where I is a set of moments of time, and J is a set of possible flows of history (time). So, $t = (i, j) \in T$ is the ith moment of time in the jth possible history.

The objects of each world are built up from a set of basic elements D. D is the same for all possible worlds. If x is an element of a world t, we express the fact that x is built up from D by saying $x \subseteq D$. We require that x be infinite. So if 'U_t' denotes the universe of the world t, then $U_t \in 2^D$; we of course require that $\sim(\varnothing \in U_t)$ ($\varnothing$ the empty set).

For each j, $I \times \langle j \rangle$ represents the set of moments of time of the jth history. The elements of the jth history are functions of the form:

$$f: I \to U_i U_{(i,j)} U\{\varnothing\} \text{ such that } f(i) \in U_{(i,j)} U\{\varnothing\}$$

If $f(i) = \varnothing$, we say that f does not have a temporal part in (i). With each history j, we associate a set E_j of elements existing in that history. The functions $f \in E_j$ are regarded as the elements, and the objects $f(i)$ are regarded as their temporal parts.

Axioms may be imposed to characterize various types of objects. For example, $f(i) = f(k)$, for $i, k \in I$, etc. (i.e., persistence for f). For further exaplanation, we define the *sum* of two objects f, g as $f \cup g$, and require that $(f \cup g)(i) = f(i) \cup g(i)$. Of course, if f, $g \in E_j$, $f \cup g$ may not be a member of E_j. For example, if f and g denote persons, $f \cup g$ may not be in E_j.

A common noun G_j or a mass term M_j is a family of f's; i.e., $G_j, M_j \subseteq E_j$. So 'sheep' is represented by the family of all sheep and 'water' by the family of all "collections" of water. The difference is of course that if f, $g \in M_j$, then $f \cup g \in M_j$; however, if f, $g \in G_j$, then we may have that $\sim(f \cup g \in G_j)$.

Turning to adjectives, we distinguish two kinds: one like, e.g., 'yellow', and one like 'big'. The first class is represented by functions of the form $A_j: I \times \{j\} \to 2^{E_j}$. The 2nd class is represented by functions of the form $B_j: I \times \{j\} \to (2^{E_j})^{2^{E_j}}$. That is, A gives you for each (i, j) the set of all objects that are A's; B gives you for each (i, j) the function (e.g., big) that gives you for each family of objects (e.g., sheep), those which are "big sheep."

Of course, each A gives rise to a B_A by taking: $B_A(i, j)(S) = S \cap A(i,j)$. That is, B_A intersects 'sheep' with the set of yellow things. Some adjectives may have the property that, if they hold for an f at a moment, then they always hold for that f. Classes of adjectives of the first kind, and classes of mass or common terms, can also be represented in a natural way.

Turning to proper names (e.g., $n =$ the king of France) we have two options. First, following the usual practice of modal logic, we could take the semantical meaning (or assignment) for a proper name as a function $n_j \colon I \times \{j\} \to E_j$. However, we think it is more intuitive to take a proper name n to be a function more like elements f; i.e., $n(i, j) \in U_{ij}$. The reason for that is that we regard a "name" (e.g., the president) as an office, just like an individual, filled up by various temporal cross sections of possibly several individuals.

Formally our language contains variables x, y for subsets of D, variables f, g, for elements of $U_j E_j$, binary relation $\approx$ for coincidence, variables A_1, A_2, for adjectives of first kind variables C, M (for common or mass terms), variables X, Y for classes of mass or common terms, variables B_1, ... for 2nd kind adjectives, and individual constants $n_1, n_2. \ldots$

The atomic formulas of the language are the following: $x \approx y$, $x \approx f$, $f \approx g$, $n \approx x$, $n \approx f$, $n \approx n'$, $A(f)$, $A(n)$, $C(f)$, $C(n)$, $B(C(f))B(C(n))$, $X(m)$. The nonclassical connectives are L and $\square$.

A function α is an assignment from the language into the model iff α assigns to the various variables values as follows:

(1) $\alpha(x) \subseteq D$.
(2) $\alpha(f) \in U_j E_j$.
(3) $\alpha(n)$ is a function such that $\alpha(n)(j) \in E_j$.
(4) $\alpha(A)$ is a function such that $\alpha(A)(i, j) \subseteq E_j$.
(5) $\alpha(C)$ is a function such that $\alpha(C)(j) \subseteq E_j$.
(6) $\alpha(B)$ is a function such that $\alpha(B)(i,j) \in (2^{E_j})^{2^{E_j}}$.
(7) $\alpha(X)$ is a function such that $\alpha(X)(j) \subseteq 2^{E_j}$.

A formula Π with free variables that include $x_1, \ldots, x_{k'}, f_1, \ldots, f_k$ is said to have truth value at (i,j) iff $\alpha(x_p) \in U_{i,j}$ for $p \leq k$ and $\alpha(f_p) \in E_j$, for $p \leq k'$. If Π has a truth value at (i,j) [notation $\|\Pi\|_{i,j}$] then it is computed as follows:

(a) $\|x \approx y\|_{i,j} = 1$ iff $\alpha(x) = \alpha(y)$.
(b) $\|x \approx f\|_{i,j} = 1$ iff $\alpha(x) = \alpha(f)(i)$.
(c) $\|f \approx g\|_{i,j} = 1$ iff $\alpha(f)(i) = \alpha(g)(i)$.
(d) $\|n \approx f\|_{i,j} = 1$ iff $\alpha(n)(i,j) = \alpha(f)(i)$.
(e) $\|n \approx x\|_{i,j} = 1$ iff $\alpha(n)(i,j) = \alpha(x)$.

(f) $\|n \approx n'\|_{i,j} = 1$ iff $\alpha(n)(i,j) = \alpha(n')(i,j)$.

(g)   All other atomic formulas have the intuitive truth definition.

(h) $\|L\Pi\|_{i,j} = 1$ iff, for all $i_1 \in I$, if $\|\Pi\|_{i_1,j}$ is defined then it is 1.

(i) $\|\square \Pi\|_{i,j} = 1$ iff, for all $j' \in T$, if $\|\Pi\|_{i,j'}$ is defined then it is 1.

(j)   For the classical connectives, we take the usual definition, with $U_{i,j}$ and E_j being the domains. If we want we can add connectives L_i to the language, with $\|L_i\Pi\|_{i*,j*} = 1$ iff $\|\Pi\|$ is defined at $i, j*$ and $\|\Pi\|_{i,j*} = 1$.

EXAMPLES

0. $f \approx g$ holds at time t iff f and g have a common temporal part. $L(f \approx g)$ means that, in the history of t, they always have the same temporal part. $\square\ (f \approx g)$ means that in all histories they must have the same temporal part at time t.

1.   This ring is gold (or this is $f \wedge$ is a ring of gold): "$f \in$ ring $\wedge$ $f \in$ gold."

2. f is the same metal as g: $(\forall m)(m \in X \rightarrow f \in m$ iff $g \in m)$. (i.e., X is a collection of properties, i.e., the kinds of metals).

3. f is the same coin as g: $L(f \approx g) \wedge f \in$ coin $\wedge\ g \in$ coin.

4. a is the same person b who killed the dog ten years ago: $(\exists f)[f \approx a \wedge$ ten years ago $f \approx b \wedge f$ is a person $\wedge$ ten years ago f killed the dog].

5.   Ice melts: $m_{\text{ice}} \subseteq m_{\text{melts}}$.

6.   This statue is bronze; either $f \in$ Bronze, or, if we refer to the temporal copy of the statue, then, $(\exists f)[f \in$ statue $\wedge f \approx x \wedge f \in$ Bronze].

NOTES

* We are indebted to several persons commenting on a draft of this paper at the 1972 Stanford Metaphysics Colloquium, among them David Kaplan and Thomas Schwartz. We are also grateful for helpful comments from John Perry.

[1] *Reference and Generality* (Ithaca, N.Y.: Cornell, 1962), pp. 39 *passim*.

[2] 'The Same F', *Philosophical Review* 79, 2 (April 1970): 181–200.

[3] Let us explore briefly an issue that does not affect the controversy between unitarians and pluralists. This is the issue of equalities of differing strengths. These will be illustrated, and their structure incorporated in the formal semantics to be given in the appendix of this paper. These differences, however, do not affect the issue of whether Geach's formula has application, and whether sameness is relative to predicates.

The explication of these equalities requires the following basic notions. We conceive of a variety of relations between entities that have histories in time and that figure in possible as well as actual states of affairs. Thus we have individuals in the actual as well as in possible worlds, with their actual as well as possible histories.

The weakest case of equality is that of contingent coincidence between two entities through a part of their histories. For example, Richard Nixon is only contingently the president, and he has this role only through a part of his history. Again, construing the office of the president as composed of a series of stages, it is contingent that one of these should coincide with Nixon, and it is only a small part of the history of the office that intersects with Nixon in this way. This is , then, the analysis for

(A)   Nixon is now the president of the USA.
Then there may be cases in which this partial overlap between the histories of two entities is not contingent: i.e., it holds in all the possible worlds in which the two entities exist.

(B)   The young religious ruler in Tibet is necessarily the saddest child in Tibet.
In different possible worlds different people will rule Tibet. Likewise, different people will be spending their childhood as the saddest child in Tibet. But, if (B) is true, in all the possible worlds in which Tibet has a religious ruler and has children among its citizens, the partial overlap between the history of the ruler and that of the man who in his youth is the saddest child, will hold.

Passing from partial overlaps to total coincidence through history, we note that there are cases in which this coincidence is contingent. For example,

(C)   Joe Smith is the only lawyer in Dexter.
In this case Joe Smith need not have chosen this particular career, and in its different possible histories the town of Dexter has different individuals as its only lawyer.

The strongest case is that in which two entities coincide through their histories in all the possible worlds in which they exist. For abstract entities such as properties, this would mean the class of all possible worlds; and the same would hold for God, if he exists and does so necessarily. For other entities, such as most particulars, this type of equality would hold in all those possible worlds in which they exist. Opinions vary as to which, if any, types of statements about particulars exemplify this type of equality which is called "absolute identity." Among the candidates would be:

(D)   Tully is Cicero.   (D') The Evening Star is the Evening Star.
[For this view on names see S. Kripke, 'Identity and Necessity' in M. Munitz (ed.), *Identity and Individuation* (New York: NYU Press, 1971), pp. 135–164.]

These four types of case require only two basic notions of equality: coincidence and absolute identity – as will be shown in the appendix. These distinctions can be accepted by what we have called the "unitarian" position, and they do not require any relativization of 'same'.

[4] There is a close link between these notions in Aristotle's treatment of sameness: see, e.g. *Metaphysics* Bk. V, Ch. 9.
[5] R. Chisholm, "Problems of Identity" in Munitz, *op. cit.*, pp. 3–30.
[6] For an able exposition of this view see H. M. Cartwright, 'Quantities', *Philosophical Review* 79, 1 (January 1970): 25–42.
[7] For a discussion of how the + − count distinction cuts through the + − abstract distinction, see J. Moravcsik, "Subcategorization and Abstract Terms," *Foundations of Language*, 6, 4 (November 1970): 473–487.

H. C. BUNT

ENSEMBLES AND THE FORMAL SEMANTIC PROPERTIES OF MASS TERMS

1. INTRODUCTION

The purpose of this paper is to present an analysis of the formal semantic properties of mass terms. What is meant by formal semantic properties will be explained in section 2; in the present section a characterization in syntactic terms is given of the phenomena that go by the name of mass terms.

The most familiar kind of mass terms are those known as mass nouns. Words like "water", "wine", "furniture", "news", "time", "garbage", etc., are called mass nouns to distinguish them from words like "book", "table", "story", "apple", "dream", etc., which are called count nouns. There are certain evident syntactic differences between the words of these two groups, and the words listed are relatively clear cases. To say precisely what distinguishes in general a mass noun from a count noun, however, is notoriously difficult, and to my knowledge no one has yet succeeded in doing so. In other words, an adequate syntactic characterization of the terms *mass noun* and *count noun* is lacking. A serious complication is caused by the fact that the count/mass distinction is not really a distinction among words, but a distinction among ways of using them. Practically every noun can be used both as a count noun and as a mass noun. For instance, the "mass noun" *wine* is used as a count noun in:

(1)   Hungary produces many excellent wines,

and the "count noun" apple is used as a mass noun in:

(2)   Don't put too much *apple* in the salad.

I will continue to speak of "mass nouns", following the usual terminology, but it should be understood that this is a shorthand for "mass way of using a noun"[1]. What makes us decide whether a noun is used as a count noun or as a mass noun? For sentences (1) and (2), this seems clear enough: "wines" in (1) is a count noun because it is plural, and combined with "many"; "apple" in (2) is a mass noun because it is

F. J. Pelletier (ed.), *Mass Terms*, 249–277. *All Rights Reserved.*
Copyright © 1979 by D. Reidel Publishing Company, Dordrecht, Holland.

combined with "much". But these criteria do not help us for such sentences as:

(3)   Hungary produces excellent wine.
(4)   Don't put any apple in the salad.

One can find other criteria, besides the ones used for sentences (1) and (2), but there will always remain sentences like (4), in which there is no overt criterion for deciding whether the nouns should be classified as count or as mass. For this reason, I propose the following two-stage decision procedure for classifying nouns as count or mass:

1. Establish a list of classification criteria. If a noun occurs in an expression in which one of these criteria is present, it is classified accordingly.

2. If a noun occurs in an expression S_1 which does not contain one of the criteria of the list, construct an expression S_2 which does contain such a criterion and in which the noun is used in the same sense as in S_1. The classification obtained from S_2 is also the classification of the noun as it occurs in S_1.

Two remarks are in order concerning this procedure. Firstly, it cannot be guaranteed that the procedure will always work, for there is no guarantee that an S_2-expression, containing one of the established classification criteria, can always be found. In other words, in proposing this procedure I do not claim that the count/mass classification of noun occurrences is exhaustive[2].

Secondly, the requirement that the noun in the expression S_1 is used in the same sense in the expression S_2 implies that semantic considerations play a part in the classification: whether the noun is used in the same sense in S_1 and S_2 depends on the interpretations assigned to these expressions.

With respect to the establishment of a list of count/mass classification criteria, it should be noted that such a list is language dependent. I do not claim to have a perfectly satisfactory list for any particular language, but I think the following list is sufficient for by far the largest number of cases in English:

1. A singular[3] noun, preceded by the indefinite article, is a count noun.

2. A singular noun, preceded by an amount expression, is a mass noun. By an amount expression I mean expressions like "10 kilogrammes of", "less than 5 litres of", "half a cup of", and expressions like "much", "little", "a little bit of", etc.

3. A noun, preceded by a number expression, is a count noun. By a number expression I mean expressions like "1", "two", "3", "$12\frac{1}{2}$", "$\frac{3}{4}$", and expressions like "many", "few", "more than 3", "several", "numerous", etc.

In section 5 of this paper I will tentatively propose an additional criterion, based on the observation that certain adjectives cannot be combined with mass nouns. The more criteria one has, the larger is the number of noun occurrences that can be classified directly by stage 1 of our decision procedure.

Applying this procedure to the nouns "wine" and "apple" in (3) and (4), we find that "wine" is classified as a mass noun in view of (5):

(5)   Hungary produces much excellent wine,

and that "apple" is classified as a mass noun if it is interpreted as being used in the same sense as in sentence (2), and classified as a count noun if it is interpreted as being used in the same sense as in (6):

(6)   Don't put an apple in the salad.

This is a clear illustration of the fact that an interpretation of the expression is indispensable for classifying the nouns occurring in it. Of course, in practical language use such interpretations are provided by the context of use.

There have been some suggestions in the literature (see Moravcsik, 1973) to extend the count/mass distinction to other syntactic categories, in particular to adjectives. I will consider this possibility in section 5; for the time being, my considerations are restricted to nouns.

A restriction throughout this paper is that only extensional interpretations will be considered. I think this is a fruitful approach because the specific problems that mass terms pose can be separated from the problems connected with intensional vs. extensional meaning. Once a satisfactory treatment of the extensional semantics of mass nouns has been established, the addition of intensional considerations is analogous to the count noun case.

2. SEMANTIC ASPECTS OF MASS NOUNS

2.1. *Formal Semantic Properties*

Having established a working definition of the terms mass noun and count noun, the question can be faced whether there is a systematic semantic difference between mass nouns and count nouns. In order to answer this question, I will investigate the formal semantic properties of mass nouns. By the formal semantic properties of an expression I mean those semantic properties which the expression has by virtue of the way it is built up from subexpressions.

For instance, the sentence

(8a)   All ice creams are cold

has the formal semantic property of logically implying the sentence

(9a)   All Italian ice creams are cold,

and this implication holds independently of the particular words "ice creams", "cold", and "Italian": it only depends on the formal structure of the sentences (8a) and (9a)[4]. The formal semantic properties of an expression can be made explicit by translating the expression into a formal language, the logical properties of whose expressions are exactly known. It is instructive to consider how this could be done for sentence (8a), and how it could be done for sentence (8b), which is obtained from (8a) by replacing the count noun "ice creams" by the mass noun "ice cream":

(8b)   All ice cream is cold.

Corresponding to (9a) we have, in this case:

(9b)   All Italian ice cream is cold.

Sentence (8a) can be translated into a formal language of predicates and sets: interpreting "ice creams" as referring to the set of all ice creams, and "cold" to a predicate, an appropriate translation of (8a) is:

(10a) $(\forall x)(x \in \text{ICECREAMS} \rightarrow \text{COLD}(x))$.

This expression obviously implies:

(11a) $(\forall x)((\text{ITALIAN}(x)\ \&\ x \in \text{ICECREAMS}) \rightarrow \text{COLD}(x))$

which would be the corresponding translation of (9a)[5]. Can we make a similar translation of (8b), and see that it implies (9b)? We can, if we can interpret the mass noun "ice cream" as referring to "the set of all ice cream" – but here we have a problem: a set is characterized by its elements, but what are the elements that constitute this set? Certainly not the things that we call ice creams: sentence (8b) says that every bit of ice cream, of whatever size or shape, is cold.

Here we hit upon the fundamental difference between count nouns and mass nouns. The difference is that count nouns, as opposed to mass nouns, "possess built-in modes of dividing their reference" (Quine, 1960), that is to say inherent in a count noun, like "ice creams" or "books", is the determination of what counts as a single instance: as "one ice cream", "one book", whereas in the case of a mass noun, like "ice cream" in (8b), or "water", there is no inherent determination of what could count as a single ice cream instance or a single water (it is even incorrect English to say "one m", if "m" is a mass noun). It seems, rather, that a mass noun refers to an object in a "homogeneous" way, without focussing on particular parts or elements. This means that, for describing the way that mass nouns refer, we cannot use sets like we can for count nouns. A fundamental problem for the semantic analysis of mass nouns is what can be done instead. It is an important part of my proposal for the semantic analysis of mass nouns not to use the notion of a set, but a somewhat different notion, developed specifically for this purpose. This notion, which I call the "ensemble" notion, is explained in section 3.

It was already noted that the relation between the sentences (8a) and (9a) is independent of the particular nouns and adjectives that appear; it is an instance of the general scheme: All x's are P, therefore All Q x's are P. Similarly, the pair of sentences (8b), (9b) is an instance of the general scheme: All M is P, therefore All Q M is P. I assume the intuition that this scheme represents a necessary truth to be strong enough to take it as one of the formal semantic properties of mass terms that a semantic theory must account for. In later sections of this paper an account will be given of the following schemes:

	S1.	All M is M
	S2.	All P M is M
(12)	S3.	All P M is P
	S4.	If all M is P, then all Q M is P
	S5.	If all M is P, and m is M, then m is P.

2.2. *Cumulative and Distributive Reference*

Most of the work that has been done on mass nouns in recent years (see Pelletier, 1975) takes Quine's discussion of mass terms in *Word and Object* (1960) as the point of departure. Quine gives a semantic characterization of mass terms as those terms that "refer cumulatively", a notion which is explained as: "any sum of parts that are water is water". Formulated more generally, a term W refers cumulatively if:

(13)   Any sum of parts that are W is W.

This is known as the *cumulative reference condition*. A problem with this condition is that it is too vague as long as the notions "sum", "part" and "to be W" are not defined. It may be true that, in some intuitive sense, the sum of parts that are water is again water, but in much the same way the sum of parts that are books is again books. It remains to be seen whether the notions in question can be made precise in such a way that a criterion is obtained for distinguishing mass nouns from count nouns. In section 3 a precise definition of these notions will be proposed in terms of ensembles, and it will be seen that in this interpretation the cumulative reference condition holds for count nouns as well as for mass nouns.

Another possible criterion, mentioned by Cheng (1973), is what he calls Cheng's condition: "any part of the whole of the mass object which is W is W." The notion of a "mass object", occurring in this condition, is introduced by Cheng as: "the object to which a mass term applies." I disagree with Cheng's view that mass terms refer to a particular kind of object.[6] However, Cheng's condition can be brought on a par with Quine's condition, viz. as a condition on the way in which terms refer, as follows: a term W with the property that:

(14)   Any part of something that is W is W,

is said to refer distributively, and I call (14) the *distributive reference condition*. Evidently, this condition has the same degree of vagueness as the cumulative reference condition. Again, when formalizing the notions "part of" and "to be W", it will turn out that the distributive reference condition expresses a semantic property which holds for count nouns as well as for mass nouns.

2.3. *Minimal Parts and Homogeneous Reference*

In *Word and Object* (p. 99), Quine made an observation which has had a particularly great influence on recent work on mass nouns. Quine observes that "there are parts of water, sugar, furniture too small to count as water, sugar, furniture". This observation is made in order to argue that the copula "is" in a sentence like "this is water", "this is sugar", "this is furniture", cannot be interpreted as expressing a general part-of relation, because such a part-of relation would have to behave differently for increasingly small water-parts than for increasingly small sugar-parts, and again differently for increasingly small furniture-parts.

The general idea implied by this observation is the following:

(15)   For each mass noun there is a specific minimal size that parts of its referent can have.

I call this the *minimal parts hypothesis.*

In view of the great impact that this hypothesis has had on the work on mass nouns (e.g. Moravcsik, 1973, p. 281, Parsons, 1970, p. 366, Pelletier, 1974, p. 87, Burge, 1977, part III), it is worth considering precisely what it asserts. In my opinion the minimal parts hypothesis is ambiguous as to what it is about:

– is it an assertion about the real world? As such, it is correct in many cases: the parts of a H_2O molecule are not water, the nails of a chair are not furniture, and of the parts of an energy quantum nothing can be predicated whatsoever. On the other hand, no minimal parts of time, freedom, ambrosia, or love are known to exist; in these cases the assertion is incorrect, unless parts with size "zero" are also considered as minimal parts.

– is it an assertion about the use of mass nouns in English? As such, it seems to be incorrect. For instance, the mass noun "water" has been used for centuries when there was no knowledge about H_2O molecules, and even today the accumulated knowledge about molecules, atoms, energy quanta, photons, phonons, and bits of information does not affect the use of nouns like "air", "water", "money", "energy", "labour", "light", "sound", "music", "news", etc. In fact, the opposite appears to be the case: mass nouns provide a way of talking about things as homogeneous entities, as if they do not consist of certain smallest parts. For some words and some speakers, this way of talking may reflect their real beliefs about the world, e.g. in the case of "time", "water", or "energy". In other cases, like "furniture", "footwear", and "computing equipment", it is unlikely that any speaker really believes that the mass noun refers to something "homogeneous". However, nothing in the use of these words indicates a presupposition on the existence of minimal parts.

Since this paper is concerned with the analysis of language, and not with the analysis of the real world, the first interpretation of the minimal parts hypothesis is irrelevant here; the second interpretation appears to be simply incorrect, and I indicated that in fact the opposite view seems to be called for. I formulate this view as the following hypothesis, which I call the *homogeneous reference hypothesis*:

(16)   A mass noun refers in such a way that no particular articulation of the referent into parts is presupposed, nor the existence of minimal parts.

This expresses how a mass noun differs semantically from a count noun. The difference is not in the kind of objects that mass nouns and count nouns refer to, but in the way in which they refer. "Furniture" and "articles of furniture" are examples of referring to the same things in different ways, by using a mass noun and a count noun, respectively.

2.4. *The Formal Description of Mass Noun Referents*

As remarked earlier, to describe precisely the way that mass nouns refer we cannot use the notion of a set, and it was announced that the notion of an "ensemble" would be developed for this purpose. Before turning to ensembles, let us recapitulate the requirements they should fulfill.

1. According to the homogeneous reference hypothesis, ensembles must be objects of which parts can be taken in any arbitrary way, without any commitments as to the existence of minimal parts.

2. For these ensembles, formal concepts corresponding to the "sum" and "part of" notions must be defined, and the notion "to be W" (with W a mass term) must be defined, such that the cumulative and distributive reference conditions hold. The notion of an ensemble is introduced somewhat informally in the next section; a formal, axiomatic treatment of ensemble theory in condensed form can be found in the appendix of Bunt (1976a).

3. ENSEMBLE THEORY

Ensembles are objects that are characterized by their parts. Two ensembles are identical if they have the same parts. The part-of relation, symbolized as $\subseteq$, is a primitive notion in the theory of ensembles. In set theory there is also a part-of relation $\subseteq$ (usually called subset relation) which is not primitive, but defined in terms of the primitive element relation $\in$: $A \subseteq B$ means that all elements of A are elements of B. Since the $\subseteq$ relation in ensemble theory is primitive, its transitivity (which in set theory can be proved from the definition) must be postulated by means of an axiom[7]:

(17)   AXIOM I. AXIOM OF TRANSITIVITY
$$(\forall x,y,z)((x \subseteq y \ \& \ y \subseteq z) \rightarrow (x \subseteq z))$$

This $\subseteq$ relation will play the role of the formalization of the part-of notion, occurring in the cumulative and distributive reference conditions.

The notion "sum", occurring in these conditions, is formalized as the operation called *merging* or *taking unions*. The merge (or union) of two ensembles x and y is the ensemble, denoted by $x \cup y$, which is defined by having both x and y as parts, and being contained in all other ensembles with the same property. In formula:

(18) $x \subseteq x \cup y \ \& \ y \subseteq x \cup y \ \& \ (\forall z)((x \subseteq z \ \& \ y \subseteq z) \rightarrow$
$(x \cup y \subseteq z))$

In other words, the union of x and y is the smallest ensemble in which both x and y are contained, smallest in the sense of the part-of relation. The existence of the union of x and y is guaranteed by the Axiom of Unions (see below, Axiom IV). It is easy to prove that the union, defined in this way, is uniquely determined. Of course, there is no reason to restrict the operation of merging to just two operands. A more general definition of merging will be given later. Similarly, the intersection of two ensembles x and y can be defined as the smallest ensemble that includes all the common parts of x and y. If x and y are disjoint, i.e. they have no common parts, their intersection is *empty*. The empty ensemble, denoted by $\varnothing$, is defined by the property of having no other parts than itself.

It was said in the beginning of this section that two ensembles are identical if they have the same parts. The conditions under which two ensembles are identical are determined by the Axiom of Extension plus the definition of equality. In order to formulate the Axiom of Extension it is useful to first introduce the notion of *proper part*. The proper part relation, symbolized as $\subset$, is defined as follows:

(19)   DEFINITION 1. $x \subset y \underset{D}{=}^8 x \subseteq y \ \& \ \neg(y \subseteq x)$

The Axiom of Extension says that whenever all proper parts of an ensemble x are parts of an ensemble y, x is part of y:

(20)   AXIOM IIa. AXIOM OF EXTENSION
$$(\forall x, y)((\forall z)(z \subset x \rightarrow z \subseteq y) \rightarrow x \subseteq y)$$

(We will see below that this form of the axiom is not completely adequate, but (20) expresses the basic idea most clearly[9]).

Equality between two ensembles is defined as mutual inclusion:

(21)   DEFINITION 2. $x = y \underset{\text{D}}{=} x \subseteq y \ \& \ y \subseteq x$

We thus see that two ensembles are equal if they have the same proper parts.

In the definition of union and intersection, the notion "smallest in the sense of the part-of relation" was used. This notion occurs frequently in ensemble theory, and it is convenient to have an abbreviated notation for saying that there exists an ensemble x which is the smallest ensemble with a certain property $\psi(x)$. For this purpose I use the notation $(\underset{-}{\exists} x)\psi(x)$ defined by:

(22) $(\underset{-}{\exists} x)\psi(x) \ (\underset{\text{D}}{=} \ (\exists x)\psi(x) \ \& \ (\forall y)(\psi(y) \to x \subseteq y))$

Note that the smallest ensemble with a certain property is always uniquely determined.

One of the fundamental theorems in ensemble theory is the following.

THEOREM 1.   Given an ensemble x and a property $\psi(z)$ there exists the smallest ensemble including all parts z of x with the property $\psi(z)$. In formula:

(23) $(\forall x)(\exists y)(\forall z)((z \subseteq x \ \& \ \psi(z)) \to z \subseteq y)$

This ensemble is denoted by:

(24) $[z \subseteq x | \psi(z)]$

Notice the analogy of Theorem 1 with the Axiom of Subsets in set theory[10], which guarantees the existence of the set $\{z \in x | \psi(z)\}$ for any set x and property $\psi(z)$.

There is, however, also an important difference between set theory and ensemble theory, because in set theory we have:

$a \in \{z \in x | \psi(z)\}$ if and only if $a \in x \ \& \ \psi(a)$

but in ensemble theory we only have:

$a \subseteq [z \subseteq x | \psi(z)]$ if $a \subseteq x \ \& \ \psi(a)$

The corresponding only if-clause is missing here, because it cannot be guaranteed for every property $\psi(z)$ that, whenever two parts of the ensemble (24) have this property, their intersection and their union will also have the property[11]. Only "half" of the only if-clause holds in ensemble theory as well: all parts of the ensemble (24) can be proved to be part of the ensemble x. This implies, according to the Axiom of Extension:

(25)   THEOREM 2. $[z \subseteq x | \psi(z)] \subseteq x$.

Of particular interest are those ensembles that have the property that one can continue indefinitely to take ever smaller parts. I call these ensembles *continuous*. In order to define this notion of continuity precisely, it is convenient to first introduce the *genuine part* relation, symbolized as $\sqsubset$:

(26)   DEFINITION 3. $x \sqsubset y \underset{D}{=} x \subset y \ \& \ \neg(x = \varnothing)$

An ensemble x is now defined as being continuous if it has a genuine part, and if every genuine part has again a genuine part.

Clearly, every non-empty part of a continuous ensemble is itself a continuous ensemble. I believe that continuous ensembles are appropriate for modelling the logical properties of truly continuous entities, such as time.

Not all ensembles are continuous. For instance, an ensemble need not have any genuine part at all. Such an ensemble, if it is not empty, is called *atomic*.

(27)   DEFINITION 4.   ATOM $(x) \underset{D}{=} \neg(x = \varnothing) \ \&$
       $\neg(\exists y)(y \sqsubset x)$

Notice that, if x, y, and $\varnothing$ in (27) were to stand for sets rather than ensembles, the sets that are called atomic would be those sets that have exactly one element.

The ensembles that result from merging two or more atomic ensembles play a very interesting role. I call these ensembles *discrete*. Notice that it follows from the definitions that an ensemble cannot be both continuous and discrete. To see the role that discrete ensembles play, we must consider the second primitive relation in ensemble theory. I call this relation the *unicle relation*, and denote it by $\in$. The role of this relation in the theory is expressed by the following axiom:

(28)   AXIOM III.   AXIOM OF UNICLES
       $(\forall x)((\text{ATOM}(x) \rightarrow (\exists! y)(y \in x)) \ \& \ (\neg \text{ATOM}(x) \rightarrow$
       $\neg(\exists y)(y \in x)))$

This axiom says that every atomic ensemble has exactly one "unicle" (the notation $(\exists !y)$ abbreviates: there is exactly one y), and all other ensembles do not have unicles. As atomic ensembles can be compared with sets with one element, the $\in$ relation can be compared with the relation that the single element of such a set has to that set, in other words as the relation between S and {S}.

In terms of the two primitive relations of ensemble theory, a new relation can be defined which I call the *element relation*, symbolized as $\in$, as follows:

(29)   DEFINITION 5. $y \in x \underset{D}{=} (\exists z)(z \subseteq x \ \& \ y \subseteq z)$

In other words, the elements of an ensemble are the unicles of its atomic parts.

Notice that, since a continuous ensemble has no atomic parts, it has no elements!

It can be proved that the $\in$ relation, defined by (29), has exactly the same properties as the $\in$ relation in set theory. If we add to the axiom system, which defines the ensemble notion (see the appendix for the complete list of axioms), one extra axiom which says that all ensembles are discrete, i.e. we restrict the notion of ensembles to the discrete case, this axiom system can be proved to be equivalent to the Zermelo-Fraenkel axiom system for set theory. In other words, *discrete ensembles are sets*.

From the fact that an ensemble need not have any genuine part, it follows that the axiom of extensionality, given in (21), is not adequate: it does not cover the case of atomic ensembles. For atomic ensembles the following addition is needed:

(30)   AXIOM IIb.
            $(\forall x,y)(\mathrm{ATOM}(x)(x \subseteq x \ \&(((\forall z)(z \in x \rightarrow z \in y)) \rightarrow x \subseteq y))$

Now that we have the $\in$ relation among ensembles at our disposal, the merging of arbitrarily (possibly infinitely) many ensembles can be defined. This is done via the following axiom:

(31)   AXIOM IV.   AXIOM OF UNIONS
            $(\forall x)((\exists y)(y \in x) \rightarrow (\exists u)(\forall z)(z \in x \rightarrow z \subseteq u))$

The ensemble u in (31) is the union of all the ensembles that are elements of x. This union is denoted by $\cup (x)$. The general definition of merging allows us to define the notion of *discreteness* precisely: an ensemble x is discrete if:

(32) $(\exists y)((\exists z)(z \in y)\ \&\ (\forall z)(z \in y \rightarrow \mathrm{ATOM}(z))\ \&\ \cup (y) = x)$

This states formally that x is obtained by merging a number of atomic ensembles (the elements of the ensemble y). In the use of ensemble theory that will be made below, it is necessary to know that every ensemble has a *power set*. This is asserted by the following axiom:

(33)   AXIOM V.   AXIOM OF POWERS
            $(\forall x)(\exists y)(\forall z)(z \subseteq x \rightarrow z \in y)$

The ensemble y in (32) is the power set of x, also written as $\mathscr{P}(x)$; it can be proved that it is a discrete ensemble.

Since the axiom system, upon which ensemble theory rests, reduces to the Zermelo-Fraenkel axiom system when extended with one axiom (saying that all ensembles are discrete), it follows that ensemble theory is a logically consistent formalism.

4. THE SEMANTIC PROPERTIES OF MASS NOUNS FORMALIZED

4.1 *Cumulative, Distributive, and Homogeneous Reference*

The concepts of ensemble theory can be used for describing the semantic properties of mass nouns with formal rigour and preciseness. The basic assumption in doing so is that ensembles are appropriate for describing the objects that mass nouns refer to. I do not restrict the use of ensembles for this purpose to ensembles that are continuous. According to the homogeneous reference hypothesis, mass nouns are used to refer to entities in such a way that no particular division of the entities into parts is presupposed and no minimal parts are presupposed to exist. If we interpret a mass noun as referring to an ensemble, without any presupposition about the kind of ensemble (continuous, discrete, or mixed), we are precisely in agreement with the homogeneous reference hypothesis. Count nouns, on the other hand, are interpreted in the usual way as referring to sets, i.e. discrete ensembles.

What does ensemble theory tell us about the cumulative and distributive reference conditions, as candidates for characterizing mass nouns semantically?

The informal notions "part of" and "sum" have already been formalized as $\subseteq$ and $\cup$; I furthermore formalize the notion "to be W", as it occurs in these conditions, as "to be part of the ensemble that W refers to". Calling this ensemble E_W, the cumulative and distributive reference conditions are formalized as:

(33) $(\forall x,y)((x \subseteq E_w \ \& \ y \subseteq E_w) \to (x \cup y \subseteq E_w))$[12]
(34) $(\forall x)((\exists y)(y \subseteq E_w \ \& \ x \subseteq y) \to (x \subseteq E_w))$

According to ensemble theory, condition (33) is true for all ensembles E_w. This follows immediately from the definition of merging (see (18)). So *all* ensembles satisfy the cumulative reference condition.

Condition (34) is also true for all ensembles E_w; this follows immediately from the transitivity of the part-of relation. Therefore, in this formalization neither the cumulative nor the distributive reference condition captures a semantic property which is characteristic of mass nouns.

The only semantic difference between count nouns and mass nouns that remains is that the latter refer homogeneously and the former do not: count nouns are taken to refer to discrete ensembles, which do have minimal parts (their atomic subensembles), while mass nouns may refer to any kind of ensemble, with or without minimal parts.

4.2. *Ensemble Language*

Next I proceed to define a formal language which is based on the notion of an ensemble, and which I will use to translate mass noun expressions into so as to make their formal semantic properties explicit. I call this language Ensemble Language (EL).

EL is a simplified version of a formal language that is used for the semantic representation of English sentences in the question-answering system PHLIQA 1 (Medema et al., 1975).[13]

EL is defined by a grammar which is a 4-tuple $\langle T, C, S, F\text{-ROLES} \rangle$, where T, C, and S are countable sets and F-ROLES is a function from C into the set of finite subsets of S.

The elements of T are called "terminal symbols", those of C "syntactic constructions", and those of S "semantic roles". The function F-ROLES assigns a set of semantic roles to each syntactic construction.

The set of expressions of EL is recursively defined by the following rules:

(i)   all terminal symbols are expressions;
(ii)   if $e_1, e_2, \ldots, e_n$ are expressions, c is a syntactic construction, and F-ROLES $(c) = \{role_1, role_2, \ldots role_n\}$, then the pair $(c, \{(role_1, e_1), (role_2, e_2), \ldots, (role_n, e_n)\})$ is an expression.

A language defined in such a way is called a *construction language*. The expressions of a construction language are abstract mathematical objects that explicitly display their syntactic structure: the way in which they are constructed from immediate subexpressions. The semantics of a construction language is defined by a set of rules, one for each syntactic construction, that define how the denotation of an expression constructed with that syntactic construction (i.e. the entity which the expression denotes), is derived from the denotations of the immediate subexpressions. The *semantic* structure of the expressions of an construction language thus corresponds directly to its *syntactic* structure.

The simple construction language EL, which I want to use, has seven syntactic constructions, described by the EL grammar as follows:

C = {function application, quantification, selection, relation
      application, quantity, negation, conjunction}

S = {function, argument, for, variable, holds, head, modifier,
      $argument_1$, relation, $argument_2$, number, unit, not,
      and_1, and_2}

F-ROLES = {⟨function application, {function, argument}⟩,
            ⟨quantification, {for, variable, holds}⟩,
            ⟨selection, {head, variable, modifier}⟩,
            ⟨relation application, {$argument_1$, relation,
             $argument_2$}⟩,
            ⟨quantity, {number, unit}⟩,
            ⟨negation, {not}⟩,
            ⟨conjunction, {and_1, and_2}⟩}

In the set T of terminal symbols I distinguish the following subsets:

– a set F of function symbols: $F = \{F_1, F_2, F_3, \ldots\}$
– a set E of ensemble symbols: $E = \{E_1, E_2, E_3, \ldots\}$
– a set U of unit symbols: $U = \{u_1, u_2, u_3, \ldots\}$
– a set of M of "measure" symbols (see below):
    $M = \{\mu_1, \mu_2, \mu_3, \ldots\}$
– a set of X of variables: $X = \{x_1, x_2, x_3, \ldots\}$

The semantics of the function application-, relation application-, negation- and conjunction-constructions are as suggested by the names. For instance, the semantic rule associated with the function application construction says that the function in question should be applied to the argument in question in order to obtain the value of the expression in question. The selection construction serves to form the smallest part of a given ensemble (the "head") that includes all parts with a given property (expressed by the "modifier"; cf. formula (24)). The quantification construction expresses the familiar universal quantification over a certain set (here: discrete ensemble). A general notion of quantification over ensembles, which is needed for the representation of quantified mass noun expressions, will be introduced below, in combination with the explanation of the quantity construction. This completes the definition of EL.

Because the expressions of a construction language explicitly display their syntactic and semantic structure, they can conveniently be used for formal symbolic (possibly mechanical) manipulation, and this also makes construction languages attractive as semantic representation languages. The construction language which is used for this purpose in the PHLIQA 1 system has more syntactic constructions than EL, and makes use of a system of semantic *types* in order to restrict the set of expressions, defined by the grammar, to meaningful ones. A construction language is particularly suited for being combined with a system of types because of the explicitness of the structure of its expressions. In this paper I will only make a very restricted use of types and describe their incorporation in EL informally; the reader is referred to Scha (1975) for a formal description of the incorporation of a type system in the grammar of a construction language.

The use of types in EL is as follows. Let the EL grammar assign to each ensemble E_i of E a type t_i, different ensembles being allowed to have the same type. It is convenient then to index the elements of E according to their types: those ensembles having type t_i are indexed as E_{i1}, E_{i2}, E_{i3}, ..., etc. The $\subseteq$ relation is type-preserving: all genuine parts of an ensemble have the same type as the ensemble. It follows immediately that ensembles with different types do not intersect.

The terminal symbols of the set M, which were called "measure symbols", denote *measure functions*, functions from $\bigcup_j \mathscr{P}(E_{i_j})$ into

$\mathbb{R} \times \{u_i\}$, i.e. functions applicable to all ensembles with type t_i and having as values pairs (n, u_i) with n a real number[14] and u_i a certain element from U, a so-called "unit". The use of measure functions is explained below. In the context of this paper it is convenient to use an abbreviated notation for EL-expressions and to rely on the reader's ability to reconstruct the unabbreviated forms if needed. I will use the following abbreviations:

$F(a) \quad \underset{\text{D}}{=}$ (function application, {(function, F), (argument, a)}),

$(\forall x \in E)P \underset{\text{D}}{=}$ (quantification, {(for E), (variable, x), (holds, P)}),

$[x \subseteq E|\ P] \underset{\text{D}}{=}$ (selection, {(head, E), (variable, x), (modifier, P)}),

$xRy \quad \underset{\text{D}}{=}$ (relation application, {(argument$_1$, x), (relation, R), (argument$_2$, y)}),

$(n, u) \quad \underset{\text{D}}{=}$ (quantity, {(number, n), (unit, u)}),

$\neg e \quad \underset{\text{D}}{=}$ (negation, (not, e)),

$e_1,\ \&\ e_2 \quad \underset{\text{D}}{=}$ (conjunction, (and$_1$, e_1), (and$_2$, e_2)).

4.3 Amounts

The quantity construction in EL is included for the representation of amount terms like "25 kilogrammes", "3.5 dollars", etc., that occur in sentences like:

(35a)   The cheese in this box weighs 25 kilogrammes
(35b)   This box contains 25 kilogrammes of cheese (books, apples. .)
(35c)   These coins have a value of more than 3.5 dollars
(35d)   It took me less than 10 minutes.

I will present a simplified treatment of amounts, containing just as much as I minimally need for handling quantified mass noun expressions.[15]

I consider an amount term like "25 kilogrammes", which will be translated into EL as (25, kilogrammes) in its abbreviated form and in its unabbreviated form as (quantity, {(number, 25), (unit, kilogrammes)}), as referring to an abstract entity, an "amount", that can be used for characterizing the size of objects in terms of their weight. One of the most conspicuous features of amounts is that they have an *arithmetic*. Certain units can be mutually converted, such as kilogrammes, pounds, ounces and grammes, and amounts expressed in these units can be compared, added, and subtracted. I will neglect the phenomena of convertability entirely. I also leave complex units, like "dollars per gallon" out of consideration. I feel it is justified to do so, since in the present paper I do not pretend to give an analysis of amount terms per se. In fact, having accepted these limitations, there seems to be little point in considering more than one way to measure the size of an ensemble.

Therefore, I will assume from now on that for each type t_i there is just one measure function μ_i that expresses the sizes of ensembles with the type t_i in terms of a unit u_i. The application of the measure function μ_i to an ensemble x with type t_i will be denoted by $|x|$.

In order to be suitable for measuring the size of ensembles, a measure function is required to have the following properties:

(i) The size of a non-empty ensemble is larger than zero units:

$$(36) \qquad (\forall x)(\forall E_{ij})(x \subseteq E_{ij} \ \& \ x \neq \varnothing) \to (|x| > (o, u_i))$$

(ii) The size of the union of two disjoint ensembles is the sum of the two sizes:

$$(37) \qquad (\forall x, y, E_{ij}, E_{ik})((x \subseteq E_{ij} \ \& \ y \subseteq E_{ik} \ \& \ x \cap y = \varnothing) \to (|x \cup y| = |x| + |y|))^{16}$$

From these properties of measures the following theorems follow:

THEOREM 3. An ensemble has a size of zero units if and only if it is empty.

This theorem follows from (37) since $\varnothing = \varnothing \cup \varnothing$ and $\varnothing \cap \varnothing = \varnothing$.

(38) THEOREM 4. For any two ensembles A and B, if $A \subseteq B$, $|A| = |B|$ and $|A|$ is finite then $A = B$.

Since, trivially, $A = B$ implies $|A| = |B|$, it follows from this theorem that the identity of two finite ensembles is equivalent to the equality of their sizes, provided that one is part of the other.

4.4 *Simple quantified mass noun expressions*

Let us now consider some examples of the analysis of mass noun expressions, using EL as semantic representation language and ensemble theory for establishing formal semantic properties. More complex examples are given in section 5.2. As a first example, I take one of the "problem sentences" listed by Parsons (1970):

(39a)   Most gold is still unmined.

I agree with Parsons that, neglecting the word "still", a correct analysis of this sentence is:

(39b)   The amount of unmined gold exceeds the amount of mined (i.e. not unmined) gold.

If GOLD[17] is the EL name for the ensemble of all gold, and UNMINED stands for the EL translation of the corresponding predicate, an EL representation of (39b) is:

(39c) $|[x \subseteq \text{GOLD}|\text{UNMINED}(x)]| > |[x \subseteq \text{GOLD}|$
        $\neg\text{UNMINED}(x)]|$

A sentence with a quantification that involves a definite amount is analysed similarly, for instance the sentence:

(40a)   5000 tons of gold are (still) unmined

is represented in EL as:

(40b) $|[x \subseteq \text{GOLD}|\text{UNMINED}(x)]| = (5000, \text{tons}).$

Similarly, for the corresponding sentence with a universal quantification:

(41)   All gold is (still) unmined

the following EL representation is appropriate[18]:

(42) $|[x \subseteq \text{GOLD}|\text{UNMINED}(x)]| = |\text{GOLD}|$

Since, according to Theorem 2 of ensemble theory, the ensemble occuring in the left-hand side of (42) is contained in the ensemble GOLD, Theorem 4 can be applied to reduce (42) to:

(43) $[x \subseteq \text{GOLD}|\text{UNMINED}(x)] = \text{GOLD}$

Equality between ensembles is defined by mutual inclusion, and from the transitivity of the part-of relation it follows from (43) that:

(44) $(\forall x)(x \subseteq \text{GOLD} \to x \subseteq [y \subseteq \text{GOLD}|\text{UNMINED}(y)]).$

So every piece of gold is a piece of unmined gold, which is, intuitively, a more satisfactory analysis than the one in terms of sizes.

Another of Parsons' problem sentences is: "All blue styrofoam is styrofoam". This is an instance of the formal scheme S2, mentioned in section 2.1: "All P M is M". I will analyse this scheme by taking, in the spirit of my original example "All ice cream is cold"/"All Italian ice cream is cold", the sentence:

(45)   All Italian ice cream is ice cream.

This sentence is similar in structure to "All gold is still unmined", and accordingly we get, by analogy with (43):

(46) $[x \subseteq \text{ITALIAN-ICE}|x \subseteq \text{ICE}] = \text{ITALIAN-ICE}$

where

(47) $\text{ITALIAN-ICE} \underset{D}{=} [y \subseteq \text{ICE}|\text{ITALIAN}\,(y)]$

Since, according to Theorem 2, ITALIAN-ICE $\subseteq$ ICE, all parts of ITALIAN-ICE are parts of ICE, and therefore the property $x \subseteq$ ICE in the left-hand side of (46) is not restrictive. Therefore, the left-hand side is equal to ITALIAN-ICE, which means that (46) is reduced to:

(48)   ITALIAN-ICE = ITALIAN-ICE

This is a tautology in ensemble theory. Therefore, upon this analysis, sentence (45) is an analytic sentence.

The formal scheme S1: "All M is M", is in fact simpler than the one just considered. In its tasty icy instance, it is

(49)   All ice cream is ice cream

The EL representation of this sentence is:

(50) $|[x \subseteq \text{ICE}|x \subseteq \text{ICE}]| = |\text{ICE}|$

Theorems 2 and 4 can again be used to reduce this to the equality between the two ensembles, and by the same reasoning as applied to (46), the left-hand ensemble can be shown to be equal to the right-hand ensemble. So all ice cream is ice cream. We see that, upon this analysis, the schemes S1 and S2 represent tautologies. The schemes S3-S5 will be considered in section 5.2; we first take a look at the semantic aspects of the application of adjectives as restrictive modifiers on mass nouns.

5. ADJECTIVES AND THE COUNT/MASS DISTINCTION

5.1. *The Classification of Adjectives*

In this section I briefly present a tentative view on the possibility of distinguishing between "count adjectives" and "mass adjectives", and some of the consequences of this view. It was noted by Quine (1960) that the cumulative reference condition: "any sum of parts that are W is W," which he proposes as the semantic criterion for the count/mass distinction, is satisfied by some adjectives and not by others. For instance, any sum of parts that are red, heavy, or expensive seems to be red, heavy, expensive, but the sum of parts that are spherical, light, or cheap, is in general not spherical, light, or cheap. This has led to the suggestion to classify adjectives accordingly as mass or count.

However, a classification such that, e.g., "heavy" and "expensive" belong to one category, and "light" and "cheap" to another, does not seem to have any relation to the count/mass distinction among nouns. It seems to me that a classification which is more interesting for the present discussion can be obtained by conjoining the conditions of cumulative and distributive reference. What I mean by that is the following. I call a property P *homogeneous* if it satisfies the following conditions:

(51)
    (i)   the sum of any parts that have the property P has the property P.
    (ii)   any part of something that has the property P has the property P.

Formalized in terms of ensembles, these conditions read:

(52a) $(\forall x, y)((P(x)\ \&\ P(y)) \rightarrow P(x \cup y))$
(52b) $(\forall x)(P(x) \rightarrow (\forall y)(y \subseteq x \rightarrow P(y)))$

Notice that, according to the conjoined condition (51), "heavy" and "light", as well as "expensive" and "cheap", belong to the same category because either they do not refer cumulatively or they do not refer distributively. There are not many adjectives of which it can be maintained categorically that they satisfy (51); most adjectives can be used in a sense in which they do, and also in a sense in which they do not. Color adjectives are good examples: a "yellow pear" can either mean a pear which is yellow at the outside, or a pear which is yellow throughout. In the latter sense a homogeneous property is denoted, in the former sense not. My suggestion is to use the "homogeneous reference" condition (51), formalized as (52), for classifying adjective-senses into count and mass: those adjective-senses that satisfy the condition are called *mass adjectives*, those that do not are called *count adjectives*[19]. I think this classification is of more interest here than the one based on the cumulative reference condition alone, because it seems that, as a rule, only *homogeneous* properties can sensibly be predicated of mass noun referents.

This claim is supported by such examples as:

(53a)   *I smeared 50 grammes of spherical cheese on my bread
(53b)   *The salad contains large apple
(53c)   *Most water is heavy
(53d)   *I like big ice cream.

What emerges from these and related observations is the tentative claim:

(54)   Count adjectives do not combine with mass nouns.

I will refer to (54) as the *homogeneous combination principle*. The homogeneous combination principle has an intuitive understanding, based on the observation that count adjectives like "large", "small", "heavy", "weighing less than 200 grammes", are typically used to indicate properties of individual physical objects; a mass noun, on the other hand, refers homogeneously, and not to a well-established class of objects; therefore, their combination does not make sense.

An obvious consequence of the homogeneous combination principle is that it yields a new criterion for classifying nouns as count or mass. Certain adjectives, like size adjectives (large, small, big, tiny, huge, . . .), are always count; if we meet a noun combined with such an adjective, it must be classified as a count noun.
For instance, in the sentence

(55)   I can't find any apple in the salad

the word "apple" is ambiguous; it can be understood as a count noun or as a mass noun. But when a count adjective is added, as in:

(56)   I can't find any big apple in the salad

the ambiguity disappears: "apple" in (56) is a count noun. The count adjective "big" has a markedly different effect, in this respect, from a mass adjective like "sweet".

5.2. *Quantification and Adjectives*

I now turn to the formal semantic properties captured by the formal schemes S3, S4 and S5. In the ice cream paradigm, S3 is instantiated as:

(57)   All Italian ice cream is Italian.

Maintaining the systematic correspondence between English sentences and their EL representations, built up in (39) through (50), we have the following EL representation of this sentence:

(58) $|[x \subseteq \text{ITALIAN-ICE}|\text{ITALIAN}(x)]| = |\text{ITALIAN-ICE}|$

with ITALIAN-ICE as in (47).

Now there are two important questions to face:

1. what do the logical properties of the EL representation (58) tell us about the question whether sentence (57) is analytic?

2. what does the sentence (57) imply for individual pieces of Italian ice cream, according to the logical properties of (58)?

I will show that, according to the analysis (58), the sentence is analytic and implies that every piece of Italian ice cream is ice cream; therefore, this analysis accounts for the formal semantic properties that the sentence intuitively seems to have.

By applying the theorems 2 and 4, as before, we see that (58) is equivalent to the proposition (59) in ensemble theory:

(59) $[x \subseteq \text{ITALIAN-ICE}|\text{ITALIAN}(x)] = \text{ITALIAN-ICE}$

According to the homogeneous combination principle, ITALIAN is a homogeneous property. This implies that *all* parts of ITALIAN-ICE have this property. Therefore, the property ITALIAN (x) in the ensemble at the left-hand side of (59) is not restrictive, so the ensemble is simply equal to ITALIAN-ICE.

This argument was identical to the one used for example (45): "All Italian ice cream is ice cream", except that the latter did not require the homogeneous combination principle because "to be W" is a homogeneous property for purely logical reasons. It was noted that "All Italian ice cream is ice cream" is formally identical to Parsons' example "All blue styrofoam is styrofoam". The example just considered: "All Italian ice cream is Italian", would correspond to "All blue styrofoam is blue". In Parsons' analysis, the analyticity of both sentences would follow from the same argument. It apparently escaped Parsons that this is untenable, and that it is in fact caused by the logical inconsistency of the "substance" notion, which is the basis of his analysis. I have shown the inconsistency of the substance notion in some detail elsewhere (Bunt, 1976a; 1976c)[20]. Sofar, I have not seen any correct account of the analyticity of S3-type sentences.

With respect to the second question raised above, the homogeneity of the property ITALIAN implies that all parts of the ensemble at the left-hand side of (59) have the property. It then follows from the equality

(59) that all parts of the ensemble at the right-hand side also have this property; all parts of Italian ice cream are Italian.

The S4 schema: if all M is P, then all Q M is P, is instantiated in the ice cream paradigm as the inference of (61) from (60):

(60)   All ice cream is cold
(61)   All Italian ice cream is cold.

The question is whether there is a logical consequence-relation between the EL representations (62) and (63):

(62) $|[x \subseteq \text{ICE}|\text{COLD}(x)]| = |\text{ICE}|$
(63) $|[x \subseteq \text{ITALIAN-ICE}|\text{COLD}(x)]| = |\text{ITALIAN-ICE}|$

As before, by using theorems 2 and 4, this question can be reduced to the one in terms of ensembles:

(64) $[x \subseteq \text{ICE}|\text{COLD}(x)] = \text{ICE}$
(65) $[x \subseteq \text{ITALIAN-ICE}|\text{COLD}(x)] = \text{ITALIAN-ICE}$

According to the homogeneous combination principle, COLD is a homogeneous property. It follows from (64) that all parts of ICE are cold. Since all parts of ITALIAN-ICE are parts of ICE, they must also be COLD. Therefore, the property COLD (x) in the left-hand side of (65) is not restrictive, and the ensemble in question is simply identical to ITALIAN-ICE. So we are again left with the tautology ITALIAN-ICE = ITALIAN-ICE.[21]

It may be worth noting that the homogeneity of the properties COLD and ITALIAN implies that the representations (64) and (65) of the sentences (60) and (61), respectively, have the following logical consequences:

(66) $(\forall x)(x \subseteq \text{ICE} \rightarrow \text{COLD}(x))$
(67) $(\forall x)(x \subseteq \text{ICE} \& \text{ITALIAN}(x)) \rightarrow \text{COLD}(x))$.

So every piece of ice cream is cold, and every piece of ice cream that is Italian is cold. So it seems that the analysis given here does indeed match our intuitions concerning the formal semantic properties of the sentences in question.[22]

Finally, we investigate the logical validity of the S5 scheme: if all M is P, and m is M, then m is P. For instance: "All ice cream is cold" and "this little bit is ice cream" therefore "this little bit is cold". The EL representations of the two antecedent sentences are:

(68) $|[x \in ICE| \; COLD \; (x)]| \; = \; |ICE|$

(69) $b \subseteq ICE$

("b" stands for the EL representation of "this little bit".) From (68) we obtain, by applying theorems 2 and 4 as before, the equality of the two ensembles in question. According to the homogeneous combination principle, this implies that all parts of ICE have the property COLD. So in particular the part "b" has this property: COLD (b).

This is a solution to Quine's classical semantic puzzle: all water is wet, this puddle is water, therefore this puddle is wet.

SUMMARY

In this paper an analysis is presented of the formal (i.e. non-lexical) semantic properties of mass terms. This analysis is also an *explanation* of these properties, in the sense that it is carried out by applying a formal framework which is developed on the basis of assumptions concerning the fundamental, defining characteristics of mass terms. As defining characteristics of mass terms are taken: for nouns the property of *homogeneous reference*, for adjectives the property of denoting a *homogeneous property*. Both these characteristics are formalized in the main part of the framework, called *Ensemble Theory*. The framework is completed by the addition of a simple treatment of amounts and the postulation of the homogeneous combination principle. The power and the soundness of the framework are demonstrated by applying it to a number of important cases and showing that it correctly accounts for the semantic properties of the expressions involved.

ACKNOWLEDGEMENTS

I owe many thanks to my colleagues at the PHLIQA project for numerous stimulating discussions on mass terms. This paper benefited greatly from comments on an earlier paper, in particular from Remko Scha and Jan Landsbergen at the PHLIQA project, from several colleagues at the Institute for Perception Research, from Julius Moravcsik at Stanford University, and from Anna Szabolcsi at the Institute of Linguistics in Budapest.

APPENDIX

List of axioms for ensemble theory

The notation is used that was developed in section 3.
1. Axiom of Transitivity.

$$(\forall x, y, z)((x \subseteq y \ \& \ y \subseteq z) \rightarrow (x \subseteq z))$$

2. Axiom of Extension.

$$(\forall x, y)(((\forall z)((z \subseteq x \ \& \ z \neq \varnothing) \rightarrow (z \cap y \neq \varnothing)) \rightarrow$$
$$(x \subseteq y)) \ \& \ \text{ATOM}(x) \rightarrow (x \subseteq x))$$

3. Axiom of Unicles.

$$(\forall x)((\text{ATOM}(x) \rightarrow (\exists ! y)(y \in x)) \ \& \ (\neg \text{ATOM}(x) \rightarrow$$
$$\neg(\exists y)(y \in x)))$$

4. Axiom of Substitutivity.

$$(\forall x, y, z)((x \in z \ \& \ x = y) \rightarrow (y \in z))$$

5. Axiom of Unions.

$$(\forall x)((\exists y)(y \in x) \rightarrow (\exists u)(\forall z)(z \in x \rightarrow z \subseteq u))$$

6. Axiom of Replacement.

Let ψ be any well-formed expression with 2 free variables, such that $(\forall x, y, z)((\psi(x, y) \ \& \ \psi(x, z)) \rightarrow (y = z))$ i.e. ψ represents a function.

$$(\forall x)(\exists y)(\forall z)(z \in y \rightarrow (\exists u)(u \in x \ \& \ \psi(u, z))$$

7. Axiom of Powers.

$$(\forall x)(\exists p)(\forall z)(z \subseteq x \rightarrow z \in p)$$

8. Axiom of Pairs.

$$(\forall x, y)(\exists p)(x \in p \ \& \ y \in p)$$

9. Axiom of Infinity.

Let $\{z\}$ denote the atomic ensemble with unicle z.

$$(\exists x)((\exists y)(y \in x) \ \& \ (\forall z)(z \in x \rightarrow \{z\} \in x))$$

10. Axiom of Regularity.

$$(\forall x)((\exists y)(y \in x) \rightarrow (\exists z)(z \in x \ \& \ z \cap x = \varnothing))$$

NOTES

[1] The above considerations and those that follow are not restricted to bare nouns, but apply also to complex noun phrases like "pure orange juice", "Italian ice cream", "furniture imported from Denmark", etc.

[2] Some nouns seem to resist a classification as either count or mass, simply because it is odd to use them in contexts in which one of the classification criteria is present. For instance, it seems about equally odd to say "much relativity" as "many relativities". See also Ware (1975), p. 380.

[3] I consider a noun as singular if it governs singular verb forms.

[4] I use the term "formal semantics" in opposition with "lexical semantics" or "referential semantics". The importance of the distinction formal/lexical (referential), also known as the distinction between "sentence semantics" and "word semantics", has recently been emphasized by several authors, e.g. Bartsch & Vennemann (1972, p. 39), Landsbergen (1976, p. 1), Thomason (1974, p. 48).

[5] The "formal language of predicates and sets", used in (10a) and (11a), is just first-order predicate language with notations borrowed from set theory. The symbol "$\in$" represents formally a 2-place predicate.

[6] An adequate criticism of Cheng's view has been given by Moravcsik (1973b).

[7] The axioms and other formulae of Ensemble Theory are formulated in standard first-order predicate logic. All variables range over ensembles.

[8] The symbol "$\underset{D}{=}$" can be read as: abbreviates.

[9] The axiom given in (20) only covers the case that the ensemble "x" has a non-empty proper part; the other case is covered by Axiom IIb, stated in (30). Together, (20) and (30) are a notational variant of the Axiom of Extension given in Bunt (1976a). In the mean time I have discovered, however, that a stronger Axiom of Extension is needed; see the appendix.

[10] See e.g. Fraenkel et al. (1973), p. 36.

[11] Take for instance for $\psi(z)$ the property $z \cap a \neq \varnothing$, where "$a$" is some part of x. There is no reason why the ensemble $[z \subseteq x | z \cap a \neq \varnothing]$ should not contain parts disjoint with a.

[12] Formula (33) is the formulation for the case of two parts. The general formulation follows immediately from the definition of the union of arbitrarily many ensembles.

[13] The work reported in this paper was to a large extent conducted as part of the PHLIQA 1 project. The semantic analysis of mass noun expressions, performed by the PHLIQA 1 system, is based on the theoretical foundations presented here.

[14] This formulation is not quite accurate in two respects. Firstly, as the empty ensemble belongs to $\bigcup_j \mathscr{P}(E_{ij})$, the domain of a measure function is the set of all ensembles of a certain type t_i extended with the empty ensemble. Secondly, by $\mathbb{R}$ I mean the set of real numbers extended with $+\infty$ and $-\infty$. This set, sometimes called the extended set of real numbers, is commonly used in measure theory, see e.g. S. Berberian, *Theory of Measure and Integration*.

[15] A more extensive treatment of amounts is given in Bunt (1978), pp. 10–18.

[16] Notice that $|x|$ and $|y|$ are pairs (n_x, u_i), (n_y, u_i), with $n_x, n_y \in \mathbb{R}$. By $|x| + |y|$ is denoted the pair $(n_x + n_y, u_i)$.

[17] Capital letters are used to indicate EL constants.

[18] Another possible analysis of universally quantified mass noun expressions like (41), that one might think of, is in terms of parts rather than amounts, e.g. $(\forall x \subseteq GOLD)$ UNMINED (x), which would be more closely analogous to the traditional way of analysing universally quantified count noun expressions as exemplified by (10a) (cf. also Bunt (1978), p. 19). The logical relation between these two ways of analysing universal quantification over a mass term is explored in some detail in section 5.2. If 'unmined' is assumed to be a mass adjective in the sense defined in section 5.1. (as seems most plausible), it is easily seen that the two ways of analysing (41) are logically equivalent.

[19] As in the case of nouns, most of the considerations also apply to complex phrases.
[20] The simplest paradox that can be constructed is by considering the substance $s = \sigma x[\overline{} \mid x \, Q \, x]$. For this substance there holds: $yQs \leftrightarrow \overline{}]yQs$. Cf. note 11.
[21] The proof that (64) implies (65) can also be given without making use of the homegeneity of COLD, but then a little more ensemble theory is needed. In particular, what is needed is the following equality:

$$[x \subseteq \text{ITALIAN-ICE} \mid \text{COLD } (x)] = [x \subseteq \text{ICE} \mid \text{ITALIAN } (x) \ \& \ \text{COLD } (x)] =$$
$$= [x \subseteq \text{ICE} \mid \text{ITALIAN } (x)] \ \cap \ [x \subseteq \text{ICE} \mid$$
$$\text{COLD } (x)]$$

This equality, which is not difficult to prove, reduces to (65) when (64) is substituted at the right-hand side, Theorem 2 is applied, and it is recognized that $A \cap B = A$ if $A \subseteq B$.
[22] Note that (66) and (67) are the exact counterparts of (10a) and (11a)! The only difference between the analysis of the count noun case (8a)/(9a) and the mass noun case (8b)/(9b) is that the role of the $\in$-relation in the count case is taken over by the $\subseteq$-relation in the mass case.

REFERENCES

R. Bartsch, Th. Vennemann (1972), *Semantic Structures*.

Bunt, H. C. (1976a), 'The formal semantics of mass terms', *Papers from the IIIrd Scandinavian Conference of Linguistics*, Helsinki 1976.

Bunt, H. C. (1976b), 'The semantic interpretation of mass nouns in the PHLIQA 1 system', Paper read at the 14th Annual Meeting of the Association for Computational Linguistics, San Francisco 1976.

Bunt, H. C. (1976c), 'Some recent developments in semantics', *IPO Annual Progress Report* **11**.

Bunt, H. C. (1978), 'A formal semantic analysis of mass terms and amount terms', in J. Groenendijk and M. Stokhof (eds.), *Amsterdam Papers in Formal Grammar*, Vol. II.

Burge, T. (1977), 'A theory of aggregates'.

Cheng, Ch. Y. (1973), 'Response to Moravcsik', in Hintikka *et al.* (1973).

Fraenkel, A. A., Bar-Hillel, Y., Levy, A. and Dalen, D. van (1975), *Foundations of Set Theory*.

Hintikka, J., *et al.* (eds.), (1973), *Approaches to Natural Language*, D. Reidel, Dordrecht.

Landsbergen, S. P. J. (1976), *Syntax and Formal Semantics of English in PHLIQA 1*. COLING 76 papers, Ottawa.

Medema, P., Bronnenberg, W. J., Bunt, H. C., Landsbergen, S. P. J., Scha, R. J. H., Schoenmakers, W. J. and Utteren, E. P. C. van (1975), 'PHLIQA 1: Multilevel semantics in question answering,' *American Journal of Computational Linguistics*, microfiche 32.

Moravcsik, J. M. E. (1973), 'Mass terms in English,' in Hintikka *et al.* (1973).

Moravcsik, J. M. E. (1973b), 'Reply to comments', in Hintikka *et al.* (1973).

Parsons, T. (1970), 'An analysis of mass terms and amount terms,' *Foundations of Language* **6**. Reprinted in this volume, pp. 137–166.

Pelletier, F. J. (1974). 'On some proposals for the semantics of mass terms,' *Journal of Philosophical Logic* **3**, 87–108.

Pelletier, F. J. (1975), 'A bibliography of recent work on mass terms', *Synthese* **31**, Nos. 3/4. Reprinted in this volume, with additions, 295–298.

Quine, W. V. O. (1960), *Word and Object*.

Scha, R. J. H. (1976), 'Semantic types in PHLIQA 1', COLING 76 papers, Ottawa.

Thomason, R. H. (ed.) (1974), *Formal philosophy: selected papers of Richard Montague*.

Ware, R. X. (1975), 'Some bits and pieces', *Synthese* **31**, Nos. 3/4. Reprinted in this volume, pp. 15–29.

PREDICATION AND MATTER

This paper is divided into four sections. First, I will pose what may be called the metaphysical problem of matter. Then, I will describe a related problem: the logico-linguistic problem of mass terms. Third, I will outline the standard solutions to these problems. Fourth, I will suggest a new solution.

1. THE METAPHYSICAL PROBLEM OF MATTER

Things would be pleasantly simple if everything were a universal or a particular. Universals, for our purpose, may be thought of as having four essential properties:

(a)   universals are jointly (i) eternal, (ii) uncaused and (iii) abstract
(b)   universals are intensional entities
(c)   universals may be expressed in language by general terms
(d)   universals are never said of themselves only; that is, no universal U is such that, for all A, A is U iff $A = U$.[1]

In contrast to universals, particulars do not in general have these properties. Every particular B is such that, for all A, A is B iff $A = B$. Particulars *are* said of themselves only. Moreover, particulars cannot be expressed in language by general terms; also, particulars are not intensional entities, and particulars are seldom, if ever, jointly (i) eternal, (ii) uncaused, and (iii) abstract.

Now what about stuffs? Gold? Water? Concrete? Egg nog? Matter, itself? Are stuffs universals or particulars, or are they members of an altogether different metaphysical category?

Given the foregoing criteria, stuffs do not seem to qualify as particulars on at least two counts. First, if S is a stuff, it is not the case that, for all A, A is S only if $A = S$. That is, it is not the case that stuffs must be said of themselves only. For example, if gold exists, then something besides gold must be gold (e.g., a nugget, a gold ring or perhaps just a bit of gold dust).

279

F. J. Pelletier (ed.), Mass Terms, 279–294. All Rights Reserved.

The second reason for thinking that stuffs are not particulars is that stuffs *seem* to correlate with general terms in the same way that universals do. *Prima facie*, it seems that the stuff gold bears the same relation to the sentence 'this is gold' as the universal red bears to the sentence 'this is red'.

At the same time, however, stuffs do not seem to qualify as universals. First, stuffs need not be eternal, uncaused, and abstract. Many stuffs are caused and in fact created and, hence, are not eternal; here are some examples: plutonium, Saran Wrap, Coca Cola. Relatedly, some stuffs don't even exist: e.g., phlogiston and kryptonite (i.e., the fictional element that Superman is allergic to). Further, there is some sense – though perhaps not the relevant sense – in which stuffs are concrete. Secondly, stuffs, unlike universals, may well be extensional entities. I have some serious reservations about this point. But isn't it true that, if whatever is composed of S_1 is composed of S_2 and conversely, then $S_1 = S_2$? It may well be the extensionality of stuffs that leads us to assert identities such as water $= H_2O$. Nothing analogous happens with, say, the property of being a creature with a kidney and the property of being a creature with a heart.

Thus, we are faced with a metaphysical problem. Given that stuffs appear to qualify neither as universals nor as particulars, what are they?

2. THE LOGICO-LINGUISTIC PROBLEM OF MASS TERMS

In Chapter III of *Word and Object* Quine introduces the metalinguistic notion of mass term. The difference between mass terms and sortal words (or count nouns) is usually brought out as follows:

(a)   if 'm' is a mass term, it is natural to ask 'how much m?' but not 'how many m?': 'how much water?' not 'how many waters?'

(b)   if 's' is a sortal, it is natural to ask 'how many s?' but not 'how much s?': 'how many pencils?' not 'how much pencil?'

Now consider the sentences 'Socrates is a man' and 'man is rational'. In traditional logic the logical form of these sentences is thought to be 'A is B'. The numerous problems that confront traditional logic led modern logicians, under the leadership of Frege and Russell, to propound a different logical grammar. According to the modern theory, 'Socrates is a man' has the form '$M(s)$', where 'M' is a predicate or general term and 's' is a concrete singular term. And 'man is rational' has the form of a universal conditional, '$(\forall x)(Mx \rightarrow Rx)$'. Thus, the abstract singular term of traditional logic entirely disappears from the sentences under consideration.

Analogous to 'man' above, mass terms, e.g., 'chalk', seem to occur in two ways, namely, as predicates and as abstract singular terms. The following sentences illustrate this fact:

(i) a is chalk
(ii)   chalk is messy.

The logico-linguistic problem of mass terms results from the fact that not all the sentences in which mass terms occur before the copula can be analyzed as universal conditionals. For example, 'water is widespread' is not equivalent to 'whatever is water is widespread'. Hence, the modern theory must be adjusted.

Thus, we are are faced with a logico-linguistic problem. What is the logical form of sentences whose surface grammar contains mass terms? What is the correct way to parse sentences that seem to contain mass terms?

Before going further I should make two points of clarification. First, not all mass terms determine stuffs. For example, the expressions 'motion' and 'music' can be used as mass terms, but motion and music are certainly not stuffs. I should also state that I will not count things like furniture, footwear, traffic, or information as stuffs in my sense. In this paper I will not suggest any theory about the nature of non-stuffs that are determined by mass terms. Inevitably, then, I will leave a number of questions open.

Second, it is best to view our inquiry as analysis, not ontology. We are not trying to determine whether stuffs really exist or not. Rather we are trying to determine whether stuffs, if they exist or were to exist, would be universals, particulars or something else. We are not trying to determine whether various positive forms of mass-term sentences are true (or pragmatically required for the statement of scientific facts). Instead we are trying to determine what are the real logical forms of the various kinds of mass-term sentences. It is not crucial to our discussion that such sentences should be true (or indispensible to science) or that stuffs should exist.

3. THE STANDARD SOLUTIONS

We will now examine the three standard solutions to the metaphysical problem of mass and the logico-linguistic problem of mass terms. These standard solutions are (a) Quine's analysis, (b) the general-term analysis and (c) the abstract-singular-term analysis.[2]

(a) *Quine's Analysis*

According to Quine's ingenious analysis, mass terms in ordinary language are ambiguous. The logical forms of our sample sentences (i) '*a* is chalk' and (ii) 'chalk is messy' are:

    (i') $C(a)$
    (ii') $M(c)$

In (i') the entity that correlates with the predicate 'C' is of the kind that normally correlates to a general term. Thus, for Quine, the correlatum of 'C' is a set, namely, the set of things that are composed of chalk. (Given Quine's parsing, platonists such as Russell would say that correlatum of 'C' is the *property* of being composed of chalk.) In (ii') the correlatum of the singular term 'c' is the fusion of all particulars that are composed of chalk. That is, 'c' names a kind of *particular* which Nelson Goodman calls a scattered particular. Thus, Quine's proposal allows us to retain the view that everything is either a universal or a particular.

    There are two kinds of difficulty with Quine's proposal. Consider four sample sentences:

> Chalk is used for writing on blackboards
> Champagne creeps up on you
> Plastic is inexpensive
> Plutonium is heavier than hydrogen

    The problems here are obvious. For example, although plastic is inexpensive, the fusion of all things composed of plastic is certainly not inexpensive.

    The second kind of difficulty with Quine's proposal is *logical*. Consider the following apparently valid argument:

> *a* is gold
> gold is malleable
> ∴ *a* is malleable

On Quine's proposal, there is no clue of how to bring this argument within reach of contemporary methods of logic. The following sentence creates a related problem:

> White chalk is white.

One would think that this sentence is logically true. But again, there is no clue of how to make it so.

(b) *The General Term Analysis*

The second solution to the metaphysical problem of mass and the logico-linguistic problem of mass terms may be called the general-term analysis. This analysis has been suggested by Richard Grandy and Tyler Burge.[3]

According to this view our sentences (i) and (ii) are to be treated in the standard fashion prescribed by modern logic. Thus, (i) and (ii) have the following logical forms:

(i') $C(a)$
(ii') $(\forall x)(Cx \rightarrow Mx)$

The entity that corresponds to the general 'C' is of the kind that usually correlates to a general term, i.e., a set or a property. So far, then, the general term view allows one to hold the view that everything is either a universal (or a set) or a particular.

The general-term view has the additional advantage of solving the second kind of problem that confronts Quine's view:

> *a* is gold $G(a)$
> gold is malleable $\Rightarrow$ $(\forall x)(Gx \rightarrow Mx)$
> ∴ *a* is malleable   ∴ $M(a)$
> White chalk is white $\Rightarrow$ $(\forall x)((Wx \,\&\, Cx) \rightarrow Wx)$

Both of the symbolic translations are valid.

Now what about the troublesome sentences that lead Quine to reject the general term view in the first place. Richard Grandy has suggested that the recalcitrant sentences be analyzed as being about sets whose names contain only the predicative use of mass terms. For example 'water is widespread' should be analyzed as '$P(\{x:x \text{ is water}\})$' where '$P$' is a predicate somehow determined by the word 'widespread'. Hence, '$P\{x:x \text{ is water}\}$' might be cashed out as '$\{x:x \text{ is water}\}$ has widespread-membership' or '$\{x:x \text{ is water}\}$ is a widespread-set'. Or take another example. 'Gold has atomic number 79' is to be analyzed as '$\{x:x \text{ is gold}\} = \{x:x \text{ has atomic number 79}\}$'.

I will suggest two objections to this treatment of mass terms. First, in its details it is unintuitive. Consider the last example. It seems simply false that any particulars besides atoms have atomic numbers. The second and very serious objection is based on some further examples:

(1)   Chalk is easy to find.
(2)   Chalk is easy for children to find in Holland.
(3)   Hot water is in the water heater only when it is not in the tub.

Presumably, these sentences get analyzed as follows:

(1') $\{x:x \text{ is chalk}\}$ is an easy-to-find-set
(2') $\{x:x \text{ is chalk}\}$ is an easy-for-children-to-find-in-Holland-set
(3') $\{x:x \text{ is hot } \& \ x \text{ is water}\}$ is an in-the-water-heater-only-if-not-in-the-tub-set

The problem I want to point out is this. If these hyphenated expressions are to be introduced as new undefined primitives, then the hope of a systematic treatment of mass terms must be abandoned. For, an infinite number of such primitives is required and an infinite number of primitives can't be managed by humans. On the other hand, if the hyphenated expressions are to be counted as syntactically and semantically complex, new logical machinery must be introduced for dealing with this new complexity. In this case, however, it would look as though the most difficult problems of mass terms have merely been swept under the rug. We must wait for the hypothetical logical machinery to solve the problems. Incidentally, even if such machinery can be provided, it is not clear that the present view, with these complications, would be simpler than the abstract-singular-term analysis.

As I mentioned, besides Richard Grandy, Tyler Burge also recommends the general-term view. Roughly speaking, Tyler Burge chooses to use *fusions* in place of Grandy's sets. For example,

> gold has atomic number 79

is to be analyzed as:

> ean 79 = the fusion of all particulars that are gold

where 'ean 79' abbreviates the analysis of the definite description 'the element whose atomic number is 79'.

One possible problem with this approach arises in connection with producing something appropriate for 'ean 79'. Perhaps difficult problems are being swept under the rug.

Another problem is that fusions seem to have the wrong kind of identity conditions. If all jewelry were made of gold and all gold were forged into jewelry, we would not be inclined to say that jewelry = gold and, hence, that jewelry is the element whose atomic number is 79. Perhaps, however, this problem can be fixed up.

A third and possibly more serious difficulty with the proposed view is that it appears unable to handle some of the harder cases. One such case seems to call for something like predicate variables whose substituends can be mass terms. For example,

> Gold is malleable, and *it* has atomic number 79 and *it* is hard.

Whereas Grandy is free to represent this sentence as follows:

$$(\forall x)(Gx \to Mx) \ \& \ (\exists F)(F = (\lambda x)(Gx) \ \& \ F = (\lambda x)(x \text{ has atomic number 79}) \ \& \ (\forall x)(Fx \to Hx))$$

Burge is not, since fusions of particulars are not suitable values for predicate variables. The following examples illustrate complex variations on this problem:

(1)   Although Plutonium was discovered in Berkeley, it is produced mainly in Los Alamos because it is so unstable and, hence, a threat to urban populations.

(2)   Although salt is an essential mineral, none of it is better than too much because it ionizes so readily that it can cause severe dehydration.

(3)   Although marble is widespread it is difficult to mine in large pieces because it is very hard and hard stone is difficult to cut without shattering.

(4)   Although Andre's beef is the most special food in the house, it is not the specialty of the house because it is too difficult to make in large quantities.

(5)   Ascorbic acid causes orange juice to be tart and glucose causes it to be sweet; either way it is healthy.

(6)   Many people prefer Uncle Ben's rice to brown rice because it is white and they believe that whatever is white is pure.

Now we come to a fourth objection. Let us assume (and this is a significant assumption) that the proposed view can handle such sentences in a *piecemeal fashion*. Nonetheless, in order to solve the metaphysical problem of mass and in order to solve the logico-linguistic problem of mass terms, what is called for is not a piecemeal approach but rather a *unified method*. Even with our strong assumption, there is no special reason for thinking that the present approach could provide a unified method.

This is where the abstract-singular-term analysis comes in: it has promise of providing a unified method.

(c) *The Abstract-Singular-Term Analysis*

According to this analysis all occurrences of mass terms are occurrences of singular terms. Hence, in our sample sentences (i) and (ii), 'chalk' occurs as a singular term:

(i′) aRc
(ii′) Mc

where 'R' is a relational predicate.

Terry Parsons has propounded the singular term analysis.[4] From a metaphysical point of view, mass terms such as 'chalk' are names of stuffs, where stuffs are neither universals nor particulars. The advantage of this view is obvious: the sentences that were problematic for the general term view are easily handled, they simply say what they seem to say. That is, they ascribe properties to or assert relations among *stuffs*.

This analysis has been criticized for having an excessive ontology.[5] However, this criticism seems to be based on a confusion between analysis (metaphysical and logico-linguistic) and ontology. The following analogy should dramatize my point. Someone who declares that the sentence 'red is a color' has the logical form of a singular predication and that colors are not particulars need not be ontologically committed to to the universal red. He may hold that 'red' is a vacuous name and, hence, that 'red is a color' is not strictly true (or perhaps that it is strictly neither true nor false). At the same time, he may hold that for practical matters like science near *paraphrases* (e.g., 'whatever is red is colored'), as opposed to analyses, can always be supplied piecemeal (or perhaps even systematically). It is simply off target to criticize Parson's analysis (or the analysis that will be suggested in this paper) for ontological excess.

In order to characterize the logic for names of stuffs, Parsons introduces three primitives: two predicates – "is constituted of" and "is a quantity of" – and a *substance-abstraction* operator. This approach has two non-fatal shortcomings. First, it is not very plausible that these expressions are primitives, in the sense of being undefinables. One would hope that a complete analysis of stuffs and mass terms would include definitions of these expressions. The second and related shortcoming is that, if these expressions are adopted as primitives, then new axioms which characterize their logical properties must be added to logic. Of course, it would be desirable to obtain the logical principles for stuffs from the logic that we already have. The view that I will now suggest accomplishes this to a much greater extent than Terry Parson's approach.

4. A PROPOSAL

From the logico-linguistic point of view, the proposal I will make is a version of the abstract-singular-term analysis. From the metaphysical point of view, my theory takes the stand that stuffs are neither universals nor particulars. The following is the metaphysical picture:

extensional entities			intensional entities: universals			
...(species?)	stuffs	particulars	propositions	qualities	relations	...

In discussing stuffs, I shall use a somewhat technical expression, '*A* is composed of *B*'. The composition relation differs from the constitution relation. We may say that an ice cube is composed of H_2O but not that it is composed of a volume of H_2O or that is composed of Hydrogen *and* Oxygen.

As I mentioned, the logico-linguistic theory which I shall propose is a version of the abstract-singular-term analysis. The unique aspect of my version is its treatment of the *copula*. I adopt a special theory of the copula as it occurs in Indo-European languages. This theory is foreshadowed by the theory held by Peter Abelard and, in certain fragments, by Leibniz. Further, the theory of the copula that is incorporated in Lesniewski's 'Ontology' and also the treatment of the 'ε'-relation in Quine's set theory *ML* are not entirely foreign to the theory that I will now propose.

According to this theory, it is the same univocal copula that occurs in each of the following sentences:

> Socrates is wise
> The teacher of Plato is Socrates
> Wisdom is good
> *a* is chalk
> Chalk is messy
> Chalk is calcium carbonate.

The logical form of each of these sentences is:

> *A* is *B*.

Thus, our sample sentences (i) and (ii) have the forms:

(i′)   *a* is *c*
(ii′)   *c* is *m*.

An open-ended list of principles should help to impart the suggested reading of the copula:

(i)   If *B* is a quality, '*A* is *B*' is true *iff* *A* is qualified by *B* (i.e., *A* has *B*)

(ii)   If *B* is a particular, '*A* is *B*' is true *iff* *A* is identical to *B*[6]

(iii)   If *B* is a stuff, '*A* is *B*' is true *iff* *A* is composed of *B*.

I must stress that these principles in no way constitute a definition of the copula. The copula cannot be defined. It is a primitive logical constant. In fact it is a primitive in terms of which the other constants in the principles are, hopefully, to be defined.

Against the proposed theory it may be asserted that the so-called 'is'-of-predication is being confused with the so-called 'is'-of-identity and an 'is'-of-composition. In reply I would suggest that this criticism is based on a theory that is a dogma. Despite what the logic texts say, it is simply not obvious that there even exists a *sense* of 'is' that may be called the 'is'-of-identity, for there is an entirely plausible and natural alternative way of looking at the matter. Sentences such as 'red is red' are *structurally ambiguous*. On the reading that makes 'red is red' false, 'red is red' has the form '*A* is *B*'. On the other hand, given the reading that makes 'red is red' true, 'red is red' is elliptical for, i.e., a syntactical transformation from, 'red is identical to red'. The latter sentence has the form '*A* is *B*', and '*B*', i.e., 'identical to red', names a property. Analogously, there is no *sense* of 'is' that may be called the 'is-of-composition such that 'is' in 'the ring is gold' is synonymous to 'is composed of'. 'The ring is gold' and 'the ring is composed of gold' both have the form '*A* is *B*'. In the former '*B*', i.e., 'gold' names a stuff; in the latter '*B*', i.e., 'composed of gold' names a property.[7]

Now I will attempt to give a definition of what it is to be a stuff. Five metaphysical intuitions are utilized in my definition. *First*, stuffs are necessarily not particulars. *Second*, it is necessary that whatever is composed of a stuff is itself a stuff or a particular.[8] For example, the only things composed of water are stuffs (e.g. ice, steam, snow) and particulars (e.g. drops, ice cubes, clouds of steam, snowballs). I shall express this fact by saying that only stuffs and particulars *are comprehended by stuffs*. *Third*, a stuff cannot exist unless there is some particular which is composed of it.[9] For example, chalk exists only if there is some particular piece or bit of chalk. I will express this fact by saying that each stuff is such that some particular *is comprehended by* it. *Fourth*, a stuff is composed of itself. (A contrast will help to clarify this point. When the sentence 'red is red' is read as elliptical for 'red is identical to red', it is true. When it is not elliptical for 'red is identical to red', it is false. Now consider the sentence 'chalk is chalk'. On *both* readings the sentence is true. Given one reading it is to be true only if chalk is identical to chalk. Given the other reading it is to be true only if chalk is composed of chalk). I will express this fact by saying that each stuff *comprehends* itself. The *fifth* intuition concerns a transitivity property. Necessarily, if *A* is composed of *B* and *B* is composed of *C*, then *A* is composed of *C*. For example, the ice cube is composed of ice; ice is composed of water; therefore, the ice cube is composed of water. I shall express this fact as follows: for each stuff *S*, if *A*, *B*, and *C* are comprehended by S and if A is comprehended by B and B is comprehended by C, then A is comprehended by C.[10]

We begin with two preliminary definitions:

(1) $A = B$ iff$_{def}$. For all C, A is C iff B is C

(2) B is (a) particular iff$_{def}$. For all A, A is B iff $A = B$.

The following, in a nutshell, is the intuition behind definition (2): what is particular about particulars is that they are particular (i.e., they are truly said of themselves and themselves only). Now consider a hypothetical counterexample to this definition. If the property of being an object of thought is the only object of thought, then despite the fact that it is not a particular, it would satisfy the definition. This hypothetical counterexample could be avoid simply by prefixing the definiens with 'necessarily'. If this modification is required, then what is particular about particulars is that they are necessarily particular. Conceivably, however, the modification will not be needed, for thought – like truth – might require ramification in order to avoid antinomy.

Now we give one more preliminary definition.

(3)   Inductive definition of 'A is comprehended by B':
           (a) if $A = B$, A is comprehended by B
           (b) for all C, if C is comprehended by B and
                   if A is C,
                   then A is comprehended by B.

This inductive definition can be turned into a direct definition of 'A is comprehended by B'. To do this we use Frege's method for turning inductive definitions into direct definitions except that the class-membership relation 'ε' is replaced by the copula 'is'. I will omit this step.

Given these preliminary definitions and the previously listed essential properties of stuffs, we advance the following definition:

(4) S is a stuff iff$_{def}$
           (a) S is not a particular &
           (b) For all C, if C is comprehended by S, then
                   (i)   there exists a particular P such that P is C
                   (ii) C is C
                   (iii) for all A and B, if A is B and B is C, then A is C.[11]

Now what about the original logical problems created by names for stuffs?

Consider the argument:

a is chalk

chalk is white

∴ *a* is white.

This argument has the form:

a is *c*

c is *w*

∴ *a* is *w*

This is not a valid argument form as the following example shows:

this is chalk

chalk is found in Dover

∴ this is found in Dover

I suggest that, in addition to its standard use, the sentence 'chalk is white' can be used elliptically for the sentence:

whatever is chalk is white.

This elliptical use makes the above argument valid.

a is *c*

$(\forall x)\,(x \text{ is } c \rightarrow x \text{ is } w)$

∴ *a* is *w*[12]

Now we come to the sentence 'white chalk is white'. Of course, there is an elliptical use of this sentence which is short for:

Whatever is white and chalk is white.

This sentence is valid. $(\forall x)\,((x \text{ is } c \,\&\, x \text{ is } w) \rightarrow x \text{ is } w)$. By contrast, the non-elliptical use of the sentence is not used for making a statement about the things that are composed of white chalk; rather, it is making a statement about white chalk itself. Symbolically, the sentence is represented as follows:

$(\imath x)\,(x \text{ is a stuff} \,\&\, (\forall y)\,(y \text{ is } x \equiv (y \text{ is white} \,\&\, y \text{ is chalk})))$ is white.

So represented, the sentence is *not* logically valid. But I contend that we should not expect the sentence to be logically valid any more than we should expect the sentences 'purple phogiston is purple' or 'the present king of France is a king' to be valid. What ought to be valid is: 'If it exists, white chalk is white'. Given my method of representing *this* sentence, it indeed turns out to be valid in standard first-order quantification theory.[13]

I shall conclude the paper by suggesting three further definitions. Consider that general notion of *material object* which does not disallow that some material objects may have psychological or intentional properties as well as material properties:

(5)   *A* is a material object *iff*$_{def}$
         A is a particular & $(\exists S)$ (*S* is a stuff & *A* is *S*).

Consider the notion of composition which was used earlier in our informal discussion:

(6)   *A* composes *B* *iff*$_{def}$ *A* is a stuff & *B* is *A*.

Lastly, consider the notion of matter according to which, e.g., gold is matter, steam is matter, the stuff of which electrons are composed is matter and also the stuff of which protons are composed is matter:

(7)   matter $=_{def}$ the stuff *B* which is such that, for each stuff *A*,
         A is *B*.

Matter is the stuff which all stuffs are.

The definitions I have proposed should be viewed as extremely tentative for there remain a number of questions about which we have weak or inconclusive intuitions. For example, just as there might be species and genera of particulars, there might be species (or families) and genera of stuffs and, hence, mass terms might double as such species or genera terms. E.g., we say both that gold is metal and that gold is a metal. It is plausible that 'matter', too, has such a dual use. If this is in fact so, I should hope that by methods akin to those used in this paper we could define what it is to be a species of particular and what it is to be a species of stuff and that matter, of the second kind, could be defined as the most general species of stuff. In any case, I consider this and several other questions to be entirely open.

Since there are numerous open questions, the thesis to which I wish to be committed is that it is possible to give successful definitions along the suggested or related lines. It should be noted, moreover, that even if all such definitions should break down in the end, the proposed theory of categories and composition may be correct as a metaphysical theory and the proposed theory of predication may be both correct and useful as a logico-linguistic theory. If it is true that successful definitions can be given in terms of logical constants such as 'is', an interesting consequence results. Just as our concept of number and our concepts of the various numbers and operations are, in a well-defined sense, logical concepts[14], the concepts of material object and matter are, in the same well-defined sense, logical concepts. Hence, an expanded form of logicism.

Reed College

NOTES

[1] This Fourth property may be confusing. Much more will be said about it later in the paper.

[2] The name 'abstract-singular-term analysis' is misleading, for according to this view, stuffs are in a sense both concrete and general.

[3] Richard Grandy, 'Response to Moravcsik', in Hintikka *et al.*, *Approaches to Natural Language*, D. Reidel, Dordrecht, 1973. Tyler Burge, 'Truth and Mass Terms', *Journal of Philosophy* **64** (1972), 263–282.

[4] 'An Analysis of Mass Terms and Amount Terms', *Foundations of Language* 6 (1970) 362–388.

[5] Cf., Tyler Burge, *op. cit.*, pp. 268–269, 271.

[6] Consider the sentence form '*A* is *B*' that is associated with the standard reading of the sentence 'Frege is smart'. By replacing '*A*' with 'the teacher of Plato' and '*B*' with 'Socrates', we obtain a sentence concerning whose truth value we have unfortunately weak intuitions. What is plain is that (a) the sentence is not obviously false and (b) it would be difficult to show that it is false. Such questions must, I am afraid, be adjudicated by our best metaphysico-logico-linguistic theory. It should be noted that even if this sentence is false, there are alternative ways to treat particulars. Insofar as the theory of mass terms and matter proposed in this paper depends on a treatment of particulars, such an alternative treatment would suffice.

Incidentally, in this paper I will not take a stand on the thesis that in 'Socrates is (a) man' – another '*A* is *B*' sentence – 'man' is the name of a species or natural-kind and not the name of a quality. Nonetheless, I do find this thesis plausible.

[7] In my forthcoming book *Properties, Relations and Propositions* it is shown how syntactically complex property-names (such as 'identical to red' and 'composed of gold') as well as relation names and proposition names (i.e., 'that'-clauses) can be defined in a fully extensional, first-order theory for the copula.
theory for the copula.

It will be noticed that 'identical to red' and 'composed of gold' are adjectival in form.

The noun forms of these names are 'identity to red' and 'composition of gold'. The properties named are identity to red and composition of gold.

8 The definition that I am going to propose could be tightened up if 'particular' in this condition were replaced with 'concrete particular'. I believe that I can define 'concrete particular' with methods akin to those used in this paper. However, that definition must await another paper.

9 Again, the definition that I am going to propose could be tightened up if 'particular' in this condition were replaced with 'concrete particular'.

10 There are further properties of stuffs which could be cited. However, for a trial run the above five properties should serve our purposes.

11 This definition could be tightened up by prefixing clause (b) with 'necessarily'.

12 I find this solution inelegant. The following is an alternative line. It might be logically necessary that the copula is transitive with respect to a, c and w if w belongs to a certain category q (e.g., the category of physical qualities). If so, the following would be a valid argument:

$$a \text{ is } c$$
$$c \text{ is } w$$
$$\underline{w \text{ is } q}$$
$$a \text{ is } w$$

This suggestion, however, requires much further study before its value can be determined.

13 It should be noted that nothing I have said prohibits the elimination of all syntactically primitive names in favor of syntactically complex names whose constituent nonlogical constants are all predicates. For example, 'gold' could be an abbreviation for 'the stuff which goldizes' or 'the stuff all and only instances of which goldize', where 'goldize' is a predicate that expresses, e.g., the essential properties of gold or the properties required in order to be (composed of) gold.

14 In 'The Axiom of Extensionality Can Be Dropped: Numbers Can Be Universals', *Journal of Symbolic Logic* **39** (1974), 401, I show, by an adaptation of Frege's definitions together with a first-order 'no-class' theory, that these concepts can be defined in terms of the copula. Accordingly, 'There are five apples' is a transformation from 'the apples are five', where the latter sentence is of the form 'A's are B' and 'A's and 'are' are the plurals of 'A' and 'is', respectively.

FRANCIS JEFFRY PELLETIER

A BIBLIOGRAPHY OF RECENT WORK
ON MASS TERMS

The following is a reasonably complete bibliography of work done on mass terms in the past twenty years or so. There are some omissions; hopefully all of them are intentional, and follow these general guidelines. First, the 'Linguistic' group is purposefully slight – I have included only those works I think have direct bearing on some philosophical problems. Second, while there are a number of works on the notion of a sortal in which there is normally some discussion of mass terms, unless the discussion is lengthy or central, I have not included these references. The same could be said for works on the notions of identity, change, matter, individuals, individuation, particulars, etc. Third, I have not bothered to completely specify all the points of a long work where mass terms are discussed. E.g., in *Word and Object* mass terms are discussed at more places than I have cited.

Bacon, John (1973), 'Do Generic Descriptions Denote?', *Mind* **82**, 331–347.
Bealer, George (1975), 'Predication and Matter', *Synthese* **31**, 493–508; reprinted in this volume, pp. 279–294.
Bunt, H. C. (1979), 'Ensembles and the Formal Semantic Properties of Mass Terms', in this volume, pp. 249–277.
Burge, Tyler (1971), *Truth and Some Referential Devices*, unpublished Ph.D. thesis, Department of Philosophy, Princeton University.
Burge, Tyler (1972), 'Truth and Mass Terms', *Journal of Philosophy* **69**, 263–282.
Burge, Tyler, 'A Theory of Aggregates', *Noûs*, forthcoming.
Burge, Tyler (1975), 'Mass Terms, Count Nouns, and Change', *Synthese* **31**, 459–478: reprinted in this volume, pp. 199–218.
Carlson, Gregory (1973), *Superficially Unquantified Plural Count Noun Phrases in English*, unpublished M.A. thesis, Department of Linguistics, University of Iowa.
Cartwright, Helen (1963), *Classes, and Non-Singular Reference*, unpublished Ph.D. thesis, Department of Philosophy, University of Michigan.
Cartwright, Helen (1965), 'Heraclitus and the Bath Water', *Philosophical Review* **74**, 466–485.
Cartwright, Helen (1970), 'Quantities', *Philosophical Review* **79**, 25–42.
Cartwright, Helen (1972), 'Chappell on Stuff and Things', *Noûs* **6**, 369–377.
Cartwright, Helen (1975), 'Some Remarks about Mass Nouns and Plurality', *Synthese* **31**, 395–410; reprinted in this volume, pp. 31–46.

F. J. Pelletier (ed.), Mass Terms, 295–298. All Rights Reserved.
Copyright © *1975 and 1979 by D. Reidel Publishing Company, Dordrecht, Holland.*

Cartwright, Helen, 'Amounts and Measures of Amount', *Noûs* **9**, 143–164; reprinted in this volume, 179–198.

Celce, M. and Schwartz, R. M., *Counting, Collecting' Measuring and Quantifying in English*, System Development Corporation document SP-3378, Santa Monica, California.

Chappell, Vere (1970–71), 'Stuff and Things', *Proc. Arist. Society* **71**, 61–76.

Chappell, Vere (1973), 'Matter', *Journal of Philosophy* **70**, 679–696.

Chellas, Brian (1975), 'Quantity and Quantification', *Synthese* **31**, 487–491; reprinted in this volume, pp. 227–231.

Cheng, Chung-Ying (1973), 'Response to Moravcsik', in Hintikka *et al.* (eds.), *Approaches to Natural Language* (Synthese Library), D. Reidel Publishing Company, Dordrecht and Boston, 1973, pp. 286–288.

Chomsky, Noam (1965), *Aspects of the Theory of Syntax*, M.I.T. Press, Cambridge, Mass., 1965, Chapter 2.

Clarke, D. S. (1970), 'Mass Terms as Subjects', *Philosophical Studies* **21**, 25–29.

Cook, Kathleen (1975), 'On the Usefulness of Quantities', *Synthese* **31**, 443–457; reprinted in this volume pp. 121–135.

Cresswell, Max (1976), 'The Semantics of Degree', in Barbara Partee (ed.), *Montague Grammar*, Academic Press.

Dudman, V. H. (1970), 'Divulsion', *Australasian Journal of Philosophy* **48**, 107–115.

Fiengo, Robert (1974), *Semantic Conditions on Surface Structure*, unpublished Ph.D. thesis, Department of Linguistics, Massachusetts Institute of Technology.

Geach, P. T. (1962), *Reference and Generality*, Cornell University Press, Ithaca, N.Y., 1962, esp. 38–42, 149–160.

Gibbons, P. C. (1969), 'Heteromerity', *Australasian Journal of Philosophy* **47**, 296–306.

Gibbons, P. C. (1971), 'Divulsion?', *Australasian Journal of Philosophy* **49**, 68–70.

Gleason, H. A. (1965), *Linguistics and English Grammar*, Holt, Rinehart & Winston, 1965, esp. 135 ff.

Grandy, Richard (1973), 'Reply to Moravcsik', in Hintikka *et al.* (eds.), *Approaches to Natural Language* (Synthese Library), D. Reidel Publishing Company, Dordrecht and Boston, 1973, pp. 295–300.

Grandy, Richard (1975), 'Stuff and Things', *Synthese* **31**, 479–485; reprinted in this volume, pp. 219–225.

Jespersen, Otto (1924), *The Philosophy of Grammar*, reprinted 1965 by W. W. Norton & Co., esp. 198 ff.

Laycock, Henry (1972), 'Some Questions of Ontology', *Philosophical Review* **81**, 3–42.

Laycock, Henry (1973), 'Chemistry and Individuation', unpublished, read at Canadian Philosophical Association meetings 1973.

Laycock, Henry (1975), 'Theories of Matter', *Synthese* **31**, 411–442; reprinted in this volume, pp. 89–120.

McCawley, James D. (1975), 'Lexicography and the Count-Mass Distinction', *Proceedings of the First Annual Meeting of Berkeley Linguistics Society*, pp. 314–321.

Montague, Richard, 'Reply to Moravcsik', in Hintikka *et al.* (eds.), *Approaches to Natural Language* (Synthese Library), D. Reidel Publishing Company, Dordrecht and Boston, 1973, pp. 289–294; reprinted in this volume as 'The Proper Treatment of Mass Terms in English', pp. 173–178.

Moravcsik, J. M. E. (1970), 'Subcategorization and Abstract Terms', *Foundations of Language* **6**, 473–487.

Moravcsik, J. M. E. (1973), 'Mass Terms in English', in Hintikka *et al.* (eds.), *Approaches to Natural Language* (Synthese Library), D. Reidel Publishing Company, Dordrecht and Boston, 1973, pp. 263–285.

Moravcsik, J. M. E. (1973), 'Reply', in Hintikka *et al.* (eds.), *Approaches to Natural Language* (Synthese Library), D. Reidel Publishing Company, Dordrecht and Boston, 1973, pp. 301–308.

Moravcsik, J. M. E. and Gabbay, Dov: (1973), 'Sameness and Individuation', *Journal of Philosophy* **70**, 513–526; reprinted in this volume, pp. 233–247.

Parsons, Terence (1970), 'An Analysis of Mass and Amount Terms', *Foundations of Language* **6**, 363–388; reprinted in this volume, 137–166.

Parsons, Terence (1975), 'Afterthoughts on Mass Terms', *Synthese* **31**, 517–521; reprinted in this volume, pp. 167–171.

Pelletier, Francis Jeffry (1971), *Some Problems of Non-Singular Reference: A Logic for Mass, Sortal, and Adverbial Terms*, unpublished Ph.D. thesis, Department of Philosophy, U.C.L.A.

Pelletier, Francis Jeffry (1974), 'On Some Proposals for the Semantics of Mass Terms', *Journal of Philosophical Logic* **3**, 87–108.

Pelletier, Francis Jeffry (1975), 'Non-Singular Reference: Some Preliminaries' *Philosophia* **5**; reprinted in this volume, pp. 1–14.

Pelletier, Francis Jeffry (1976), 'Sharvy on Mixtures', read to Pacific APA.

Pelletier, Francis Jeffry (1979), 'Sharvy on Mass Predication', in this volume, pp. 55–61.

Quang Phuc Dong 'Three Lexicographic Notes on Individuation', *Quarterly Regress Report* No. 38, South Hanoi Institute of Technology.

Quine, W. V., (1950), 'Identity, Ostension, and Hypostasis', in Quine, *From a Logical Point of View*, Harper & Row reprint, 1963, originally in *Journal of Philosophy* **47**.

Quine, W. V. (1958), 'Speaking of Objects', in Quine, *Ontological Relativity*, Columbia, University Press, 1969, originally in *Proc. Amer. Phil. Assn.* 1958.

Quine, W. V. (1960), *Word and Object*, M.I.T. Press, Cambridge, Mass., 1960, esp, 90–124.

Quine, W. V. (1964), 'Review of Geach, *Reference and Generality*', *Philosophical Review* **73**, 100–105.

Sharvy, Richard (1976), 'Mixtures' read to Pacific APA.

Sharvy, Richard (1979), 'The Indeterminacy of Mass Predication', in this volume, pp. 47–54.

Sharvy, Richard: forthcoming, 'Maybe English has No Count Terms' (unpublished paper).

Strawson, P. F. (1953–54), 'Particular and General', *Proc. Arist. Soc.*, 233–260.

Strawson, P. F. (1959), *Individuals*, Methuen, London, 1959, esp. 208 ff.

Van Heijenoort, Jean (1974), 'Subject and Predicate in Western Logic', *Philosophy East and West*, 253–268.

Wald, Jan David (1976), *Mass Terms in English*, unpublished Ph.D. thesis, Brandeis University.

Wallace, John (1964), *Philosophical Grammar*, unpublished Ph.D. thesis, Department of Philosophy, Stanford University.

Ware, Robert X. (1975), 'Some Bits and Pieces', *Synthese* **31**, 379–393; reprinted in this volume, pp. 15–29.

Woolhouse, R. S. (1972), 'Things', *Philosophy and Phenomenological Research* **33**, 199–206.

Zemach, Eddy (1970), 'Four Ontologies', *Journal of Philosophy* **67**, 213–247; reprinted in this volume, pp. 63–80.

Zemach, Eddy (1975), 'On the Adequacy of a Type Ontology', *Synthese* **31**, 509–515; reprinted in this volume, pp. 81–87.

University of Alberta, Edmonton

INDEX OF NAMES

INDEX OF SUBJECTS

SYNTHESE LANGUAGE LIBRARY

Texts and Studies
in Linguistics and Philosophy

Managing Editors:

JAAKKO HINTIKKA
Academy of Finland, Stanford University, and Florida State University (Tallahassee)

STANLEY PETERS
The University of Texas at Austin

Editors:

EMMON BACH (University of Massachusetts at Amherst)
JOAN BRESNAN (Massachusetts Institute of Technology)
JOHN LYONS (University of Sussex)
JULIUS M. E. MORAVCSIK (Stanford University)
PATRICK SUPPES (Stanford University)
DANA SCOTT (Oxford University)